MUTUALITY

A Formal Norm for Christian Social Ethics

Dawn M. Nothwehr

Wipf & Stock
PUBLISHERS
Eugene, Oregon

Wipf and Stock Publishers
199 W 8th Ave, Suite 3
Eugene, OR 97401

Mutuality
A Formal Norm for Christian Social Ethics
By Nothwehr, Dawn M.
Copyright©1998 Nothwehr, Dawn M. and The Sisters of St. Francis –
Academy of Our Lady of Lourdes of Rochester, MN
ISBN: 1-59752-313-5
Publication date 7/25/2005
Previously published by Catholic Scholars Press, 1998

DEDICATION

> Jesus was radical not in his lust for sacrifice, *but in his power of mutuality*. Jesus' death on the cross, his sacrifice, was no abstract exercise in moral virtue. His death was the price he paid for refusing to abandon the *radical activity of love*--of expressing solidarity and reciprocity with the excluded ones of his community. Sacrifice, I submit, is not a central moral good of the Christian life. Radical acts of love--expressing solidarity and bringing mutual relationships to life--are the central virtues of the Christian moral life. . . . [I]t is risky to live as if the commonwealth of the living God were present--that is, to live by radical mutuality and reciprocity. . . . Those in power believe such love to be "unrealistic" because those touched by the power of such love tend to develop a reluctance to accept anything less than mutuality and self-respect, anything less than human dignity, anything less than authentic relatedness.[1]

May this work in some small way enable more of us to analyze moral and ethical dilemmas by probing the dynamics of power involved, and then consciously choosing the path of mutuality, thereby being faithful to the Lord Jesus.

---

[1] Beverly Wildung Harrison, "The Power of Anger in the Works of Love: Christian Ethics for Women and Other Strangers," *Union Seminary Quarterly Review* 36 (1981 Supplement): 52-3. Emphasis is Harrison's.

TABLE OF CONTENTS

COMMENDATORY FORWARDS xi
PREFACE xvii
ACKNOWLEDGEMENT ixx
INTRODUCTION MUTUALITY: A FORMAL NORM FOR
CHRISTIAN SOCIAL ETHICS 1
    WORKING DEFINITION OF "MUTUALITY" 3
    DEFINITION OF "NORMS" 5
    DEFINITION OF "BALANCE OF POWER" 6
    CONTEXT: THE WHOLE OF CREATION 8
    FOUR FORMS OF MUTUALITY 9
    RELATIONSHIP BETWEEN LOVE,
    JUSTICE, AND MUTUALITY 12
    MUTUALITY: A CORRECTIVE AND
    COMPLEMENTARY NORM 12
        Critique of Love 16
        Critique of Justice 16
    RESTATEMENT OF THE THESIS 18
    PROCEDURE 18
CHAPTER 1 MUTUALITY DEFINED IN SELECTED WORKS
          OF FOUR CHRISTIAN FEMINISTS 21
    INTRODUCTION 21
    PART ONE: EXPOSITION OF THE FOUR FEMINISTS
    DEFINITIONS OF MUTUALITY 22
        Rosemary Radford Ruether:
        Stated Definition of Mutuality 23
            Ruether's Feminist Theological Context 24
                Anthropology:
                Woman Image/Image of God 24
                Sin 27
                Redemption 28

- Christology 28
- Ecological Ethics 30
- Ruether's Basic Definition of Mutuality 33
- Further Analysis of Mutuality 34
  - Cosmic Mutuality 34
  - Gender Mutuality 35
  - Generative Mutuality 36
  - Social Mutuality 37
  - Normative Status 37
  - Distinctions/Relationship of Mutuality to Equality, Friendship, Reciprocity, Solidarity 38
  - Relationship of Mutuality to Love and Justice 39

(Isabel) Carter Heyward:
Stated Definition of Mutuality 41
- Feminist Theological Context 41
  - Theology 42
  - Christology 43
  - Anthropology 46
- Heyward's Basic Definition of Mutuality 47
- Further Analysis of Mutuality 48
  - Cosmic Mutuality 49
  - Gender Mutuality 50
  - Generative Mutuality 52
  - Social Mutuality 54
  - Normative Status 56
  - Distinctions/Relationship of Mutuality to Equality, Friendship, Reciprocity, Solidarity 57
  - Relationship of Mutuality to Love and Justice 59

Beverly Wildung Harrison:
Stated Definition of Mutuality 61

    Feminist Theological Context 61

        Socialist Feminist Theory 61

        Theology 64

        Christology 66

    Harrison's Basic Definition of Mutuality 66

    Further Analysis of Mutuality 67

        Cosmic Mutuality 67

        Gender Mutuality 69

        Social Mutuality 70

        Normative Status 71

        Distinctions/Relationship of
        Mutuality to Equality, Friendship,
        Reciprocity, Solidarity 72

        Relationship of Mutuality
        to Love and Justice 73

Elizabeth A. Johnson:
Stated Definition of Mutuality 76

    Feminist Theological Context 77

    Johnson's Basic Definition of Mutuality 78

    Further Analysis of Mutuality 78

        Cosmic Mutuality 78

        Gender Mutuality 79

        Generative Mutuality 81

        Social Mutuality 82

        Normative Status 83

        Distinctions/Relationship of
        Mutuality to Equality, Friendship,
        Reciprocity, Solidarity 85

        Relationship of Mutuality
        to Love and Justice 88

PART TWO: MUTUALITY DEFINED - TOWARD
A CHRISTIAN FEMINIST CONSENSUS................... 90

    Consensus on Distinction/Relationship of
    Mutuality to Equality, Friendship,
    Reciprocity, Solidarity 90

    A Consensus: Relationship of
    Mutuality, Love, and Justice 91

    A Feminist Consensus for
    Four Forms of Mutuality 92

        A Consensus for Cosmic Mutuality 92

        A Consensus for Gender Mutuality 93

        A Consensus for Generative Mutuality 93

        A Consensus for Social Mutuality 94

    A Consensus for
    the Normative Status of Mutuality 94

    Redefinition of Mutuality:
    A Formal Norm for Christian Social Ethics 95

CHAPTER 2 CLASSICAL ANTECEDENTS:
    CHRISTIAN FEMINISTS' NOTION OF MUTUALITY .. 99

    INTRODUCTION 99

    TWO VIEWS IN HISTORICAL CONTEXT:
    COSMIC INTERDEPENDENCE AND FRIENDSHIP 100

    Context for Cosmic Interdependence
    and Friendship 100

    Hugh of St. Victor 104

        Incarnation 104

        Virgin Birth 105

        The Presence of God in All Creation 106

        The Sacrament of Marriage 107

    Aelred of Rievaulx: Spiritual Friendship 108

    Mutuality in Hugh of St. Victor
    and Aelred of Rievaulx 109

    THOMAS AQUINAS 111

    Friendship With God 112

- Anthropology 113
- God: Exemplar Cause 114
- Thomas's Use of Friendship in Aristotle 115
- God as Friend 117
- Trinitarian Relations: Analog of Mutuality 119
  - Aquinas's Metaphysics of Divine Being 120
  - Relations: *ad intra/ad extra* 120
  - Names of God 121
  - The Divine Missions 122
- The Incarnation 124
  - The Economy of Salvation 124
  - Love Incarnate 126
- Feminists' Notion of Mutuality and Aquinas's Thought 129
  - Cosmic Mutuality 131
  - Gender Mutuality 131
  - Generative Mutuality 132
  - Social Mutuality 132

JOHN DUNS SCOTUS 133

- Mutuality in Scotus: Mary Elizabeth Ingham's Thesis 133
- The Basis for Mutuality: Scotus's Philosophy .. 136
  - *Haecceitas* 136
  - Cognitive Theory 136
  - Moral Theory 140
- Paradigms of Mutuality in Scotus's Theology ... 143
  - Trinity 144
  - Creation and *imago Dei* 146
  - Incarnation 146
  - Divine *acceptatio* and the Order of Merit .. 147

Feminists' Notion of
Mutuality and Scotus's Thought 150

    Cosmic Mutuality 150

    Gender Mutuality 150

    Generative Mutuality 152

    Social Mutuality 153

CONCLUSIONS 155

CHAPTER 3 TWENTIETH CENTURY ANTECEDENTS TO CHRISTIAN FEMINISTS'S NOTION OF MUTUALITY: MARTIN BUBER AND H. RICHARD NIEBUHR 157

INTRODUCTION 157

MARTIN BUBER: MUTUALITY IN HIS DIALOGICAL PHILOSOPHY 157

    Buber's Basic I - Thou Philosophy 158

        Word Pairs (Wörtpaare): I-It (Ich-Es) and
I-Thou (Ich-Du) 158

        The World of Relation 159

            The Three Primary Spheres 159

            The Dynamics of Relating:
Meeting and Dialogue 159

    Martin Buber's Notion of Mutuality 162

        Definition and Translation Issues 162

        Mutuality: Its Modes in Buber's Three
Spheres of Relation 162

            Sphere of Human Relations 162

                Helping Relations 163

                Friendship 166

            Mutuality in the Nonhuman
Spheres of Relations 167

                Threshold of Mutuality 168

                Prethreshold of Mutuality 170

                The Subthreshold of Mutuality 171

   Mutuality in the Sphere of
   geistige Wesenheiten 171
    Mutuality and Art 172
    Mutuality and the Eternal Thou 173
  Summary of Buber's Notion of Mutuality 176
  Mutuality as a Norm in Buber's Work 177
 H. RICHARD NIEBUHR'S RESPONSIBILITY:
 ANTECEDENT TO MUTUALITY 179
  Niebuhr's Key Theological Assumptions/
  Theory of Responsibility 180
   From Natural Faith to Monotheism 180
   Humanity the Sinner/
   God the Giver of Grace 182
   Christology 184
   H. Richard Niebuhr's Theory of
   Responsibility 186
    Patterns of God's Actions
    and Human Response 191
    Normative Nature of Responsibility 193
  Responsibility: Antecedent to
  the Feminist Notion of Mutuality 197
 MUTUALITY IN BUBER, NIEBUHR, AND
 MODERN CHRISTIAN FEMINISTS 197
  Some General Considerations: Buber 197
  Some General Considerations: Niebuhr 200
  Four Forms of Mutuality:
  Modern Feminists, Buber, and Niebuhr 201
CHAPTER 4 THE MORAL STATUS OF MUTUALITY:
  A FORMAL NORM 205
 INTRODUCTION 205
 FORMAL NORM: DEFINITIONS AND DESCRIPTIONS 206
  Formal Norm: A Basic Definition 206
  Formal Norm: Timothy E. O'Connell 208

Formal Norm: Josef Fuchs 210

Formal Norm: Lisa Cahill. 214

Formal Norm: Consensus Among
Cahill, Fuchs, and O'Connell 216

ARGUMENT THAT MUTUALITY IS A FORMAL NORM 216

Four Feminists's Evidence for
the Normative Status of Mutuality 217

Distinctiveness/Relationship:
Love, Justice, and Mutuality 219

 Love 219

 Justice 221

What Mutuality as a Formal Norm
Illuminates/Delimits 223

Mutuality, Love, and Justice:
Foundational Formal Norms. 227

CHAPTER 5 MUTUALITY A FORMAL NORM FOR
CHRISTIAN SOCIAL ETHICS: A CASE STUDY 231

INTRODUCTION 231

"FROM LAST RESORT TO ENDGAME: MORALITY,
THE GULF WAR, AND THE PEACE PROCESS"
BY GEORGE WEIGEL 233

Review of the Content 233

Analysis of the Essay 234

"JUST WAR AS POLITICS: WHAT THE GULF WAR
TOLD US ABOUT CONTEMPORARY AMERICAN LIFE"
BY JEAN BETHKE ELSHTAIN 239

Review of the Content 239

Analysis of the Essay. 239

"WHOSE JUST WAR? WHICH PEACE?"
BY STANLEY HAUERWAS 244

Review of the Content 244

Analysis of the Essay 245

CONCLUSIONS: THE PROBATIVE VALUE OF MUTUALITY	249
MORE QUESTIONS	251
BIBLIOGRAPHY	253
INDEX	271

COMMENDATORY FORWARD

The evolving story of the relationship between feminism and Christianity is a complex one, fraught with turmoil and tension, yet brimming with promise and possibility. And efforts to articulate and chart the interplay between these two powerful streams of belief and practice, particularly through scholarly dialogue between feminist ethics and Catholic moral theology, to date remain preliminary and contested. To this nascent, yet critically important task, Dawn M. Nothwehr's book is a substantial and welcome contribution.

This work is marked by a salutary ambition, range, and depth. Dr. Nothwehr takes on no less than four challenging tasks, and in each case rises to the challenge. First, the author clarifies and analyzes an ubiquitous but murky term in feminist discourse. Second, through an investigation of selected classic and contempory Christian and Jewish texts, Nothwehr discovers antecedents and alternate articulations of this critical feminist norm at the heart of our religious traditions. Third, she advances a convincing case for explicitly conceiving mutuality as a formal norm in Christian social ethics, one which must operate along with love and justice as a fundamental criterion for moral analysis, judgement and action. Finally, she models a constructive, scholarly and versatile approach to what has been called "bridge discourse," the effort to draw connections between positions regarded by many as disparate or conflicting.

By selecting as her focus "mutuality," Nothwehr brings to the fore an issue of perennial importance in Christian social ethics, that of power. As she shows, feminist theology invites religious ethicists to reconceive normative questions of power from the vantage point of its dynamic, mutual sharing, a sharing that encompasses not only individual relations, but society and the natural world. She also demonstrates how attention to relations of mutuality sheds light on the spectrum of classic Christian theological and moral topics, revealing dimensions of our traditions that standard assumptions about power as domination tend to obscure.

The multifaceted character of this book make it a potential resource for a diverse audience among scholars, teachers, and educated laity. Some will especially benefit from its investigation of the writings of classic figures such as John Duns Scotus and Thomas Aquinas. Others will find illuminating its theoretical integration of sources, norms, method, and case studies. Most important, Nothwehr's work opens avenues for informed dialogue between persons who cherish our Catholic moral tradition, and persons who cherish the wisdom embodied in the experiences, practices, and thinking of women. The author of this book clearly cherishes both. For what she has accomplished, and for providing a springboard for further conversation and scholarship, we are in her debt.

Christine Firer Hinze
Associate Professor of Theology
Marquette University

COMMENDATORY FORWARD

What makes moral choices and acts right or wrong? Dawn M. Nothwehr, OSF's *Mutuality: A Formal Norm for Christian Social Ethics* replies that mutuality belongs among the criteria. Mutuality is a relational and interdependent aspect of existence that Christian feminist social ethics has brung to integrate into moral theology. Nothwehr analyses mutuality in cosmic, gender, generative (divine power healing and renewing) and social relationships. Her central thesis is that: "just as anyone ought to act lovingly and justly, so too ought one to act mutually. . . in one's relationships with God, other humans, other earthcreatures, the earth itself, and the entire cosmos." She shows how this is a credible theological opinion. This is an evaluation of the validity of her claim. Readers will want to test this judgment.

But the meaning of her arguments exceeds their probative role in two ways. This makes the book worthwhile for those who may not concur with some of the christological themes or even with the basic thesis. First, she situates moral life and theory in the context of the whole of creation. Her argument from start to finish conceives cosmos, earth, and nature as creation dependent on and manifesting the Creator. She reads Christian feminist thought (Rosemary Radford Ruether, Isabel Carter Heyward, Beverly Wildung Harrison, and Elizabeth A. Johnson) in light of Franciscan presuppositions that even fallen creation retains intrinsic being and goodness that grounds a pre-theoretical, nonscientific, appreciative relationship between human beings and the planet earth. True, the text does not address normative claims in creation theologies and spiritualities. Still, it illuminates a moral dimension in relationships with the cosmos and the earth. Part of being *imago Dei* she points out, consists in sharing the Creator's love and concern for the good of the whole of creation. This is an alternative to the common postulate blaming the *imago*

Dei theme for modern industrial exploitation of nature. Nothwehr does not make that mistake because her study of Thomas Aquinas and her familiarity with a tradition of relating to creation in categories of kinship.

This is because she has an orientation to Christian tradition as a resource for thinking about current themes. Here, too, her meaning exceeds the needs of her argument. The logic of her feminist argument is an inquiry into tradition. She dares to begin by engaging the post-modern theme of mutuality in dialogue with pre-modern Christian texts. She carefully, critically consults Hugh of St. Victor, Thomas Aquinas, and John Duns Scotus. Then she brings her findings forward to such twentieth century antecedents to the feminist notion of mutuality as Martin Buber and H. Richard Niebuhr. This provides ample context for evaluating Christian feminist social ethics and the positions of ethicists Timothy E. O'Connell, Josef Fuchs and Lisa Sowle Cahill. Through it runs readiness to consider the whole of Christian tradition open to dialogue with contemporary concerns, though she treats only part of it. Dialogue with tradition, then, is a form of mutuality: interdependence between the past and the present in the community of faith and understanding.

Thomas Hughson, SJ
Associate Professor of Theology
Marquette University

COMMENDATORY FORWARD

Until three decades ago, Catholic theology was the preserve of men, ordained men. Then with the Second Vatican Council, the doors creaked open to a new epoch. Lay men, and more importantly lay women, joined the lists of Catholic searchers in the field of theology. The full implications of this seismic shift are now only beginning to be felt. But the major import of these changes glows with a new and fresh radiance in this study. Written by a Franciscan sister with gentle strength that does credit to Francis and Clare, Dawn Nothwehr takes her place as a welcome and significant teacher of Catholic thought. This is transformative theology, a theology that does not stop at the arguments, but goes directly to the assumptions.

Assumptions are controlling. Arguments are like waves; assumptions are like tides that move the seas and all who sail on them. Underlying all talk of power, nature and society and indeed of God and gendered humankind are assumptions that long ruled with unsuspected hegemony. Some of those assumptions were full of mischief, divisive mischief that alienated men from women, humans from the rest of biological nature, affect from reason, and secular from sacred.

Sister Dawn employs a corrective category, mutuality. At first blush the term would seem too tender and nebulous to address the splits in our consciousness, but this theologian brings well informed care to its definition. It becomes in her hands a critical tool which can do healing surgery on many of the foundational categories of Catholic theology, and indeed of much modern thinking beyond the pale of Catholicism. Mutuality calls attention to the essential interdependency of all that is in our cosmos. Our cells, after all, are recycled stardust. Mutuality needs to be able to be added to the noble categories of justice and love as a reminder of our radical relatedness. Jean Paul Sartre said that the greatest evil of which we are capable is to treat as abstract that which is concrete. Even avowed commitment to love and justice have coexisted with horrible evils in the concrete world around us. While talking love and justice, we have historically been able to ignore slavery. Most theologians did not even see it as a moral issue; some busied themselves pondering the humane number of slaves that could be packed into a slave ship. Other theologians prayed during the holocaust while the smoke from their incense commingled in the sky with the smoke of the murdered dead. As Sister Dawn puts it, "in the practice of the Christian community, a hierarchical cultural conception of the relationship between men and women superseded the notion of equal regard expressed in the early baptismal formula. . ."there is neither male or female." Even today she remarks with sadness, "the Roman Catholic Church continues to be governed by a solely male presbyterate and hierarchy." Sister Dawn does not shy from the pains of application.

Mutuality as here defined and used is a call to concreteness and a solvent of all hostile alienations. It is an ecumenical theology that harmonizes beautifully with the notions of interdependence and unrationed reverence that permeate other religions such as Buddhism and the Chinese religions. Her work points insistently towards a whole new ecclesiology and a new politics and economics, all based on a full realization of our foundational relationality.

Sister Dawn's doctor-mother at Marquette University was Christine Firer Hinze, another rising star in the new Catholic world. The thought of women thinkers fill her pages--but also the thought of men. Her feminism is marked, by what else!! mutuality. Men and women--both Francis and Clare--are her teachers and sources. Her ears are open to the voices of all faiths and all beliefs. Her spirit is Franciscan and celebratory as she calls us from power over to power with. Here is theology enlivening and reconciling.

Daniel C. Maguire
Professor of Theology
Marquette University

PREFACE

Behind this study stands some twenty years of professional and pastoral practice in Minnesota, Colorado, Washington, the District of Columbia, New York, Colombia, and Nicaragua. I have been engaged in various roles working side by side with marginalized peoples struggling for peace, justice and human rights. My mentors have included: the residents of the hollers of Appalachia; abused children in residential psychiatric treatment centers; homeless Native Americans of south Minneapolis; victims of urban slum landlords; teenaged run-aways in Colorado; defense workers suffering from mysterious radiation sickness after producing nuclear warheads; refugees from Guatemala, El Salvador, and Southeast Asia; victims of war in Nicaragua; the people of *barrios invasiones* in Colombia; jobless victims of plant closings; persons with HIV disease; persons coping with schizophrenia; elderly persons suffering Alzheimer's disease.

It has also been my privilege to sit at the feet of some of the saints and prophets of our day and to observe them at work. These have included: Marjorie Tuite, OP; Rosemary Radford Ruether; Gustavo Gutierrez; Adolfo Perez Esquivel; Dom Helder Camara; Caesar Chavez; Jim & Shelly Douglas; Archbishop Raymond Hunthausen; Bishop Matthew H. Clark; Daniel C. Maguire; Kathleen M. O'Connor; Marc H. Ellis; Sr. Emmanuel Collins, OSF; Sr. Florence Zweber, OSF; Sr. Janel Crumb, OSF; Sr. Marie Nord, OSF; and Sr. Patricia Fritz, OSF--to name a few.

So, just what did I learn from all of these experiences that led me to this study? From the poor and marginalized, I learned the depths of generous love amid the most excruciating circumstances known to humankind. From the saints and prophets, I grasped the wisdom of justice rooted in covenant fidelity. From both, I gleaned the knowledge that without a recognition of the "Divine Spark" or the *imago*

Dei at the core of *all* life, attempts to practice the Christian and Jewish tenets of love and justice are worthless.

These heroic and faithful people showed me that it is not only *that* one practices love and justice toward one's neighbor, but also *how* one practices these virtues that makes the difference in the thriving of humankind. True love and justice require more than pallid liberal charity that patronizingly gives alms or blindly and passionlessly renders empirical judgments altering the lives of the poor and the marginalized. Rather, true love and justice requires impassioned radical empowerment exemplified by the Incarnation, where Jesus' choice to become powerless encountered our poverty. Such action demands first a full identification with poverty and abjectness, and then cries out for the relinquishment of power by the powerful and a taking up of power by the poor and the marginalized. This exchange of power needs to be based on the common recognition of the full personhood of the other, the concomitant valuing of the other, and a common regard marked by trust, respect and affection. In other words, the practice of love and justice requires mutuality.

Mutuality as a formal norm for Christian social ethics seemed so obvious when observing the lives of real people, yet it was never specified as an aspect of the Christian moral framework. Could it be, I asked, that my exemplars were on to something new? Or, is it that Christians have overlooked something very old and deep within the Jewish and Christian moral traditions? It seemed that modern Christian feminists were beginning to recognize mutuality as necessary for the Christian moral framework, yet they were scattered in their definitions and uses of the term. I began my research to discover if indeed, mutuality is a formal norm for Christian social ethics.

Dawn M. Nothwehr, OSF, Ph.D.
Assisi Heights
Rochester, MN.

ACKNOWLEDGMENT

This book is the culmination of my doctoral study. I am deeply aware of many persons who have supported me through the years and who assisted me in completing this journey.

I am grateful to my parents, Hubert J. Nothwehr (deceased) and Beata E. Lemke Nothwehr who first taught me the meaning of love, justice and mutuality by the example of a faith-filled and egalitarian marriage relationship. My sister, Joan Martha Nothwehr, especially in her struggles with schizophrenia, has challenged me to live out of a stance of social mutuality, relinquishing power-over so that another might have power-with. My thanks to the Nothwehr's--Don, Mary, Larry, Chris, Meaghan, Matt, Lauren Claire--who helped keep life in perspective.

My Franciscan community supported my study financially, with prayers, and wise counsel. Special gratitude goes to those at Tau Center, who graciously hosted me during visits to my mother (an Alzheimer patient). The scholars of the Franciscan Life Center--Kate Minar, Ramona Miller, Ingrid J. Peterson, and Margaret Pirkl, were vital conversation partners for the Scotus section of this study. When a family emergency threatened the completion of this project, Sr. Charlotte Hesby and Area Minister, Sr. Jennifer Corbett generously cared for me. Sr. Marisa McDonald and Sr. Rosemary Zemler assisted with the computer and printing technicalities. My Cojourner, Marie Dietrich, MD, provided me with humorous cards, letters and phone calls. This five-year journey was made bearable because Shannon Schrein, OSF (Sylvania, OH) was a loyal friend and study partner all along the way--course work, language exams, DQE's, DDO's, writing, editing, and defending--and of course, celebrating.

I am appreciative of the Faculty of the Theology Department at Marquette University who generously shared their knowledge and talent with me. The Theology office staff, Kay, Camille and Audrey always had ready answers to my questions--and a friendly word besides. To them I am grateful. I thank Marquette University's Memorial Library staff for their assistance.

My deep gratitude is to Daniel C. Maguire, my academic advisor, who taught me much--by example as well as word--what it means to be a theologian, who signed reams of forms for the department and graduate school, and who guided and supported me. My dissertation director, Christine Firer Hinze, was a partner from the inception of this study, bringing it clarity and focus. Her "eagle-eye" for editing was indispensable to this enterprise, as well. Dr. Firer Hinze responded to my needs in a timely manner and it was a privilege to work with her.

I am indebted to my Dissertation Committee for evaluation and critique of this project--and more. Bradford E. Hinze first suggested the expertise of Dr. Firer Hinze and gave a helpful assessment of my project at the dissertation seminar. D. Thomas Hughson reviewed and encouraged this study at its beginning. Wanda Cizweski-Zemler directed me to the theologies of Hugh, Aelred and Thomas and supported my efforts to comprehend them.

ABSTRACT

MUTUALITY: A FORMAL NORM FOR CHRISTIAN SOCIAL ETHICS

Notions of interdependence and mutuality have been a significant element in recent developments in the natural sciences, human sciences, and philosophy. These advances across so many fields can be viewed as recognizing the facticity of mutuality, or even its ontological status. If this is so, the ethical questions naturally follow: "Is this state of affairs a `good'?"; "How then ought we to act?". It is to these latter questions that this dissertation attends.

The central problem this study addresses is the nature of the contribution Christian feminist thinkers have made by claiming that mutuality is a necessary part of a Christian social ethical framework. The theological method employed in this dissertation is analytical and comparative toward the end of illuminating, testing, and demonstrating the thesis: mutuality is a formal norm for Christian social ethics that functions along with love and justice to promote a balance of power that is required for optimum human flourishing, a flourishing set within the interdependent context of the whole of creation.

Part one of chapter one analyzes selected primary sources of Rosemary Radford Ruether, (Isabel) Carter Heyward, Beverly Wildung Harrison, and Elizabeth A. Johnson isolating their definition and treatment of the term, "mutuality." Part two of chapter one concludes with a consensus definition of mutuality drawn from definitions by the four feminists. The conclusion is drawn that, similar to the tripartite nature of justice, mutuality has four forms--cosmic, gender, generative, and social.

Chapters two and three illustrate several moments in the history of Christian thought wherein antecedents of the feminists notion of mutuality are found. Selected primary works of Thomas Aquinas, John Duns Scotus, Martin Buber, and H. Richard

Niebuhr are examined.

Chapter four compares the four feminists' definition of mutuality with definitions of formal norm by Josef Fuchs, Lisa Sowle Cahill, and Timothy E. O'Connell. It is determined that mutuality is a formal norm for Christian social ethics.

The final chapter is a case study. Utilizing our definition, it is shown how consideration of mutuality and its four forms influences the ethical analyses of George Weigel, Jean Bethke Elshtain, and Stanley Hauerwas in determining if the Persian Gulf War was a just war. It is concluded that the probative value of the formal norm, mutuality, is multifaceted. First and foremost, it requires the moral agent to deal concretely in moral reflection and moral decision-making. Specific and careful attention needs to be given to the reality revealing questions--what?, why?, how?, who?, where?, when?, What are the foreseeable effects?, What are the viable alternatives?--in the concrete, as well as in the abstract. Second, mutuality requires the moral agent to probe the dynamics of power in an ethical dilemma and to seek out ways to shape those dynamics to serve power-with. It is a complement to and corrective of love and justice. Third, engaging the norm of mutuality presses the moral agent toward inclusivity drawing into the process of moral reflection concern for the thriving and flourishing of all involved. More than the norms of love and justice, mutuality places humans in a perspective within the whole of creation.

INTRODUCTION
MUTUALITY: A FORMAL NORM FOR CHRISTIAN SOCIAL ETHICS

Notions of interdependence and mutuality have been a significant element in recent developments in the natural sciences, human sciences, and philosophy. These advances across so many fields can be viewed as recognizing the facticity of mutuality, or even its ontological status.[1] If this is so, the ethical questions naturally

---

[1] For a small sample of this huge literature see the following: In the natural sciences--Fritjof Carpa, *The Turning Point: Science, Society, and the Rising Culture* (New York: Simon and Schuster, 1982); Fritjof Carpa, *The Tao of Physics: An Exploration of the Parallels Between Modern Physics and Eastern Mysticism* (New York: Bantam, 1977); Nigal Calder, *The Key to the Universe: A Report on the New Physics* (New York: Viking, 1977); Steven Weinberg, *The First Three Minutes* (New York: Basic Books, 1977); John Boslough, *Stephen Hawking's Universe* (New York: Avon, 1985); Anne H. Ehrlich and Paul R. Ehrlich, *Earth* (New York: Franklin Watts, 1987); Thomas Berry, *Dream of the Earth* (San Francisco: Sierra Club Books, 1988); Anne H. Ehrlich, Paul R. Ehrlich, and John P. Holdren, *Human Ecology: Problems and Solutions* (San Francisco: W.H. Freeman, 1973); Brian Swimme, *The Universe is a Green Dragon: A Cosmic Creation Story* (Santa Fe, NM: Bear and Company, 1985); Brian Swimme, "How to Heal a Lobotomy," in Irene Diamond and Gloria Orenstein, eds., *Reweaving the World: The Emergence of Ecofeminism* (San Francisco: Sierra Club Books: 1989); In law--Roderick F. Nash, *The Rights of Nature: A History of Environmental Ethics* (Madison: University of Wisconsin Press, 1989); Christopher Stone, *Should Trees Have Standing?: Toward Legal Rights For Natural Objects* (Los Altos, CA: Sierra Club Books, 1974); In psychology--James Serpell, *In the Company of Animals: A Study of Human-Animal Relationships* (London: Basil Blackwell, 1986); In philosophy--David Rothenberg, "The Individual and the Community: Two Approaches to Ecophilosophy in Practice," a paper presented at the Fifth Annual Casassa Conference, March 14-15, 1991, Loyola Marymount University, Los Angeles, CA; Erazim Kohak, *The Embers and the Stars: A Philosophical Inquiry into the Moral Sense of Nature* (Chicago: The University of Chicago Press, 1984); In urban planning--Marcia D. Lowe, "Rethinking Urban Transport," in *State of the World, 1991* (New York: Norton, 1991); In political science--Jeremy Rafkin, *Biosphere Politics: A New Consciousness for a New Century* (New York: Crown Publishing, 1991); In agriculture--Wes Jackson, *New Roots For Agriculture* (Lincoln: University of Nebraska, 1987); In economics--Michael Renner, "Converting to a Peaceful Economy," in *State of the World, 1990* (New York: Norton, 1990).

follow: "Is this state of affairs a 'good'?"; "How then ought we to act?". It is to these latter questions that this work attends.

Love and justice have been perennially considered constitutive norms for Christian social ethics. However, in recent years there has been a perceptible movement among Christian feminists toward defining mutuality as a formal norm for Christian social ethics, as well.[2] The notion of mutuality is a term common to nearly all Christian feminist literature. Feminist scholars use the idea of mutuality in various ways. To date, no feminist scholar has given sustained attention to the meaning of the term "mutuality," nor has anyone explicitly called mutuality a formal norm for Christian social ethics. The central problem which this study addresses is the nature of the contribution Christian feminist thinkers have made to Christian social ethics by claiming that mutuality is also a necessary feature of a Christian ethical framework. Drawing on the thought of Christian feminist scholars, particularly the work of

---

[2] For a small sample of this literature, see: Eleanore Humes Haney, "What is Feminist Ethics?: A Proposal For Continuing Discussion," *Journal of Religious Ethics* 8 (1980): 115-24; Carol S. Robb, "A Framework For Feminist Ethics," *Journal of Religious Ethics* 8 (1981): 48-68; Daniel C. Maguire, "A Feminist Turn in Ethics," *Horizons* 10 (1983): 341-47; Margaret A. Farley, "Feminist Ethics in the Christian Ethics Curriculum," *Horizons* 11 (1984): 361-72; Leonard Swidler, "Mutuality The Matrix For Mature Living: Some Philosophical and Christian Theological Reflections," *Religion and Intellectual Life* 3 (1985): 105-19; Ruth L. Smith, "Morality and Perspectives of Society: The Limits of Self-Interest," *Journal for the Scientific Study of Religion* 26 (1987): 279-93; Lisa Sowle Cahill, "Notes on Moral Theology 1989: Feminist Ethics," *Theological Studies* 51 (1990): 49-64; Mary Grey, "Claiming Power-in-Relation: Exploring the Ethics of Connection," *Journal of Feminist Studies in Religion* 7 (1991): 7-18.

Beverly Wildung Harrison,[3] (Isabel) Carter Heyward,[4] Elizabeth A. Johnson,[5] and Rosemary Radford Ruether,[6] this study will illuminate, test and demonstrate the following thesis: Mutuality is a foundational formal norm for Christian social ethics that functions along with love and justice to promote a balance of power that is required for optimum human flourishing, a flourishing set within the interdependent context of the whole of creation.

WORKING DEFINITION OF "MUTUALITY"

Specifically, what is meant by "mutuality?" As is the case with "love" and "justice," understandings and usages of this term vary greatly. Indeed, it is a substantial task of this study to clarify these diverse understandings and usages of

---

[3]The analysis of Harrison's works will be based primarily on the following sources: "Agendas for a New Theological Ethics," in *Churches in Struggle: Liberation Theologies and Social Change in North America*, ed. Wm. K. Tabb (New York: Monthly Review Press, 1986), 89-98; "Dream of a Common Language: Toward a Normative Theory of Justice in Ethics," *The Annual of the Society of Christian Ethics* (1983): 1-25; "Human Sexuality and Mutuality: A Fresh Paradigm," *Journal of Presbyterian History* 6 (1983): 142-61; *Making the Connections: Essays in Feminist Social Ethics*, ed. Carol S. Robb (Boston: Beacon Press, 1985); "Misogyny and Homophobia: Unexplored Connections," *Church and Society* 73 (1982): 20-33; *Our Right to Choose: Toward a New Ethic of Abortion* (Boston: Beacon Press, 1983); "The Politics of Energy Policy," in *Energy Ethics*, ed. Dieter T. Hessel (New York: Friendship Press, 1979), 56-71; "The Power of Anger in the Works of Love: Christian Ethics for Women and Other Strangers," *Union Seminary Quarterly Review* 36 (1981 Supplement): 41-57.

[4]The selected works by Heyward are: *The Redemption of God: A Theology of Mutual Relation* (New York: University of America Press, 1982); *Our Passion For Justice: Images of Power, Sexuality and Liberation* (Cleveland: The Pilgrim press, 1984); *Touching Our Strength: Erotic as Power and the Love of God* (San Francisco: Harper and Row, Publishers, 1989); *Speaking of Christ: A Lesbian Feminist Voice* ed. Ellen C. Davis (New York: The Pilgrim Press, 1989); and *Staying Power: Reflections on Gender, Justice, and Compassion* [uncorrected 12/1/94 page proofs] (Cleveland: The Pilgrim Press, 1995).

[5]Selected works by Johnson are: *Consider Jesus: Waves of Renewal in Christology* (New York: Crossroad, 1992); *She Who Is: The Mystery of God in Feminist Theological Discourse* (New York: Crossroads, 1992); *Woman, Earth, Creator Spirit*, 1993 Madeleva Lecture (New York: Paulist Press, 1993).

[6]Selected sources by Ruether are: *Disputed Questions: On Being Christian*, Journeys in Faith, ed. Robert A. Raines (Nashville: Abingdon, 1982); *Gaia and God: An Ecofeminist Theology of Earth Healing* (San Francisco: Harper, 1992); *Sexism and God-Talk: Toward a Feminist Theology* (Boston: Beacon Press, 1983); *To Change the World: Christology and Cultural Criticism* (New York: Crossroad, 1989). Also included is Eugene C. Bianchi and Rosemary Radford Ruether, *From Machismo to Mutuality: Essays on Sexism and Man-Woman Liberation* (New York: Paulist Press, 1976).

"mutuality." When otherwise unmodified, I assume Margaret Craddock Huff's definition as the working definition of "mutuality." Huff states that mutuality is:

> . . . a dynamic situation within relationship in which one is simultaneously open to the influence of the other or others, influencing the other or others, and aware of influencing the other or others. Both receptivity and active initiative are required, as are recognition and appreciation of the others' wholeness and particular experience.[7]

In this understanding of mutuality, there is assumed a set of boundary lines that demarcate the person from her/his environment and, significantly, a line that if crossed, indicates a harmful violation of personal integrity.

Though some authors tend to use "equality," "solidarity," and "reciprocity" synonymously with "mutuality," I treat these as distinct terms, bearing significant nuances that differentiate them from "mutuality." Equality is distinguished by definite boundaries and a marked one-to-one correspondence in the relationship or the exchange between the parties of an affiliation; an exchange of like for like.[8] In a relationship characterized by reciprocity, there are clearly designated boundaries between the parties involved, and any action, influence, or giving/receiving is conditioned by the expectation by the other party(ies) that what is received is of equal value to what is given.[9] In the case of solidarity, boundary lines are distinct. Yet, there is a desire to be with the other that strains boundary lines between persons toward one another. Each person's desire exceeds his/her ability to fully participate

---

[7] Margaret Craddock Huff, "The Interdependent Self: An Integrated Concept from Feminist Theology and Feminist Psychology," in *Philosophy and Theology* 2 (1987): 163.

[8] *Oxford English Dictionary*, 2nd ed., s.v. "equality." "The condition of being equal in quantity, amount, value, intensity, etc.; The condition of having equal dignity, rank, or privileges with others, the fact of being on equal footing; In persons: Fairness, impartiality, equity. In things: Due proportion, proportionateness."

[9] Ibid., s.v. "reciprocity." "The state or condition of being reciprocal; a state or relationship in which there is mutual action, influence, giving and taking, correspondence, etc., between two parties or things; Mutual or correspondent concession of advantages or privileges, as forming a basis for commercial relations between two countries."

in the act or experience to be undergone by the other.¹⁰ The straining toward the other, however, does not break individual boundaries. In the case of mutuality, boundaries are distinct, but the critical difference is that they are determined *with* the other(s) and thus, they are more flexible and fluid.¹¹ The means and the end of exchange must be geared to the common flourishing of all parties involved.

DEFINITION OF "NORMS"

Generally, moral norms are defined as "the criteria of judgment about the sort of persons we ought to be and the sort of actions we ought to perform."¹² For Christians, sources for moral norms include scripture, natural law, regulations or laws of the church, experiences of the value of persons and their social relationships and the ongoing life of discernment of the faithful people of God.¹³ According to Timothy O'Connell, "formal norms" are norms which:

> . . . describe the form, the style, the shape that one's life should have in a particular area of ethical concern. Although material norms try to grapple with the concreteness of the situation, with its material, in order to assess various values, formal norms try to point out, in a specific area of moral choice, the character, the form, the successful

---

¹⁰Ibid., s.v. "solidarity." "The fact or quality on the part of communities, etc., of being perfectly united in interests, sympathies, or aspirations; community or perfect coincidence of (or between) interests."

¹¹Heyward, *Touching Our Strength*, 112. Heyward cites a conversation with Margaret Craddock Huff in which Huff stated that boundaries can serve to either connect us or separate us from others: "Boundaries are important, but we cannot create them unilaterally if they are to help us experience strong, empowering connectedness. To sustain mutuality we must create our boundaries *with* one another. This is true whether we are individuals or nations. We learn, with one another's support, how to respect boundaries. We learn, with one another, how to cross them and how to expand them, how to strengthen them and how to loosen them. In Great Britain, `no trespassing' signs do not mean `keep out,' as they do in the United States. Rather, they mean simply, 'You are welcome to enter, but do no harm.' Crossing boundaries is not assumed to be synonymous with danger or harm. In fact, to refuse to cross them, to wall ourselves off from honest connectedness, can, and often does, damage us as well as others."

¹²Richard M. Gula, *What Are They Saying About Moral Norms?* (New York: Paulist Press, 1982), 1. See also Andrew C. Varga, *On Being Human: Principles of Ethics* (New York: Paulist Press, 1978), 10. "A norm, standard or criterion of morality . . . means a measure which can be compared with the human act, thus revealing the goodness or badness of the act."

¹³For a discussion of sources for moral norms see Karl Rahner, *The Dynamic Element in the Church* (New York: Herder and Herder, 1964), 63 and Richard M. Gula, *Reason Informed by Faith: Foundations of Catholic Morality* (New York: Paulist Press, 1989), 283-97, particularly 284-85.

moral agent will possess . . . formal norms proclaim the goal to which every script ought to conform, the dream that every script ought to incarnate. Or, again, although material norms tell us what we should do, formal norms tell us who we should be.[14]

Using O'Connell's definition of a formal norm, I submit that just as one ought to act lovingly and justly, so too one ought to act mutually. One ought to be just, loving and mutual in one's relationships with God, other humans, other earth- creatures, the earth itself, and the entire cosmos.

DEFINITION OF "BALANCE OF POWER"

In common parlance, the term "balance of power" is associated with "an equilibrium of power between two or more nations sufficient to prevent any one from being strong enough to make war or otherwise attempt to impose its will upon the other."[15] In this work however, the meaning of this term is nuanced by the more specific definitions of each element of the phrase--"balance" and "power." Two notions included among the standard definitions of "balance" are "an aesthetically pleasing integration of elements: "harmony" and "physical equilibrium."[16] A notion suggested by the term "equilibrium," is "the normal oriented state of the animal body

---

[14]Timothy E. O'Connell, *Principles For A Catholic Morality* Revised Edition, (San Francisco: Harper, 1990), 180-84 . See also Lisa Sowle Cahill, "Contemporary Challenges to Exceptionless Norms," in *Moral Theology Today* (St. Louis: Pope John XXIII Medical-Moral Research and Education Center, 1984), 123-24 and Josef Fuchs, *Personal Responsibility and Christian Morality Responsibility and Christian Morality* (Washington, DC: Georgetown University Press, 1983), 143.

[15]*Webster's Seventh New Collegiate Dictionary* s.v. "balance of power." See also Reinhold Niebuhr, *The Nature and Destiny of Man* Vol. 2, (New York: Charles Scribner's Sons, 1949), 257-69. For Niebuhr, the concept of the balance of power in domestic (national) relations represented the attainment of order which is enforced by the authority and force of a dominant group. In international relations a balance of power meant an accommodation of interests of nations relative to their power which was adequate to prevent wars. It falls to major countries to maintain a tolerable degree of order, because the international sphere lacks the organization which can provide coercion requiring that the interests of the system be protected. For Niebuhr, the equilibrium of power was not "brotherhood," but rather a situation of tension. He views the principle of balance of power as "a principle of justice insofar as it prevents domination and enslavement; but it is a principle of anarchy and conflict insofar as its tensions, if unresolved, result in overt conflict." Ibid., 266.

[16]*Webster's*, s.v. "balance."

in respect to its environment."¹⁷ Implicit in the process of determining both what is "aesthetically pleasing" and the point of "equilibrium" is a fluid orientation of each party in the relationship to the other. The over-all effect of the fluid orientation is that each party in the relationship gives over or receives something for the betterment of all involved in the relationship. "Balance," thus, implies a shared dynamic "power-to" flourish.

Two prominent understandings of "power" are relevant here: (1) "a possession of control, authority, or influence over others" and (2) "capacity for being acted upon or undergoing an effect."[18]

The meaning of the term "balance of power," as used in this study, is constructed by gleaning the significant nuances of harmony, physical equilibrium, relation to the environment, and shared power from definitions of the components of the term. For the purposes of this project, "balance of power" indicates an organismic and dynamic homeostatic relationship in which there is a relatively stable state of equilibrium or a tendency toward such a state between distinct, but interdependent parties.[19] Assumed in my definition is the feminist notion of "power-to" or "power-

---

[17]Ibid., s.v. "equilibrium."

[18]Ibid., s.v. "power." See also Bernard Loomer, "Two Kinds of Power," *Criterion* 15 (1976): 12-28. Loomer discusses "unilateral power" and "relational power." In addition see Beverly Wildung Harrison, "The Politics of Energy Policy," in *Making the Connections*, 174: "The feminist insight that power is enhanced when power is shared, reciprocal, and constrained by the limits that respectful interrelationship imposes has been widely, and properly, invoked over against other more typical images of social power in our western intellectual tradition. Power has long connoted the capacity to control others. Furthermore, power as a social resource has been interpreted primarily as a fixed and static "zero sum" that can only be traded off, coerced or seized. . . . I believe that in situations of genuine conflict of interest, power does take on a zero sum dynamic, but it is the goal of a genuinely transformative social ethic to identify social policies that will enhance shared, reciprocal, accountable social power so as to press beyond zero-sum power toward more inclusive shared power and participation." See Carter Heyward, *Touching Our Strength*, 191: "Power is the ability to move, effect, make a difference; the energy to create or destroy, call forth or put down. Outside of a particular context, power bears neither positive or negative connotations. Power can be used for good or for ill. Using power-with others is good. Using power-over others is evil."

[19]The notion of peace in St. Augustine's *De Civitate Dei*, Book XIX.13 in *Patralogia latina* 41, is similar to my notion of the "balance of power." He, however, assumes a hierarchy within society and I do not. See also St. Augustine, *City of God*, trans. Marcus Dods (New York: Modern Library, 1950), 690.

with" in which one's "ability to move, effect, make a difference" is "shared, reciprocal and constrained by the limits that respectful interrelationship imposes."[20] The sort of balance of power envisioned here is one in which reciprocity is prized and pursued.

CONTEXT: THE WHOLE OF CREATION

Mutuality is a foundational formal norm for Christian social ethics that functions along with love and justice to promote a balance of power that is required for optimum human flourishing, a flourishing set within the interdependent context of the whole of creation. We now examine more closely how mutuality concerns the whole of creation.

Christian modes of promoting human flourishing have frequently shown little conscious regard for the fact that humans are but part of the creation. Many have construed Christianity's tendency toward anthropocentrism as contributing to the ecological ravaging of the earth. Some interpretations of the Genesis 1 creation myth, with its command to *adam* to ". . . fill the earth and subdue it; and have dominion over every living thing that moves upon the earth . . ." (Gen 1:28), which remove the text from its broader context of Covenant, have been erroneously utilized as the justification for abuse to the ecosystem of the earth.[21] Human status as dominant over the created world has been emphasized in many theological interpretations of the relationship of humans to other animals, plants, the earth, and the cosmos to the near exclusion of the crucial truth that humans are but part of the ecosystem of the entire created universe. The fact that humans bear the image and likeness of God does not exclude the fact that *all* creation bears the mark of the Creator. Thomas Aquinas perhaps put it best. Thomas's macro-ordering of the universe does not place humans as the isolated created good. While it is God's proper place to be concerned with the

---

[20]Harrison, "The Politics," in *Making the Connections*, 175 and Heyward, *Touching Our Strength*, 191. The term, "power-with" appears early in feminist literature. See Mary Parker Follett, *Creative Experience* (New York: Longman, Green & Company, 1924) and her *Dynamic Administration* (New York: Harper and Brothers, 1942).

[21]See James Nash, *Loving Nature: Ecology, Integrity and Christian Responsibility* (Nashville: Abingdon Press, 1991).

universe, as friends of God and lovers of God humans must be concerned with the whole of creation because that is what love requires.[22] This implies that, contrary to prevalent assumptions, neither love, justice, or mutuality can be understood or attained without attention to the interdependent context of human life in its largest and most local dimensions.

FOUR FORMS OF MUTUALITY

Mutuality is difficult to define, both because of its complexity and because of the widely diverse ways it is used in ethics literature. Consistently visible in the Judeo-Christian tradition, both in antecedent and analogical notions in Thomas Aquinas, John Duns Scotus, Martin Buber and H. Richard Niebuhr, and more explicitly treated in the works of (Isabel) Carter Heyward, Beverly Wildung Harrison, Elizabeth A. Johnson and Rosemary Radford Ruether are several forms of mutuality.[23] This work will explore four forms of mutuality as they are suggested in the works of these eight scholars.[24]

---

[22]Thomas Aquinas, *Summa theologiae*, Black Friars Edition (New York: McGraw-Hill Book Company, 1968). See II-II.25.4, Responsio: "Or we can discuss charity in terms of its special character, in other words according as it is friendship, for God chiefly, and consequently for whatever belongs to him." In daily life, issues that concern our friends become our concern, as well. Thus, since all creation belongs to God, we must also be "friend" to all in creation. See also Jean Porter, *The Recovery of Virtue: Relevance of Aquinas For Christian Ethics* (Louisville: Westminster/ John Knox, 1990), 170: "... for Aquinas the claim that charity makes us friends of God is no metaphor. He means it literally, his strong sense of the infinite gap between creature and Creator notwithstanding. In II-II.23.1, he assures us that charity is true friendship because it is based on mutual communication between God and the justified (cf. II-II.24.2).... Elsewhere Aquinas speaks even more strongly. He asserts that through the theological virtues, we become partakers in the divine nature (I-II.62.1). Through charity in particular, we enjoy a 'certain intimate conversation' with God (I-II.65.5). Still more strongly, the grace of God, by which faith, hope and charity are bestowed, can be said to deify (*deificet*) us (I-II.112.1). In short, charity can be described as the friendship of women and men with God, because charity transforms its subjects into participants in the very mind and will of God." Insofar as we are "god-like," God's concerns are our concerns; the well-being of creation is thus our concern.

[23]Peter A. Angeles, ed. *Dictionary of Philosophy* (New York: Barnes and Noble Books, 1981), s.v. "form." "That aspect under which a thing is conceptualized or appears and by which it is classified."

[24]The four forms of mutuality were educed from the careful study of the use of the term "mutuality" in key primary texts of these authors. For each use of the term by an author the location, the use, the context, and a descriptive definition of the term in each context was charted. The four forms of mutuality emerged from drawing comparisons and contrasting the information charted.

Mutuality in these works is discernible in four forms. First, mutuality is seen as recognition of interdependence among, and a reverence for, all things and all beings in the cosmos. This is suggested in Buber's understanding of the relationship of all elements of creation to one another in that all bear the mark of the same Creator. This form is also indicated in Ruether's "ecological ethic." In this form, all in creation is potentially both subject and object. Second, mutuality is understood as relationship to the divine and participation in the on-going co-creation/redemption of the world. (Isabel) Carter Heyward points to this form in her explication of the Incarnation and the covenant relationship between God and Israel. Here the focal subjects and objects of mutuality are God and human persons. However, because of the delicate balance of the ecosystem necessary to sustain maximum human flourishing, the entire cosmos is also included in Heyward's notions of redemption/creation. In a third form, mutuality is seen as undergirding egalitarian relationships between women and men. Beverly Wildung Harrison and Rosemary Radford Ruether demonstrate the grounds for equal and embodied participation of both male and female human beings in the *imago Dei*. Ruether's work contrasting mutuality and *machismo* is particularly relevant here. Harrison stresses the notion of embodiment as a way of being and doing, seen particularly in sexual relationships, as giving expression to the *imago Dei*. Elizabeth A. Johnson demonstrates how the trinitarian relationships stand as a paradigm for the relationships between women and men. Pointing to the fact that the persons of the Trinity are "persons precisely *as* mutual relations" and that "there is no subordination, no before, or after, no first, second, and third, no dominant and marginalized," she infers the necessity of mutuality in human relations.[25] Human

---

[25]Johnson, *She Who Is*, 216-23. See particularly 219: "There is no subordination, no before or after, no first, second and third, no dominant and marginalized. There is only `a trinity of persons mutually interrelated in a unity of essence.' The trinitarian symbol intimates a community of equals, so core to the feminist vision of ultimate shalom. It points to patterns of differentiation that are non-hierarchical, and to forms of relating that do not involve dominance. It models the ideal, reflected in so many studies of women's ways of being in the world, of relational bonding that enables the growth of persons as genuine subjects of history in and through the matrix of community, and the flourishing of community in and through the praxis of its members. In this vision, personal uniqueness flourishes not at the expense of relationship but through the power of profound companionship that respects differences and values them equally: an aim mirrored in the symbol of the Trinity."

beings, male and female, are both subjects and objects in mutual relation. Fourth, mutuality is described as radical solidarity, reciprocity and identification with the least ones of the world. This form is implicit in Harrison's expansion upon H. Richard Niebuhr's notion of responsibility, which poses Jesus' suffering and death as embodied power of mutuality as the central moral goal of the Christian life. All human persons are both subjects and objects for mutuality in Harrison's understanding. All human persons are in some way both oppressed and oppressor. However, Christians have a particular obligation to work toward the empowerment of the economically poor.[26]

It appears that the notion of "mutuality" is similar in its complexity to the notion of "justice." Traditionally, a tripartite nature--commutative, social and distributive--has been ascribed to justice.[27] Similarly, mutuality seems to have four key loci of expression--cosmic, gender, generative, social. Cosmic mutuality is seen in the relation between God and the whole of creation, and in the fact that humans are mutually related to everything in the entire cosmos by virtue of their relationship with

---

[26] All of these authors use scripture as a foundational source in developing their notion of mutuality. See e.g. in: Johnson, *She Who Is*, 70-71; Harrison, *Our Right*, 57-90; Ruether, *Gaia and God*, 20-22; and Heyward, *Redemption of God*, 149-78. The biblical texts that are widely accepted as undergirding the Christian doctrines of creation, redemption, *imago Dei*, covenant, Trinity, Incarnation, as well as the notions of community, love, justice, or friendship are readily visible in the arguments offered by these authors. Biblical sources used by these authors are assumed in my analysis of mutuality, though a complete analysis of the biblical texts is beyond the limits of this work. Where scriptural grounding is particularly significant, I have noted the relevant texts and/or the sources of biblical analysis upon which the scholar relies.

[27] A thorough discussion of the nature of justice is found in Daniel C. Maguire, *A New American Justice* (Minneapolis: Winston Press, 1980), especially 55-84. Maguire notes (page 194, n.4) an excellent treatment of the tripartite nature of justice found in Joseph Pieper, *Justice* (New York: Pantheon Books, 1955), 48-55. See especially page 50, where Pieper refers to Thomas Aquinas's explanation of the forms of justice: ". . . Justice rules in a community or state whenever the three basic relations, the three fundamental structures of communal life, are disposed in their proper order: firstly, the relations of individuals to one another *(ordo partium ad partes)*; secondly, the relations of the social whole to the individuals *(ordo totius ad partes)*; thirdly, the relations of individuals to the social whole *(ordo partium ad totum)*. These three basic relationships correspond to the three basic forms of justice: reciprocal, or mutually exchanged justice *(iustitia commutativa)*, which orders the relation of individual to partner; ministering justice *(iustitia distributiva)*, which brings order to the relations between the community as such and the individuals who are its members; legal or general justice *(iustitia legalis, iustitia generalis)*, which orders the members' relations to the social whole." See also Aristotle, *Nicomachean Ethics* Book V:1129a3 -1138b14 where he describes and defines the scope and external nature of justice, as well as its internal nature. For Thomas Aquinas's treatment of justice, see his *ST* II-II.57-122, especially Questions 58, 61, 79, 80, and 122.

God. Gender mutuality is found in the relation between women and men as embodied, egalitarian relations. Generative mutuality is located in human/divine partnership in ongoing co-creation and redemption. Insofar as each human person bears God's image and likeness within his/her own flesh, each enjoys mutuality with God as creator and redeemer. Social mutuality is pinpointed in the relations of radical solidarity, reciprocity and identification with the poor and oppressed, the least ones in the world. All four loci are interrelated in a manner similar to the interrelationship of social, distributive and commutative justice.

RELATIONSHIP BETWEEN LOVE, JUSTICE, AND MUTUALITY

Two formal norms, love and justice, have traditionally been viewed as foundational for all Christian ethics. While at times either love or justice has been more heavily stressed, both have been perennially presented as measures of Christian morality. As Daniel C. Maguire points out, it is significant that throughout the canon of Scripture love and justice are viewed as coordinates of the same plane. He states:

> . . . `Sow for yourselves justice and reap the fruit of steadfast love' (Hos. 10:12). The dichotomy between love and justice is spurious. The two are naturally related. Justice goes before love, insisting on the minimal prerequisites for survival. But then it makes common cause with love upon discovering that surviving without thriving is not surviving at all.[28]

MUTUALITY: A CORRECTIVE AND COMPLEMENTARY NORM

It is precisely in the consideration of what behavior constitutes "thriving" that the need arises for mutuality as a formal norm to complement and correct love and justice in the Christian social ethical framework. Failure to consider mutuality as a norm has left many significant questions unexplored or inadequately considered, including those involving the concrete aspects of the reality revealing questions (what?, why?, how?, who?, where?, when?, What are the foreseeable effects?, What are the viable alternatives?); the dynamics of power and the shaping of those dynamics to serve "power-with;" and concern for the thriving and flourishing of *all* involved in

---

[28]Daniel C. Maguire, "The Primacy of Justice in Moral Theology," *Horizons* 10 (1983): 77.

the situation. Thus, some interpretations of the Christian tradition in relation to enormously complex issues permitted, tolerated or even promoted all sorts of violation of human well-being, yet were considered ethically adequate in their time.[29] For example, slavery was ignored as a theological issue or even defended by clergymen such as Cotton Mather.[30] Women were treated as material property even as late as 1917, when the Roman Catholic Code of Canon Law portrayed women as functionally subordinate, morally sinful and seductive, intellectually inferior, and emotionally unstable.[31] In the practice of the Christian community, a hierarchical cultural conception of the relationships between men and women superseded the notion of equal regard expressed in the early baptismal formula, ". . . there is neither

---

[29]Some would contend that mutuality was part of a Christian culture and that it was submerged by a post-Cartesian and increasingly technological modernity with its centralizing of scientific knowledge. See for example Kirk Koerner, *Liberalism and Its Critics* (New York: St. Martins, 1985); Irving Greenberg, "Cloud of Smoke, Pillar of Fire: Judaism, Christianity, and Modernity After the Holocaust," in *Auschwitz: Beginning of a New Era?*, ed. Eva Fleischman (New York: KTAV, 1977); Jonathan Schell, *The Fate of the Earth* (New York: Knopf, 1982); or Joan Casanas, "The Task of Making God Exist," in *The Idols of Death and God of Life: A Theology*, ed. Pablo Richard, trans. Barbara E. Campbell and Bonnie Shepherd (Maryknoll: Orbis Books, 1983). In this case, also, the significant point remains: mutuality has been absent in both traditional and modern evaluations, whether considered "Christian" or "reasonable" in their time.

Needless to say, the historical examples of slavery, women's canonical status, and the role of U.S. and Vatican state diplomacy in the Holocaust are each complex. Any claim that a lack of mutuality alone detracts from their proper moral resolution would take much greater development than is possible here. My point here is to merely suggest situations in which many would agree moral failure occurred and to invite the reader into the process of reflection I unfold in the following chapters. As I show in Chapters 4 and 5, mutuality has probative value in that it illuminates and delimits loving and just behavior. Consideration of mutuality causes us to ask different questions concerning love and justice, thereby making it more possible to discern moral good and evil.

[30]James H. Cone, *God of the Oppressed* (New York: Seabury Press, 1975), 45-53. "Unfortunately, American theology from Cotton Mather and Jonathan Edwards to Reinhold Niebuhr and Sherbert Ogden including radicals and conservatives, have interpreted the Gospel according to the cultural and political interests of white people. . . . During slavery the social limitation of white theology was expressed in three main forms: (1) some white theologians ignored slavery as a theological issue; (2) others justified it; and (3) only a few spoke out against it."

[31]Rose Dermott, "The Legal Condition of Women in the Church: Shifting Policies and Norms'" (JCD diss., The Catholic University of America, 1979). See also D. Morrison, *The Juridic Status of Women in Canonical Law and in United States Law* (Rome: Gregorianum, 1965).

male *and* female."[32] Even today, the Roman Catholic Church continues to be governed by a solely male presbyterate and hierarchy.[33] Similarly, the "Double Love Command" has been noted in Christian moral tradition for centuries. Yet, from within that same tradition, Christian leaders within the Vatican State and the U. S. government found the leeway to play a questionable role in relation to the Holocaust.[34] In all of these instances, disregard for mutuality as a formal norm along

---

[32]For a succinct discussion of the issues of the interpretation of this text, see Elizabeth Schüssler Fiorenza, "Justified by All Her Children: Struggle, Memory and Vision," *Concilium* (1990/1): 27-34. For extensive bibliographical references refer to H. D. Betz, *Galatians* (Philadelphia: Fortress Press, 1979). See also D. R. MacDonald, *There is No Male or Female* (Philadelphia: Fortress Press, 1987). For a methodological discussion and execution of the reconstruction of Gal 3:26-28, see Elizabeth Schüssler Fiorenza, *In Memory of Her: A Feminist Theological Reconstruction of Christian Origins* (New York: Crossroad, 1983), 204-41.

[33]Elizabeth McDonough, "Women and the New Church Law," *Concilium* 85 (1986): 73-81. Although women are considered part of the laici and the christifideles in the 1983 Code of Canon Law, there remain significant restrictions, for example (Can. 230.1) the stable ministries of lector and acolyte are restricted to men; (Can. 667.3) only monasteries of nuns must observe the extensive and strict norms for papal cloister; all women are excluded from the ministri sacri because they are not men (Can. 1024). These differences are significant because they bar women from participation in all aspects of the life and ministry of the Church. Ibid., 79: "In Canon 208, the 1983 Code qualifies its affirmation of 'true equality' for all chrisitfideles by adding the phrase, 'according to one's own condition and function.' Within this qualification, it can be said that laity are not juridically equivalent to clergy and women are not juridically equivalent to lay men. The former inequality is solidly based on the divine institution of ministri sacri; the latter is not so solidly founded."

[34]In the vast literature on these complex issues, most authors acknowledge both the moral failure of the state and the saintly heroism of some individuals and groups. I would argue that saintly heroism involved fidelity to love and justice, informed by mutuality. See: John F. Morley, *Vatican Diplomacy and the Jews During the Holocaust 1939-43* (New York: KTAV, 1980), esp., 209; Owen Chadwick, "The Pope and the Jews in 1942," in *Persecution and Toleration: Papers Read at the 22nd Summer Meeting and 23rd Winter Meeting of the Ecclesiastical History Society*, Studies in Church History 21, ed. W.J. Sheila (London: Basil Blackwell, 1984), 435-72; Edward H. Flannery, "Anti-Zionism and the Christian Psyche," *Journal of Ecumenical Studies* 6 (1969): 173-84; Edward H. Flannery, *The Anguish of the Jews: Twenty-three Centuries of Anti-semitism* (New York: Macmillan, 1965) {Revised Edition (New York: Paulist Press, 1985)}; John Pawlikowski, *Catechetics and Prejudice: How Catholic Teaching Materials View Jews, Protestants, and Racial Minorities* (New York: Paulist Press, 1973); Jules Isaac, *The Teaching of Contempt* (New York: Holt, Reinhart, Winston, 1984); Thomas F. Stransky, "Holy Diplomacy: Making the Impossible Possible," in *Unanswered Questions: Theological Views of Jewish - Catholic Relations* ed. Roger Brooks (Notre Dame: University of Notre Dame Press, 1988), 51-69; Yehuda Bauer, et.al., eds., *Remembering the Future: Working Papers and Addenda - Jews and Christians During and After the Holocaust*, 3 vols., (New York: Pergamon Press, 1989), esp. in vol. 3, 2973-85; and in vol. 1, 93-108; 156-170; 248-53; 254-65; 266-80; and 584-97; Debrah E. Lipstadt, "Moral Bystanders," *Society* 20 (1983): 21-26; Raul Hillberg, *The Destruction of European Jews* (Chicago: Quadrangle Books, 1961); A. Roy Eckardt, *Elder and Younger Brothers* (New York: Schocken, 1973); Daniel C. Maguire, "The Violence of Anti-Semitism," in *The Moral Revolution: A*

with love and justice, significantly contributed to the thwarting of human thriving and even the unnecessary loss of human life, while the behavior of key decision-makers was judged to be morally adequate according to the existing Christian ethical norms of the time.[35] When only love and justice are considered, some of the conditions for optimum human flourishing remain obscured. When mutuality is added to the equation, the conditions for optimum human flourishing are more adequately revealed and measured.[36]

Christian Humanist Vision (San Francisco: Harper & Row, Publishers, 1986), 63-66; Robert G. Weisbord and Wallace P. Sillanpoa, *The Chief Rabbi, the Pope, and the Holocaust: An Era in Vatican-Jewish Relations* (New Brunswick: Transaction Publications, 1992); Alan Cowell, "Vatican Disavows Suggestion of Church Guilt in Holocaust," *New York Times* 143 (May 27, 1994): A3(N), col. 4; Archbishop Lipscomb, "Commemorating the Liberation of Auschwitz," *Origins* 24 (1995): 561-64; German Bishops, "Opportunity to Re-examine Relationship With the Jews," *Origins* 24 (1995): 585-86; or Polish Bishops, "The Victims of Nazi Ideology," *Origins* 24 (1995): 586-88.

The terrible moral failure of the policy of U.S. (and other governments) is exemplified in the U. S. Holocaust Museum exhibit on the USS St. Louis. See: Saul S. Friedman, *No Haven for the Oppressed: United States Policy Toward Jewish Refugees, 1938-1945* (Detroit: Wayne State University Press,1973); Frank W. Brecher, *Reluctant Ally: United States Foreign Policy Toward the Jews From Wilson to Roosevelt* (New York: Greenwood Press, 1991); David S. Wyman, ed., *America and the Holocaust*, 13 vols. (New York: Garland Publishing, 1989); Davis S. Wyman, *The Abandonment of the Jews: America and the Holocaust 1941-1945* (New York: Pantheon Books, 1984).

In addition see: Lucy S. Dawidowicz, *The War Against the Jews, 1933-45*, First Edition (New York: Holt, Reinhart and Winston, 1975); Stephen Ross, interview by Debbie Dunn, in *Stephen Ross: Holocaust Survivors Project* (New York: William E. Wiener Oral History Library, American Jewish Committee, 1975); and Abraham J. Peck, ed., *Jews and Christians After the Holocaust* (Philadelphia: Fortress Press, 1982).

[35]The obvious objection to my claim is that these atrocities were tolerated because individuals did not follow existing moral norms. I affirm the feminist argument that predominant moral frameworks available in those times were deficient because they were grounded in theology(ies) rooted in a hierarchical world view, Greek philosophical dualism, and an almost entirely transcendent image of God- -all of which obscure mutuality as a value. The notions of love and justice employed were rooted in the unreality of a false consciousness that failed to consider what constitutes the concrete necessities for the flourishing of all involved.

[36]Needless to say, the historical examples above are each complex. I do not claim that a lack of mutuality alone detracts from their proper resolution, nor do I claim that consideration of mutuality alone would insure moral integrity. Any such claims would take much greater development than is possible here. My point here is to merely suggest situations in which many would agree moral failure occurred and invite the reader into the process of reflection I unfold in the following chapters. As I show in Chapters 4 and 5, mutuality has probative value in that it illuminates and delimits loving and just behavior.

Critique of Love

At many points in Christian history, sacrificial love has been stressed to the neglect of mutual love. In a number of Christian traditions, any love of self was suspect and *agape* at times came to be understood as void of a healthy self-love, pride in one's own goodness or any self-interest. In Catholicism, it seems that the tendency to understand love as nearly exclusively sacrificial is a bequest of some forms of medieval passion mysticism.[37] As Christine Gudorf claims, Christian love must not be presumed to be disinterested or set apart from other love as self-sacrificing. "All love involves sacrifice and aims at mutuality. . . . Much love is mutual; all love is directed at mutuality. It could not be any other way, for we find love rewarding."[38] Mutuality functions as a corrective to a one-sided emphasis on sacrificial love.

Critique of Justice

Justice has long been considered a complex multifaceted reality.[39] The influential Aristotelian and Thomistic theories of justice state that justice has a

---

[37] Christine E. Gudorf, "Parenting, Mutual Love and Sacrifice," in *Women's Consciousness, Women's Conscience: A Reader in Feminist Ethics* ed. Barbara Hilkert Andolsen, Christine E. Gudorf, Mary D. Pellauer, (Minneapolis: Winston Press, 1985), 175-91. See particularly 182 n. 9 where Gudorf discusses a split in the dominant understanding of love by Catholic and Protestant theologians. Gudorf cites Anders Nygren, *Agape and Eros*, trans. Philip S. Watson, (New York: Harper and Row, 1969), 712-13, in which he advances the idea that Luther considered love of neighbor to necessitate completely dispossessing and annihilating self-love. Gudorf indicates that S. Kierkegaard, *Works of Love*, trans. Howard and Edna Hong, (New York: Harper and Row, 1965), 68 is in full agreement with Nygren's reading of Luther. Prior to Luther and in the patristic period Christian love was regularly referred to in terms such as eros or mutual love--see Aquinas's *ST* II-II.26.9-12. Contrary to Nygren's claim that his explication of *agape* was the normative *New Testament* understanding for all Christians, his interpretation was a phenomenon nearly exclusive to Protestant ethics. See Gerald Gilleman, *The Primacy of Love in the Moral Life* (New York: Newman Press, 1959).

[38] Gudorf, "Parenting," in *Women's Consciousness*, 182, 185. Most feminists see value in sacrificial love that is chosen freely, consciously, and with the full integrity of the lover intact which moves the relationship toward greater mutuality or has mutuality as its goal.

[39] For a discussion of the relationship of love and justice see Gene Outka, *Agape: An Ethical Analysis* (New Haven: Yale University Press, 1972), 73-92. He includes Rawls, Frankena, Fletcher, Brunner, Ramsey and others in these remarks.

tripartite nature --commutative, social and distributive.[40] Some contemporary ethicists's renderings of that theory assume reciprocal influence of varying degrees in each form of justice. Several of these ethicists, for example, Daniel C. Maguire, clearly assume mutuality as part of their notion of justice.[41] There is a burgeoning movement among feminist scholars, however, toward considering mutuality as an absolute criterion for Christian social ethical behavior. Increasingly, feminist ethicists are drawing mutuality to the foreground to stand as a distinct and normative consideration in the ethical process.

Generally, theories of justice can be classified in three categories: Rationalist[42] and natural law theories, analytical and positivist theories, and utilitarian and other theories.[43] Mutuality functions as a complement and challenge to natural law theories

---

[40]See *Justice*, and *New American Justice*, 55-84 where Maguire defines "justice." See also Daniel C. Maguire and A. Nicholas Fargnoli, *On Moral Grounds: The Art/Science of Ethics* (New York: Crossroad, 1991), 27-32, 33-37.

[41]Maguire, *New American Justice*, 74.

[42]Peter A. Angeles, *Dictionary of Philosophy*, s.v. "rationalism:" "In general, the philosophic approach which emphasizes reason as the primary source of knowledge, prior or superior to, and independent of sense knowledge." Key rationalists are Plato, Aristotle, and Descartes.
  Ibid., s.v. "law, natural:" "The set of obligations or principles (laws, maxims, duties, codes, commands, etc.) binding upon one's conduct which are obtained by reason from examination of the universe (nature) in contrast to those obtained by revelation, intuition, innate moral conscience, authority, feelings, inclinations." Key figures are Thomas Aquinas, Cicero, Ulpian.
  Ibid., s.v. "analytic philosophy:" "A twentieth-century philosophic movement . . . that concentrates on language and the attempt to analyze statements (or concepts, or linguistic expressions, or logical forms) in order to find those with the best and most concise logical form which fits the facts or meaning to be presented. Central to analytic philosophy is the forming of definitions--linguistic or non-linguistic, real or contextual." Key figures are Bretrand Russell, G.E. Moore, Ludwig Wittgenstein.
  Ibid., s.v. "positivism, logical:" ". . . The acceptance of the verifiability principle, which is a criterion for determining that a statement has cognitive meaning. The cognitive meaning of a statement (as opposed to its emotive or other levels of meaning) is dependent upon its being verified. A statement is meaningful if-and-only-if it is, at least in principle, empirically verifiable. Some rock-bottom sense experience (positive knowledge) must be reached before a statement can have cognitive meaning." Two key figures are Thomas Hobbes and Chiam Perelman.
  Ibid., s.v. "utilitarianism:" ". . . One should act so as to promote the greatest happiness (pleasure) of the greatest number of people." Key figures are Jeremy Bentham, John Stuart Mill, and John Rawls.

[43]*Encyclopedia of Philosophy*, s.v. "justice." This article presents a discussion of major theories of justice.

in that it requires a more critical view of hierarchy than is commonly found in natural law traditions, entailing the elimination of relationships of unilateral submission and subjugation. Mutuality functions as a corrective to the positivists in that it shifts the criterion for justice from pure legalism to include the concrete and dynamic needs of the other as basic to thriving. Mutuality functions as a corrective to utilitarianism in that it requires consideration of the good/needs of all beings and elements of the universe in relation to one another, not merely the greatest good for the greatest number.

RESTATEMENT OF THE THESIS

I submit that mutuality is a foundational formal norm for Christian social ethics that functions along with love and justice to promote a balance of power that is required for optimum human flourishing, a flourishing set within the interdependent context of the whole of creation. Mutuality serves as a complement and corrective to love and justice. To the extent that mutuality is absent in a power relationship, condescension or oppression occurs. To the extent that love is absent, hate or indifference exists. The lack of mutuality in the creation and sustenance of a just situation can result in mere coercion and condescension. Lack of mutuality in a relationship of love can result in a kind of sacrifice that may be ultimately harmful to all involved. Lack of justice in a relationship can result in extravagant indulgence on the part of one party in the relationship at the expense of the other(s). Lack of love in a relationship may result in a mechanistic balance, which some would call justice, but which would not necessarily produce the maximum conditions for human flourishing.

PROCEDURE

The theological method employed in this study will be analytic and comparative toward the end of illuminating, demonstrating and testing the thesis concerning mutuality as a formal norm. Four issues will be investigated.

First, I will analyze selected writings of Harrison, Heyward, Johnson and Ruether to isolate their treatments of the term, mutuality. Several questions will be addressed to the selected works of each scholar. My first query will determine precisely how the term "mutuality" is defined: (a) Does "mutuality" intend the interdependent relatedness of all cosmic elements, including human beings? (b) Does "mutuality" encompass the concrete and full embodiment of women and men in the *imago Dei*? (c) Does "mutuality" connote human participation in the on-going creation and redemption of the world? (d) Does "mutuality" denote the relinquishment of "power-over" by those more powerful and a claim to "power-with" by those less powerful toward the flourishing of all in any situation?[44] My next inquiry will be: In what context(s) does the author use the term, "mutuality?" Finally I will seek to determine if the author of the particular text perceives that "mutuality" functions as a norm in Christian social ethics. Based on common points discovered in the analysis, my working definition of mutuality will be refined.

Second, in order to illustrate the grounding within the Christian tradition for the status of mutuality as a norm, I will compare the feminists' understanding of mutuality with analogs found in selected works by Thomas Aquinas, John Duns Scotus, Martin Buber and H.R. Niebuhr.

Third, I will return to the works of Harrison, Heyward, Johnson and Ruether. Here, relying on definitions of "formal norm" by Josef Fuchs, Lisa Sowle Cahill and Timothy E. O'Connell, I will consider the extent to which mutuality functions as a foundational formal norm in the feminist works.

---

[44]This inquiry seeks to probe the dynamics of the voluntary relinquishment of power by "the powerful" in order to empower the whole for the greater good of all. This dynamic was modeled by the two saints of Assisi, Clare and Francis who were both *majores*, but who chose to identify with the *minores*. Their choice influenced revolutionary change for centuries to come. See Ingrid J. Peterson, *Clare of Assisi: A Biographical Study* (Quincy, IL: Franciscan Press, 1993), 62, 122-23, 134, 177, 195, 215-16. See also Omer Englebert, "A Time For War, A Time For Servitude," in *The Francis Book: Eight Hundred Years With the Saint From Assisi*, ed. Roy M. Gasnick (New York: Collier Books, 1980), 12-14. In addition see Marie Dennis, et. al., *St. Francis and the Foolishness of God* (Maryknoll: Orbis Books, 1993), 28-40. The responsibility of "the less powerful" or poor to assert their personhood and human dignity when oppressed is also investigated. This dynamic is exemplified in Paulo Freire's notion of *conscientização*. See Paulo Freire, *Pedagogy of the Oppressed*, trans. Myra Bergman Ramos (New York: Herder and Hereder, 1970), 27-55. See also Ruether, *Sexism and God-Talk*, 163-64, 180-81. In addition see James H. Cone, *Black Theology and Black Power* (New York: Seabury Press, 1969), 137-38. Finally, see Gustavo Gutierrez, *The Power of the Poor in History*, trans. Robert R. Barr (Maryknoll: Orbis Books, 1983), 90-101.

Fourth, the argument for mutuality as a formal norm (along with love and justice) for Christian social ethics will be advanced. I will make the case for mutuality as a foundational formal norm by arguing that when only love and justice are considered, some of the conditions for optimum human flourishing remain obscured. When mutuality is included in moral deliberation, the conditions for optimum human flourishing are more adequately revealed and measured.

In the final chapter, I will provide a practical application of the thesis. In order to demonstrate my argument that there is probative value in maintaining mutuality as a formal norm for Christian social ethics, I will examine three moral analyses of the application of the just war criteria to the Persian Gulf War. Using the definition of mutuality established in Chapter One, I will evaluate how (if at all) each author's consideration of the notion of mutuality affects his/her judgment whether or nor the Gulf War was a just war. Conclusions will be drawn concerning the probative value of mutuality for moral decision-making.

CHAPTER 1
MUTUALITY DEFINED IN SELECTED WORKS OF FOUR CHRISTIAN FEMINISTS

INTRODUCTION

The objective of this chapter is three-fold: first, to analyze the definition of "mutuality" found in selected works by Beverly Wildung Harrison, (Isabel) Carter Heyward, Elizabeth A. Johnson, and Rosemary Radford Ruether; second, to identify their common definition of the notion; and third, to determine if it is evident from the texts that these thinkers view mutuality as a formal norm for Christian social ethics. The chapter is divided into two parts.

In Part One, I first, review the theological context in which the author uses the term "mutuality" and provide each scholar's basic definition of the term. I then analyze how the meaning of "mutuality" is nuanced by the different contexts and various ways each author employs the word. The analysis is focused by means of five questions, each concerning a particular form of mutuality, which I address to these texts. For each author, I inquire (a) Does "mutuality" intend the interdependent relatedness of all cosmic elements, including human beings [cosmic mutuality]? (b) Does "mutuality" encompass the concrete and full embodiment of women and men in the *imago Dei* [gender mutuality]? (c) Does "mutuality" connote human participation in the on-going creation and redemption of the world [generative mutuality]? (d) Does "mutuality" denote the relinquishment of "power-over" by those more powerful and a claim to "power-with" by those less powerful in a situation toward the flourishing of all [social mutuality]? and finally, (e) Does mutuality function as a formal norm in Christian social ethics?. Because these feminists use terms that are potentially synonymous with "mutuality," I then, briefly consider how and to what extent each author distinguishes or relates mutuality, equality, friendship, reciprocity, solidarity, love, and justice.

In Part Two I identify points of consensus among the four feminists on the aforementioned issues. Then, based on common points discovered in the analysis, I reformulate the working definition of "mutuality" that was given in the Introduction.

The selected works of Heyward, Harrison, Johnson and Ruether were chosen because they constitute a balanced representation of both Protestant and Catholic feminist thought. Each scholar stresses a different aspect of "mutuality." Heyward's theology of mutual relation builds upon Buber's concepts of "I and Thou" and of the biblical understanding of covenant between Yahweh and Israel. Harrison expands upon H. R. Niebuhr's notion of responsibility and poses mutuality, modeled upon Jesus' embodied power of mutuality, as the central moral goal for the Christian life. Insofar as Jesus as the Christ expresses fullness of what Christian moral life ought to be, Johnson's "Jesus-Sophia" and her treatment of the Trinity provide a substantial theological basis for mutuality as central to Christian social ethics. Ruether's pioneering work in historical theology is foundational for contemporary feminist theology; particularly relevant here are her ecological ethics and her work contrasting mutuality with *machismo*.

PART ONE:
EXPOSITION OF THE FOUR FEMINISTS' DEFINITIONS OF MUTUALITY

Before we can begin the analysis of the four feminists' understandings of mutuality, it is necessary to provide a brief exposition of key elements of each author's theology to demonstrate the grounding of the definition in Christian thought. Because Rosemary Radford Ruether is a "founding mother" of contemporary Christian feminist theology, I begin with her. In different ways, Harrison, Heyward, and Johnson each build upon Ruether's fundamental insights concerning Christianity from a feminist perspective. I treat (Isabel) Carter Heyward and Beverly Wildung Harrison next and in sequence, because although they approach the notion of "mutuality" from different perspectives, they readily acknowledge their reliance upon one another's works.

Elizabeth A. Johnson is treated last, as one who is of a second generation of contemporary feminist scholars benefitting from the work of earlier feminists. Johnson's own contributions bring greater depth to the claims advanced by earlier feminists and interpret classical Christian theology from her Catholic Christian liberationist feminist perspective.

Rosemary Radford Ruether: Stated Definition of Mutuality

Rosemary Radford Ruether is a feminist liberationist historical theologian who is widely acknowledged as a "founding mother" of modern feminist theology.[1] As early as 1967 she began raising questions which subsequently laid the groundwork for her most systematic work, *Sexism and God-Talk: Toward a Feminist Theology*. In this work that she lays the foundation for her ecological ethic, an ethic she weaves through nearly all of her other major works and which she elaborates in even greater detail in her 1992 work *Gaia and God: An Ecofeminist Theology of Earth Healing*. While the premises for Ruether's ethics are most clearly set forth in these works, her use of the term "mutuality" is infrequent. What is foundational to Ruether's ecological ethics, however, is the recognition of a radical relatedness of all things. This relatedness Ruether defines as "biophilic mutuality."[2] When Ruether does use the term "mutuality," she does so in a manner that seems to presume the reader is aware of her broader liberationist and ecofeminist theological assumptions which are detailed in *Sexism and God-Talk*.

---

[1] See Kathryn Allen Rabuzzi, "The Socialist Feminist Vision of Rosemary Radford Ruether: A Challenge to Liberal Feminism," *Religious Studies* 15 (1989): 4-8. See also Rebecca S. Chopp, "Seeing and Naming the World Anew: The Works of Rosemary Radford Ruether," Ibid., 8-11. In addition see Rosemary Radford Ruether, "Beginnings: An Intellectual Biography," in Gregory Baum, ed., *Journeys: The Impact of Personal Experience on Religious Thought* (New York: Paulist Press, 1975), 34-56.

[2] Ruether, *Gaia and God*, 265.

Ruether's Feminist Theological Context
Anthropology: Woman Image/Image of God

The starting point for Ruether's theological reflection is the experience of women.[3] She analyzes her sources seeking to glean that which supports women as full human beings. Next, she utilizes the gleanings to reconstruct the tradition raising to high relief that which illuminates the full humanity of women (equal to men) as a divine mandate. Only those understandings that fully include and liberate women are considered legitimate. Ruether also presumes that God's defense of the oppressed (the prophetic tradition) can be applied to women (as well as men) because it can be demonstrated that they are the most oppressed. In the light of these presumptions, Ruether holds that there is truth to be drawn from Gnostic, "pagan" religions and classical theology.

In Ruether's view, the oppressed status of women in modern Western society can be traced to a dualistic traditional Christian anthropology in which a distinction was made between *essence* and *existence*.[4] Historically, human nature is fallen and its original authentic nature and potential has been obscured. While patriarchal Christianity never fully denied the status of *imago Dei* to women, the ambiguous

---

[3] Ibid., 12-46. That there is no homogeneous woman's experience presents a definite challenge to feminists to sustain a dialogue among all women in order to discern what is unique and what is common in the experience of women. See Barbara Hilkert Andolsen, Christine E. Gudorf, and Mary D. Pellauer, "Introduction," in *Women's Consciousness*, xi-xvii. See also Alison M. Jaggar, "Feminist Ethics: Some Issues For the Nineties," *Journal of Social Philosophy* 20 (1990): 91-107.

[4] Ruether, *Sexism and God-Talk*, 95-99. Ruether illustrates this point citing: Augustine's *De Trinitate* 7.710; Thomas Aquinas's *ST* I.92.1; Martin Luther's "Lecture on Genesis, Gen.2:18;" and Karl Barth's *Church Dogmatics* Vol. 3, Sec. 4. In Ruether's *New Woman/New Earth: Sexist Ideologies and Liberation* (New York: Seabury, 1983), 33 she cites Aquinas's *ST* I.99.2.1.92, Plato's *Timaeus* 50-51, 91; Aristotle's *Politics* 1:1-2; *On the Generation of Animals* I: 729b, II: 731b, 737a, 738b in support of her claim.

For critical discussions of these issues, see: Anne Carr, review of *New Woman, New Earth: Sexist Ideologies and Human Liberation*, by Rosemary Radford Ruether, *Journal of Religion* 57 (1977): 336-38; John A. Coleman, review of *New Woman, New Earth: Sexist Ideologies and Human Liberation*, by Rosemary Radford Ruether, *Union Seminary Quarterly Review* 32 (1977): 192-94; Mary Mullins, review of *New Woman, New Earth: Sexist Ideologies and Human Liberation*, by Rosemary Radford Ruether, *Horizons* 6 (1979): 129-30; and M. Cleophas Costello, review of *New Woman, New Earth: Sexist Ideologies and Human Liberation*, by Rosemary Radford Ruether, *Theological Studies* 37 (1976): 358-60.

structure of Christian anthropology expresses males' projection of their "lower selves" onto women.[5] Woman in her essential nature was seen as having less spiritual (higher) nature and more physical (lower) nature. In this projection, it was stressed that woman holds a "greater aptness" for sin and achieves a lesser level of spirituality. Women should thus defer to men who represent the greater fullness of the "headship" of the (male) God at the level of mind and reason.[6] In the erroneous thinking of Tertullian, Augustine, or Aquinas (for example) women were considered more responsible for sin in the world.[7] According to Ruether, the continuing influence of the thought of Luther, Calvin, Barth, and the Roman pontiffs has carried this misguided interpretation of the Fall into the present day.

Parallel to this oppressive and patriarchal Christian anthropology, egalitarian forms of Christian anthropology asserting women's equality with men as created in the divine image and redeemed in Christ Jesus always existed.[8] An eschatological feminism grew up in the first two centuries of Christianity (Gal. 3:28) that supported a trend to form an egalitarian Christian counter culture.[9] Unfortunately, egalitarian movements in a number of historical eras--early Christian Gnostics, the Shakers, and the Quakers--have been condemned as heretical.[10] These egalitarian sources are among those to which Ruether turns in constructing a feminist Christian anthropology.

Ruether constructs a feminist anthropology that is intended to be egalitarian, whole (inclusive of a healthy state of all dimensions of humanness--psychological,

---

[5]Ruether, *Sexism and God-Talk*, 93-94.

[6]Ibid., 94-95.

[7]Ibid., 95-99, 167. Ruether quotes Tertullian's *de Cultu Feminarum* 1.1, which defines women as "the devil's gateway."

[8]Ruether, *Sexism and God-Talk*, 99-102.

[9]Ibid., 99. Ruether cites the scholarship of Elizabeth Schüssler Fiorenza.

[10]Ibid., 100-102.

physical, etc.) and fitting for redeemed humanity. Christ is the model for this new humanity. Here, the fullness of humanity is defined as the true self, known and understood by oneself and others, as one is known and understood by God, bearing the fullness of the *imago Dei*.[11] Through encounters with others, humans become more whole as the meaning of their personhood unfolds in additional dimensions of their various relationships. Thus, gradually people reconnect with the *imago Dei* by receiving their full psychic potential, transforming social roles and rediscovering relationality that has been lost amid erroneous patriarchal projections of Christian anthropology. One particularly significant reconnection to be made is between humans and all beings in the universe.[12] To the extent that persons are able to come to their whole selves, being neither ones who are oppressed nor oppressors, they are in fact free.

While asserting gender equality, Ruether does not deny gender distinction, but values it as any other characteristic, as a feature of the person's humanity. Genuine mutual relationship is possible based upon the common power of the shared humanity of males and females.

Ruether understands God as the "primal matrix," "the great womb," and Tillich's "ground or power of being." She uses three different terms to refer to the divine: Gods/Goddesses, God, and God/ess.[13] When she refers to the deities of the Ancient Near East, she uses the capitalized form of gods and goddesses as a way of rejecting the traditional Christian assumption that these deities were false and that their stories hold no truth. She uses "God" to name the divine in the Judeo-Christian

---

[11] Ibid., 109-13, 191.

[12] Ibid., 87. See also Ruether, *To Change the World*, 59 and Ruether, *Gaia and God*, 251.

[13] Ruether, *Sexism and God-Talk*, 45-46. For critical discussions of this point see the following: Ursula King, review of *Sexism and God-Talk: Toward a Feminist Theology*, by Rosemary Radford Ruether, *Religious Studies* 20 (1984): 699-702; June O'Connor, review of *Sexism and God-Talk: Toward a Feminist Theology*, by Rosemary Radford Ruether, *Religious Studies Review* 12 (1986): 202-205; and Carol S. Robb, review of *Sexism and God-Talk: Toward a Feminist Theology*, by Rosemary Radford Ruether, *Union Seminary Quarterly Review* 40 (1985): 59-72.

tradition. Ruether considers the male generic form inadequate to express the vision of the divine in her theology. Her preferred term is "God/ess," which she also recognizes as inadequate, but which is heuristic and evocative. The strength of the term "God/ess" is that it points to the male and female forms of the English word for the divine, while preserving the Judeo-Christian affirmation the God is one.

Sin

Ruether reconstructs the definition of sin from the viewpoint of women. She defines personal sin as "the capacity to set up prideful, egotistical, antagonistic relations with others," but *also* as the passivity and acquiescence of individuals (particularly women) to the group ego.[14] The primary social sin (frequently manifested in the personal realm as well) is sexism, the myth that the female is inferior and evil. Social sin also encompasses any other form of structural alienation and oppression.[15] Among men and in male culture, macho-masculinity is the most frequent manifestation of sexism, which includes: (1) violence against women (2) a hierarchical and anti-communitarian bias (3) abstraction (4) consequentialism, and (5) misogyny.[16] For women, the most frequent manifestation of sin is their cooperation in their own subjugation, and peer violence--subjugating those (especially women) over whom they hold power.[17] When this difference in the kind of sinful behavior predominant in women and men is recognized, women are found to be equal in sinfulness with men; and not to be placed upon a pedestal as sweet idyllic virgins or condemned as the evil temptresses. Sinfulness is a common weakness of a common humanity shared by male and female alike.

---

[14]Ruether, *Sexism and God-Talk*, 164.

[15]Ibid., 174: "Sexism as sin centers on distortion of relationality." See also Ibid., 215.

[16]Ibid., 179. Here Ruether cites Daniel C. Maguire's classification in his "The Feminization of God and Ethics," *Christianity and Crisis* 42 (1982): 63-64.

[17]Ruether, *Sexism and God-Talk*, 180.

Redemption

Ruether severely criticizes traditional understandings of redemption which stress individual spirituality to the near total neglect of the historical, socio-economic aspects of human life. She proffers a renewed understanding of redemption based upon the fact that God/ess is the source of both redemption and creation.[18] Ruether believes: "We must recognize sin precisely in this splitting and deformation of the our true relationships to creation and to our neighbor and find liberation in an authentic harmony with all that is incarnate in our social, historical being."[19] Ruether stresses that the divine/human relationship is mutual in that humans are capable of making critical choices in daily life that determine, in part, the progress or regress of their relationship to God, one another and the entire creation.

Christology

Jesus the Liberator (of women in particular) holds the focal place in Ruether's Christology.[20] Ruether emphasizes that, as portrayed in the synoptic gospels, Jesus life and ministry sets a standard for all Christians to emulate. In his personal suspension of the cultural barrier forbidding the public association of women and men in Jewish society, his criticism of religious and social hierarchies, and his proactive stance toward the poor and marginalized he demonstrated a moral preference for relationships characterized by mutuality (this will be elaborated further, below). Significant in Ruether's Christology is the notion that we can encounter Christ in the form of our *sister*, as well as our brother.

---

[18]Ibid., 214-34.

[19]Ibid., 215-16.

[20]Ibid., 116-38. See also Ruether, *To Change the World*, 56: "His ability to be liberator does not reside in his maleness, but, on the contrary, in the fact that he renounced this system of domination and seeks to embody in his person the new humanity of service and mutual empowerment."
For a critical discussion of this point see: Marianne H. Micks, review of *To Change the World: Christology and Cultural Criticism*, by Rosemary Radford Ruether, *Theology Today* 39 (1992): 214-15; and John Carmody, review of *To Change the World: Christology and Cultural Criticism*, by Rosemary Radford Ruether, *Horizons* 9 (1992): 372-73.

Orthodox Christian exegesis of the Jesus story picks up on the pre-exilic tradition of the Davidic Messiah where the king was an instrument of God's salvation, leading the people to fulfillment of the covenant with God. Ruether notes the important fact that Jesus always resisted the crowds that wanted to make him a king. What is most significant, in Ruether's view, is that Jesus radicalized the Messiah concept. His vision of the Reign of God was neither nationalistic nor other-worldly, but it was universal and focused on *this world*.[21] The focus on the Messianic mission as an objective to be fulfilled in history militates against philosophical dualism that pits the lesser valued "earthly" against the more valuable "heavenly," the historical against the eternal. The Reign of God was to be a time of servant leadership and vindication of the poor and the oppressed (among whom women were frequently the most burdened). Jesus also freed religion from fossilization in past traditions while respecting them, renewing them and interpreting their significance for the future. In a word, Jesus restored the concept of God's salvific activity taking place *here and now*, as well as the significance of God's future actions.[22]

This restoration returned a sacred status to the concrete, cooperative, embodied aspects of life that had been lost with the image of the Goddess. The paradigm for mutual relations returned--heaven *and earth* (Matt. 25), male *and female* (Gal. 3:28) were *both* again significant. This balanced restoration had been expressed with the Hebrew notion of *shalom*, but it was nearly lost in the militant triumphalism that accompanied the image of the Messianic Warrior King.[23]

---

[21]Ruether, *Sexism and God-Talk*, 121. Ruether cites Albert Nolan, *Jesus Before Christianity: The Gospel of Liberation* (Capetown: Philip David, 1976). See also Ruether, *To Change the World*, 12-14. Ruether cites Geza Vermes, *The Dead Sea Scrolls in English* (New York: Penguin Books, 1962), 121 and Geza Vermes, *Jesus the Jew* (New York: Collins, 1973, 160-91.

[22]Ruether, *Sexism and God-Talk*, 123. Ruether claims that the spirit of Jesus' intent concerning the character of the Reign of God is preserved in his sayings in the *New Testament* which can be traced to the earliest days of the Jesus movement. She cites Joachim Jeramias, *The Parables of Jesus* (New York: Scribner's, 1955), 70-74; Constance Parvey, "Women in the New Testament," in *Religion and Sexism: Images of Women in Jewish and Christian Traditions*, ed. Rosemary Radford Ruether (New York: Simon and Schuster, 1974), 138-42.

[23]Ruether, *To Change the World*, 69-70.

Because of the subordinate role of women in Jewish society, Ruether views Jesus' ministry to and among women as evidence of a radical interpretation of the Messianic role.[24] While the Jewish prophetic tradition generally expressed denunciations of injustice and tyranny, it had little to say concerning women specifically--the mandate to care for widows being the one exception. Jesus' use of women as examples of faith, his frequent association with them, and the biblical witness of women as the first apostles of the resurrected Christ--all represent for Ruether an affirmation by Jesus of women as equal with men as bearing the *imago Dei*.[25] Thus, the oppression of women in any form is sinful. The ancient truth of the *imago Dei* (God/ess) as inhering in both *female* and male was indeed vindicated.

Ecological Ethics

In my judgment, a personalist (as opposed to a physicalist) approach to natural law is presumed in Ruether's ecological ethics.[26] In order to support this general framework for her ecological ethics, Ruether returns to her analysis of the roots of the Christian tradition in the religions of the Ancient Near East and the Jewish messianic tradition.[27] There, she retrieves two images of God: (1) God as Messianic King and (2) God as Divine Wisdom. Ruether stresses that in both cases the evolution of the divine as female is central to an understanding of how theology determined the

---

[24]Ibid., 35-37. Ruether stresses that to claim that Jesus reinterpreted and revolutionized some aspects of Judaism is not to be anti-Semitic. In fact, Hillel and his Pharasitic school made some of the same claims Jesus made. Ruether cites Asher Finkel, *The Pharisees and the Teacher of Nazareth* (Leiden: E. J. Brill, 1964), 134-75.

[25]Ruether, *To Change the World*, 47-56. Ruether claims that the Christology of Eusebius of Ceasarea and Constantine blessed at Nicea in 325 AD. was a construct based on the warrior king image of God, the body/spirit dualism and the hierarchy of being. She cites Aristotle's *Politics* I: 1-2; E. Goodenough, "The Political Philosophy of Hellenistic Kingship," in *Yale Classical Studies* Vol. 1, 1928 and Eusebius of Pamphilis's *Oration in Praise of the Emperor Constantine*. Alternative Christologies have always existed within Christianity. Ruether cites *The Second Epistle of Clement* 12.2. In *Gaia and God*, 235-37 she cites Ireaneus's *Ad. Haer.* v.22; v.34.2.3; and v.36.3.

[26]Gula, *What About Moral Norms*, 35. "Personalism" is "characterized by placing an emphasis on the dimensions of the human person and human actions which extend beyond the physical and biological to include the social, spiritual, and psychological dimensions as well." Ibid.

[27]Ruether, *Sexism and God-Talk*, 116-17.

development of ethics. Parallel to the demise of the female, wisdom oriented image of God is a loss of egalitarianism as a measure of ethical goodness.[28]

In Canaanite and other Ancient Near Eastern traditions the world was dependent on the Goddess' annual renewal of the dying vegetation king.[29] Similarly, in Eastern Mediterranean cultures divine Wisdom is represented by the Goddess.[30] The Wisdom figure is carried into the Hebrew Scriptures (Pov. 8) and enters Christian scriptures in the Logos of the New Testament.[31] In orthodox Christianity, however, the Logos became the (male) Son, while in Gnostic Christianity (defined as unorthodox) the Wisdom figure remained female.[32] This definitive interpretation of God as male by the orthodox Christian community had dire consequences for the lived experience of women as bearers of the *imago Dei*.

The Messianic King was transformed in prophetic Hebrew thought.[33] The idea of renewal of the earth in agrarian times took on wider meanings of moral and historical proportions. Over time, the Messianic King became known as the conquering warrior king who liberated the people and then reigned over the renewed kingdom. The king was expected to win, not to be self-sacrificing. The entire concept of a female consort was deemphasized, nearly lost. The female image of the divine was preserved in Israel primarily through the influence of conquered and

---

[28]Ibid., 47. Ruether cites E.O. James, *The Cult of the Mother Goddess: An Anthropological Documentary Study* (New York: Barnes and Noble, 1959), 24.

[29]Ruether, *Sexism and God-Talk*, 48. Ruether cites James Ibid., 23-46.

[30]Ruether, *Sexism and God-Talk*, 56-57. Ruether cites Raphael Patai, *The Hebrew Goddess* (Philadelphia: KTAV, 1967), 36-45, 49-50 and Phyllis Trible, *God and the Rhetoric of Sexuality* (Philadelphia: Fortress Press, 1978), 48.

[31]Ruether, *Sexism and God-Talk*, 58.

[32]Ibid., 59. Ruether cites "The Gospel of Hebrews" in Edger Hennecke and Wilhelm Schmeemelcher, eds., *New Testament Apocrypha* Vol. 1 (Philadelphia: Westminster Press, 1963), 164. She also cites "The Gospel of Philip," in *The Nag Hammadi Library in English* ed. James M. Robinson (New York: Harper and Row, 1977), 134.

[33]Ruether, *Sexism and God-Talk*, 119. Ruether cites Sigmund Mowinchel, *He That Cometh* (New York: Blackwell and Abingdon, 1955), 96-154.

assimilated peoples. Again, Ruether stresses, this loss of a female image of the divine held serious negative ramifications for the practical acceptance of women as conveyers of the *imago Dei*.

Ruether's Christology shows how Jesus' life and ministry affirmed women as bearers of the *imago Dei*. From the foundational premise that women are created as whole, fully human persons, equal in status with men before God, Ruether derives several notions that frame her ecological ethics.[34] First, women model relationships based on mutuality rather than on hierarchy.[35] Second, the traditional dualism that separates spirit/mind/male from matter/body/female, which has been embraced by dominant strains of Christianity and Western culture, is no longer valid.[36] Raising the status of matter to that equal to the spiritual, necessitates the reconsideration of all relationships as defined by the classical dualistic standards. Thus, a third element is that domination, manipulation and abuse can have no place in a Christian feminist ecological ethical system. Positively stated, humans must live in relationship with God, other humans, other earth creatures, the earth itself and the entire cosmos in a manner that promotes mutual well-being. Finally, the biblical preference for the poor and the oppressed as well as the obligation of the wealthy and the powerful to provide for the entitlement of the poor to a life of dignity needs to be extended to the entire ecosystem, if indeed humanity is to survive and flourish.[37] Ruether explains: "The

---

[34] Ruether, *Sexism and God-Talk*, 85-92.

[35] Bianchi and Ruether, *From Machismo to Mutuality*, 114. Such relations are implicit in "sisterhood." See Ruether, *Sexism and God-Talk*, 89-91 and 111-13 where she cites Sally P. Springer and George Deutsch, *Left Brain, Right Brain* (San Francisco: Freeman, 1981), 121-30 and Jeanette McGlone, *The Behavior and Brain Sciences* 3 (1980): 215-63.

[36] Ruether cites Lynda M. Glennon, *Women and Dualism: A Sociology of Knowledge Analysis* (New York: Longman and Green, 1979), 97-115.

[37] Ruether, *Gaia and God*, 265-74, esp. 268. For a critical discussion of this point see: Ann Swahnberg, review of *Gaia and God: An Ecofeminist Theology of Earth Healing*, by Rosemary Radford Ruether, *Journal of Religion* 74 (1994): 508-81; Wendy Farley, review of *Gaia and God: An Ecofeminist Theology of Earth Healing*, by Rosemary Radford Ruether, *Theology Today* 50 (1993): 461-64; and Sonya A. Quitsland, review of *Gaia and God: An Ecofeminist Theology of Earth Healing*, by Rosemary Radford Ruether, *Journal of Ecumenical Studies* 31 (1994):190-92.

notion of dominating the universe from a position of autonomy is an illusion of alienated consciousness. . . . An ecological ethic must always be an ethic of eco-justice that recognizes the interconnection of social domination and the domination of nature."[38] With this theological grounding in mind, we now turn to Ruether's definition of "mutuality."

Ruether's Basic Definition of Mutuality

Rosemary Radford Ruether uses the term, "mutuality" in several of her works, but she usually does not define it. She leaves the reader to employ contextual definition and draw upon her more systematic efforts for an interpretation of "mutuality."

Ruether's main contribution toward defining "mutuality" in the broad sense, is her reconstruction of Christian history which seeks to reclaim the status of women as bearing the *imago Dei*, to reinterpret Christian doctrines to reflect the equality of women as *capax Dei*, and promote women's contributions to theology and praxis. In her reconstructed version of Christian history and the role of women within it, Ruether lays a foundation for a theology in which "mutuality" emerges as a normative principle that governs the Christian understanding of God (*ad intra*) and relationships between the divine and human.

A "new ecological ethic" follows from Ruether's theology, which requires humans to live relationally on the basis of mutuality.[39] Not only are relationships between humans the subject of this ethic, but also the relationships between humans and all elements of the cosmos and the entire ecosystem. This ecological ethic is generated from an understanding of anthropology that is egalitarian and inclusive of women; a Christology that stresses Jesus as a critic of dominance; and a morality that

---

[38]Ruether, *Sexism and God-Talk*, 89, 91.

[39]Ruether, *Sexism and God-Talk*, 85-92.

requires a conversion of heart away from sexist and other dominating attitudes, and to the cause of universal community.[40]

Ruether's early definition of "mutuality" seems to stand as paradigmatic for her use of the term elsewhere. Just as she sees sexism as the root metaphor for all oppressive relationships (sin), so too, it seems that she understands "mutuality" in relation to gender parity or androgyny. Ruether defines "mutuality" this way:

> People don't hear with their vaginas and think with their penises. Men and women equally have organs of psychic activity and receptivity. Psychically men and women are not complementary but mutual. Mutuality means not only that men speak and women hear, but that women also speak and men hear. It means that men and women cease to be half personalities. Both must grow to unite the many sides of themselves through multiple relationships with other people. . . . Relations center upon personal respect and mutual development.[41]

This gender focused understanding of "mutuality" is also normative in her ecological ethics.[42] Ruether speaks of gender equity as an aspect of "biophilic mutuality," the total systemic interdependence of everything and everyone. Ruether grounds this notion in data from the natural sciences and a philosophy similar to the ancient worldview that considered the human body the microcosm and the world the macrocosm.[43]

Further Analysis of Mutuality
Cosmic Mutuality

Ruether's social analysis of the three classical creation stories (the *Enuma Elish*, *Genesis* 1 and 2, Plato's *Timaeus*) which shaped the cosmology of the Christian world and evidence from natural sciences (such as astrophysics, ecology, and quantum physics) have led her to conclude that most fundamental to any ethical system is the

---

[40]Ibid., 72-92, 93-115, 116-38, 159-92, 214-34, 164.

[41]Bianchi and Ruether, *From Machismo to Mutuality*, 84.

[42]Ruether, *Gaia and God*, 171-72, 258.

[43]Ibid., 48-58.

acknowledgment of the interrelation of all things.⁴⁴ She claims the Christian doctrine of creation is ambiguous concerning the actual relationship of humans to the rest of the cosmos. Some interpretations of Christian cosmology ultimately serve to maximize the well-being of humans *and* all of creation more than others, for example, the notion of familial relationship of all things purported by St. Francis of Assisi.

Ruether claims that an ethical framework rooted in the interrelatedness of all can be retrieved from Christian sources. Such a framework includes four basic assumptions: (1) Nature is not completely capable of fulfilling all human desires for goodness because it is not totally benign for them; (2) Humans are capable of love and care for others that draws them beyond themselves and that points to the meaning and source of life; (3) Humans can relate to both evolutionary consciousness and goodness and the organic mortality they share with plants and animals; (4) While humans can reshape nature to reflect human ideals, they are limited by the laws of the interdependence of the ecosystem.⁴⁵ Ruether states: "Human ethics should be a more refined and conscious version of this natural interdependency, mandating humans to imagine and feel the suffering of others, and to find ways in which interrelation becomes cooperative and mutually life-enhancing for both sides."⁴⁶ Ruether is certain that mutuality needs to characterize all relationships so as to maximize the flourishing of humans and the entire cosmos. In her view, it is contradictory to think that any one element of creation can flourish without the rest of the creation, because everything is held in a delicate balance in the ecosystem.

Gender Mutuality

Within Ruether's early and more explicit definition of "mutuality" it is clear that she considers men and women equal in their psychic capacity and humanity. Yet, men and women are distinct as persons, not only different animal bodies with complementary genitalia. As Ruether's definition of mutuality indicates, in any

---

⁴⁴Ibid., 15-48.

⁴⁵Ibid., 31.

⁴⁶Ibid., 57.

genuine relationship, there is an exchange of power between persons in speaking and hearing that is formative of both persons. Neither of the persons objectify any one aspect as constitutive of the entire personality of the other. The conditions of the relationship are respectful and growthful for both parties alike.

Generative Mutuality

Traditional dualism in Western society has strained gender relationships, and much blame has been cast by both sides, male and female.[47] Based upon the Genesis portrayal of humans in the image of God as male and female, as well as the notion of conversion in the Hebrew prophetic tradition, Reuther submits that there is another option. The process of "restructuring of society to maximize the incentives for mutuality" is a means by which people can redeem the personal and social sin of sexism, and be co-creative by converting structures rooted in dualism to structures grounded in harmony between humans, the divine and humans, and humans and the cosmos.[48]

What is required to achieve mutuality in society is clear, concrete, transformative action by all people to structure new forms of gender parity, by dismantling oppressive hierarchies. Ruether believes the critical starting point for this transformation to mutuality is for men and women to genuinely share *both* the parenting of children from birth and domestic work associated with daily life.[49] In addition, women need to "enter into all the strongholds of male militarism" (sports, business, government, etc.), assert their talents and creativity, and transform the male

---

[47]Traditional or classical dualism refers to Plato's philosophy which held that the sensual world is not the real world. Rather, there are two realms: the realm of Perfect Unchanging Ideas (forms) know only by our intellect, and illusionary, or less real realm of the concrete, individual, changing objects known by our senses and existing as imperfect copies of the Perfect Ideas. See Peter A. Angeles, *Dictionary of Philosophy* (New York: Barnes and Noble Books, 1981), s. v. "Platonism." For Ruether's more detailed explication of the effects of Platonic dualism on the development of Christianity see her *New Woman/New Earth*, 186-214. In Ibid. 3-35, particularly 32 n.'s 7 and 8, she notes dualism in Plato's *Timaeus*, 50-51, 91; *Phaedo*, and *Phaedrus*.

[48]Ruether in Robert A. Raines, ed., *Disputed Questions on Being Christian*, Journeys in Faith, (Nashville: Abingdon, 1982), 139-40.

[49]Ruether, *Gaia and God*, 171-72.

37

bastions by modeling equally effective, and less destructive strategies of mutual relations. Males need to cultivate their "feminine" dimension, respect homosexuals as human persons, and regard women as diverse but equal others with whom they relate for mutual growth, not male aggrandizement.[50]

Social Mutuality

Ruether believes mutuality is a goal of feminists; the recognition of interrelatedness with difference between the genders and all elements of the cosmos. Insofar as gender relations are both interpersonal and social, mutuality also bears implications for social behavior. What Ruether claims for women in relationships with men, she extends to all who are oppressed. She draws upon her Christology in which, as the Christ, Jesus is the representative of humanity liberated. He is the liberating Word of God who manifests the "*kenosis* of patriarchy." He announced a new humanity in which hierarchical casts and privileges have no place, mutual relationships marks moral excellence, and the "lowly" are valued by virtue of their participation in the *imago Dei*. Therefore, as Christ lived in mutual relation to all persons, particularly those oppressed, mutuality must distinguish the relationships of Christians. This means that those more powerful in a situation need to relinquish power to others less powerful in order to achieve the optimal flourishing for all. The "power-over" relinquished by the more powerful needs to be seized and transformed by the less powerful into "power-with" through their active participation in forming a consensus for the common good.

Normative Status

Ruether joins many other liberation theologians in the belief that "some social systems are closer to the kingdom than others. Some situations disclose greater justice and mutuality; some systems allow for greater justice and mutuality."[51] Since Ruether understands mutuality as a relation free of sexism and oppression, as vital for

---

[50]Bianchi and Ruether, *From Machismo to Mutuality*, 99, 120.

[51]Ruether, *To Change the World*, 22.

biophilic community and ultimately as necessary for the survival of the planet, mutuality both contributes to and is a characteristic of liberation.[52] Ruether believes: "The task of the follower of Christ is to move human society a little farther from the kingdom of Satan, the kingdom of alienation and oppression, and closer to God's kingdom, a society of peace, justice and mutuality."[53] Insofar as Ruether believes that Christians are obligated to work for the coming of God's Reign, a reign characterized and formed by mutuality, mutuality must be a norm for Christian ethics.

Distinctions/Relation of Mutuality to Equality, Friendship, Reciprocity, Solidarity

Ruether has consistently used "equality" to denote the fundamental common humanity of both genders and as the opposite of gender "complementarity," a notion that stresses biological differences between genders.[54] Ruether goes a bit further when she calls for a principle of equity as the starting point of the good society.[55] In this context, she judges equity upon the basis of the fundamental relatedness of all members of the biotic community and of all present and future generations. Ruether uses "equality" to express the fact that all members of the biophilic community are the same in their status as valuable and necessary and "mutuality" as the dynamic of the relationships that contribute to the maximum flourishing of all forms of life.

Ruether's discussion of "friendship" is found within her broader treatment of healthy sexual relations in marriage. She views friendship as a committed relationship characterized by mutual growth and intimacy between partners.[56] Friendship is the psycho-social aspect of the relationship that enables the creation of "our bodies,

---

[52]Ruether, *Gaia and God*, 265, 269.

[53]Ruether, *To Change the World*, 23.

[54]Ruether, *Sexism and God-Talk*, 93-115. Cf. Gula, *What About Moral Norms*, 35 concerning the physicalist approach to natural law. See also Bianchi and Ruether *From Machismo to Mutuality*, 104-07.

[55]Ruether, *Gaia and God*, 258.

[56]Bianchi and Ruether, *From Machismo to Mutuality*, 85.

ourselves" as the "sacrament of personal communication" along with physical intimacy in a marriage.[57] Friendship then, is a paradigm of mutuality in personal relationships, particularly in marriage.

Ruether rarely uses "reciprocity" except to designate a one-for-one exchange in a relationship between parties of different genders toward the achievement of the wider goal of gender parity.[58] Ruether stresses that the conversion to gender mutuality first requires change on the part of both genders to recognize and accept the equal and full humanity of both women and men.

Finally, Ruether uses "solidarity" to name Jesus' stance in relation to the poor of his day.[59] She also uses "solidarity" to indicate the stance Christians must take in relation to all religious belief systems which bear fruit toward human flourishing.[60] In Ruether's view, relationships of solidarity involve a struggle of the oppressed together with those less oppressed toward mutuality. In mutual relations, boundaries are readily crossed upon the agreement of the parties involved; in the case of solidarity, boundaries remain impermeable because of the oppression.

Relationship of Mutuality to Love and Justice

Ruether sees love and justice as intimately related in the process of liberation of the oppressed, particularly women. She sees love as a "primal virtue" that is manifested in healthy self-esteem and self-confidence, grounded in the knowledge of one's dignity as a person who is loved by and created in God's image and likeness.[61] Ruether defines love as a relationship in which "both partners . . . [seek the] total welfare and personal growth of the other."[62] Ruether's understanding of love is

---

[57]Ibid.

[58]Ibid., 79. See also Ruether, *Gaia and God*, 265.

[59]Ruether, *To Change the World*, 21.

[60]Ibid., 43.

[61]Bianchi and Ruether, *Machismo to Mutuality*, 108.

[62]Ibid., 81.

rooted in the concept of divine love found between the Canaanite deities, Anath and Baal.[63] She accents the fact that these lovers were equal and capable of an equal love. It is this prototype of divine love that is carried into the Hebrew idiom and onto the human plane in the *Song of Songs*. In that Hebrew poem, according to Ruether, the equality of the lovers (maiden and the king) and their mutual love stood as a model of the relationship between God and humankind. Of particular note is the fact that the love was *both* like the affection between sister and brother *and* sensual, erotic passion.[64] Thus, Ruether's concept of love is mutual love, not the objectified dispassionate love of some interpreters of Christian *agape*. As a liberationist, Ruether affirms Gustavo Gutierrez's definition of love as possible "only among equals . . . the gift of oneself to another."[65] In Ruether's concept, love recognizes injustice as incongruent with itself and is moved to anger and involved in *conscientization*.[66] Then love and justice make common cause in judging all forms of oppression as inadequate and sinful, because it is unworthy of the beloved of God--either the oppressed or the oppressor.[67]

Ruether affirms Gutierrez's claim that justice is the counter cultural righteousness of the Hebrew prophets (Is. 32:17; Ps. 85).[68] It is the establishment, with a preferential option for the poor, of the conditions under which there is no more

---

[63]Ruether, *Sexism and God-Talk*, 40.

[64]Ruether cites Phyllis Trible, *God and the Rhetoric of Sexuality*, (Philadelphia: Fortress, 1978), 45ff.

[65]Gustavo Gutierrez, *A Theology of Liberation: History, Politics and Salvation*, trans. Caridad Inda and John Eagleson, Revised Edition with New Introduction (Maryknoll: Orbis Books, 1988), xxxi and 6.

[66]Bianchi and Ruether, *From Machismo to Mutuality*, 108. See Paulo Freire, *Pedagogy of the Oppressed*, 54.

[67]Bianchi and Ruether, *From Machismo to Mutuality*, 109.

[68]Gutierrez, *Theology of Liberation*, 97. See Rosemary Radford Ruether, "Rich Nations/Poor Nations: Towards a Just World Order in the Era of Neo-Colonialism," in Francis A. Eigo, ed., *Christian Spirituality in the United States: Independence and Interdependence* (Villanova, PA: Villanova University Press, 1978), 86. See also Ruether, *Gaia and God*, 214-15.

oppression, servitude or alienation (Is. 65:21-22; Is. 29:18-19; Matt. 11:5; Lv. 25:10ff; Lk. 4:16-21). In her view, the biblical linkage (Is. 24) between the "covenant of society" and the "covenant of creation" where society and nature cohere in a single created community under the sovereignty of God, is vital to understanding the full implication of justice.[69] Thus, for Ruether, a more accurate term for justice is "eco-justice."[70]

Ruether has illustrated how ecological exploitation is a byproduct of social exploitation.[71] Devastation of the earth and social injustice are two expressions of the same apostasy, namely, dualism.[72] By contrast the biblical vision of the Reign of God is *shalom*, where righteous is measured and found worthy by the standard of justice. The establishment of eco-justice requires conversion to one another and to the earth. The paradigm Ruether suggests for this process is the Jubilee Year (Lev. 25), which is also the vision Jesus referred to in the Lord's Prayer (Matt. 6:9-13).[73] Mutuality is a condition for biblical justice.

(Isabel) Carter Heyward: Stated Definition of Mutuality

Feminist Theological Context

Carter Heyward is a professor of theology at Episcopal Divinity School, Cambridge, MA, and one of the first eleven women ordained to the priesthood in the Episcopal Church.[74] She writes from a lesbian liberation perspective and she is attempting to develop a theology of mutual relation. Her central claim is that the

---

[69]Ruether, *New Woman/New Earth*, 188. See also Ruether, *Gaia and God*, 207-214.

[70]Ruether, "Rich Nations/Poor Nations," 81. See also Ruether, *Gaia and God*, 3, 4, 213.

[71]Ruether, "Rich Nations/Poor Nations," 82-83.

[72]See also Rosemary Radford Ruether, *Liberation Theology: Human Hope Confronts Christian History and American Power*, (New York: Paulist Press, 1972), 16-22.

[73]Rosemary Radford Ruether, "Witness to Hope in a Demonic World," *Sojourners* 20 (1991): 22-23. See also *Gaia and God*, 214.

[74](Isabel) Carter Heyward, *A Priest Forever*, (New York: Harper and Row, 1976).

original and fundamental relatedness of all being is liberated and redeemed in history through the recreation of mutuality and justice.

Heyward undergirds her notion of mutuality with concepts drawn from three areas of theology: (1) understanding of God (2) understanding of Jesus (3) understanding of the human person, particularly human sexuality.

Theology

Heyward understands God as primarily immanent and relational.[75] Her fundamental criticism of traditional Christian theology is that for nearly two millennia it has predominately fostered transcendent images of God (Almighty, All Powerful, King, etc.). God was set above the world in such a way that in order to experience God's favor, humanity had to divert attention from this world and concentrate on the next. What was lost in the transcendent imagery was the immanence of God, and at Chalcedon (451 CE), Christians lost the ultimacy of the voluntary character of the human/divine relationship when the option was made for the hypostatic union of the two natures of Christ.[76]

Heyward claims that the God of Israel was essentially a God of covenant fidelity and righteousness (*hesed, emeth*) revealed through acts on behalf of the people.[77] According to Heyward, human righteousness was manifested in voluntary acts done in the context of community according to the covenant. In Heyward's view, the New Covenant defined righteousness in terms of the spiritual/intellectual/ conceptual as something already effected by the Messiah; faith was significant, not works. According to Heyward, where this world was, for the Jews, a realm in which to bring about righteousness, for the Christians it became a waiting room for the *parousia*.

---

[75]For a critical discussion of this point see: Virginia Remey Mollenkott, "Who's Redeeming Whom?," review of *The Redemption of God: A Theology of Mutual Relation*, by Isabel Carter Heyward, *Christianity and Crisis* 43 (1983): 123-24.

[76]Heyward, *Redemption of God*, 3-5.

[77]See Stephen Charles Mott, *Biblical Ethics and Social Change* (New York: Oxford University Press, 1982), 60-63.

Relationality is central to Heyward's theological reflection. "Mutuality" is the term she explicitly uses to distinguish that particular relationality between and among God, humans, all earthcreatures and the earth itself which marks the conditions for the maximum flourishing of all involved.[78] "Mutuality" for Heyward is at once a theological and an ethical term. It is ethical in that it defines the divine presence incarnate in us, embodied in our relational selves such that without our cooperation, the realm of God will be lacking.[79] It is a theological term in that it defines God in relation.

Christology

Consistent with her preference for an image of God as one who is immanent, Heyward argues for a "low" Christology on the basis of the negative and ambiguous historical consequences yielded by traditional "high" Christologies.[80] Heyward holds that the foundation of Christology must be the interaction of the human and divine in a single relational dynamic.[81] "Christ" is found in genuine human "justice-making with compassion, courage, and integrity, which can be interpreted as either 'human' or 'divine' and is, in fact, both at once."[82]

---

[78] Heyward, *Staying Power*. 107-108.

[79] Heyward, *Touching Our Strength*, 33.

[80] Heyward, *Speaking of Christ*, 14. See also Heyward, *Redemption of God*, 189-92 where she discusses her understanding of the negative influence of Platonic dualism and Aristotelian hierarchy on Christology, philosophy, anthropology and ecclesiology. For a critical discussion of this point see: Rita Nakashima Brock, review of *Speaking of Christ: A Lesbian Voice*, by Carter Heyward, *Journal of Religion* 72 (1992): 130-31.

[81] Heyward, *Speaking of Christ*, 21. See also Heyward, *Our Passion For Justice*, 29. See also Carter Heyward, "Can Anglicans Be Feminist Liberation Theologians?" in *The Trial of Faith: Theology and the Church Today*, ed. Peter Eaton (West Sussex: Churchman Publishers, Ltd., 1988), 39.

[82] Heyward, *Speaking of Christ*, 21. Heyward's Christology also relies on a process of re-imaging Jesus as an exemplary historical figure (rather than salvific in the orthodox sense) who fully embodies this unique human/divine relation. This is similar to Ruether's re-encounter with the Jesus of the Synoptic Gospels. See Ruether, *Sexism and God-Talk*, 117-138. In *Redemption of God*, 47, Heyward states: "Everyone can incarnate God . . . Everyone can, but not everyone does." In *Speaking of Christ*, 89, n. 24, Heyward credits Tom F. Driver, *Christ in a Changing World: Toward an Ethical Christology*, (New York: Crossroad, 1982) as a major influence on her Christology.

Heyward relies on the Gospel of Mark to illustrate these essential characteristics concerning Jesus' relation with God and other persons: intimacy--"the centering of human relation in the depth of human being;" immediacy--"the unmediated" sense of power in present relation; and passion--sustaining and "bearing up" human life.[83] Here Heyward stresses the distinction of two kinds of power: *exousia* (authority) and *dunamis* (power).[84] Jesus heals by empowering the sick to claim their own power in relation and extends *dunamis* even toward death itself; relational "power-with" is more powerful than controlling power.[85]

It is his use of *dunamis* as relational "power with" that distinguishes Jesus and enables his followers to recognize him as the "Christ". He extends his power in deep intimate mutual relation and the disciples reply, "You are the Christ."[86]

Jesus' relationship to *Abba* (his source of power) indicates a strong mutuality between the two. Jesus "grows *with* God in love" into voluntary and mutual interdependence and Jesus enables God's growth by bringing God into the world through his own human relations and activities.[87] When God is understood, as Heyward claims, as the power in all just and mutual relation, humanity is divinized by participation in those relations. Just as Jesus is fully divine because his human relations are fully just and mutual, so too, it is the potential of each human person to

---

[83] Heyward, *Redemption of God*, 44, 49, 54-9.

[84] Ibid., 41. See also Heyward, *Touching Our Strength*, 172, n. 6: "*Dunamis* is the Greek word for power. In the New Testament it is used in contrast to *exousia*, which is the Greek for authority. Jesus had power rather than authority in the eyes of the religious leaders of his time. . . . " *Dumamis* would seem to suggest Heyward's understanding of "power-with," not "power-over," since nearly every government of Jesus' day was structured according to a hierarchical model.

[85] Heyward, *Redemption of God*, 51-52.

[86] Ibid., 36. Heyward comments on Mark 8:27-29.

[87] Ibid., 37-39.

be divinized by virtue of their humanness. This notion rests on an understanding of the human person as constituted as a self precisely by and through relationality.[88]

While Heyward acknowledges Jesus as the most complete manifestation of this divinization (Jesus is completely manifested as "Christ"), she contends that the relation itself cannot be unique in him for all time.[89] Jesus' uniqueness lies in his bearing forth into history, through voluntary mutual relation, concrete evidence of the essential human relation to God in a manner that required a radical shift in consciousness. In the course of his life and at his death he thus engaged in the work of redemption, not completing it, but handing it on to others. This "Christic power" of Jesus is fundamentally relational power that transforms wrong-relation into right-mutual and just-relation.[90] "Christic power" is efficacious power in relation which is God, and which Christians recognize as the source, ground, inspiration and movement toward right-relation, that is, toward mutuality and justice as inseparable.

For Christians, Jesus is the singular human exemplar of relationality in that his relation with God was *fully* mutual. Jesus incarnates in history the divine power itself, which is mutual empowerment that is both paradigmatic and redemptive. To be fully human is to live in mutual relation with the divine and with others. The "Christic power" of mutual relation creates, sustains and enlivens human existence in this world. While indeed there are tensions, limitations and abuses (sin) involved in relationships, Christic power mediated through concrete lives manifests and actualizes mutuality, love and justice and transforms human life by evidencing and encouraging

---

[88]Heyward, *Touching Our Strength*, 33. See also Heyward's notion of "self-in-relation" demonstrated in her *Touching Our Strength* and her *Speaking of Christ*, passim.

[89]Heyward, *Redemption of God*, 47. Marking Jesus as uniquely divine for all time blocks dialogue and solidarity with non-Christians, especially Jews and post-Christians. Calling him "Christ" *for Christians* distinguishes the experiential particularity that is one of the preconditions for dialogue. See also Ibid., 211-19 where Heyward compares her Christology with the Christologies of Bonhoeffer, Sobrino, and Sölle.

[90]Heyward, *Speaking of Christ*, 21-22.

the inherent possibility of every human person's ever fuller embodiment of that same power.[91]

Anthropology

Heyward's anthropology is rooted in the notion that because humans are created in the divine image and likeness of a relational God, the human person is constituted as a self precisely by relationality.[92] Heyward draws upon findings of the Stone Center, an interdisciplinary women's studies institute at Wellesley College, to posit that: "In a word, growth fostering relationship is mutual" and "disconnection one from the other is what leads to violence in relationships."[93] There is no healthy person who stands outside of mutual relation; in isolation humans are nobodies. As human persons, we create one another: "our we-ness literally creates my I-ness and this is a very great good."[94] Often fear is aroused in our knowing the need for mutuality. Thus, the path to mutuality, which necessitates the sharing of power, is frequently a difficult one, fraught with tension between letting go or holding onto our power in relation. Fear can be diverted into practices or social structures that falsify or bar mutual relations, such as patriarchy in advanced capitalism. Heyward contends that it is in this very struggle for mutuality with the other that the sacred is being born among us.[95]

---

[91] Heyward, *Redemption of God*, 200: "It is not that Jesus was unique; rather that his relationship to God was uniquely and singularly the *only* liberating relationship a person can have to God. . . . the way is a relational, active life in the world; . . ."

[92] Heyward, *Touching Our Strength*, 33. For critical discussion of this point see: Rita Nakashima Brock, review of *Touching Our Strength: The Erotic as Power and the Love of God*, by Carter Heyward, *Journal of Religion* 72 (1992): 130-31; and James Lassen-Williams, review of *Touching Our Strength: The Erotic as Power and the Love of God*, by Carter Heyward, *Anglican Theological Review* 72 (1990): 346-51.

[93] Heyward, *Touching Our Strength*, 14-15. Heyward cites the work of Jean Baker Miller, "What Do We Mean by Relationships?," Work in Progress, no. 22 (Wellesley: The Stone Center Working Paper Series, 1986), 3. She also relies on Martin Buber's notion of "I" and "Thou," and Scottish moral philosopher John Macmurray's notion of the "person and personal" as "social-rational."

[94] Heyward, *Staying Power*, 18. See also Heyward, *Touching Our Strength*, 21.

[95] Heyward, *Touching Our Strength*, 33-34.

Common sense wisdom holds that those things which are most painful, joyful and intimate are also common in the experience of most people. I submit that if, as Heyward contends, God is our power in mutual relation, and if each human person is created in the Divine Image and Likeness, then at the very essence (the most intimate core) of our humanity must be a desire for mutuality.

While Heyward agrees that "Intimacy refers to a fundamental bonding between persons' innermost senses of identity,"[96] she is also firm in her conviction that she has experienced intimacy and mutuality with total strangers; through brief conversations with strangers following a lecture, for example.[97] All of this suggests that if mutuality can be achieved between strangers on a one-to-one basis, then some process(es) could be developed for groups and nations to utilize to harness that potential for the good of the whole.[98]

Heyward's Basic Definition of Mutuality

Like many feminist thinkers, Carter Heyward's notion of mutuality has evolved over the years.[99] Her most complete and detailed definition of "mutuality" is given in the "Glossary" of her *Touching Our Strength*, where she states:

> Mutuality is a way of loving and is a way of speaking of Love. It is the experience of being in right relation. *Mutuality is sharing power in such a way that each participant in the relationship is called forth more fully into becoming who she is—a whole person, with integrity.*
>
> Experientially, mutuality is a process, a relational movement. It is not a static place to be, because it grows with/in the relationship. As we are formed by mutuality, so too does the shape of our mutuality change as our lives-in-relation grow. We become bearers with one another of the justice of God. Not perfectly, but authentically.[100]

---

[96] Heyward, *Redemption of God*, 44.

[97] Heyward, *Touching Our Strength*, 153.

[98] Ibid., 116-22. See also Gudorf, "Parenting," in *Women's Consciousness*, 175-91.

[99] Heyward, *Touching Our Strength*, 185, n. 7.

[100] Heyward defines "mutuality" and "power" in the glossary of her *Touching Our Strength*, 191. "Power" is defined as "the ability to move, effect, make a difference; the energy to create or destroy, call forth or put down. Outside of a particular context, power bears neither positive nor negative

Heyward supports her definition with references to the work of Margaret Craddock Huff of the Stone Center, particularly Huff's understanding of mutuality as:

> A dynamic situation within relationship in which one is simultaneously open to the influence of the other or others, influencing the other or others, and aware of influencing the other or others. Both receptivity and active initiative are required, as are recognition and appreciation of the other's wholeness and particular experience.[101]

Since 1987, Heyward has been collaborating with psychologist Janet Surrey in the study of "mutuality." Heyward reports their conclusions:

> Mutuality is *relational movement*, not a static way of being. It is a dynamic process generated by a shared assumption that all parties in relationship can, and should be empowered through the relational process.
>
> From an ethical perspective, mutuality is the creative response to alienated power and offers our only hope for transforming alienated power into energy for making justice. In the context of alienated power, mutuality means struggling against forces that silence, separate, and shatter us. The ongoingness of the struggle against these forces is what keeps our visions of mutuality from being sentimental ideals that cannot be realized.[102]

Further Analysis of Mutuality

A major difficulty associated with analyzing Heyward's use of "mutuality" lies in the fact that her limited published works are mainly unsystematic, the result of addressing a wide variety of audiences with varied agendas. Numerous rhetorical styles shape her works making it perplexing at times to determine her precise meaning. Nonetheless, when placed in the light of her more complete theological statements, some definite patterns do emerge.

---

connotations. Power can be used for good or for ill. Using *power-with* others is good. Using *power-over* others is evil." All emphasis is Heyward's.

[101] See Huff, "The Independent Self," 163, cited in Heyward, *Touching Our Strength* 185, n. 7.

[102] Heyward, *Staying Power*, 87-88. Surrey is a Stone Center psychologist.

Cosmic Mutuality

Undoubtedly, Heyward would affirm the interrelatedness of all cosmic elements, including humans. Heyward holds that because God loves, God by definition is in relationship with humanity. God's involvement in the world is total; consequently there is no unnecessary or unimportant element, person, or entity. This means that everything in the world must be considered part of the ethical life. Every human decision cosmically effects all other beings, enabling their existence or disrupting their survival potential. While remaining distinct from God, creation, through the Incarnation, shares God's life in a co-creative relationship, mutuality.

From this understanding of God and humanity Heyward has concluded further that texts which are God's word (an extension of God) must be congruent with the image of God as our power in mutual relation who is concerned with the entire cosmos, not just humans. ". . . No text is sacred that is used to abuse violate or trivialize human and other earthcreatures. . . . [the Bible] is holy only in so far as we who read, study, preach or teach it do so in a spirit of collaborative, critical inquiry steeped in collective struggle for radical mutuality between and among us all on earth".[103] Texts (scriptural or praxis) are authoritative for Christians only insofar as they inspire "us to envision and embody justice and resist domination, subordination, violence and greed."[104] Heyward's point is well taken that, contrary to claims implicit in Platonic dualism that human flourishing is simply individual and spiritual, human well-being is in fact tied up with bodily existence and survival, relationships to humans, and relationships to non-humans.[105]

---

[103] Heyward, *Touching Our Strength*, 81-3. See Elizabeth Schüssler-Fiorenza's *Bread Not Stone: The Challenge of Feminist Biblical Interpretation* (Boston: Beacon Press, 1984) and her *In Memory of Her* as well as Ruether, *Sexism and God-Talk* for other feminist discussions of the thesis that the Bible is to be read and heard as *a* word of God.

[104] Heyward, *Touching Our Strength*, 81.

[105] Heyward, *Our Passion For Justice*, 174. For a critical discussion of this point see: John A. Kater, review of *Our Passion For Justice: Images of Power, Sexuality, and Liberation* by Carter Heyward, *Anglican Theological Review* 67 (1985): 207-10.

Gender Mutuality

Heyward holds that the concrete demonstration of equal participation by women and men in the *imago Dei* is a foundation upon which mutuality rests. Heyward is highly critical of the traditional and nearly exclusive portrayal of God as the transcendent One who stands "above" as a power of hierarchical relation (rather than a power of mutual relation). She maintains that this traditional hierarchical paradigm is directly related to church teaching which places human sexuality in a negative rather than a positive light.[106] Heyward argues:

> [W]e have not been able to experience this very natural and moral stirring in ourselves, between and among us as good--related to God, of God, empowered by God. . . . The power of mutual relation is creative sensual power, which is redemptive of our isolation and brokenness in its carrying us in relation with others.[107]

Mutual relation is broader than sexuality and it is the way in which we come to know ourselves as both lover and beloved. It is in this very radical yearning for mutuality that the boundaries of the human and the divine are revealed--there is both affirmation and lament for the "yet/not yet" nature of our mutuality.[108] It is in movement toward mutual relation, known through the erotic served up to us by our senses of taste, smell, touch, sight and hearing that we know the divine who is embodied between and

---

[106] Heyward, *Touching Our Strength*, 44-42. Here Heyward relies on the analysis of Samuel Laeuchli, *Power and Sexuality: The Emergence of Canon Law at the Synod of Elvira* (Philadelphia: Temple University Press, 1972). Laeuchli argues that clergy relied on Aristotelian and Platonic interpretations of the Fall in *Genesis* 3 that made human sexuality something unholy and in need of strict regulation. See also Heyward, Ibid., 167, n. 9. Heyward cites Haunani-Kay Trask, *Eros and Power: The Promise of Feminist Theory* (Philadelphia: University of Pennsylvania Press, 1986), 56. She also cites Jeffery Weeks, *Sexuality and Its Discontents: Meanings, Myths and Modern Sexualities* (London: Routledge and Kegan Paul, 1985), 44.

[107] Heyward, *Our Passion For Justice*, 246-47.

[108] Heyward, *Touching Our Strength*, 91.

among us.[109] Central to Heyward's understanding of embodiment is that it is our most excellent experience of the love of God (I Jn. 4:7ff).[110]

The opposite is also true. Insofar as mutuality is squelched between and among us, the sacred is also bridled and disempowered. When there is no mutual calling forth toward each becoming more fully who we are to be. Power is diminished, creative energy is lost, and redemption is rendered impossible.

This suppression of human potential and of the sacred is what makes sexism so tragic. Sexism, and particularly heterosexism,[111] is a perfect example of the non-mutual relations that Heyward claims are blessed by misguided Christians. Ironically, it is in a lesbian relationship, a relationship traditionally named as sinful by Christianity, that Heyward has personally found mutuality.[112] Heyward does not naively believe in the perfection of gays and lesbians, but she does claim that gay/lesbian relationships are free of the oppressive need for the domination of women

---

[109]Ibid., 94. See Ibid., 187: "Erotic [is] our desire to taste and smell and see and hear and touch one another. It's our yearning to be involved--all "rolled up"--in each other's sounds and glances and bodies and feelings. The erotic is the flow of our senses, the movement of our sensuality, in which we experience our bodies' power and desire to connect with others. The erotic moves transpersonally among us and also draws us more fully into ourselves. *Although, to some extent, everyone's eroticism is distorted by abusive power relations (of domination and control), the erotic is the sacred/godly basis of our capacity to participate in mutually empowering relationships.*" Emphasis is Heyward's. See also Heyward, *Our Passion For Justice*, 198.

[110]Ibid., 99. See also Christine E. Gudorf, *Body, Sex, and Pleasure: Reconstructing Christian Sexual Ethics* (Cleveland: The Pilgrim Press, 1994).

[111]Heyward, "Heterosexism: Enforcing Male Supremacy," *The Witness* 69 (1986):18-19. In her *Touching Our Strength*, 50, Heyward defines heterosexism as: "the basic structure of gay/lesbian oppression in this and other societies. Heterosexism is to homophobia what sexism is to misogyny and what racism is to racial bigotry and hatred. Heterosexism is the *structure* in which are generated and cemented the *feelings* of fear and hatred toward queers and dykes, and toward ourselves if we are lesbians or gaymen. Dialectically, such feelings serve also to secure the structure. They thereby strengthen not only such traditional patriarchal religious institutions as christianity, which have helped set the structure of compulsory heterosexuality in place; but also more deeply personal 'institutions,' such as the self-loathing of homosexual youths and the hatred of such youths by others." Heyward also cites Adrienne Rich, "Compulsory Heterosexuality and Lesbian Existence," *Blood, Bread and Poetry: Selected Prose 1979-85* (New York: W.W. Norton, 1986), 63-64.

[112]Heyward, *Our Passion For Justice*, 90. Heyward readily affirms her lesbian identity and views it as an asset providing an important perspective for her theology. See her *Speaking of Christ*, 11.

by men, which in her view is most characteristic of the social order in the Christian west.

Generative Mutuality

In Heyward's view, "mutuality" identifies and defines who Jesus was and how he related to people. According to Heyward, the "Christic," redemptive power of mutuality, borne into the world by believers, has been suppressed by the tradition and must be recognized in our time.[113] In short, she believes that only by re-imaging God, particularly the person of Jesus, as our power in mutual relation will we be able to truly know God and participate fully in redemption, by living as God lives--in mutuality with all in the world.

In contrast to what she calls a traditional dualistic view--that in relationship to God, humans are less good and less important than the divinity--Heyward contends that humans and all of creation participate in the redemption of the world, along with Jesus of Nazareth.[114] Significant in Heyward's interpretation of redemption is her apprehension of the contrasting assumptions held by Irenaeus of Lyons and Augustine of Hippo concerning the divine conceived as omnipotent, omnipresent, and "wholly other" and the implications those assumptions hold for the human role in redemption and creation[115].

Augustine, in her view, assumed that nature itself is not evil, yet he pessimisticly stressed the sin of fallen humanity. Further, she notes that; following Augustine, orthodox Christianity identified the fallen human condition with loneliness, separation, division and estrangement. Heyward accentuates the fact that Platonic influence upon Augustine's theology shaped an anthropology that understood humans as *non posse non peccare* and a Christology in which Jesus alone carried out the task

---

[113] Heyward, "Lent, Easter: Seasons Upside Down," *Christianity and Crisis* 51 (1991): 75-76.

[114] Heyward, *Speaking of Christ*, 24. See also Heyward, *Speaking of Christ*, 90 n. 2, where she quotes F. D. Maurice, *Theological Essays* (London: James Clarke, 1957), 67.

[115] Heyward, *Redemption of God*, 107-47. Heyward discusses the theodicies of Iraeneus and Augustine in detail.

of redemption. Classical orthodox Christian notions of redemption followed Augustine. Because human corrupt free will can choose no good, according to Augustine, humans are given the grace to become more God-like and even more isolated (apart from matter) "higher" state like God's own. Heyward claims then, that for Augustine, salvation was from human bodily existence as well as sin. His view thus deemphasizes human agency and responsibility in promoting, sustaining, nurturing human development and growth.

By contrast, Heyward understands Iraeneus's view of humanity to be optimistic and to presume the goodness of creation. Following Iraeneus, Heyward views sin as both individual choice and involuntary involvement with structures which frame and limit the actual possibilities of individual choice.[116] Redemption takes place precisely in the struggle to transform situations and structures of injustice and creative right-relation. Thus, rather than a state that can be achieved, redemption is a journey with God through time, always "in dissonant tension with counterforces."[117] It requires a kind of "revolutionary patience" to continue to engage in the struggle, since immediate gratification is often not to be had. Even though mutuality and justice are never totally fulfilled in this world, they draw us forward, because we do know them in part: "through imitations and glimpses, intuitions and relationships . . . [we are drawn to] our beginnings--into the heart of our creation/creativity, into our relatedness."[118]

Heyward also speaks of mutuality in co-creation.[119] God is most appropriately described as a dynamic or a process; one affected by human relations, strengthened

---

[116]Ibid., 111. See also Heyward, "Heterosexist Theology: Being Above It All," *Journal of Feminist Studies in Religion* 3 (1987): 34.

[117]Heyward, *Our Passion For Justice*, xiv, 205.

[118]Heyward, *Touching Our Strength*, 91-92.

[119]Heyward, *Redemption of God*, 9: "With us, by us, through us, God lives, God becomes, God changes, God speaks, God acts, God suffers, and God dies in the world. . . . The constancy of God is the activity of God in the world wherever, whenever and for whatever reason, *humanity* acts, creates, liberates, and blesses humanity."

by human co-operation, who suffers when creatures suffer.[120] For Heyward, the boundary between the human and divine is one of quality, not kind. The power which is God is limitless in depth, scope, constancy, and goodness, always available, always creative, always coming into being, "the source and constant resource of good in our lives."[121] Human power is often misdirected and limited, but the power of God provides "radical re-encouragement" in the face of human restrictions and distortions, because there is a radical and foundational connection between the human and divine.[122] Human persons are understood to be co-creative agents with God and all creation by virtue of their very constitution.

Social Mutuality

Heyward asserts that control (power-over) alienates power in relation while mutuality transforms it into co-creative dynamism.[123] Since, on the one hand, a goal of the Christian community is that "there [be] no one in need" (Acts 4:34), and on the other hand, it is important that the "whole body" functions together to maximize the gifts of each for the common good (Eph. 4:15; 1 Cor. 12:7), then it appears only logical that every means possible should be tapped to achieve those goals. Certainly, Heyward would agree that "mutuality" necessitates that the contribution and participation of the lesser party(ies) in a relationship significantly influence the optimal flourishing of all.[124]

---

[120]Heyward distinguishes her theology from process theology in that process thought begins with speculation and uses speculative abstractions (where she does not) to thematize the concrete. See Carter Heyward, "An Unfinished Symphony of Liberation: The Radicalization of Christian Feminism Among White US Women - A Review Essay," *Journal of Feminist Studies in Religion* 1 (1985): 108 passim.

[121]Heyward, *Touching Our Strength*, 190.

[122]Heyward, *Our Passion For Justice*, 118.

[123]Heyward, *Redemption of God*, 56.

[124]Heyward, *Staying Power*, 88: "Genuine mutuality emerges only when [there is] . . . a shared capacity to experience our voices although we have been silenced; [we experience] our connectedness although we have been separated; and [we realize] our integrity as persons although we have been shattered."

While boundaries are important for maintaining personal identity, Heyward contends that, like a knife, a boundary can shape or sever a relationship. If the setting of boundaries is to shape a relationship and not destroy it, they need to be set *with* one another, no matter whether we are speaking of individuals or nations. Such a stance opens far-reaching implications for the meaning of flourishing and the moral life:

> Where there is no effort toward mutuality there is no love. This means that Christians can't love people we don't respect. We cannot love those whom we don't invite to be with us as sisters and brothers. We may pity them; we may treat them charitably; but we cannot love them. . . . Only together, in mutual relation, is there any common personal power, any love, any actual God. . . . The difference between liberal charity and radical love is that, while the former is condescending, the later is mutual.[125]

Once we recognize our common power with others and with God, barriers fall away as causes of disempowerment and become definitive of distinct persons or groups that can empower one another.

It is upon an understanding of God as "the power that moves toward the creation of mutual relation in a just world"[126] that Heyward rests her claim that concrete "love of neighbor as self"--*rather than* love of God--is "*the* norm for Christian life and theology."[127] This neighbor love or "praxis of relational cooperation" mirrors and is enlightened by "faith in a just god/ess whose justice is made known in relations characterized by mutuality and justice."[128] Faith and praxis form and inform each other in a continuous mutual process.[129]

---

[125] Heyward, *Our Passion For Justice*, 167.

[126] Ibid., 194.

[127] Ibid., 227. See also "An Unfinished Symphony of Liberation," 102. See also *Redemption of God*, 1-2, 44, 48.

[128] Heyward, *Speaking of Christ*, 21.

[129] Heyward stands with Gustavo Gutierrez in this regard as stated in his *Theology of Liberation*, xxxiii-xxxiv.

Normative Status

In Heyward's work, we see mutuality used normatively in three ways. First, she shows mutuality as the way God relates to all of creation, particularly to human beings. Thus, insofar as humans are created in God's image and likeness, humans have the innate capacity for mutuality. Secondly, she shows how Jesus is mutual in all of his relations and how he is *more* than a human exemplar because his relation with God is *fully* mutual. Insofar as Jesus is the norm for Christian ethics, mutuality as modeled by Jesus must be a norm for Christian ethics. Finally, Heyward argues that human relations are healthy to the extent they are mutual. Heyward illustrates the normative nature of mutuality using numerous examples of good, healthy, holy relationships in which mutuality holds a central place, as well as examples of abusive and oppressive relationships in which mutuality is absent.[130]

From Heyward's understanding of the image of God, human/divine relation, and human agency, it also follows that "this intrinsic mutuality . . . should be the foundation of--our ethics, pastoral care and theology."[131] Any violation of mutuality, be it in interpersonal relations or between humans and other earthcreatures, constitutes evil and sin in Heyward's view.[132] This evil takes on a variety of forms including patriarchy, crossing sexual boundaries, or destroying personal power to create in relation to others.

On the positive side, Heyward understands mutuality as a natural and moral bond which requires an ethical response that promotes mutual relations as well as the transformation of non-mutual situations. Jesus' life, teaching and ministry provides the foundation and example for Heyward's construal of normative behavior:

> The experience of mutuality can strengthen us also to live prophetically as enablers of mutuality.

---

[130]Heyward, *Touching Our Strength*, 96.

[131]Carter Heyward, "How My Mind Has Changed: The Power of God-With-Us," *Christian Century* 107 (1990): 275. See *Our Passion*, 124.

[132]Heyward, *Redemption of God*, 162.

> . . . When we are really present with someone, we know and are known by this person. We are able to share forgiveness as mutual blessing and in so doing, to provide a resting place for one another close to the heart of God.[133]

Heyward holds that one's realization and acceptance of mutuality as fundamental for a healthy life makes one morally responsible for creating and maintaining mutual relations.[134]

Given all of this, it seems fair to propose that the notion of mutuality functions as a formal norm for Christian social ethics in Heyward's works, even though she never explicitly makes such a claim.

Distinctions/Relationship of Mutuality to Equality, Friendship, Reciprocity, Solidarity

Heyward's understanding of mutuality is further illuminated when considered in relation to her use of four analogous terms, equality, reciprocity, solidarity, and friendship. For Heyward, "Equality denotes a sameness of position or status, while mutuality describes a dynamic relational movement into a vision of ourselves together."[135] She holds that neither mutuality nor equality necessarily assure or imply one another. Mutuality is dynamic in that it "signals relational growth and change and constitutes an invitation into shaping the future together."[136] Mutuality is, in effect, what prevents equal relationships from breaking down into unequal and abusive relationships.

Heyward asserts that "mutuality is not merely reciprocity, a *quid pro quo* give and take of benefits or sexual pleasure."[137] She is clear that mutuality is beyond merely reciprocal relations.[138] Sadly, in Heyward's view, traditional Christianity has

---

[133]Heyward, *Touching Our Strength*, 142 and 147.

[134]Heyward, *Our Passion For Justice*, 243-44.

[135]Heyward, *Touching Our Strength*, 34.

[136]Ibid.

[137]Ibid., 14-106 passim.

[138]Ibid., 104.

modeled, blessed and enforced relationships and practices that are reciprocal--merely a one for one exchange, which remains open to unrestricted "power-over." This choice for merely reciprocal relationships, Heyward contends, violated the model of mutual relationship established by God at the time of creation--the fluid exchange between parties in relation toward the flourishing of all. Some reciprocal relationships that pass for "goods" are non-mutual parenting, religious leadership, physical/emotional/spiritual healing, and teaching.[139]

Heyward uses the term "solidarity" infrequently, but quite specifically, defining it as: "a voluntary act of standing with those who suffer--offering them no pretense, no magical solutions, no theological rational for suffering, no feigned lightheartedness or denial of pain and fear."[140] Whenever the term is used, solidarity indicates a stance or tendency toward using "power with" or on behalf of the other, yet *also*, it signals the *inability* to overcome some boundary in order to actually *be with* the other.[141]

Interpreting contextually, one can conclude that Heyward understands "solidarity" as a power which awakens the desire for powerful person(s) to move toward less powerful person(s) and which tends toward mutuality in that it allows the more powerful to see her/his commonness with the other. Yet, there are real barriers which preclude the powerful person(s) from acting upon this realization, and which inhibit mutuality where all boundaries are fluid and dynamic.

Heyward defines "friendship" as "the most exact experience we have of mutual relationship." She uses the experience and concept of friendship as a "paradigm for mutual relation, for justice in the small daily places of our lives as well as an image for

---

[139]Ibid., 57. Heyward is highly critical of abusive "power-over" relationships that do not clearly result in the thriving and well-being of all parties. See also Ibid., 35: ". . . unless it [parent/child] is a mutual relationship in which both are growing and changing in relation to the other, the parent/child bond is abusive."

[140]Heyward, *Speaking of Christ*, 37.

[141]Ibid., 25, 29, 30, 40, 41, 83-4. Persons with AIDS, cancer, battered women, victims of apartheid or genocide, and the people of Nicaragua are subjects of "solidarity."

mutual relation, for justice in the small daily places of our lives as well as an image for justice and "godding" in the world."[142] Elsewhere, Heyward suggests that both goodness and mutuality constitute friendship. It is mutuality that provides friendship with power. It is mutuality that provides "the fulcrum of our capacity to survive and affect the world around us."[143] So, for Heyward, mutuality is a component of friendship.

Mutuality then, in Heyward's view, signals something more than equality and reciprocity. In mutuality the movement is toward a union as in a single human body. In society or in the church community, Heyward sees this unity in the metaphor of the Body of Christ--when any part of the body suffers, all suffer.[144] Extending this body metaphor, Heyward finds in the erotic a more perfect model of the fluid, energizing and creative power that is mutuality.[145]

Relationship of Mutuality to Love and Justice

Though Heyward recognizes a flexible relationship between mutuality, love and justice at the practical level, conceptually she does hold them distinct. Heyward asserts that "where there is no effort toward mutuality, there is no love."[146] In turn, she observes, "Love creates righteousness or justice, here on earth. To make love is to make justice."[147] In addition, ". . . justice is right relation, and right relation is mutual relation."[148]

---

[142]Heyward, *Touching Our Strength*, 188.

[143]Ibid., 56.

[144]Heyward, *Speaking of Christ*, 25, 50. Just as various organs of the body have particular functions, but are interdependent, so too, while maintaining individual identity, humans can engage in mutual relations.

[145]Heyward, *Our Passion For Justice*, 192.

[146]Ibid., 167.

[147]Ibid., 186.

[148]Heyward, *Touching Our Strength*, 22-23.

Heyward contends that *acts* of love involve agapic, philial, and erotic *integrity*. She counters Outka by focusing on the *act* of love, rather than on the *concepts* of love. "Put otherwise, the Christian love of one's neighbor as self, the mutuality of friendship, and the sexual dynamic that draws us into relation are revealed, *in practice* as one act of love."[149]

For Heyward, the strongest metaphor for mutuality is the erotic power of sexual love-making.[150] As in love-making, the recognition of mutuality (a common power) must precede the establishment of true justice or love.[151] Without a recognition of mutuality, love-making is subject to corruption by relations of dominance, subjugation or oppression, and justice-making is open to the mere exertion of "power-over" that is self-serving and oppressive.

In Heyward's view, justice or right relationship is the form in which God is concretely manifest in history, "the pattern of the Sacred in our life together."[152] Right relation is God's logos, or complete self-expression. Heyward believes that truly mutual relation or interconnectedness, and thus true human being requires justice. She draws her concept of justice from the Jewish and Christian traditions of Hebrew, *hesed* of God, which she interprets as "righteousness."[153] While keeping love, justice and mutuality conceptually distinct, Heyward's discussion emphasizes the

---

[149] Heyward, *Redemption of God*, xxvi, n. 17.

[150] Heyward, *Touching Our Strength*, 3, 4, 17, 34. Heyward understands the term, "love-making" very broadly as an expression of embodied relational inclinations. Included here are inclinations ranging from embodied feelings most would call sensuality, to the erotic pleasures of genital love-making. See her definitions of "sensuality" and "sexuality," Ibid., 193-94.

[151] Heyward, *Our Passion For Justice*, 167: "Only in mutual relation is there any common personal power, any love, any actual God. I have no power without you. God is ours to share, to give into and receive from, to experience together or not at all. The difference between liberal charity and radical love is that, while the former is condescending, the latter is mutual."

[152] Heyward, *Touching Our Strength*, 22, 74. Using the doctrine of the trinity, Heyward relates justice to the being of God, see Ibid., 23, 189.

[153] Heyward, *Our Passion For Justice*, 190-91.

interplay between the three notions in the dynamism of relationships that result in the maximum flourishing of all involved.

Beverly Wildung Harrison: Stated Definition of Mutuality

Beverly Wildung Harrison is a socialist feminist Christian ethicist who has taught at New York's Union Theological Seminary since 1972.[154] She has been a pioneer in the development of feminist ethics that is motivated by social consciousness and based upon a thorough critique of current forms of the political economy in relation to the Christian tradition.[155] Her feminist liberationist analysis utilizes the social sciences, philosophy and theology. Harrison believes the biological likenesses between women and men exceed the differences. Gender, therefore, does not supply a sufficient basis for unequal participation by women and men in society or economy. Central to Harrison's method is the concept of "embodied reason" as the way norms are critically tested. Her effort is to overcome the body/mind split in both intellectual and social life; to teach the necessity of attending to our bodies and emotions as sources of moral data and power; and challenging traditional dualistic sexual ethics with ideas of body-mediated reasoning.

Feminist Theological Context

Socialist Feminist Theory

In her landmark article, "The Power of Anger in the Work of Love: Christian Ethics For Women and Other Strangers," Harrison proposes three basepoints for a feminist moral theology: (1) activity as a mode of love (2) our bodies, ourselves[156] as

---

[154] See Carol Robb, "Introduction," in *Making the Connections*, xi-xxii.

[155] See *Journal of Feminist Studies in Religion* 9 (1993). This is a special issue in honor of Harrison. It includes over a dozen critical articles treating all aspects of her work. A comprehensive annotated bibliography is also included.

[156] The term, "our bodies, ourselves" originated in The Boston Women's Health Collective, *Our Bodies, Ourselves* (New York: Simon and Schuster, 1973). James B. Nelson elaborated on the definition and significance of the term in his *Embodiment: An Approach to Sexuality and Christian Theology* (Minneapolis: Augsburg Publishing House, 1979). See note 163, below for a definition of "embodiment."

agents of love, and (3) the centrality of relationships in ethical decision-making.[157] Here we see both the influence of liberation theology (Heyward) and Harrison's socialist feminist critique (Marx) combining to forge a new framework of analysis.[158]

Harrison recalls the fact that women's lives have historically exemplified the power of activity, experimentation and risk-taking. Cross culturally, women bear the biological and active reality of child-bearing and child-rearing, and are more often than not the bread winners and traders in the society, as well. Given this, she contends that women could not have been the source of a theology that values the static, passive, contemplative qualities as holy, while viewing the mundane routine activity of day-to-day life as a religious disvalue.[159] In contrast to traditional natural law theologies that "fail to do justice to the fact that the power of nature passes through, what Marx called, the `species-being of human nature'," she claims that loving as a mode of activity (along with "being" loving) needs to be recognized as a characteristic of a feminist ethical framework.[160] This is necessary because it is

---

[157]Harrison, "Power of Anger," 41-57.

[158]For a description of "socialist feminism" see Carol S. Robb," A Framework For Feminist Ethics," *Journal of Religious Ethics* 9 (Spring 1981): 60-62. Robb states: "Theorists ally themselves with that trend within Marxist theory which emphasizes the connections between culture, politics, and the economic base, with attendant organizing implications, and oppose that trend which emphasizes the primacy of workplace organizing on economic issues." Harrison consistently cites the following as among the most important sources for socialist-feminist theory: Rosalind Pollack Petchesky, *Abortion and Women's Choice: The State, Sexuality, and Reproductive Freedom*, (New York: Longman, 1984; Zellah R. Eisenstein, ed., *Capitalist Patriarchy and the Case For Socialist Feminism* (New York: Monthly Review Press, 1979); Batya Weinbaum, *The Curious Courtship of Women's Liberation and Socialism* (Boston: South End Press, 1978); Nannerl O. Koehane, Michelle Z. Rosaldo, Barbara Gelpi, eds., *Feminist Theory: A Critique of Ideology* (Chicago: University of Chicago Press, 1982).

[159]Harrison, "Power of Anger," 45-46.

[160]Ibid., 46: "A feminist moral theology needs to root its analysis in this realm of radical moral activity. Such freedom is often abused, but the power to create a world of moral relations is a fundamental aspect of human nature itself. In my opinion, the metaphor of Be-ing does not permit us to incorporate the radicality of human agency adequately. Do-ing must be as fundamental as Be-ing in our theologies... we can never make sense of what is deepest, "wholist," most powerfully sacred in the lives of women if we identify women only with the more static metaphor of being, neglecting the centrality of praxis as basic to women's experience."

through our human activity that our world and our beliefs are transformed from theory to actuality.

Women, on the other hand, must not make the error of totally neglecting "be-ing," placing it in a polarity with "do-ing;" both are necessary for good ethics and ethical living. At this point, however, the dualism promoted through the disvaluing of "do-ing" must be corrected. Women have been deeply involved in the construction of human dignity and community for centuries and they have much to bring to Christian ethics. Women have (have had) the power to build and bring forth community.[161] Love needs to be understood as "the power to act-each-other-into-well-being or we will continue to thwart and maim each other."[162] For women the power for such activity is found in *our bodies, ourselves*.

A second basepoint that Harrison submits centers on the understanding and appreciation of embodiment, and the effort to defeat the dualistic thinking that creates the body/mind split at every level of social and intellectual life.[163] Traditional (disembodied) Christian thought has held that "detachment" and "disinterestedness" are foundational qualifications for sound moral decision-making and action. Harrison holds, to the contrary, that all knowledge, including moral knowledge, is body-

---

[161]Ibid., 47.

[162]Ibid.: "Through acts of love--what Nel Morton has called 'listening each other into speech'-- we literally build up the power of personhood in one another." See also Beverly Wildung Harrison, "H. Richard Niebuhr: Towards a Christian Moral Philosophy" (Ph.D. diss., Union Theological Seminary, 1974), 170-203. Harrison discusses H. Richard Niebuhr's notion of faith expressed as co-creative action that forges new relationships in the world, and breaks open new possibilities for resolving existing contradictions.

[163]Carol S. Robb, "Introduction," in *Making the Connections*, xix-xx: "The term 'embodiment' with respect to feminist theory and specifically feminist ethics means, minimally five things: (1) Our sexuality and body-selves are to be celebrated rather than deprecated, and are to be respected as the ground of our personhood. (2) Mutuality, rather than control, ownership or paternalism, is a major moral norm for social, including sexual communication. (3) Sex role rigidity is destructive of possibilities for mature interpersonal relations; hence sex role fluidity is practiced. (4) We are to recognize and honor all expressions of sexual communication between people who care for each other in mutuality and regard, whether they are homosexual or heterosexual relations. (5) At the level of social policy, a woman's moral agency should be trusted above anyone else's to decide what responsibility requires, especially with respect
to the predicaments of procreation."

mediated knowledge. Foundational to the conception of ideas is body-mediated perception of experience.[164] Harrison believes that the notion of body mediated knowledge is a significant corrective to the Western intellectual heritage which created the body/mind dualism that has been the root cause of negative attitudes toward women. Affirming bodily mediated knowledge has been a source of renewed self-respect and empowerment for women, particularly as it concerns issues of sexuality.[165] Harrison stresses that every one of our senses--including and our emotions and sense of touch--mediate the world to us. Our minds and bodies work together as an integrated system enabling us to interact with our world as whole persons.

Harrison illustrates the empowerment of women that results from their revitalized understanding of embodied knowledge in her discussion of the constructive use of the emotion of anger. She contends that Buber was correct in concluding that anger is a signal that something is wrong in a relationship. When one realizes that s/he is angry one can choose to "avoid, ignore, condemn or blame" or "we can act to alter the relationship toward reciprocity, beginning a real process of hearing and speaking to each other."[166] Thus, embodied ways of knowing (such as feeling anger) are viewed by Harrison as having a central place in feminist ethics.

Theology

Harrison's third basepoint follows Heyward in maintaining the centrality of relationship. Harrison states: "A feminist moral theology insists that relationality is

---

[164]Harrison, "Power of Anger," 48: "Ideas are dependent on our sensuality. Feeling is the basic bodily ingredient that mediates our connectedness to the world. . . . All power including intellectual power is rooted in feeling. If feeling is damaged or cut off, our power to image the world and act into it is destroyed and our rationality is impaired." Cf. Harrison, "Keeping the Faith in a Sexist Church: Not For Women Only," in *Making the Connections*, 219-21. While Harrison unequivocally condemns Aquinas's misguided views on the biologically determined and inferior nature of women, she enthusiastically endorses his affirmation of the senses as constitutive of human intelligence and proper humanity.

[165]Harrison, "Human Sexuality and Mutuality," 151-52.

[166]Harrison, "Power of Anger," 50. See also Martin Buber, *I and Thou*, trans. Walter Kaufmann (New York: Scribner's Sons, 1970), 67-68.

at the heart of all things."[167] Harrison cites Heyward's *Redemption of God* as a fine articulation of the major criticisms of traditional theology, and credits Heyward with offering the sorely needed corrective of a "God of mutual relation." Harrison claims: "Where our image of transcendence is represented to us as unrelatedness, as freedom from reciprocity and mutuality, the experience of God as living presence grows cold and unreal."[168] Such an unrelated God leaves humans in a posture of either the heroic--needing to make grand gestures to gain God's attention; or on the other hand, in the position of "sniveling gratitude of the weak toward the strong who grant favors."[169] When these stances are translated into human behaviors and dynamics the result is a disastrous loss of human dignity by all involved.

"Mutuality," on the other hand, is a quality of God that is a desired quality for humanity and human relations. Harrison's (also Heyward's) image of God is influenced by F. D. Maurice and H. R. Niebuhr in that she understands obedience to God (a relationship of "power-over") and morality before God (a relationship of "power-to" or "power-with") as opposing images of God/human relations.[170] Obedience and morality involve two different dynamics and entail two different images of God. Morality allows the embrace of mutuality ("power-to") acting with the other toward a common end; while obedience requires subordination and subjugation ("power-over"), a kind of doing for the other. In order for our moral language to "embrace

---

[167]Harrison, "Power of Anger," 50.

[168]Ibid., 51.

[169]Ibid.

[170]Harrison, "Sexism and the Language of Christian Ethics," in *Making the Connections*, 38-39: "Theological images that portray God as Lord or King, even those who describe God as Mother/Father, teach us that the holy power is not a reciprocal power. By contrast, metaphors that locate and identify holiness in sister/brother relations teach us to long for a "holy One" who is a companion, one not diminished by our growth, power, and fulfillment, one who does not need to rule by dictum. Such images and metaphors teach us social relations of mutuality . . . my well-being and yours are not inherently at odds. As relational beings, we need each other for our common well-being, and in our mutual relation we experience God/ess."

mutuality and support the whole spectrum of human fulfillment, autonomy, and as yet unrealized possibility, all of us must envision all action as genuine *inter*action."[171]

Christology

Harrison's Christology is never systematically discussed in her works. However, she clearly supports the "low" Christologies of Heyward, Segundo, Sölle, and Miranda in the context of her discussion of Liberation Theology.[172] Most significant for Harrison, in each of these Christologies is the fact that Jesus stands primarily as the exemplary proclaimer of the "commonwealth of God;" not as the *one* redeemer. Harrison prefers these Christologies because they *also* call forth believers to active embodied relationships with others and the world in order to complete the redemption and bring about the reign of God in history.

Harrison's Basic Definition of Mutuality

Beverly Harrison is not as clear in distinguishing "mutuality" as a unique concept as is Carter Heyward. She readily acknowledges her dependence on Heyward's work in demonstrating the theological and Christological foundations for "mutuality," so we can presume some similarity in the meaning of the term for the two scholars.[173] However, while Heyward's definition of "mutuality" primarily follows her analysis of sexism and heterosexism, Harrison's definition results from combining socialist feminist theory with the traditional analytic models of the discipline of Christian social ethics.[174] She thus defines "mutuality" in terms of the functional role it plays in eliminating structural subjugation or subordination of marginal groups or individuals in society, particularly women.

---

[171] Ibid., 39. The emphasis is Harrison's. Cf. H. Richard Niebuhr, *The Responsible Self: An Essay in Christian Moral Philosophy*, ed. Richard R. Niebuhr, Paperback edition (New York: Harper and Row, 1978), 60-68.

[172] Harrison, "Theological Reflection in the Struggle for Liberation: A Feminist Perspective," in *Making the Connections*, 262-63.

[173] Harrison, *Making the Connections*, 262, 271 n. 28, 272 n. 5, 274 n. 34, 287 n. 9, 300 n. 20, 25.

[174] Carol S. Robb, "Introduction," in *Making the Connections*, xiii-xxii.

Harrison defines "mutuality" as "love in its deepest radicality. It is so radical that many of us have not yet learned to bear it. To experience it we must be open, we must be capable of giving and receiving."[175] Elsewhere, she defines "mutuality" as a way of being in the world that deepens relation, embodies and extends community, and passes on the gift of life.[176] In another place, Harrison defines "mutuality" as: "the power, simultaneously, *to affect and be affected by another* . . . ."[177] Mutuality involves "the simultaneous acknowledgement of vulnerability to the need of the other, the recognition of one's own power to give and receive . . . and to call forth another's power of relation and express one's own."[178] Finally, Harrison understands "mutuality" as the heart of Christian ethics.[179]

Further Analysis of Mutuality

Cosmic Mutuality

Harrison demonstrates her belief in the interdependence of all cosmic elements, including human beings, most clearly in her two essays: "The Politics of Energy" and "Agendas For a New Theological Ethic."[180] In both articles, Harrison's first step is to show the necessity of understanding the notion of justice in biblical terms rather than in primarily institutional terms (Rawls). The biblical notion of

---

[175] Harrison, "Power of Anger," 51-52.

[176] Ibid. Mutuality is the power that enables and expresses Jesus' radical activity of love, so this phrase defines mutuality. Jesus' activity constituted this way of being.

[177] Harrison, "Human Sexuality and Mutuality," 152-53. See *Making the Connections*, 290, n. 5 where Harrison defines power as "the ability to act on and effectively shape the world around us, particularly through collective actions and institutional policy. To have power means to have access to physical resources and wealth, to knowledge, and to loci of social decision-making and to be able to impact institutional and social policy."

[178] Harrison, "Misogyny and Homophobia: The Unexplored Connections," in *Making the Connections*, 150.

[179] Harrison, "Power of Anger," 51.

[180] Harrison, "Politics of Energy Policy," in *Energy Ethics* 56-71 and Harrison, "New Theological Ethics," in *Churches in Struggle*, 89-98.

covenant, she shows, includes personal well-being, social justice, and care for the earth and other expendable resources (ecojustice).[181]

Harrison concurs with Heyward's understanding of "right-relationship" which "evokes a shared passion for justice," "a common longing for a world `where there are no excluded ones'."[182] The biblical covenant and evidence from ecological science each reveal the reciprocal nature of the relationship between the ecosystem, human beings and their activities. Using socialist feminist terms, Harrison also claims that the natural environment asserts itself as a "living part of `our bodies, ourselves.'"[183]

Harrison turns next to consider how "power" is understood within social analysis.[184] How power is construed is critical to whether or not the analysis contributes to a life-giving outcome for all--including the ecosystem. In the course of her discussion, Harrison renounces as inadequate any analysis of power that "takes account of *power* in an institutional matrix" and "groups already in ascendancy" while excluding an analysis of the effect of power on "those already most disadvantaged in society."[185] In her view, an adequate analysis of power is executed from a position that includes the viewpoint of society's most disadvantaged.

In the ecological context, Harrison develops her notion of mutuality by appealing to Jesus as the paradigm of mutual relationship (more below). The logic

---

[181]Harrison, "Politics of Energy Policy," in *Energy Ethics* 58-59. See also Harrison, "New Theological Ethics," in *Churches in Struggle*, 90-92.

[182]Harrison, "New Theological Ethics," 90. Harrison refers to Heyward's *Our Passion For Justice*, and her own essay, "Human Sexuality and Mutuality," in Judith L. Weidman, ed., *Christian Feminism: A Vision of a New Humanity* (San Francisco: Harper and Row, 1984). Another version of the latter essay has been cited above as "Human Sexuality and Mutuality."

[183]Harrison, "Politics of Energy Policy," in *Energy Ethics* 57. Just as alienation from embodied knowledge distorts one's world view, so too, failure to recognize the capacity of the ecosystem to "answer back" to human demands upon it is devastating to the well-being of our world.

[184]Ibid., 57-58.

[185]Ibid., 58-59. See also "The Politics of Energy Policy," in *Making the Connections*, 174-90, 293, n. 3. In Robb's edition of the essay, Harrison makes explicit her reliance on Heyward's concept of divine/human relationship and covenant; her critique of orthodox Christologies; and the notion of power-in-relation.

of Jesus' radical mutuality with the marginalized of his day would make little sense if he did not (at least tacitly) also take account of power relations governing ecological resources that were necessary to provide for their optimal survival and thriving.[186] Harrison summarizes this argument in terms of the modern ecological crisis and the need to care for the thriving of the earth and the "least ones" when she declares:

> [E]conomic well-being . . . requires a *conjoining* of sensuous human labor with human dignity and self-direction, and involves *participation* in decisions about the use of *socially* produced wealth. We must challenge the commoditization of all human activity and all *social* relations which is the consequences of the capitalist hegemony over *all* aspects of life.[187]

It is my judgement that, in light of Harrison's reliance on Heyward, her own understanding of the terms "conjoining," "participation," and "socially" connote mutuality, the notion that power is shared "in such a way that each participant in the relationship is called forth more fully into becoming . . . whole . . . with integrity."[188]

Gender Mutuality

Harrison is a self-proclaimed dialectical materialist who is certain that in order to transform traditional biases and the oppression of women, women must be understood (along with men) as autonomous moral agents. She adamantly resists natural law theories that claim sex role differences are biologically determined and thus, mirror God's intentions for human behavior.[189] Biological dimorphism has been classically interpreted according to a Platonic dualism that defines women (body/matter) as inferior to men (spirit/intellect). Because the language used to define and describe the obvious distinction between male and female is so psychologically influential, what is implicit in classical language rooted in Platonic dualism-- male/spirit/intellect/good; female/matter/affect/evil--has frequently been acted out in

---

[186]Harrison, "Politics of Energy Policy," in *Energy Ethics*, 59.

[187]Harrison, "New Theological Ethics," 96-97. The emphasis is mine.

[188]Heyward, *Touching Our Strength*, 191.

[189]Carol Robb, "Introduction," in *Making the Connections*, xvi-xvii.

a matter-of-fact subordination of women to men.[190] Harrison claims that there is ample biogenic and sociocultural evidence to challenge the erroneous claims of classical dualism.[191] But most centrally at issue in the oppression of women, in Harrison's view, is the use of power in social, political, economic, and sexual relationships.

Social Mutuality

Once again Harrison aligns herself with Heyward and declares Jesus as the paradigmatic source of mutuality:

> Jesus was radical not in his lust for sacrifice, *but in his power of mutuality*. Jesus' death on the cross, his sacrifice, was no abstract exercise in moral virtue. His death was the price he paid for refusing to abandon the *radical activity* of love-- of expressing solidarity and reciprocity with the excluded ones of his community. Sacrifice, I submit, is not a central moral good of the Christian life. Radical acts of love--expressing solidarity and bringing mutual relationships to life--are the central virtues of the Christian moral life.[192]

Harrison believes that Christians need to live as Jesus lived, with a commitment to mutuality, and in so doing, bear God into the world. Fidelity to mutuality, she stresses, frequently requires making sacrifices for the cause of radical love, creating and sustaining relationships, or righting wrong relationships. Persons in recent history who illustrate this fidelity to mutuality include Archbishop Oscar Romero, Dr. Martin Luther King, Jr., and countless women who have suffered for the sake of mutuality, but remained nameless.

> [I]t is risky to live as *if the commonwealth* of the living God were present--that is, to live by radical mutuality and reciprocity. . . . Those in power believe such love to be "unrealistic" because those touched by the power of such love tend to develop a reluctance to accept

---

[190]Harrison, "Sexism and the Language of Christian Ethics," in *Making the Connections*, 24-25.

[191]Ibid., 30-31, 274, n. 25. Harrison cites Robert Green *Sexual Identity Conflict in Children and Adults* (New York: Basic Books, 1974) and John Money and Patricia Tucker, *Sexual Signatures* (Boston: Little, Brown, 1975).

[192]Harrison, "Power of Anger," 52. Emphasis is Harrison's.

> anything less than mutuality and self-respect, anything less than human dignity, anything less than authentic relatedness.[193]

Harrison is clear that mutuality is key to radical active involvement with the disempowered of the world because it delimits love as positive activity, which serves the well-being of all involved, and it empowers both the lover and the beloved.

Normative Status

In Harrison's discussion of love, justice, passion, power, solidarity, equality, reciprocity and mutuality it is most significant that she constantly uses "mutuality" to qualify the relation under consideration. It signals a condition that normally needs to be present when, for example, authentic love or power is utilized as "power-with." When one analyzes Harrison's language surrounding the notion of "mutuality" her intent becomes plain.

> All of us, then, literally call forth each other in relationship, and our power of being and capacity to act emerges through our sensuous interaction in relation. If our modes of relationship are not grounded in bodily integrity, and if our ways of being with each other preclude mutuality--which is the power, simultaneously, *to affect and be affected by another*--we cannot and will not have not have *either* personal well-being *or* community, which is to say, relations of mutuality, shared empowerment and common respect.[194]

In Harrison's thought, mutuality sets the conditions for both justice and love. Before one can truly be loving or just, one must recognize the common power within each person and the necessity of sharing power for the optimal flourishing of all. Generally, Harrison considers mutuality a function of our sociality as human persons created in the image and likeness of God: ". . . our relationship to God is intrinsically related to our relationship to each other."[195] Our social relations are not separate from our relationship with God; implied in God-relation is social relation.

---

[193] Ibid., 53. Emphasis is Harrison's.

[194] Harrison, "Human Sexuality and Mutuality," 152-53.

[195] Ibid., 158.

In Harrison's view, not only does mutuality set the conditions for love and justice in human relationships generally, but like Heyward, she regards mutuality as a moral norm particularly important in sexual relations. The giving and receiving of touch and the sharing of erotic pleasure, sexual communication at its best creates strong bonds between persons and enhances self-respect. A feminist Christian sexual ethic condemns bodily communication when it is characterized by inequities of power and the lack of mutuality, because it results in loss of self-esteem and the devaluing everyone involved. Harrison declares:

> The moral norm for sexual communication in a feminist ethic is radical mutuality--the simultaneous acknowledgment of vulnerability to and need of another, the recognition of one's own power to give and receive pleasure and to call forth another's power of relation and to express one's own.[196]

In conclusion, Harrison is certain that "mutuality both of responsibility and of control" and "equal dignity-in-relation and in-power" are normative for relationships. I suggest in light of Harrison's definite affirmation of Heyward's notion of power-in-relation, and in order to complement her own notion of justice, Harrison would agree that mutuality, as such, most clearly meets the criteria she describes. Thus, it is clear that mutuality is considered normative for her Christian feminist ethics.[197]

Distinctions/Relationship of Mutuality to
Equality, Friendship, Reciprocity, Solidarity

Harrison defines equality in terms of the ability of all people to claim the same fundamental human rights. That understanding reflects her desire to correct the romantic perceptions of women as the superior gender, on the one hand, and sexist biases against women, on the other. By extension, she wishes to avoid the association

---

[196]Harrison, "Misogyny and Homophobia: The Unexplored Connections," in *Making the Connections*, 149-50.

[197]Harrison, "Theological Reflection on the Struggle For Liberation: A Feminist Perspective," in *Making the Connections*, 252-56 passim. At 253: "We must treat norms for what they are: human constructs that state our presumptions about what constitutes the general direction acts should take to qualify as 'moral.' Since norms are conceptual formulations of envisioned values, they may be expressed as principles of action."

of human inequality with any other human differences such as race, creed, or national origin. Harrison's focus is on *equal* valuation of the people involved, as well as on what is exchanged through the relationship.[198] Mutuality, by contrast, places the focus on the dynamics of the giving and receiving in a relationship.

Harrison understands "reciprocity" as a significant element in human rights. Reciprocity for her means that all people can claim (and receive) what they need for their well-being, with the understanding that *all* such claims carry with them the *obligation* to recognize the *same* claim from all other persons.[199] Here Harrison is in agreement with Heyward when she stresses the *quid pro quo* nature of the notion of "reciprocity." Harrison also implies that "mutuality" is different from reciprocity, though the distinction is not always made clear.

"Solidarity" is consistently used by Harrison to address a relationship between persons engaged in a struggle for social change--between those more and those less powerful. Harrison's idea of solidarity also includes a shared fidelity, accountability, and resistance to evil.[200] Even though Harrison indicates an exchange between partners as one aspect of solidarity, it is not identical with mutuality. Rather, mutuality is a relationship that is achieved once the parties move beyond the stage of struggle and conflict and they are in fact, accountable to one another, influencing one another, and influenced by one another.[201]

Relationship of Mutuality to Love and Justice

The task of analyzing Harrison's understanding of "mutuality" is made more complex by the fact that she uses love and justice interchangeably and synonymously throughout her work. An example of such usage is her presidential address to the Society of Christian Ethics in 1983. She states: "It is hardly novel to suggest that love

---

[198]Harrison, *Making the Connections*, 24-25, 29, 30-31, 169.

[199]Harrison, *Our Right to Choose*, 197. The emphasis is mine.

[200]"Theological Reflection in the Struggle for Liberation: A Feminist Perspective," in *Making the Connections*, 244.

[201]Ibid.

is the doing of justice."[202] Later she suggests that in order to do justice, "we must make love passionately in the world."[203] The implication is that love is synonymous with justice. In her efforts to reclaim the relational aspects of justice as well as her desire to set forth embodiment as a legitimate epistemological source for ethical analysis, she apparently loses sight of the need to clearly define her terms.[204]

What Harrison *does* accomplish through this usage is to make a break with the false separation of love and justice that is in continuity with the feminist notion of embodiment (as discussed above). She states: "I do believe . . . that women struggling for liberation have something critical to teach, especially about the role of the body, and of passion, in forging the connections between love, power and justice."[205] Her inclusion of "passion" serves to move the discussion to the heart of the controversy surrounding sexuality and sexual ethics, which also symbolizes the crux of non-mutual relations between genders. It is in the context of that discussion that Harrison becomes clear about her notion of mutuality (more on gender, below).

Harrison agrees with Heyward that our power to act, to do justice, comes from our passion. Passion also traditionally implies a deep intensity, which may relate to its being perceived as powerful here. Love responds to the longing for justice, which is experienced through our passion. For Harrison, love is no purely intellectual exercise to be accomplished in isolation. Passion produces the longing to make right relation, and love is the activity which people engage in as a result of this longing.[206] Here love can only refer to *mutual* love, because it is being used in reference to passion, the longing for right relation which, in biblical terms, includes a kind of

---

[202]Harrison, "Dream of a Common Language," 19.

[203]Ibid., 21.

[204]Ibid., 4, 19.

[205]Ibid., 19.

[206]Harrison, "Dream of a Common Language," 20.

mutuality.[207] It can thus be concluded that in relationships which do not operate mutually, love is not present. Harrison claims: "Love is a praxis of being actively engaged in mutual and respectful cocreation in community."[208] Elsewhere she states that love is "the power to act-each-other-into-well-being."[209]

Harrison's reason for insisting that mutual love is the only authentic love is that understandings of love which are non-mutual have been the occasion for the subordination and subjugation of women. Harrison levels strong criticism against Anders Nygren and Reinhold Niebuhr for their denigration of mutuality as "mere mutuality."[210] Authentic mutual love promotes the well-being of all involved in relationship. Love understood as a theological symbol of sacrifice or as romantic worship of women, does not challenge the dualism (of traditional Christianity) which undergirds non-mutual relations, it rather, creates, affirms and supports it.[211]

Ultimately, for Harrison, love and justice are the same. Both are right relationship. In order to do justice, we must love passionately in the world. This understanding of love and justice serves the heuristic purpose of breaking a false separation between public and private morality. The disadvantage however, is that the terms cease to be able to support and illuminate one another because they become two names for the same concept. What is gained in countering the dualistic paradigm may be lost in having only a murky distinction between love and justice.

---

[207]Harrison, "Power of Anger," 51: "Mutual love, I submit, is love in its deepest radicality. . . . To experience it, we must be open, we must be capable of giving and receiving." See also "Politics of Energy," 59.

[208]Harrison, *Our Right to Choose*, 115. This emphasis on activity stresses the Hebrew notion of loving activity, and counters erroneous notions rooted in Aristotelian biology and Platonic dualism that women are passive, and less capable of genuine love.

[209]Harrison, "Power of Anger," 47.

[210]Ibid., 27-28. In contrast to those two ethicists, Harrison believes mutuality stands at the heart of ethics. This view of "mutuality" is dangerous and inaccurate because it is based on dualism rather than embodied reality. See "Power of Anger," 51. See also Anders Nygren, trans. Philip S. Watson *Agape and Eros* (Philadelphia: Westminster Press, 1953), 75-85. In addition see Reinhold Niebuhr, *Nature and Destiny of Man: A Christian Interpretation* Vol. II (New York: Charles Scribner's Sons, 1943), 247-48.

[211]Harrison, "Sexism and the Language of Christian Ethics," in *Making the Connections*, 41.

Harrison asserts that justice is the central theological metaphor for Christian ethics. "Right relationship" is *the* principle of justice. In order to discover the meaning of justice in connection to mutuality, it is necessary to first understand what Harrison means by "right relationship." She declares:

> Justice in a liberation perspective is not a secondary and proximate norm, a mere social norm that poorly approximates a love that is personal. On the contrary, justice and the struggle for justice are *foundational to love itself.* It is naive to believe that genuine love can live and flourish where unjust social relations prevail.[212]

Like Heyward, Harrison assumes the "*doing* of justice" in her definition of "justice." That is, she presumes a solidarity with the marginalized and mutual accountability to them. Liberal theories of justice as "a juridical notion," a "regulative ideal," or even as "a first virtue of social relationships" are, in Harrison's view, inadequate. She comments: "Justice is more that all of these--it is our central theological image, a metaphor of right relationship, which shapes the *telos* of a good community and serves as the animating passion of the moral life."[213] Here again, Harrison's exact definition of justice is not given.

Elizabeth A. Johnson: Stated Definition of Mutuality

Elizabeth A. Johnson is a Roman Catholic Christian systematic theologian who utilizes a feminist liberationist methodology.[214] She believes that the Christian doctrine of God can accommodate a thoroughgoing feminist approach and that classical theological discourse about God can provide some insights useful to feminist theological discourse.[215] Johnson shows how feminist theology, drawing on women's

---

[212] Harrison, *Our Right to Choose*, 115.

[213] Harrison, "Dream of a Common Language," 4.

[214] Johnson, *She Who Is*, 11.

[215] For critical discussion of Johnson's work see: Mary Aquin O'Neill, review of *She Who Is: The Mystery of God in Feminist Theological Discourse*, by Elizabeth A. Johnson, *Religious Studies Review* 21 (1995): 19-21; Mary McClintock Fulkerson, review of *She Who Is: The Mystery of God in Feminist Theological Discourse*, by Elizabeth A. Johnson, *Religious Studies Review* 21 (1995): 21-25; Cynthia S.W. Crysdale, review of *She Who Is: The Mystery of God in Feminist Theological Discourse*, by Elizabeth A. Johnson, *Journal of Religion* 74 (1994): 414-15; Sonya A. Quitslund, review of *She Who*

interpretive experience and a critical retrieval of elements in scripture and tradition, can enable speech about God previously closed to the imagination. In Johnson's view, feminist theology can inform the classical Western Christian tradition concerning its inadequate androcentric understanding of God and uncover language for naming God that is genuinely liberating. Johnson's work also illustrates how the classical tradition can add density to feminist speech about God, directing attention to the vast scope of divine activity. Women's reality is portrayed by Johnson as fully *capax Dei*, fully capable of receiving, bearing and symbolizing the divine. It is her understanding of God, particularly the inner Trinitarian life and the divine manifestation in the Incarnation that shapes her notion of mutuality.

Johnson's works are systematic in the traditional sense and she is consistent in the use of both classical and contemporary sources to underpin her claims. She draws upon women's interpreted experience, Christian and Hebrew Scriptures and classical theology to demonstrate the foundation for her assertions.[216] While being faithful to the texts, she is also insightful and innovative in her interpretation of the sources.

Feminist Theological Context

The various contexts for Johnson's use of the term "mutuality" include her systematic treatments of speech about God, of resources for emancipatory speech about God, of the movement of the Living God throughout history, and her

---

Is: The Mystery of God in Feminist Theological Discourse, by Elizabeth A. Johnson, *Journal of Ecumenical Studies* 31 (1994): 190-92; John H. Wright, review of *She Who Is: The Mystery of God in Feminist Theological Discourse*, by Elizabeth A. Johnson, *Theological Studies* 54 (1993):371-73; Luke Timothy Johnson, review of *She Who Is: The Mystery of God in Feminist Theological Discourse*, by Elizabeth A. Johnson, *Commonweal* 120 (1993):17-22; Susan K. Roll, review of *She Who Is: The Mystery of God in Feminist Theological Discourse*, by Elizabeth A. Johnson, *Louvain Studies* 18 (1993): 374-75; and Amy Plantinga Pauw, review of *She Who Is: The Mystery of God in Feminist Theological Discourse*, by Elizabeth A. Johnson, *Christian Century* 110 (1993): 1159-60.

[216]See Johnson, *She Who Is*, 9 where she defines "classical theology."

examination of the dense symbols of the Trinity, the Living God, and the Suffering God.[217]

Johnson's Basic Definition of Mutuality

Johnson defines mutuality as a particular pattern of relationship which is consistently promoted in feminist ethical discourse:

> This signifies a relationship marked by equivalence between persons, a concomitant valuing of each other, a common regard marked by trust, respect, and affection in contrast to competition, domination, or assertions of superiority. It is a relationship on the analogy with friendship, an experience often used as a metaphor to characterize the reciprocity/interdependence dialectic at the heart of all caring relationships.[218]

In her 1993 Madeleva Lecture, Johnson further qualifies this definition, stating that it is a "give and take according to each one's strength and weaknesses" and that it is "a relationship patterned like friendship, an experience often used to characterize the freedom-connection dialectic at the heart of all mature caring."[219]

Further Analysis of Mutuality

Cosmic Mutuality

Johnson holds that the world exists in mutual, though asymmetrical, relation with Sophia-God. Certainly, the world is not necessary to God; yet, God could not be described as creator, vivifier, redeemer, liberator, companion and future without it.[220] "God in the world and the world in God: this is one way to summarize these radically distinct yet mutually related realities."[221]

---

[217] These categories outline the contents of Johnson's *She Who Is*. These areas are also addressed in her *Woman, Earth, Creator Spirit* and in most of her articles.

[218] Johnson, *She Who Is*, 68.

[219] Johnson, *Woman, Earth, Creator Spirit*, 27.

[220] Johnson, *She Who Is*, 232.

[221] Ibid., 228. See her criticism of Aquinas's thought concerning God as a friend to humanity, Ibid., 145.

Mutuality between God and the world exists insofar as each is directed toward the other with reciprocal intimacy and interest. That the moral horizon needs to be extended to consider non-human species follows from this truth. Once humans realize their living, ongoing, and interdependent, mutual kinship with the earth it readily follows that the command to love one's neighbor includes nature itself.[222]

Gender Mutuality

Johnson claims that God-talk within feminist liberationist circles poses a challenge not only to traditional literal understandings of God as male, but also to the patriarchal vision of community.[223] According to Johnson, the female image of God contests patriarchy by attesting to the divine as ultimate power residing equally within the females and males. Such an image legitimates the full dignity of women, as well as men, in the world. Johnson argues that if women and men are to bear equal dignity, oppressive structures need to change to ensure right relations within the community. Such a community, Johnson claims, is characterized by mutuality as well as love and justice.

Community in this world is the imperfect shadow of the Reign of God; the "not yet" of the eschatological dream of the "new heavens and the new earth." Johnson observes: "The genius of feminist theology has been to see that for the

---

[222] Johnson, *Woman, Earth, Creator Spirit*, 66-67. Johnson quotes Brian Patrick, as cited in Michael Dowd, *Earthspirit: A Handbook for Nurturing an Ecological Christianity* (Mystic, CT: Twenty-Third Publications, 1991), 40: "Who is our neighbor; The Samaritan? the outcast? the enemy? Yes, yes of course. But it is also the whale, the dolphin and the rainforest. Our neighbor is the entire community of life, the entire universe. We must love it all as our self . . . ." Johnson contrasts this view with a Greek philosophical worldview that arranges the world in a hierarchy and dualistic thinking that negates the importance of non-human elements of creation. The rational human spirit is viewed as superior to irrational matter and non-human components of creation are disvalued. In her *Woman, Earth, Creator Spirit*, 59-60, Johnson states: "A theology of the Creator Spirit overcomes the dualism of spirit and matter with all of its ramifications, and to the rationalization of the sacredness of the earth. The Spirit of God dwelling in the world with quickening power deconstructs dualism and draws in its place a circle of mutuality and inclusiveness. Instead of matter being divorced from spirit and consigned to a realm separate from the holy, it is an intrinsic part of the cosmic community, vivified, indwelt, and renewed by the Creator Spirit."

[223] Johnson, *She Who Is*, 6. Johnson cites Paul Ricoeur's axiom, "the symbol gives rise to the thought." See Paul Ricoeur, *The Symbolism of Evil* (Boston: Beacon Press, 1967), 347-57.

traditional eschatological dream to become reality at all, the liberation of women as genuine human persons in communities of mutuality is essential."²²⁴

The church traditionally has been understood as the paradigm of the Reign of God on earth. Thus, in the church (as in the Reign of God) men and women must be recognized not only symbolically, but actually and in practice, as having the same dignity since a mark of the Reign of God is a condition in which all are one in Christ, and because all humans bear the *imago Dei*. Johnson cites numerous texts from Christian and Hebrew Scriptures that illustrate a line of discourse about God and which name God in female terms. This conversation is directly related to and sheds light upon the full consequences of the New Testament concept of a "discipleship of equals." Allowing feminine symbols to speak with an equally powerful voice as male symbols creates the possibility for "new building blocks for emancipatory discourse about the mystery of God."²²⁵

Not insignificant among the "building blocks" is an altered understanding of the importance of the maleness of Jesus.

> The social location of the distorted interpretation of Jesus' maleness in the Christian tradition is the ecclesial community where official voice, vote, and visibility belong by law only to men. Rising to intellectual expressions that support the status quo, this patriarchy is bedrock for the androcentric construction of gender differences shaping and misusing Christology.²²⁶

Like Ruether, Johnson insists that what is theologically significant about Jesus is not his maleness, but the cross. As the "*kenosis* of patriarchy," the cross illustrates the exact opposite of the ideal patriarchal image of the powerful man. In his birth, life, ministry and death Jesus reveals himself as the Christ, the Wisdom of God-Sophia--

---

²²⁴Johnson, *She Who Is*, 32.

²²⁵Ibid., 103.

²²⁶Ibid., 154: "Envisioning a different kind of community laced by relationships of mutuality and reciprocity allows feminist thought to rethink anthropology in an egalitarian gestalt to practical and critical effect. Then Jesus' maleness is open to interpretation at once less theologically important and more liberating."

and is confessed as such by believers (1 Cor. 1:24). Insofar as Jesus provides the norm for all Christian behavior, this female image of Jesus is yet another way of calling forth genuine mutuality in the community (especially the church).[227] Jesus-Sophia disallows any interpretation of Christology in support of sexism or non-mutual relation in the community of the baptized (Gal. 3:28), and thus, the image challenges the institutional church (as well as all institutions) to genuine mutuality, as opposed to patriarchy as the form for its structures.[228]

Generative Mutuality

The Incarnation provides the paradigm for God\human relations. It attests once and for all time to the concrete embodiment of God in the world, in suffering and delight, compassion and liberation. Through the Incarnation, "Long-standing dichotomies are [herein] brought into mutual coinherence: creator and creature, transcendence and immanence, spirit and body, all splits which have fed into patriarchal obsession with power-over."[229] Acting in a spirit of *koinonia* humans are, according to Johnson, not only to praise God for the wonders of creation, but they are called to be friends of God passionately involved in what is necessary for the world's flourishing--to engage, in our terms, in generative mutuality.

The image of God as Mother is also a source for understanding mutuality between God and humanity. The human experience of gestation within the mother's body, as well as the notion of a mother being ever near her child, are readily associated with a mutuality between divine and human partners.[230] The Mother image shows the passion of God for fullness of life for the whole world and her desire for a kinship within creation that unites the universe in delightful harmony. Mother-

---

[227]Ibid., 167. See also Johnson, *Consider Jesus*, 97-112.

[228]Johnson, *She Who Is*, 165-67. See also Elizabeth A. Johnson, "Marian Tradition and the Reality of Women," *Horizons* 12 (1985): 116-35, esp. 118-19.

[229]Johnson, *She Who Is*, 169.

[230]Ibid., 185-86.

Sophia's nurturing thus moves humanity forward to become mature co-creators mutually involved in bringing about the world's flourishing and salvation.[231]

Social Mutuality

Johnson suggests that the existence and activity of the person of the Holy Spirit disallows an understanding of God that is predominantly aloof and transcendent, patriarchal and neutral in the face of oppression.[232] Johnson illustrates the rich tradition of Spirit-Sophia acting as the one who vivifies, renews, empowers, and graces all, but who acts as an advocate for the poor (Jn. 15:26-27; 16:7-11; I Jn. 4). It was by the power of the Spirit that Jesus fasted, prayed, healed, taught, lived in solidarity with the poor, died and rose again--demonstrating God's ultimate mutuality and solidarity with humanity. The Spirit continues to provide the power of mutuality to the church in the modern world.[233]

It was this immanent function of the Spirit that Aquinas recognized as the action which enables humans to be friends of God. In Aquinas's terms, friends can only desire the good for one another. Thus, human concern for the common good extends ultimately to all of creation. Since participation and self-determination enhances human self-esteem, mutuality requires the participation of the least ones in determining the flourishing of the whole.

Understanding the relations of all persons of the Trinity is critical to comprehending how Johnson's notion of mutuality applies to human relationships. Johnson surveys Aquinas's treatment of "subsistent relations" to support her contention that the Trinity serves as a paradigm of mutuality.

---

[231]Ibid., 185.

[232]Ibid., 143. Johnson cites *ST* I.42.2. Although the notion of the procession of the Spirit (whether understood in the East as proceeding from the Father; or, as in the West as proceeding from the Father and the Son) raises a tension, in that the classical doctrine of the Trinity has insisted that the three persons are coeternal and equally divine, Aquinas resolved the problem of the doctrine of coequal persons and the analogy used to describe it by posing a series of analogies, each of which corrects the other.

[233]Johnson, *She Who Is*, 140-41.

> The persons of the Trinity are persons precisely *as* mutual relations and not as anything else apart from their mutual bonding. Relationality is the principle that at once constitutes each trinitarian person as unique and distinguishes one from the other. It is only by their reciprocal and mutually exclusive relationship that the divine persons are really distinct from each other at all. Their uniqueness arises only from their *esse ad*, from their being toward the others in relation. Holy Wisdom *is* a mystery of real, mutual relations.[234]

Thus, the Triune God we meet in history dwells in a community of love. Johnson submits that total equality amid mutuality and respect for difference is visible in God's creative mediating and liberating activity. She claims that the Trinity which exists essentially in mutual inner relationships, models a community in which differences thrive among true equals and where supremacy and subjugation are unknown. A human community, following a paradigm of the equal and mutual Trinitarian relationships would enable the contribution and participation of those ordinarily considered "lesser" for the maximum flourishing of all. In order to maintain the exchange in the relationship, the "lesser" parties would also need to lay claim to the power relinquished to them as rightfully theirs or accept a definition of themselves as less than human. To be fully human is to be a bearer of the *imago Dei*. To be a person in the image of God is to be equal to all other human persons in one's humanness.

Normative Status

As a feminist theologian, Johnson affirms the fact that mutuality and deep patterns of affiliation are at the heart of women's experience, and indeed, at the core of all existence. From a feminist liberationist perspective, grounded in her understanding of trinitarian relations, Johnson criticizes interpretations of classical theism in which isolation and dualistic patterns are valued over mutuality in relations.

---

[234]Ibid., 216. Johnson cites *ST* I.29.4 and I.30.1. In "The Incomprehensibility of God and the Image of God Male and Female," *Theological Studies* 45 (1984): 463, Johnson states: "Beyond particular images for each of the divine persons, the Trinity in a formal way gives a model of relationship marked by total equality and reciprocity, rather than dominance and subordination. All that the first person is is communicated to the second; all that the second person receives is returned to the first; and the life of mutuality which they are is the third person, powerful Spirit of love. All uniquely give, all uniquely receive, all hold together a shared life. Creator, Word, and Spirit are simply, mutually one."

In the trinitarian relation *ad extra*, Johnson sees a "fundamental vision of mutual coinherence in which Holy Wisdom is present throughout the universe while everything is embraced in her inclusive freedom and compassionate love" that is highly compatible with feminist values.[235] Mutual love of Spirit-Sophia expressed as existence "with and for" surfaces as the "highest value as the Spirit of God dwells within and around the world . . . ."[236] The mutual relations of the persons of the Trinity as different equals "appears as the ultimate paradigm of personal and social life," in Johnson's view.[237] Not only in human relations is mutuality a normative factor, but mutuality is ". . . at the heart of all reality . . . borne out in an uncanny way by contemporary science, from the macro scale of astrophysics to evolutionary biology to the micro world of quantum theory."[238]

Because it is necessary and constitutive of the life of the Trinity and all creation humans ought to strive to achieve mutuality in daily living. Clearly mutuality is interpreted in Johnson's work in a normative fashion. At the heart of her critique of traditional theism is its lack of mutuality, particularly as that is expressed in patriarchy.[239] She extends the criticism concerning the absence of mutuality to explain the oppression and injustices in interpersonal, social, and ecological relations. She forcefully argues that if the image of God is the ultimate reference point for the values of a community, then mutuality needs to characterize not only relationships within society, but within the church, as well. She asserts:

---

[235] Johnson, *She Who Is*, 232.

[236] Ibid., 147.

[237] Ibid., 222. See also page 208 where Johnson states: "Accordingly, the triune God whom we encounter in history as the origin, mediator, and driving force of liberation dwells as a community of love wherein there is total equality amid mutuality and respect for difference. The triune symbol thus understood is a model of the highest ideal for humanity."

[238] Johnson, *Woman, Earth, Creator Spirit*, 32.

[239] For a criticism of Johnson's view see Robin Darling Young, "She Who Is: Who Is She?," *The Thomist* 58 (1994): 323-33.

> [T]he structure of the triune symbol stands as a profound critique, however little noticed, of patriarchal domination in church and society. The power of an interpersonal communion characterized by equality and mutuality, which it signifies, still flashes like a beacon through the dark night rather than shining like the daytime sun. Human community in relationships of equals has yet to be realized save in isolated and passing instances.[240]

This vision of ethical behavior, grounded in the mutual coinherence of Holy Wisdom and supported by orthodox panentheism is central to feminist values. Therefore, insofar as Christians are obligated to live and act as God lives and acts, in Johnson's view, mutuality is normative for Christian ethics.

Distinctions/Relationship of Mutuality to Equality, Friendship, Reciprocity, Solidarity

Equality is used primarily in two ways in Johnson's work. First, Johnson establishes how the *hypostases* of the Trinity transcend gender identity, and how, therefore the three *persons* are equal. The *hypostasis* can be named in female (as well as male) terms.[241] Having established this premise, she then uses "equality" to address the humanity of women. She claims the full humanity of women is equal to the full humanity of men. Johnson is careful to stress that this equality "does not obviate the differences" but rather, refers to "an intrinsic valuation of women as human beings, created, sinful, redeemed, with all the dignity, rights, and responsibilities that accrue as a consequence."[242]

Johnson's definition of mutuality includes the idea of friendship as a characterization of the kind of reciprocity and interdependence that she believes is at the heart of all caring relationships. However, in light of John's Gospel, Johnson recognizes a serious problem in associating "friendship" with "mutuality," since in the thought of Thomas Aquinas, which dominates much of traditional theology, "God is

---

[240] Johnson, *She Who Is*, 223.

[241] Ibid., 211.

[242] Ibid., 31-32.

never named a friend in return, and thus, the mutuality inherent in the idea of friendship is not brought to full expression."[243]

Contrary to Aquinas who seems to fear a loss of divine freedom, transcendence, and distinctiveness, Johnson argues that adult friendship serves to enhance individual identity; friends are not interchangeable with one another.[244] In opposition to Aristotle's notion of friendship, Johnson asserts that in mature adult friendship, the partners are not equal in all ways. Nor, do mature adult friends control or manipulate one another's freedom and creativity. Johnson argues that to contend that God *is* a friend to humanity is distinct from holding that God *necessarily* is a friend of humanity. Thomas's rejection of the friendship of God to humanity implies a confusion of divine freedom with divine relatedness. While Aquinas correctly places God "outside" of the created order, he mistakenly identifies the divine "being" with the divine will to befriend humanity.[245]

Johnson admits that the mutuality of the friendship of God toward humanity is asymmetrical, and there is value for speaking of God as "Being itself."[246] (Indeed, to speak of God as Being Itself elicits the notion of the relatedness at the level of "being" of the universe.) Yet, in light of the Jewish and Christian emphasis on the "fundamental friendliness of God toward the world," it is appropriate to speak of a kind of friendship of God toward humans.[247] Johnson contends that whatever use Aquinas's image of a remote, unrelated God may have served in the past, it is no

---

[243]Ibid., 145. Johnson cites *Summa Contra Gentiles* 4, Chapters 21 and 22, especially 22.2 and 22.3; *ST* II-II.23; and Walter Principe, "Affectivity of the Heart," in *Spirituality of the Heart*, ed. Annice Callahan (New York: Paulist Press, 1990), 45-65. A closer examination of Thomas Aquinas's work on this subject will be included in Chapter 2.

[244]Johnson, *She Who Is*, 217.

[245]Ibid., 227. Johnson cites *ST* I.13.7.

[246]Johnson, *She Who Is*, 236-38.

[247]Ibid., 217.

longer useful in our time. Rather, a God of mutual relationship, understood in an analogy of mature human friendship opens up a life-giving paradigm.

In light of the Jewish understanding of covenant, mutual relationship with God is free, non-possessive, and inclusive. It is characterized by mutual trust in the reliability of the other (fidelity) joined in a side-by-side (distinct, yet together) journey with common interests, delights and shared responsibilities (co-creation). Both Testaments provide witnesses that illustrate how God's interests are indeed allied with humanity's flourishing or good (Wis. 7:27) and that friends of Jesus are sharers in the indwelling and knowledge characteristic of Jesus' own relationship with God (Jn. 15:15; 17:21).[248]

Johnson utilizes mature human relationships (friendship is one kind) as a metaphor for mutuality.[249] She also views mutuality identifiable in trinitarian relations, demonstrated in the ministry of Jesus and in New Testament Christian community, as well as the relationship of Adam and Eve in Genesis as paradigmatic for mature human friendships.

Johnson does not always clearly distinguish "reciprocity" from other terms.[250] In spite of this, Johnson's use of the term "reciprocity," always communicates a necessary one-for-one exchange between the parties involved. When Johnson uses

---

[248] Ibid., 235-36.

[249] Traditionally, in Western society independence and autonomy has been acknowledged as the mark of mature adulthood. Johnson counters that the experience of women, the maturing of a young girl in relationship to her mother, suggests yet another notion of maturity, namely, becoming distinct through interconnection. The relationship is a dialectic of identification and differentiation; being and growing with the other in a mutually enhancing relation. There is no room in the dialectic for oppositional dualistic thinking, but rather "both-and" thinking demonstrating unfettered interconnectedness is required. In her *She Who Is*, 68, Johnson states that what is indeed characteristic of mature adult relations is "the coinherence of autonomy and mutuality as constitutive of the adult person." Johnson cites Nancy Chodorow, *The Reproduction of Mothering* (Berkeley: University of California Press, 1978). See also Johnson, *Woman, Earth, Creator Spirit*, 26-28.

[250] Johnson, *Woman, Earth, Creator Spirit*, 27. Also Johnson, *She Who Is*, 154, 142.

"reciprocity," her focus is nearly always the transformation of language about God. Therefore, "reciprocity," for Johnson means a general relationality between parties.[251]

Solidarity for Johnson entails a migration toward a mutual relationship by choosing to stand with those who struggle or suffer in various ways against some evil.[252] In light of J.B. Metz's category of solidarity, Johnson demonstrates how Jesus' solidarity with both Wisdom/Sophia and the poor led him to the cross and, how it is therefore, necessary for the Christian community to carry on the "dangerous speech about God that frees slaves and raises up the crucified".[253] Solidarity can be both a personal or/and a communal enterprise that is formative of all involved.

Relationship of Mutuality to Love and Justice

Unlike Heyward and Harrison, Johnson treats the idea of love quite distinctly from (though definitely not unrelated to) justice. Employing Ireneaus's axiom, *Gloria Dei vivens homo* as the core of her discussion, Johnson argues that "right speaking" about God *also* entails right relationships between humans in the world.[254] Implicit in the maxim is the idea that God is not satisfied with minimalistic human survival but rather requires the maximum human thriving. Given that women indeed, are fully human, though frequently oppressed, Johnson asserts that it is quite orthodox to extend the axiom to read, "*Gloria Dei vivens mulier*," as well. Wherever God is glorified, there is "right-speaking of God," just relationships between humans in the world which provide the conditions for the flourishing of human beings, particularly women--justice and peace.

In Johnson's view, justice has the Holy Spirit as its source, and it is made visible through action on behalf of the poor. Images of women angered by injustice

---

[251] Johnson, *She Who Is*, 68, 75, 216, 225, 226, 228.

[252] Ibid., 32, 63, 146.

[253] Ibid., 66, 72, 140.

[254] Ibid., 12, 14-15, 18.

find their vindication in the justice-making image of God as Spirit-Sophia. Justice and peace reveal the dialectic of the presence of the Holy Spirit.[255]

Johnson clarifies her notion of justice when she contrasts her apprehension with the conventional understanding of moral philosophy. Commonly, moral philosophy casts justice in terms of "rights language" and the "mature moral agent [as] one who respects the rights of others while pursuing his or her own good according to the individual's own inalienable rights."[256] Johnson associates herself with Carol Gilligan and the notion of justice "promoted by the spirituality of the justice and peace movements, the Catholic social justice tradition and feminist liberation theology [which] is more closely aligned with an ethic of care than with and ethic of justice or rights . . . ."[257]

Johnson's treatment of "love" takes place within her discussion of the Holy Spirit--Spirit/Sophia. Aquinas established that the Spirit is appropriately called love, and he names "love proceeding" (*amor procedens*) and "mutual love" (*mutuus amor*) as two central characteristics of that love.[258]

Mutuus amor rules out the consideration of any relationship between "superior" and "inferior" as a relationship of "love." It is the concept of *mutuus amor*

---

[255]Ibid., 257-59, 136, 148. 122.

[256]Ibid., 184.

[257]Ibid. In an ethics of care, "moral maturity is evidenced by the moral agent's response to the needs of others while seeking to maintain the network of relationships in which all dwell. . . . the emphasis is on personal responsibility within the context of relationship rather than on individual rights against the background of the rights of others." Ibid. See Carol Gilligan, *In a Different Voice: Psychological Theory and Women's Development* (Cambridge: Harvard University Press, 1982); Carol Gilligan, "Moral Orientation and Moral Development," in E.F. Kittay and D.T. Meyers, eds., *Women in Moral Theory*, (Totowa, NJ: Rowman & Littlefield, 1987), 19-33; Carol Gilligan, N.P. Lyons, T.J. Hammer *Making the Connections: The Relational Worlds of Adolescent Girls at Emma Willard School* (Cambridge: Harvard University Press, 1989); Carol Gilligan, J.V. Ward, J.M. Taylor, eds. *Mapping the Moral Domain* Center for the Study of Gender, Education, and Human Development (Cambridge: Harvard University, 1988). See also Cynthia S.W. Crysdale, "Gilligan and the Ethics of Care: An Update," *Religious Studies Review* 20 (1994): 21-28. For an overview of modern Catholic teaching concerning "justice" see: David Hollenbach, *Justice, Peace, and Human Rights: American Catholic Ethics in A Pluralistic World* (New York: Crossroad, 1990), 16-33.

[258]Johnson, *She Who Is*, 142. Johnson cites *ST* I.36.1 and I.37.1 and 2.

that Johnson claims as highly significant for a correct understanding of the Holy Spirit for our time.[259] This understanding of love drawn from Aquinas, in Johnson's view, also precludes the kind of "sacrificial love" in human relationships that is destructive of the lover's self-esteem. Love, however, can entail suffering as a chosen expression of mutual relationship.[260]

While the paradigm of love proceeding has some limitations, it does model a living God (Spirit-Sophia) who is freely related to humanity and all of creation, and who "blesses mutuality and ongoing compassionate love among human beings, women as well as men."[261]

PART TWO: MUTUALITY DEFINED - TOWARD A CHRISTIAN FEMINIST CONSENSUS

Consensus on Distinction/Relationship of Mutuality to Equality, Friendship, Reciprocity, Solidarity

For the most part, the four feminists avoid language that designates any form of mathematical or linear measure of relatedness. While they all use "equality" to designate the fundamental identity of the humanity of both males and females, none of these scholars intends an absolute one to one correspondence between genders that eclipses actual sexual differences. Mutuality presumes an equal humanity and is distinct from equality in that there is not necessarily a simple one-for-one exchange between parties. The conditions of the exchange are agreed to by all involved.

The consensus among Ruether, Johnson and Heyward seems to be that friendship is paradigmatic of mutuality. Because mutuality is also found outside of human friendship, it is only analogous, not identical with mutuality. But like

---

[259]Johnson, *She Who Is*, 143: "Spoken in terms of mutual love proceeding, God who is Spirit cannot be used to legitimize patriarchal structures but signals a migration toward reciprocity in community as the highest good."

[260]Ibid., 265-66.

[261]Ibid., 144.

mutuality, friendship is a relationship that provides for the growth and well-being of all parties involved.

The four feminists distinguish "reciprocity" from other terms with less clarity. Generally, each scholar understands "mutuality" as somehow exceeding reciprocity in moral excellence, yet not all of them are clear about just *how* that is so. The consensus seems to be that "reciprocity" is a relationship that *requires* a one-for-one exchange between all parties involved. The relationship has a minimal kind of cohesiveness that results from the dynamism of claims being made and the *necessity* for responses to those claims on a one-for-one basis. Yet, it seems the feminists use this term uncritically and often synonymously with mutuality.

A consensus exists among these four scholars that the term "solidarity" indicates: a stance or a tendency of either peers or (often) by the more powerful directed toward using their power "with" (often) the less powerful who are engaged in a struggle against oppression or some sort of evil. Yet, while there is a migration toward an exchange of accountability, "solidarity" also signals the *inability* to totally overcome some boundary in order to actually *be with* the other(s).[262] In mutual relations boundaries are readily crossed upon the agreement of both parties, even though the risk may be high.

A Consensus: Relationship of Mutuality, Love and Justice

Mutuality is consistently projected as a necessary condition for genuine love and/or justice. When mutuality accompanies love and justice, a vast qualitative difference in each virtue is determined, namely, the dynamic of power becomes limited to "power-with."[263] Thus, any construal of justice that fails to include the participation of all parties in deciding its limits or, or any interpretation of sacrificial love that is morally destructive to any party, is excluded. While opposing love that is exclusively sacrificial, these feminists do not discount the value of sacrifice entirely.

---

[262]Harrison, "Theological Reflections in the Struggle for Liberation: A Feminist Perspective," in *Making the Connections*, 244.

[263]Cf. n. 20, Introduction.

They believe, rather, that the lover must choose to make a sacrifice in freedom, cognizant of its consequences, with full integrity of person and toward the goal of a greater mutuality in the relationship.

A Feminist Consensus for Four Forms of Mutuality

A Consensus for Cosmic Mutuality

All four feminists adduce evidence for mutuality from the natural sciences including astrophysics, ecology, and quantum physics and thereby demonstrate a foundational kinship of everything in the entire cosmos. The four scholars acknowledge eco-feminist theory which holds that the natural environment asserts itself as a living aspect of "our bodies, ourselves"--it "answers back" when humans defile nature.[264] Humans violate the ecosystem to their own detriment. The four thinkers concur that the most effective social analysis takes into account how any form of power impacts the most disadvantaged, not forgetting all elements of the ecosystem, in the interest of attaining the well-being of all. The four feminists find traditional Christian cosmology retrievable to the extent that the relatedness of the created order and the social order is stressed in light of the Hebrew and Christian Testament witnesses. The deep relatedness represented by the phrase, "God in the world and the world in God," expresses a sort of panentheism that has been recognized for centuries as orthodox. The fact that God *is* Creator, Vivifier, Redeemer, etc., only in relation to creation shows, in a certain analogous sense, need on God's part for relationship to the cosmos. If we acknowledge the kinship of all creation, then the command to "love thy neighbor" must be extended to everything and everyone (although, admittedly with varying degrees of emphasis). In short, all of these feminists point to a form of mutuality that can be defined as:

---

[264]Ruether, *Gaia and God*, 2-3: "Ecofeminism brings together . . . ecology and feminism, in their full, or deep forms and explores how male domination of women and domination of nature are interconnected, both in cultural ideology and in social structures." Ruether cites Judith Plant, *Healing the Wounds: The Promise of Ecofeminism* (Philadelphia: New Society Publications, 1989) and Irene Diamond and Gloria F. Orenstein, *Renewing the World: The Emergence of Ecofeminism* (San Francisco: Sierra Club Books, 1990). See Harrison, "Politics of Energy Policy," in *Energy Ethics*, 56.

Cosmic Mutuality - the sharing of "power-with" by and among the Creator, human beings, all earth elements, and the entire cosmos in a way that recognizes their interdependence and reverences all.

A Consensus for Gender Mutuality

Women and men are each the bearers of the full *imago Dei* (Gen. 1:27) and they are both capable of full mature moral agency. For the baptized, life *en christō* means they are part of a discipleship of equals (Gal. 3:28) that foreshadows the eschatological "New Heavens and the New Earth." Jesus' *"kenosis* of patriarchy" is significant because it precludes sexism in any form and because he is the norm for the Christian life. These writers adduce biogenic and sociocultural evidence supporting gender equality to challenge classical dualisms and physicalist interpretations of natural law. Evidence from the social sciences also shows social, political, or economic structures can be organized to purposefully empower or disempower women. Finally, all erotic, sensual, embodied knowledge (including sexuality) is a means of God's revelation of Self to us through one another. All of this points to a form of mutuality that exists between men and women and embodied in daily living, defined as:

Gender Mutuality - the sharing of "power-with" by and among women and men in a way that recognizes the full participation of each in the imago Dei, embodied in daily life and through egalitarian relationships.

A Consensus for Generative Mutuality

Insofar as each human person bears God's image and likeness within her/his own flesh, each enjoys mutuality with God as co-creator and co-redeemer. The paradigm of the Incarnation itself, Christ Jesus as both human and divine also lends support to human ability to participate with God as co-creators and co-redeemers of the world. Human friendship with God (Aquinas) and the *koinonia* of the baptized are conduits of the co-creative and co-redemptive processes. Images of God as Mother suggest understandings of human beings, created in the *imago Dei* as intimately "of my flesh" and "of my spirit." As human children are related to their birth-mother and are empowered and assisted by them to participate in those experiences she judges vital to their well-being, so too, God empowers and assists us toward engagement with Her and one another in activities that further human flourishing in the context of the whole creation. Though Christologies differ among these feminists, there is a consensus that humans continue to participate in completing the redemption of the world begun by Jesus, when they struggle in daily life to establish "right relations." In the feminists' view, practical action against sexism (the feminist paradigm for all oppression) is co-redemptive and co-creative in that it liberates all involved. All of this suggests a form of mutuality that exists among the Divine, human persons, and creation defined as:

Generative Mutuality - the sharing of "power-with" by and among the Divine, human persons, and all creation in the on-going co-creation and redemption of the world.

A Consensus for Social Mutuality

The four feminists recognize the power of mutuality as exemplified in the life and ministry of Jesus as the moral goal for the Christian life. The Holy Spirit animates and empowers people enabling them to choose to share in a common power with those less powerful or oppressed. Empowered by the Holy Spirit, people become friends with God and seek the good for their friends and, friends of friends. It is fidelity to this power of mutuality that motivates people to make sacrifices for the sake of the Reign of God, in freedom and with full integrity. Jesus demonstrated this fidelity through his *"kenosis* of patriarchy," proving that "power-with" of is greater value than "power-over" in bringing about the Reign of God in history. Given the constitutive sociality of the human person, the less powerful are obliged to assert their claim to "power-with" in order to maintain their human dignity. This evidence suggests a form of mutuality needed between the powerful and the powerless that can be defined as:

Social Mutuality - the sharing of "power-with" by and among members of society in a way that recognizes the fundamental dignity of each and the obligation to attain and maintain for each what is necessary to sustain that dignity.

A Consensus for the Normative Status of Mutuality

In light of the definition of "norm" provided in the Introduction of this study and based on the analysis of the texts just completed here, it is clear that Ruether,

Heyward, Harrison and Johnson do consider mutuality a formal norm for Christian social ethics. Mutuality is one of the definitive relationships of trinitarian life; it is a model for the relationships that ought to prevail between Christians and others. Mutuality creates the necessary conditions for love and justice insofar as it directs and limits the dynamics of the relationship toward "power-with." In sexual ethics mutuality is recognized as the norm that maintains healthy relations by delineating equity of power and dignity. Humans created in the image and likeness of God have the innate capacity for mutuality and thus, to live as God lives, in mutuality. Jesus is the exemplar and norm for the Christian moral life. His capacity for mutuality lies at the heart of who he is for Christians, and his mutuality is thus normative for the Christian life. Mutuality, finally, is a construct that is characteristic of the Reign of God. Insofar as all Christians need to work toward the coming of the Reign of God in history, relations marked by mutuality are normative. In Chapter Four of this study, I will examine the issues concerning the normative status of mutuality in greater detail. For now, however, my working assumption is that, based on the analysis of the feminists' texts thus far, mutuality is a formal norm for Christian feminist social ethics.

Redefinition of Mutuality:
A Formal Norm for Christian Social Ethics

In general, feminist theology arose as a corrective to classical theologies that stressed transcendent, patriarchal, male aspects of God to the near exclusion of immanent, egalitarian female images. The development of feminist Christian ethics has followed the development of this theology. As feminist theologies have developed, they have demonstrated that classical notions of love and justice are not adequate to accommodate the kinds and degrees of relationship that emerge as imperative if Christians are to be faithful to the immanent, egalitarian, and transcendent realities that characterize the Divine. As we have seen, there is evidence of the emergence of a formal norm that is a corrective and a complement to the traditional construal of the norms of love and justice, namely, mutuality.

Earlier, I offered Margaret Craddock Huff's definition as my working definition of mutuality:

> . . . a dynamic situation within relationship in which one is simultaneously open to the influence of the other or others, influencing the other or others, and aware of influencing the other or others.[265]

In light of our analysis of the term "mutuality" in the works of Ruether, Heyward, Harrison, and Johnson, I now wish to make several modifications of Huff's definition in order to adequately reflect the consensus we have uncovered.

These writers suggest to us that mutuality is similar in its complexity to the notion of justice. Analogous to those theories of justice which ascribe to it a tripartite nature, we have found evidence in the writings of these feminists of four forms of "mutuality." They identify four areas in which classical theology has failed to provide adequate grounding to support an ethic that serves the maximum flourishing of humanity--cosmology, divine-human co-generativity, gender relationships, human sociality. The four interrelating forms of mutuality address areas of relationship that were degraded, misunderstood, or entirely ignored because they required serious consideration of "things female" or qualities considered "feminine" in a theological system biased against women.

The **basic definition** we may adduce from these writers is:

Mutuality is the sharing of "power-with" by and among all parties in a relationship in a way that recognizes the wholeness and particular experience of each participant toward the end of optimum flourishing of all.

There are four forms noted:

Cosmic Mutuality: *the sharing of "power-with" by and among the Creator, human beings, all earth elements, and the entire cosmos in a way that recognizes their interdependence and reverences all.*

Gender Mutuality: *the sharing of "power-with" by and among women and men in a way that recognizes the full participation of each in the imago Dei, embodied in daily life and through egalitarian relationships.*

---

[265]Huff, "The Interdependent Self," 163.

Generative Mutuality: *the sharing of "power-with" by and among the Divine, human persons, and all creation in the on-going co-creation and redemption of the world.*

Social Mutuality: *the sharing of "power-with" by and among members of society in a way that recognizes the fundamental dignity of each and the obligation to attain and maintain for each what is necessary to sustain that dignity.*

This contemporary rendering of mutuality as a formal norm for Christian social ethics has deep roots within the Christian tradition. In the chapters to come, by investigating the works of Thomas Aquinas, John Duns Scotus, Martin Buber, and H. Richard Niebuhr I hope to demonstrate this claim.

CHAPTER 2
CLASSICAL ANTECEDENTS:
CHRISTIAN FEMINISTS' NOTION OF MUTUALITY

INTRODUCTION

The purpose of this chapter is modest, namely, to illustrate several moments in the history of Christian thought in the twelfth and thirteenth centuries wherein antecedents and analogs of the modern Christian feminist notions of mutuality can be found. This illustration will support my argument that the notion of mutuality has always been part of the Christian tradition.

As has been shown in Chapter One, feminists argue that frequently the Christian tradition was interpreted through conceptual modalities almost exclusively in a kind of dualism, hierarchy, patriarchy and following mathematical and linear methods of thought. Images of God were often rendered as transcendent and male, while ethical goodness was construed as preparation for the life to come. In the most well known and influential strands of the tradition, the notion of mutuality was nearly aborted from the tradition, (rather than enabled to thrive within the orthodox strains of Christianity). In spite of all of this, relationality has remained a value within Christianity and antecedents and analogs of the modern Christian feminists' notion of mutuality can be found in substantive orthodox Christian sources. One intriguing place to seek these analogs and antecedents is medieval Christian theology.

In this chapter I will first review some key aspects of the intellectual milieu of the twelfth and thirteenth centuries that served to undergird the notions of cosmic interdependence and friendship. Selected works by Hugh of St. Victor and Aelred of Rievaulx will be utilized to show how their theological understandings create antecedents and analogs to the modern feminist notions of mutuality articulated by

Rosemary Radford Ruether, (Isabel) Carter Heyward, Beverly Wildung Harrison and Elizabeth A. Johnson.

Second, I will focus on selected sections of Thomas Aquinas's *Summa theologia* friendship with God, Trinitarian relations and the Incarnation are analogous with notions of mutuality in works by Ruether, Heyward, Harrison and Johnson.

Third, conscious of the Condemnations of 1277,[1] I will employ selected works by John Duns Scotus to illustrate how his entire theological system, but particularly his understanding of covenant, Incarnation, Trinity, *imago Dei*, and *acceptatio* provide analogs to the four modern feminists' concepts of mutuality addressed in this study.

I will conclude each of the three major sections by drawing some specific linkages between the medieval notions and the four forms of mutuality treated in the Introduction and Chapter One of this work.

TWO VIEWS IN HISTORICAL CONTEXT: FRIENDSHIP AND COSMIC INTERDEPENDENCE

Context for Cosmic Interdependence and Friendship

In our own day, there is a turn to recapture the probative and normative value of interdependence.[2] Increasingly scholars from nearly every discipline are claiming that the very survival of humanity and the earth itself depends on changes in human behavior. Humans must first recognize their interrelationship with all elements of the cosmos, and then, make the consideration of interdependence a high priority in ethical

---

[1] Armand A. Mauer, *Medieval Philosophy* The Etienne Gilson Series 4, Second Edition (Toronto: Pontifical Institute of Mediaeval Studies, 1982), 204-07. The Condemnations of 1277 consisted of the prohibition against anyone teaching or holding any of 219 philosophical and theological propositions rooted in Greco-Arabic sources, especially Aristotle and Averroes, and considered as promoting necessitarianism and determinism. See Ralph Lerner and Muhsin Mahdi, eds., Ernest L. Fortin and Peter D. O'Neal, trans. *Medieval Political Philosophy: A Sourcebook* (New York: Free Press of Glencoe, 1963), 337-54 for an English version of the 219 condemnations.

[2] See Brennan R. Hill, Paul Knitter and William Madges, *Faith, Religion and Theology: A Contemporary Introduction* (Mystic, CT: Twenty-third Publications, 1993), 146-48. Many renowned theologians stress interdependence as necessary for the resolution of today's socio-economic, nuclear, and ecological crises. Also see Introduction, n. 1.

decision making.³ The broader milieu of the twelfth and thirteenth centuries holds promise as a source for insights concerning mutuality, for in that period, the dominant worldview included a profound sense of the interdependence of the entire cosmos.⁴

In the twelfth and thirteenth centuries, scholars felt a need to move from a worldview of superstitious determinism and ignorance of the operations of Nature to uncover the causes of things and understand the workings of Nature. Today, there is a widely felt need to use our vast knowledge of the causes of things to maintain and sustain a balance with nature for the maximal thriving of humanity as a participant in an interdependent creation. The world of the twelfth and thirteenth centuries faced the problem of an undifferentiated world of cause and effect. In our day, we confront the problem of knowing the cause and effect of things with such precision that we can manipulate nature and one another to our personal advantage, and with little regard for other humans, earthcreatures, the earth itself, or the cosmos.

Two widely debated concepts of the eleventh and twelfth centuries were friendship with God and spiritual friendship. The discussion within the Christian community of interdependence, spiritual friendship,⁵ and friendship with God can be

---

³See Paul Davies, *The Cosmic Blueprint: New Discoveries in Nature's Creative Ability to Order the Universe* (New York: Simon and Schuster, 1988); Bill Devall and George Sessions, *Deep Ecology: Living as if Nature Mattered* (Salt Lake City: Peregrine Smith Books, 1985); James Lovelock, *The Ages of Gaia: A Biography of Our Living Earth* (New York: W.W. Norton and Co., 1988); Lester R. Brown, et. al., *State of the World 1992: A Worldwatch Institute Report on Progress Toward a Sustainable Society* (New York: W.W. Norton and Co., 1993); Al Gore, *Earth in the Balance: Ecology and the Human Spirit* (New York: Houghton Miffflin Co., 1992).

⁴M. D. Chenu, *Nature, Man, and Society in the Twelfth Century: Essays on New Theological Perspectives in the Latin West*, ed. and trans., Jerome Taylor and Lester K. Little (Chicago: The University of Chicago Press, 1968), xv-48

⁵Brian Patrick McGuire, *Friendship and Community: The Monastic Experience 350-1250*, Cistercian Study Series 95 (Kalamazoo: Cistercian Publications, Inc., 1988), xiv-xvi. Maguire notes: "The classical definition of friendship comes from Cicero: `complete identity of feeling about all things divine and human, as strengthened by mutual goodwill and affection.'. . . According to Gregory [the Great] and Isidore [of Seville] a friend is a guardian of one's soul, *custos animi*."

traced to the Hebrew and Christian Scriptures.[6] In centuries between biblical times and the eleventh century monastic renewal one finds an oscillation in monastic writings between two views of friendship. A first view saw it as a necessary and normal human relationship which, in turn, fostered a healthy community and society; an opposing view held that particular friendships were divisive and violated the Christian concept of love for all in Christ.[7] With the renewal of monasticism in the eleventh century, and the blossoming of apostolic communities among the laity in the twelfth century, the discussion of the issues of community and friendship intensified. Two key figures in the uncovering various aspects of the discussion were Hugh of St. Victor (d.1141) and Aelred of Rievaulx (1110-1167). At the crux of the debate was the proper balance of nature and grace.

The context of this discussion was an age of expanding knowledge of the causes of things. The world was viewed as a *universitas*--all things were related in a particular order that if understood, could be managed for the good.[8] This order did not deny God's existence, but rather, revealed how God was present. Even the more conservative Hugh of St. Victor (while denouncing the doctrine of the world soul) acknowledged the mysterious power of nature which invisibly feeds and fosters all things.[9] It was a time when through advances in trade and linguistics the wisdom of the ancients--Plato, Aristotle, Cicero--was being rediscovered, renewed, and reinterpreted. The Dionysian and Eriugenist theme of "continuity" between humans

---

[6]Ibid., xvii-xxiv. See examples: Qoheleth 4: 9-12; Ps. 133:1--the classical ideal of friendship--". . . How good and pleasant it is when brothers dwell together in peace." In Sir. 6:17--spiritual friendship, the bond of human friendship is linked to the attachment to God. The theme is carried forward in the New Testament: Jn. 15:12-17 states: ". . . greater love no one has than to lay down one's life for one's friend." There is the command to love one's enemies. Jesus had personal friends: Mary, Martha, Lazarus, John. Jesus used friendship in his parables. In Acts 4:32 Christians in community shared everything in common. The notion of familial bonding is set forth in Mk. 10:30. While Christian *agape* is universal, friendship is preferential.

[7]Ibid., xxv-xxix and xl-xliii.

[8]Chenu, *Nature, Man and Society*, 24.

[9]Ibid., 23.

and cosmos emerged to qualify the Platonic concepts.[10] Humans were to understand themselves as the microcosm and the universe as the macrocosm of an ordered, dynamic and progressive chain of forces and beings.[11]

The human person was defined as a *compositum*--both matter and spirit.[12] Humans who live within Nature are themselves individually a nature. By virtue of the spiritual, humans are caught up in the mystery of salvation and free in their particular encounter with God. Nature, as Alan of Lille stressed, also requires humans to be virtuous in order to reach fulfillment.[13]

At Chartres the *Timaeus* was utilized to construct the Christian version of the macro/microcosm.[14] William of Conches (d.1154) was the key twelfth century exegete who initiated this work.[15] At St. Victor, after Hugh's death, Godfrey published *Microcosmos* which gave a full treatment of the theme.[16] Thus, the human person was understood as simultaneously an image of the world and an image of God. Numerous treatises entitled "On the Soul" incorporated consideration of the material as well as the spiritual side in the discussion of humanity.[17] Furthermore, the symbolism of St. Victor, which stressed the common destiny of the universe and humankind, allowed for the human spirit drawing nourishment from the universe.[18] The world had a sacramental character because it was "filled with God."

With humans understanding themselves as both spiritual and natural, and as a microcosm as well, the attitude about the struggle between the world and the

---

[10]Ibid.

[11]Ibid., 24.

[12]Ibid., 25-26.

[13]Ibid., 27.

[14]Ibid., 30.

[15]John Scotus Eriugena's *Periphyseon* of the ninth century is the original source in the West.

[16]Chenu, *Nature, Man, and Society*, 31. Godfrey of St. Victor (d.1195).

[17]Ibid., 34.

[18]Ibid., 35.

Gospel shifted. No longer was it a question of the idyllic monastic life of perfection and creating the "city of God" on earth; rather, it was a matter of casting evangelical leaven into the world so it could rise in a new civilization apart from feudalism. In short, as the scholastics would say later, "Grace does not vitiate nature, it perfects it!".[19]

In this changing and evolving intellectual context, the understanding of relationships between persons also shifted. The portrayal of individual's need for friendship both within and outside of the monastic community changed, and with it, the treatment of many other defining relationships such as those between the human and divine, humans and creation, and male and female. Hugh of St. Victor was among the major writers to bring together the emerging understanding of *universitas* with the doctrines of the Christian faith.[20] Hugh's understandings of the Incarnation, the Virgin Birth, the presence of God in all creation, and the sacrament of marriage are of particular interest to us here, because they illustrate a kind of mutual relation between the genders and between the divine and the human.

Hugh of St. Victor

Incarnation

In Book Two, Part I of his *De sacramentis christianae fidei* Hugh explains that his intent is to clarify the orthodox Christian teaching concerning the Incarnation.[21] Using St. Augustine as his primary source, he refutes several major Christological heresies in order to reassert that Christ is truly God and truly human,

---

[19]Ibid., 39-40. Master Gilbert of LaPorrée claimed that all of nature belongs to secular science, but all nature is sacred as well. It is only one's perspective that changes, and science and mysticism ought to complement one another. The exaltation of nature meant putting an end to one particular Christian concept of the universe.

[20]Hugh of St. Victor, *De sacramentis christianne fidei*, is the first great theological *summae*. His ideas on the works of creation and restoration as structure are presented as a *quisito*. He shows the progression of religious experience through three stages: natural law, written law, and grace.

[21]Hugh's works are found in *Patralogia latina*, CLXXV-CLXXVII (1879). The translation used here is: Hugh of St. Victor, *On the Sacraments of the Christian Faith*, trans. Roy J. Deferrari (Cambridge: Medieval Academy of America, 1951).

one person in two natures. Hugh then moves to the heart of the matter of the Incarnation and stresses Christ's human nature--flesh and rational soul. That Christ grew in wisdom and stature is a proof of his humanity.[22] His death and suffering were indeed real.[23] Hugh, implicitly also upholds an image of a compassionate God, who suffers with humanity. He refutes those who deny that image quoting Is. 53:4, "Surely he hath born our infirmities and carried our sorrows."[24] Such an empathy is an antecedent of mutuality, because a distinguishing feature of mutuality is that the boundary lines of the relationship are defined jointly by all parties in the relationship.

Virgin Birth

Hugh's most unique contribution is his explication of the Virgin Birth. In Book II, Part 1, Section viii of *De sacramentis christianae fidei* Hugh maintains that love alone can incline the human body to function as is necessary in order to conceive a child as the result of human intercourse. This love cannot be in only one spouse, but must be mutually present to consummate the work gladly and joyfully. Nature operates in a man through the love of a woman and in a woman through the love of a man. In the case of the Virgin Mary's conception of Christ through the Holy Spirit, Hugh contends that:

> Mary conceived of the Holy Spirit, not because she received the seed of the fetus from the substance of the Holy Spirit, but because of the love and operation of the Holy Spirit nature provided the substance for the fetus from the flesh of the virgin. For since in her heart the love of the Holy Spirit was especially ardent, on this account in her flesh the virtue of the Holy Spirit worked marvelous things. . . . Christ, therefore, was both born from the Virgin because He received the substance of the flesh from the flesh of the virgin, and conceived of the Holy Spirit because the virgin herself from her flesh alone without the admixture of virile seed conceived Him through the operation and love of the Holy Spirit. This was possible because of

---

[22]*On the Sacraments*, Book II, Part 1, Section vi. Cf. Lk. 2:40.

[23]Ibid., Book II, Part 1, Section vii. Hugh states: "If Christ had not suffered pain on the cross, why did he ask so much that the chalice of suffering be transferred from Him? (Cf. Matt. 20,39)."

[24]Ibid.

the ardent love that was mutually shared between her and the Holy Spirit.[25]

In contrast to Hugh's model, the later and more influential Aristotelian biological model held that the woman is entirely passive in procreation. Some interpreted that passivity as evidence of the inferiority of women. Hugh's paradigm not only places women on an active par in procreation with men, but (in the case of Mary) places her in mutual relationship with the Holy Spirit. Hugh's model expresses notions analogous to gender mutuality and divine/human mutuality found in modern Christian feminist texts. Modern feminists stress the full humanity of women as *imago Dei*, not their role in procreation.

The Presence of God in All Creation

In the final sections of Book II, Part 1, (xii and xiii) Hugh treats the union of the Word with humanity and God's universal presence in the world. Hugh refers to Jesus' prayer for unity (Jn. 17:11) and illustrates how Christ is the one mediator in whom there is union between God and humanity.[26] Jesus was able to approach humans as a human, yet retain his divinity so he would not withdraw from God. He sustained punishment, but preserved justice. He was the unity of natures and a union of person. The circle is completed in that in Christ, God and human are united, first in justice, then in glory.[27]

According to Hugh, because of the Incarnation, it is now possible to say that God is everywhere, though the presence of divinity and humanity is in God to various degrees. God is not only present to universal creation, but to every part of it, God's presence is equally whole.[28] Thus, there is unity between grace (God's self-gift of

---

[25]Ibid., Book II, Part 1, Section viii.

[26]Ibid., Book II, Part 1, Section xii.

[27]Ibid., Book II. Part 1, Section xii. Cf. Jn. 17:24.

[28]Ibid., Book II, Part 1, Section xiii: "Furthermore also what we thought could not be understood strictly, when we said God was everywhere whole, unless we added, 'in Himself,' must on this account be set forth carefully. For how 'everywhere in Himself'? 'Everywhere' surely, because He is nowhere absent, but 'in Himself,' because He is not contained by those to whom He is present, as if He could not be without them."

presence) and nature.[29] In order to attain that unity in freedom, first, a reciprocal relationship needed to be established between the human and the divine. Here we have an antecedent of the modern feminist notion of cosmic mutuality which includes a kind of panentheism.

The Sacrament of Marriage

In Book II, Part 11 of *De sacramentis christianae fidei*, Hugh treats the sacrament of marriage. Here (in light of the biological and psychological understandings of the day) Hugh extends his understanding of the mutuality of love in marriage and combines it with the positive attitude toward creation gained from his understanding of the Incarnation. Underlying all that he says about marriage and the adjudication of all that threatens marriage, is his understanding of a kind of equality between women and men.

Hugh refers to Genesis 2 and notes that since women came from *adam's* rib-- the middle of the body--she is intended to be a companion to (not above or below) *adam*.[30] Because of this equality of association any marriage agreement must be a mutual agreement. Hugh follows Ambrose in stating that: "Not the deflowering of virginity, but the conjugal pact makes a marriage. . . . Coition does not make marriage but consent and if this be lacking all things even within coition itself are made void."[31] To safeguard both partners, the Church required that there be a public witness to the marriage agreement. In cases where adjudication became necessary, the Church would give priority to what was made public (rather than secret pledges). Thus, the development of Church law had its source in scripture as well as in the practical necessities of society (grace and nature). In this instance, the mutuality of the relationship between male and female is given a clear sanction and normative status

---

[29] See Hugh of St. Victor, *De tribus diebus*. See also Wanda Cizewski, "Reading the World as Scripture: Hugh of St. Victor's *De tribus diebus*," *Florilegium* 9 (1987): 65-88.

[30] *On the Sacraments*, Book II, Part 2, Section iv.

[31] Ibid., Book II, Part 2, Section v.

by the Church.³² Here we have an analogy with the modern feminist notion of gender mutuality. Whereas modern feminists focus gender mutuality as equal participation in the *imago Dei*, for Hugh, gender parity was rooted in the divinely established order of the world.

Aelred of Rievaulx: Spiritual Friendship

Aelred of Rievaulx's (1110-1167) extensive reflection on friendship within monastic community provides another medieval analog of mutuality.³³ In Book I of his *De spirituali amicitia* Aelred treated the origin and essence of friendship.³⁴ He used Cicero's definition of friendship, "mutual harmony in affairs human and divine coupled with benevolence and charity," as a working model (I.11). For Aelred however, friendship was, at its source, the overflow of God's love (I.51-57). Upon receiving the out-pouring of God's love, humans were able to share love with God and one another. In Aelred's view, not only are humans naturally loving and rational creatures, but they were created as equals, male and female.³⁵

For Aelred there was no conflict between friendship and the love of God, because all love is one and has its source in God. Aelred's identification of spiritual friendship with the perfect love of God allowed him to go so far as to suggest that

---

³²See Marjorie Rowling, *Everyday Life in Medieval Times* (New York: Dorset Press, 1987); Brenda M. Bolton, *Women in Medieval Society* (Philadelphia: University of Pennsylvania Press, 1976); C. Klapisch-Zuber, "Zacharias; or the Ousting of the Father: The Rites of Marriage in Tuscany from Giotto to the Council of Trent," in *Ritual, Religion and the Sacred*, vol. 7, ed. R. Forester and O. Ranum, (Baltimore: John Hopkins University Press, 1982); G. Duby, *Medieval Marriage: Two Models from Twelfth-Century France* (Baltimore: John Hopkins University Press, 1978); and Zacharias P. Thudy, "Clandestine Marriages in the Late Middle Ages," in *New Images of Medieval Women: Essays Toward a Cultural Anthropology*, ed. Edelgard E. DuBruck, Medieval Studies, vol. 1 (Lewiston, NY: The Edwin Mellen Press, 1989), 303-18.

³³Aelred of Rievaulx, *De spirituali amicitia*. The translation used in this chapter is *Spiritual Friendship*, Cistercian Fathers Series 5, trans. Mary Eugenia Laker, (Washington, DC: Cistercian Publications Consortium Press, 1974). See pages 1-15. A critical edition is *De spirituali amicitia* in A. Hoste and C.H. Talbot, eds., *Aelredi Rievaullensis opera omnia: Corpus Christianorum, Continuatio medievalis, I. Opera ascetica* (CCCM I; Turnhout, 1971), 287-350.

³⁴*Spiritual Friendship*, "Prologue," Book I, 4-8. Aelred based his work on Cicero's *De amicitia*.

³⁵*Spiritual Friendship*, I:57.

"God is friendship."[36] In a similar manner, in community, which was a school of love, true friendship built up community and could only serve to unify it and thus, contributed to the maximal thriving of its members (I.28-30). Love of neighbor was no distraction from the love of God. On the contrary, we must love our neighbor if we truly love God (II.68-70). Equal regard for the other "for the love of God" was the minimum standard, and mutuality the maximum norm for human flourishing, in light of Aelred's definition of spiritual friendship: "And so spiritual friendship among the just is born out of a similarity in life, morals, and pursuits, that is it is a mutual conformity in matters human and divine united with benevolence and charity" (I.46).

Mutuality in Hugh of St. Victor and Aelred of Rievaulx

Hugh of St. Victor's view of the Incarnation, while maintaining God's transcendence, focuses on how God is with humanity. The detail of his description of the reality of Christ's human nature serves to divinize the human. Hugh's God requires humanity in order to complete salvation, as much as humanity needs divinity to enable salvation to be manifested. In this relationship, I suggest, we find an antecedent of the generative form of mutuality, which stresses human participation in ongoing creation and redemption.

Gender mutuality is suggested in Hugh's concepts of the Sacrament of Marriage and the Virgin Birth. Hugh's medieval biology not-withstanding, his interpretation discloses gender equality, equal participation and common consent of both male and female partners in marriage as constitutive and root values determining the validity and legitimacy of the sacrament of marriage. These concepts also play a major role in determining his comprehension of the Virgin Birth. Hugh's regard for these values impels him to come quite close to placing the will of the Virgin Mary on the same plane with the will of the Holy Spirit: ". . .this [conception of Jesus] was only possible because of the ardent love that was mutually shared between her and the

---

[36]*Spiritual Friendship*, I:69-70. A play on 1 Jn. 4:16.

Holy Spirit."[37] In Hugh's view, between the Virgin and the Spirit there clearly was (Margaret Huff) "a dynamic situation within relationship in which each one is simultaneously open to the influence of the other or others, and aware of influencing the other or others . . . ."[38]

An antecedent of cosmic mutuality is found in Hugh's observation of God's presence in creation, and all of creation as the occasion for doxology. There is a common power between God and the creation; they, in a sense, empower one another. Not only is God present in all things, but "He is said to be everywhere, because He is absent to no part of things. . . . Not only to universal creation but also to every part of it He is present equally whole."[39] Just as the Incarnation gives dignity to humankind, so too all of creation is sanctified by God's presence in each part. Yet, God's presence does not overcome the distinctness or particularity of each element. Rather, the distinctness within creation contributes to God's glory by providing yet other occasions for doxology. Hence, there is a reciprocal exchange and empowerment between God and creation.[40] By logical extension, since God's presence is in all of creation, then humans, who bear God's image and likeness, are also related to all of creation.[41]

The values undergirding Hugh's interpretation of marriage, as a public witness to a free agreement between a man and a woman, are analogous with social mutuality. Given the social and cultural conditions of the day, women had very few options for economic security outside of marriage.[42] Infidelity frequently placed women and children in very precarious economic positions. Thus, to claim that women must

---

[37]*On the Sacraments*, Book II, Part 1, Section viii.

[38]Huff, "The Independent Self," 163.

[39]*On the Sacraments*, Book II, Part 1, Section xiii.

[40]See Cizewski, "Reading the World," 65-88.

[41]This idea will be detailed below.

[42]See David Herlihy, "Land, Family and Women in Continental Europe, 700-1200," in *Women in Medieval Society*, 13-45.

publicly consent to marriage before a witness constituted one step toward empowering women.[43] Civil and ecclesial order requires this empowerment of women.

In Aelred of Rievaulx's spiritual friendship one finds analogs of the modern feminist notions of generative, gender and social mutuality. As recipients of the overflowing love of God, humans are empowered to be co-creators with God through the free extension of the gift of love to others. The act of loving is, in a sense, redemptive of and creative for both the beloved and the lover. Gender mutuality is analogous with Aelred's belief that women and men are capable of true friendship. True friendship consists in the relationship of women and men in embodied egalitarian relations. Unlike modern feminists Aelred does not discuss the *imago Dei* as the basis for this relationship.

The dynamism of love within community is analogous with social mutuality. Within monastic community, God-given love was for the good of all and in turn, it became praiseworthy in that it was extended to the wider community of those in need. True love of God requires true love of neighbor, even beyond the monastery walls. This love of neighbor must be directed especially to the least ones, as was modeled by the early Christian community.[44] Aelred makes no mention of the obligation for the least ones to take up the power given over to them, however.

THOMAS AQUINAS

Considerations concerning cosmic interdependence and friendship were an important part of the broader intellectual milieu inherited by Thomas Aquinas. Thomas's genius was to ask the probing questions which broke the barriers of

---

[43]Marriage was recognized as a sacrament about 1150. See Kenan B. Osborne, *Sacramental Theology: A General Introduction* (New York: Paulist Press, 1988), 9.

[44]See *Spiritual Friendship*, Book I.28-30 and Book II.68-70.

ignorance and led to the truth that friendship in community is necessary for true peace and harmony.[45]

Thomas's study of friendship out-distanced most previous analyses of the subject, however, because he fully integrated the idea into his theological system, particularly in his *Summa theologiae*. Significant for our purposes is the fact that Aquinas considers friendship as one of many relationships within the macro-ordering of the universe. Unfortunately, the Aristotelian notion of hierarchy was *also* a force at work within Thomas's system. It was thus possible for him and later interpreters to neglect the presence of non-hierarchical relationality in his scholarship. For modern feminists, Aquinas's theology is a source for relationality and sense knowledge, but an obstacle to gender equity. [46]

Friendship With God

Aquinas spells out his most mature thought concerning friendship and friendship with God in the tracts on happiness and charity in his *Summa theologiae*.[47] Since, as Aquinas indicates in the Prologue of the *Secundae pars*, the subject of happiness is a human person, Thomas's anthropology must first be examined in order to fully grasp what he claimed concerning happiness. Also, in the tract on happiness, Thomas presumes that while God is the final cause for moral action, human relationship to God is as knower to known and lover to beloved.[48] Therefore, secondly, Aquinas's apprehension of God as "exemplar cause" must be illuminated and the implications which that notion holds for the divine/human relationship must be clarified. In addition, because in his treatise on charity the Angelic Doctor makes

---

[45]See Wanda Cizewski, "Friendship With God? Variations on a Theme in Aristotle, Aquinas and Macmurray," *Philosophy and Theology* 6 (1992): 369-81 and Lewis M. Hughes, "Charity as Friendship in the Theology of St. Thomas," *Angelicum* 52 (1975): 164-78.

[46]Harrison, "Keeping the Faith in a Sexist Church:Not For Women Only," in Making the Connections, 219-21.

[47]*ST* I-II.1-5. and II-II.23-27.

[48]See *ST* I.45.7.

extensive use of Aristotle's explanation of "friendship," and in order to discover where Thomas parts from Aristotle's claim that humans cannot be friends of God, Aristotle's use of that term needs examination.[49] Finally, Thomas's notion of friendship with God will be compared with the modern feminists' notions of mutuality in order to discover the analogous relationship between the terms.

Anthropology

Thomas's anthropology is succinctly summarized in the Prologue of the *Prima secunda:* "Man is made in God's image . . . in that he is intelligent and free to judge and master himself. . . ." Thomas presumes the reader's understanding of St. Augustine's *De Trinitate,* especially Books six, seven and fourteen. There Augustine clarifies that "the image of God properly consists of the memory, understanding and love of God, and that the memory, understanding and love of self constitute a sort of potential image of God that is not the image in the full sense."[50] Early in his career, in his *Scriptum super Sententiis,* Thomas had distinguished humans as created in the *imago Dei,* not merely as *vestigium.*[51] Human likeness to God is not merely as a footprint (*vestigium*), but also as an image (*imago*), able to reflect God by knowledge and love.[52] In Question ninety-three of the *Prima pars,* Thomas had shown how God had created humans with a nature that possesses the fundamental capacity for beatitude. In other words, Thomas stresses that the human form is the *telos* of God's communication of the divine likeness in the act of creation. Now, in the *Secunda pars,* Aquinas treats the similarity of humans with God in as much as, like God, humans are the principle of their own acts. Thus, not only are humans created in the

---

[49]*ST* II-II.23.1. Thomas cites *Nicomachean Ethics.*

[50]D. Juvenal Merriell, *To The Image of the Trinity: A Study in the Development of Aquinas' Teaching,* Studies and Texts (Toronto: Pontifical Institute of Mediaeval Studies, 1990), 28, 13-35.

[51]Ibid., 41-43. Merriell cites 1 *Scriptum super sententiis* d.3,q.2,a.1,sol.

[52]See *ST* I.93. See also Ian Hislop, "The Anthropology of St. Thomas," in *St. Thomas and Nietzsche,* ed., F. C. Copleston, (Ditchling, Sussex: Blackfriars, 1955), 3-10.

image of God according to their nature, but they can also participate in God's creative acts and toward their own perfection.

In Thomas's hierarchy of created beings the likeness of the species is grounded in the distinct traits of the species.[53] Of all the creatures of creation, humans are most God-like by their nature, particularly their intelligibility. What distinguishes humans is that they are rational and intellectual by nature.[54] While God cannot be defined as of one genus, species or difference because God is pure act and pure form, there is a certain order to God's attributes that can be compared with the hierarchy of being. Therefore, a correspondence exists between the divine attribute of intelligence and the constitutive difference of intellectual creatures, who are at the highest position in the hierarchy of beings and the position closest to God.[55] Thus, Thomas concludes that, unlike non-rational creatures who do not possess the highest common attribute of intelligibility, and so cannot properly represent God's nature, humans can image God.[56] Thus, humans are both the *terminus* of God's creation and, by their intellectual nature, in a position to have a unique relationship with God.

God: Exemplar Cause

Aquinas's statement from the Prologue of the *Secunda pars* that "God is the exemplar cause . . . ." is a phrase that requires attention here. Thomas reiterates a point he has made earlier in the *Summa*, namely that the relationship of God to the whole of creation is as its sole efficient and final cause.[57] Just as an architect's mind

---

[53] *ST* I.93.2*ad*.

[54] *ST* I.3.5*ad*.

[55] *ST* I.93.2*ad*.

[56] *ST* I.93.3*ad*; I.93.4*ad*; I.93.4*ad*.1*m*.

[57] *ST* I.44. See also I.47.3, "Is There an Order of Agents Among Creatures?." The Blackfriars Edition of the *Summa* includes this article in Appendix 3, Vol. 8, 158 with editor and translator Thomas Gilby's introductory explanation that: "A codex in the Library of Monte Cassino (no. 138) introduces the Question by promising four points of inquiry. `Primo . . . secundo . . . terio, de earum ordine, quarto, de unitate mundi.' The third article is inserted with the note that it is not found in the Paris exemplar of Brother Thomas's *Summa*. Pègues takes it into the text, the Leonine includes it as a footnote. Though not found in any other extant mss and having a slight flavor not characteristic of the *Summa*

is the sole efficient cause of the house s/he builds, so God is the exemplary cause of creation. In this way, Aquinas emphasizes the relatedness of all creatures to God and places humans in their context as part of the whole creation. In addition, in the background of the Prologue lies Thomas's understanding of God's particular presence in humans through grace.[58] While this fact distinguishes humans from other creatures, the unique empowerment through grace does not set them free to follow their every whim. To the contrary, the gift of grace is to be used for the good of all.[59] Interestingly, Thomas also states that while it is not necessary that God utilize other creatures to act on one another, that is indeed the case. He states: "HENCE: . . . It is not therefore from any defect of power that he acts through the intermediary of creatures, but from the abundance of his goodness, which grants to a creature not only its own inherent goodness, but also the dignity of being to others the cause of goodness."[60]

Indeed, the interrelationship of all creation is grounded in the goodness of God, who is its cause and end. Strongly implied here is the notion that this goodness is not fulfilled unless the dignity and flourishing of all creation is secured.[61] We find here a grounding for the feminists' notion that the whole of creation must be taken into consideration as the context in which mutuality operates toward the greatest flourishing of all.

Thomas's Use of Friendship in Aristotle

Aristotle's interpretation of human friendship is the model of relationship Thomas finds useful in understanding divine/human relations, as well as the

---

'ordinary,' we translate it here as a link between the discussions on Providence and on the government of the universe. (1a.22 & 103. Vols. 5 & 14)."

[58] *ST* I.8.3*ad*.

[59] See *ST* I.112.4*ad*.

[60] See n. 57 above. *ST* I.47.3*ad*.

[61] See *ST* I.112.4*ad*.

relationship of humans to each other and other earthcreatures. However, contrary to Aristotle, Thomas claims it is possible for humans to be friends of God.[62]

Aristotle uses the terms *philia* and *philein* in his discussion of friendship.[63] *Philia* refers to several different kinds of friendship: feelings bonding family members and kinship groups,[64] the camaraderie between business persons, civic and social groups,[65] regard given the head of state by citizens.[66] In his lectures on friendship (to which Thomas refers), Aristotle designated three sorts of relationships representing various degrees of *philia*. There are relationships of pleasure which consist in good company of companions, conversation and fleshly encounters,[67] of profit in which partners utilize one another for their own interests,[68] and of worth in which the partners appreciate one another's virtue.[69]

It is the third form of friendship, the "perfect friendship" between "men who are good and resemble one another according to virtue," that is Aristotle's ideal.[70] Friendship based on virtue is long lasting and mutual in the exchange between partners, each of whom desires the goodness they know in themselves for the other and for others outside the friendship. For the purpose of our study, it is significant

---

[62]*ST* II-II.23-33. Thomas makes reference to Aristotle's *Nicomachean Ethics*, Book 8, 1159a3-5; 1635. The translation of the *Ethics* used in this chapter is found in C. I. Litzinger, trans., *Commentary on Aristotle's Nicomachean Ethics: St. Thomas Aquinas* (Notre Dame: Dumb Ox Books, 1993). In the citations that follow, the first reference is made to the *Ethics* and a second is to Thomas Aquinas's *Commentary*, [*TAC*].

[63]See Cizewski, "Friendship," 370-71 for a detailed word study.

[64]*Ethics*, 1159b25-35; 1160a10-30; *TAC*, 1657-1661; 1666-1671.

[65]*Ethics*, 1160a19-30; *TAC*, 1668-1671.

[66]*Ethics*, 1160a1; 1161a10-14; *TAC*, 1662-1666.

[67]*Ethics*, 1156b1-6; *TAC*, 1573.

[68]*Ethics*, 1156a10-19; *TAC*, 1565-1566.

[69]*Ethics*, 1156b7-8; *TAC*, 1574.

[70]*Ethics*, 1156b7-8; *TAC*, 1574.

the Aristotle used the term *isos* to indicate that the partners of the perfect friendship are equals in wealth, power and excellence, enabling them to share life reciprocally.[71]

In the case of unequal or imperfect friendships, Aristotle illustrates several degrees of inequality in relationships in which *philia* can still exist between: spouses, parents and children, king and subject or master and slave.[72] Most problematic from the Christian perspective is Aristotle's contention that friendship between God and humans is impossible since the absolute inequality cannot be overcome or mitigated. Aristotle argued that to wish one's friend to be as the gods was not really a good thing because in so doing, we distance ourselves from them, and friendship ceases.[73] The presence of at least vestigial equality was Aristotle's criterion for a relationship of *philia*.[74]

God as Friend

Thomas does not accept Aristotle's as the final word on friendship with God, but rather moves to an argument that coheres with the word of the Word, who proclaimed in John's Gospel (15:15), "I no longer call you servants, but my friends *(philoi)*." At the heart of his argument is the equation of *caritas* and *amicitia*. Thomas maintains Aristotle's qualification that perfect friendship is a lasting thing, and identifies *amicitia* with a permanent inclination, as well. However, Aquinas moves beyond Aristotle.

In II-II.23 of the *Summa* Thomas explains several grounds for charity as friendship between humans and God. First, friendship is based on more than good will; it is rooted in mutual loving, common sharing and benevolence.[75] Secondly,

---

[71] See Cizewski, "Friendship," 372.

[72] *Ethics*, 1160b33-35; 1160b25; 1162a5; 1161a10-23; 1161b7-8. See also *TAC*, 1684; 1682; 1715; 1688-1694; 1700.

[73] *Ethics*, 1158a33-36, 1159a3-5; *TAC*, 1633-1635. See Elizabeth A. Johnson's interpretation in *She Who Is*, 145.

[74] Cizewski, "Friendship," 373.

[75] *Ethics*, 1155b27-31; *TAC*, 1557-1558.

humans have both an outward life in which they communicate with others and an inward life in which they have communion with God.[76] In the interior or spiritual life, the human will is moved by the Holy Spirit, harmonizing human and divine causality.[77] In so acting, God thoroughly undergirds imperfect human charity and brings it to perfection. Humans are, thus, able to act connaturally with God.[78] The Aristotelian notion of distance between the gods and humanity as prohibiting their friendship is defeated.

> Because *caritas* is defined as friendship with God, Aquinas overturns Aristotle by means of scripture, yet absorbs him into his scripturally-based anthropology. The result is a doctrine of friendship that turns first to God in the human response to a divine initiative, but then extends itself compassionately to all other human beings . . . (see e.g., 2a2ae, q.25, a.6.).[79]

God is the supreme good.[80] It is possible with the help of God's grace to reach the goal of the Beatific Vision. True happiness consists in God, perceived in God's essence through the Beatific Vision which alone can satisfy the rational creature's longing for intelligibility. Each person's earthly journey toward happiness can be fulfilled to the degree of his/her potential. Through charity the individual is enabled to participate in the very mind and will of God to fulfill the precepts of the natural law.[81] Charity is also the basis of concord among individuals and that forms the foundation for peace within the community.

In his discussion of the theological virtues, Aquinas speaks strongly concerning human friendship with God, asserting that through the theological virtues,

---

[76] *ST*, II-II.23.1.

[77] *ST*, II-II.23.2.

[78] Ibid.

[79] Cizewski, "Friendship," 376.

[80] *ST*, I.6.

[81] *ST*, I-II.65.5.

we become partakers in the divine nature.[82] As has been illustrated, through charity in particular, humans enjoy an "intimate conversation with God." In I-II.112.1 Aquinas asserts that because of faith, hope and charity the grace of God can deify (*deificet*) us, challenge us to do what seems impossible, namely, communicate with and become more like God. Charity also unites in friendship all who share in the supreme good of friendship with God. In fact, all people are included in this friendship because everyone is an actual or a potential sharer in God's grace, which generates friendship.[83] It can be concluded that insofar as humans are "god-like," God's concerns are our concerns; the well-being of creation is thus, our concern because that is what love requires.[84]

Trinitarian Relations: Analog of Mutuality

While Thomas's paradigm of friendship with God provides a strong mandate for mutuality in human relationships, some interpreters hold that the model has one glaring shortfall, namely, the fact that humans cannot fully reciprocate God's gracing humankind.[85] In Thomas's classical understanding of the Divine, God is always the self-sufficient subject and never the needy object. The treatise on God is divided in two portions in Aquinas's *Summa*: *De Deo Uno* I.2-26 and *De Deo Trino* I.27-43. The former examines the metaphysics of God's being as such and the latter explores what pertains to the trinity of persons. The fact that the entire section is placed at the beginning of the treatment of dogmatic theology seems to stress the priority of the mystery of God as such (*theologia*) rather than the triune nature of God in the

---

[82]*ST*, I-II.62.1. See also Jean Porter, *The Recovery of Virtue: The Relevance of Aquinas for Christian Ethics* (Louisville: Westminster/John Knox Press, 1990), 170.

[83]*ST*, II-II.25.1, 6, 8, 12.

[84]*ST*, II-II.25.1.

[85]Catherine Mowry LaCugna, *God For Us: The Trinity and Christian Life*, 1993 Paperback ed., (San Francisco: Harper Collins, 1991), 143-180. Recall Johnson's critique, *She Who Is*, 145.

economy of salvation (*oikonomia*).[86] If one is to truly understand Thomas's intent, it is necessary to take the entire treatise together as one whole explanation of God.

Aquinas's Metaphysics of Divine Being

In *De Deo Uno* Aquinas established his metaphysics of divine being.[87] He demonstrated that while humans can see God's effects, they cannot know God directly.[88] God is simple, nothing but uncomposed *essentia*.[89] In I.12.2, Aquinas explains the ontological dissimilarity between God and creatures. Potentiality is the main characteristic of the creature, while pure actuality defines God. Although it is ultimately inadequate, it is possible to describe and define God analogically because there are distinct resemblances between creature and Creator. The relationship between creature and Creator is present, however distinct. The potential intimacy of the relationship is demonstrated in the *Summa* II-II.23, where Thomas claims humans can be friends of God.

Relations: *ad intra/ad extra*

The core of Aquinas's trinitarian doctrine lies in his presentation of relation.[90] Thomas avoids suggesting that God must act out of necessity by drawing a distinction between real and logical relations.[91] God's relations *ad intra* are real, while God's relations *ad extra* are logical. There are no accidents in God because God is simple, that is, uncomposed *essentia*. Trinitarian relation can be understood by examining what the three persons share in common, and in terms of the processions of the Son and the Spirit from the Father. The divine activity of procession is experienced by all

---

[86]LaCugna, *God For Us*, 149-50.

[87]*ST*, I.2-11.

[88]*ST*, I.2.2.

[89]*ST*, I.3.

[90]Thomas's notion of relation is the Aristotelian *posi* or *adaliquid*, the tenth category of being. A is relative to B, if it implies B. See Aristotle's *Categories* 4, 1b,25 and 7, 6a:36-8b:24.

[91]*ST*, I.28.1ad. Logical relation is an accidental feature of something. Real relation belongs to the very nature of something. See also *ST*, I.28.2.

persons in begetting or spirating, producing the four relations of paternity, filiation, spiration and procession.[92] These four relations give rise to the three persons: Father, Son and Spirit. Thomas called those relations subsistent, since they are not really distinct from the divine essence, being distinct only among themselves.[93] Aquinas stressed that while humans can have knowledge about God through reason, knowledge of the Trinity is possible only through revelation.[94]

Names of God

The names of God are given in the Scriptures. In the process of considering the names of God Thomas makes a significant move concerning how to understand the way the Father relates. Aquinas chose to follow the Greek category of "principle" rather than the notion of "cause."[95] Thus, the name of the Father identifies the Father as the principle of the whole Godhead and signifies a relationship with the Son *in divinis*, which does not connote the Father as unbegotten. Thomas proceeded along a similar line in defining the relation of the Son and the Spirit as known through their names. As a word results from the intellectual conception in human knowing, so too a kind of imprint emerges from the love's will. The Son processes forth from the Father who knows himself and speaks the Word (which is the proper name for the Son). Likewise, the Father and the Son spirate the Spirit as their uniting bond of

---

[92] *ST*, I.28.4.

[93] *ST*, I.29.4. See *God For Us*, 154. "Thomas follows Boethius' classic definition of person as 'individual substance of a rational nature.' Substance according to Aristotle, has two meaning: 'First substance' is what something is (quiddity), ousia, essence. 'Second substance' is the suppost or that which underlies something. The latter is equivalent to hypostasis: an individual substance. It would be technically correct to say that there are three substances in God, because 'first' substance = ousia and 'second' substance = hypostasis. However, Thomas notes, this is misleading and hypostasis should be used as an equivalent to subsistence (subsistentia), not substance (substantia). . . . 'Consequently, just as Godhead is God, so God's fatherhood is God the Father who is a divine person. Hence 'divine person' signifies relation as something subsisting.'[I.29.4]"

[94] *ST*, I.32.1.

[95] *ST*, I.33.3. See also the Blackfriars edition Vol. 7, pages 2-4, n.'s 2, c-g and the Appendix, pages 239-51 for an extensive explanation of the categories.

Love (the proper name of the Spirit).[96] In those divine activities, the relationship with creation is also established and maintained. It is in the begetting of the Word that all creation is also begotten, and in the spiration of the Spirit that Love for the primal goodness which motivates the Father's love of self and every creature is founded.[97]

The Divine Missions

The divine missions are addressed by Thomas with the intent of protecting the equality of the divine persons in one essence.[98] *In divinis* there are two processions and it is the processing persons, the Son and the Spirit who are sent into the created world of time and space, with the goal of making all creatures holy.[99] Aquinas is careful to illustrate how it is the divine persons themselves who are sent, not just their gifts or effects. This is particularly significant for our purposes of demonstrating the analogous nature of the divine/human relationship in Aquinas's understanding with the notion of mutuality in the modern feminist literature, because it is here that the aloof, self-sufficient God of the *De Deo Uno* becomes an initiating and a participating God.

God is the one who establishes contact between the human and all of creation. Even though the participation is weighted on God's side and the aim of creation is God-oriented, the intent is gracious and benevolent.[100] This Creator is distinct from creation, but certainly not separate. Continually, the universe originates from divine creativity and is sustained by divine providence; God is constantly present in all creation. The good of creation is an analogy of the divine goodness. It is precisely the nature of divine power that removes the distance between the human and the

---

[96]*ST*, I.36.1-4. See *Oxford English Dictionary*, 2nd ed., s.v. "spirate." ". . . to breathe out . . . From the Latin *spirare*, to breathe."

[97]*ST*, I.34.1; I.37.2*ad*3. See also *ST*, I.34.3: "For God knowing himself, knows every creature."

[98]*ST*, I.43.1*ad*1.

[99]*ST*, I.43.5.

[100]See LaCugna, *God For Us*, 158: "This question [*ST*, I.43.3] and this focus is the bridge to all that follows in the *Summa*. By touching God and being touched by God directly, the recipient of grace is returned to its origin. The *reditus* of the creature is made possible by God's *exitus* in the mission of the Son and the Spirit."

divine. Divine creativity is continuous and sustains all beings in their existence by an inexhaustible outpouring of energy.[101] It is Being itself that animates and nourishes all creation. Grace does not destroy nature, it perfects it.[102]

Yet, there is a tension created by Thomas's language. This relationship remains only a logical one. All creation can be said to be contained in God, but only vestiges of the Trinity can be found in creation by appropriation.[103] Creation is the emanation and self-communication of the Creator; the act of God who is the efficient, exemplary and final cause of everything.[104] The relationship of creation to God is one of dependence and reception of the self-communication. God creates as the result of a decision of the divine will and only after God necessarily wills God's own being.[105] Because God necessarily wills the divine goodness, but not other things, it can be said that God creates out of divine goodness and therefore wills the thriving of all that is created.[106] In short, God wills creation to be because of God's own goodness, but the act of willing itself is not because of God's act of willing God's own goodness. Creation is an absolutely free act, and Aquinas understands that freedom to mean a choice.[107]

Thus, Aquinas presents a self-sufficient God who chooses to relate for reasons that are ultimately unknown to the creature. To the modern reader it seems as if the Aristotelian hierarchical framework within which he labored would not allow Thomas to do otherwise. Yet, what kept the Angelic Doctor from identifying with Aristotle's position that the gods are entirely inaccessible was his presumption of the economy

---

[101] *ST*, I.103.1obj2. and I.104.3*ad*.

[102] *ST*, I.1.8obj.2.

[103] *ST*, I.93.4-5.

[104] *ST*, I.44.4.

[105] *ST*, I.19.1*ad*3; I.19.4*ad*2.

[106] *ST*, I.19.2*ad*2; I.19.10. See also *ST*, I.6.4.

[107] *ST*, I.19.10.

of redemption, understood in the light of faith. Only when the self-sufficient trinitarian God is placed in the perspective of salvation history is the distance removed.[108] In order to better understand this presumption, we now turn to a brief examination of Thomas Aquinas's treatise on the Incarnation.

The Incarnation

The Economy of Salvation

Thomas Aquinas treats the Incarnation in the *Tertia pars* of the *Summa*. To demonstrate that the free, self-sufficient, transcendent God of the *De Deo Uno* is also immanent, Thomas first addresses the fittingness of the Incarnation.[109] He concludes that the Incarnation is fitting because God is good and it is the very nature of goodness to communicate itself. In addition, since God is the highest good, God communicates himself in the highest way possible, namely, to man through the union of Word, soul, flesh in one person.[110] In communicating Godself, there was no loss or change in God, rather the creature was transformed in uniting with God. Again, it is God's goodness that justifies the Incarnation for the salvation of humanity. God can assume a created nature, because such natures are good (in spite of the fact that humans can choose to sin). Like a word spoken to an audience which is simultaneously heard by each member of the audience equally, the abiding Word of God is at once everywhere and whole.[111]

---

[108]LaCugna, *God For Us*, 168, cites Karl Rahner, *Theological Investigations*, vol. 1 (New York: Crossroad, 1961), 181: "God, while remaining immutable, 'truly comes in what [God] constitutes as something united with [God] and from [God].' In other words, God truly comes to be God in creation which is united with God and also diverse from God. . . . Rahner requires God's self-enactment in order for God to be our God. God creates and enters history not to know Godself as God, but to know Godself as *pro nobis*." Emphasis is LaCugna's.

[109]*ST*, III.1.1.

[110]Notice how this schema follows the Aristotelian hierarchy which holds that like rank communicates with like rank (humans bear the image of God), intellect is over physical (word communicates the result of intellectual process), spiritual is over matter (soul is the seat of the spiritual), and highest matter because of the ability to reason (male).

[111]*ST*, III.1.1-4.

When inquiring into the necessity of the Incarnation for the salvation of the world, Thomas did not intend to demonstrate that the Word of God *a priori* had to become incarnate in order to redeem humanity. That the Word of God became incarnate in the person of Jesus Christ is an historical, contingent fact--a truth of faith. Thomas instead attempts to understand the meaning of the redemptive act.[112] It is here that the goodness and friendship of God can be seen, changing the tone of the divine/human relationship from distance to intimacy.[113] Considering the furtherance of humans in goodness, the Incarnation was the more fitting (thus, necessary) way to achieve that because it: (1) strengthened human faith in that the Word of God was heard directly from God (2) increased human hope because the extent of God's love was revealed (3) enkindled in humans charity out of a desire to return what had been received (4) gave humans an example of right living and (5) enabled humans to share in God's divinity. More explicitly, the Incarnation was effective because it: (1) showed that the devil has no power over humanity, because he is without flesh (2) highlighted the dignity of human nature (3) undermined the presumption that humans merit grace (4) fostered humility by revealing humility on the part of God, and (5) was accomplished by Jesus Christ who was one person, but with both a divine and human nature.[114] While the "necessity" for the Incarnation is beyond human comprehension, humans can see that it made satisfaction for human sin in two ways: It did so "completely" in that God's infinite dignity countered the finite nature of sin, and it lent support to all human attempts at satisfaction ("incompletely") by its completeness.

Here again, Aquinas's language and intent can be confusing to the modern reader. It seems that ultimately, the distance remains between God and creation. Thomas relies on Scriptural evidence and asserts that the Incarnation would not have happened if *adam* had not sinned. He states: "Everywhere in scripture . . . the sin of

---

[112]This will significantly limit the extent to which Aquinas's system allows him to approach an understanding of mutuality similar to modern feminists'.

[113]See *ST*, II-II.23. Friends seek the good for friends.

[114]*ST*, III.1.2*ad*.

the first man is given as the reason for the Incarnation; thus, it is preferable to hold that the work of the Incarnation is ordered by God as the remedy for sin, in such a way that if there had been no sin, there would have been no Incarnation. Divine power, of course, is not limited to this, for God could have become incarnate even if there had been no sin."[115]

Paradoxically, it is the very self-sufficiency of God which makes God so distant from humanity, that requires Thomas to *also* be open to an interpretation of the reason for the Incarnation which includes a more optimistic view of human nature. Ultimately, he must remain open to the possibility that God simply desired to communicate Godself fully to humanity and raise human nature to its highest glory by uniting it with divine nature.[116]

Love Incarnate

When one examines closely the assumptions undergirding Thomas's position, the relationship of God and humanity is intimate and empowering. Not only is God the most real being, but God is love.[117] Created in God's image, humans are also capable of love. Thomas understands love on the model of physics. Natural love moves all things, literally.[118] The universe and all things in it are motivated by varieties of love, each in its own way, charged with divine purpose. All creatures are patterned by intelligent love that intends the good.

To describe human love, Aquinas uses the word *passio* which conveys that emotions are an effect of an agent on a patient.[119] It can be said that one suffers a passion. Passion, however, is more like an active reaction or a response to some real agent. Thus, there is a real referent to the passions. They are a response to someone

---

[115]*ST*, III.1.3*ad*.

[116]See the Franciscan position below.

[117]*ST*, I.20.1. See also 1 Jn. 4:7-18.

[118]*ST*, I-II.26.2*ad*.

[119]Ibid.

or something outside oneself, not mere internal states or moods. The passions are like motion, physical movement in the ordinary sense.

Love is the first of the concupiscible passions. For Aquinas, it is the primary passion; all other passions are forms of love.[120] The human passion of love begins with the apprehension of some good--beauty, moral good, or some other good that corresponds to a particular need or possibility. If the good of a subject is apprehended by another, the subject makes an impression upon him/her. The subject is taken in by the other, and the other is changed; the impress of the subject is left on him/her. Aquinas calls this a *coaptationem*--an adaptation of the other, or a sense of affinity, or a feeling of complacency in the other. The goodness of the other lodges in the lover's heart.[121] Then the lover's desire spontaneously moves toward the object with the purpose of actually possessing it. When the object of love is attained, the movement or process ends where it began. This then is Aquinas's description of love. It is a process that has three movements: complacency, desire, and joy. It forms a circle of interconnection between lover and beloved.

Thomas's view of the experience of interpersonal passionate love shows a connected relationship. His awareness can be illustrated by examining his conception of how love effects in each partner *mutua inhaeso*, or mutual indwelling.[122] The beloved is the lover and the lover is the beloved. When two persons love each other, they inhabit each other's knowledge and affections. With regard to knowing, the beloved is constantly present in the thoughts of the lover. Moreover, the lover attempts to gain ever deeper insight into everything about the beloved, so as to know

---

[120]*ST*, I-II.26.3. Concupiscible passions are emotions of simply wanting or desiring something good. The irascible passions are fiery emotions by which a person can overcome an evil or persevere through difficulties in order to achieve a desired good. The irascible passions serve the concupiscible aims, because by them a person summons the energy or determination to attain some good that is difficult to attain.

[121]*ST*, II-II.26.2*ad*.

[122]*ST*, I-II.28.2.

his/her inner depths.[123] With respect to affections, the beloved is constantly present in the lover's feelings because of complacency. This affective dwelling causes delight or pleasure (*delectio*) when the beloved is actually present. But when s/he is absent, the lover feels a kind of desire (*desiderium*) which may be either a longing for the presence of the beloved or desire for the beloved's good. Such desire arises from the feeling rooted deep in the lover, that complacency which is love itself.[124] That is why, writes Thomas, we speak of love as *intimus*.[125]

As we have seen, charity is the root of friendship with God. Friendship has the characteristics of directness, mutuality, equality and affection. If charity is friendship, then those same characteristics must somehow apply to the divine/human relationship. Thomas writes:

> Yet good will alone is not enough for friendship, for this requires a mutual loving; it is only with a friend that a friend is friendly. Now there is a sharing of man with God by his happiness with us, and it is on this that friendship is based. St. Paul refers to it, *God is faithful: by whom you are called into the fellowship of his Son.* (I Cor.1:9) Now love which is based on this sort of fellowship is charity. Accordingly it is clear that charity is a friendship of man and God.[126]

This communication connotes a mutual partaking and a mutual indwelling. Thus, according to Aquinas the friendship between humanity and God is a participation in the divine happiness. The living God initiates the communication, and humans respond as the beloved of the lover. In this relationship, God is "in" us and we are in God. In such intimate mutuality, boundaries are traversed without personal violation, for the friend loves the friend for the sake of the friend's good. Charity does not destroy human subjectivity, uniqueness, or individuality. To the contrary, it creates, restores, and sustains those qualities. This love is most perfectly manifested in Jesus Christ.

---

[123] *ST*, I-II.28.2*ad*.

[124] Ibid.

[125] Ibid.

[126] *ST*, II-II.23.1

Feminists' Notion of Mutuality and Aquinas's Thought

Having briefly examined Thomas Aquinas's understanding of friendship with God, Trinitarian relations and the Incarnation, several conclusions can be drawn. First, Thomas writes the *Summa* from the viewpoint of God to the world (and not the reverse). The very structure of the *Summa* reinforces a focus on the transcendence of God.[127] Second, Aquinas's language reflects the Aristotelian framework which he attempts to harmonize with Christian doctrine. Thus, unless one takes the *Summa* as a whole and assumes the intimacy of the Incarnation (as Thomas does), one can erroneously appropriate the relationship of Thomas's God to creation as distant or even hostile, due to the dependence of the creature upon the Creator, rather than as a side by side companionship. Third, while the Incarnation is a gratuitous move on God's part, (according to Thomas) best understood as due only to the weakened, fallen human condition, the role of God's love must not be forgotten. Love, the indwelling of the beloved in the lover and the lover in the beloved, mitigates the negative potential of God's dominance in that within love, humans may freely respond to the love that is given, or they may refuse it. Also, Thomas's illustration of the fact that humans are most free when they are most human, i.e. in harmony with God's will, softens the impact of God's dominating power.

For Thomas then, the divine/human relationship is an analog of the modern feminists' notion of mutuality. It is a kind of "friendship" that fits our definition of solidarity, but that strains within Aquinas's Aristotelian framework toward a kind of mutuality. In a relationship of solidarity, both parties are distinct, one from the other. However, there is a desire to be with one another that stretches the boundary lines between the parties. The desire of each person to be with the other exceeds his/her ability to fully participate in the act or experience undergone by the other. At the same time, the desire to be with the other does not unjustly cross the individual's boundaries.

---

[127]LaCugna, *God For Us*, 146-48 passim.

On the one hand, in a movement of God's will, God chose to communicate Godself in creation, particularly in the Incarnation, following the nature of goodness itself to communicate. Since God is love and since love moves toward goodness, it seems possible for love to burst the boundary lines and move from solidarity to mutuality. This fluidity, characteristic of mutuality, seems to be set in place as the lover moves within the beloved and the beloved inheres in the lover. For Aquinas, in the Incarnation, God seemingly opened Godself to a dynamic relationship with humanity wherein one is simultaneously open to the influence of others, influencing the other or others, and aware of the influence of others. Both receptivity and active initiative are part of the relationship of the Son (Jesus of Nazareth) and humanity. In the Incarnation the dignity of humanity was enhanced and the wholeness of each person was acknowledged.

Significantly, however, Aquinas never mentions that God is a friend in response to the friendship of humans. The mutuality inherent in friendship is interrupted by a constant return to the ultimate transcendence of God. It is, in the final analysis, not the natural desire for the *reditus* of the creature to the Creator that bonds the relationship of human and divine. According to Thomas, humans can never be understood as causing God to do anything, since God never acts out of necessity.[128] Thus, Thomas's notion of friendship with God remains only an analog to mutuality.

---

[128] Aquinas's contemporary, Hedewijch of Antwerp, a thirteenth century mystic, believed that in freedom and empowered by love, humans could indeed influence God, who is a lover. See John Giles Milhaven, *Hedewijch and Her Sisters: Other Ways of Loving and Knowing* (Albany: State University of New York Press, 1993), 1-72, esp. 68.

Cosmic Mutuality

Aquinas's understanding of God's operation in and through creatures is analogous with cosmic mutuality, which highlights the relationship between God, humans, other earthcreatures, and the earth itself. Aquinas's starting point is significant in that he likens the entirety of creation to the goodness of God.[129] The focus here is the common goodness shared by creatures with one another and with God. While differences in species certainly limit the kind of interaction available to each creature, they do not prevent its participation in goodness. Each creature also holds the capacity to cause goodness in other creatures.[130] Because humans have been specifically created in God's image and likeness, they are most able to communicate goodness. However, no one creature can communicate God fully, so the entire cosmos is necessary-- though even it cannot communicate its proper end (God) since for Thomas, God is not identical with creation.[131] Because all gifts are given for the good of the whole, humans must seek the maximum thriving of all of creation.[132] Thus, in order for the cosmos to exist and thrive, there must be cosmic mutuality among God, all earthcreatures, humans, and the entire cosmos. Since in Thomas's system, the more complete and the closer to its final end something is, the better it is, cosmic mutuality is normative.

Gender Mutuality

Thomas's adherence to Aristotelian biology precludes any discussion of gender mutuality in his system.[133] In addition, Aquinas's use of scripture seems to be free of any critical cultural analysis. This causes some uses of scripture that modern exegetes would regard as mistaken, as can be seen in his confusion of Gal. 3:28 and Col. 3:11

---

[129] *ST*, I.47.1.

[130] *ST*, I.47.3*ad*.

[131] *ST*, I.47.2*ad* and I.47.3*ad*.

[132] *ST*, I.112.4*ad*.

[133] *ST*, I.92.1.

in Question Ninety-three of the *Prima pars* and in Question Seventy of the *Tertia pars*. On these and other counts, innumerable feminist writers, including Harrison, Heyward, Johnson and Ruether have harshly criticized Aquinas's treatment of women.[134]

Generative Mutuality

Generative mutuality, which focuses on human/divine co-creation and co-redemption, finds its analog in Aquinas's notion of the love of God and love of neighbor. Insofar as the human will is moved by the Holy Spirit in charity to love God, harmonizing human and divine causality, humans are able to act connaturally with God.[135] On the other side, humans cannot truly love God if they do not love their neighbor.[136] Yet, in the final analysis, human love for God needs to remain greater than love for the neighbor, because we find the goodness in common with our neighbor only in so far as we know God's goodness, first.[137]

Social Mutuality

An antecedent to social mutuality may be found in Thomas Aquinas's understanding of the common good. Aquinas defines the common good in his treatise on justice.

> Now it is evident that all who are included in a community, stand in relation to that community as parts to a whole; while a part, as such, belongs to the whole, so that whatever is the good of a part can be directed to the good of the whole. It follows therefore that the good of any virtue, whether such virtue direct man in relation to himself, or in relation to other individual persons, is referable to the common good to which justice directs: so that all acts of virtue can pertain to justice, in so far as it directs man to the common good.[138]

---

[134] See the bibliography of this study for the works of these scholars.

[135] *ST*, II-II.23.2.

[136] *ST*, II-II.2ad.1.

[137] *ST*, II-II.2ad.2.

[138] *ST*, II-II.58.5.

Aquinas states further, that it is the role of law to direct the common good.¹³⁹ While it is, in general, good that people have private property, Aquinas is clear, when discussing questions of personal possession and need, that the poor have the right to the necessities of life. In fact, says Thomas, the poor may even steal in order to obtain the necessities of life.¹⁴⁰ The Angelic Doctor reasons that there is a fine line delineating what is to be held in common according to natural law. When there are poor, those who do not have the necessities of life, because some are rich, that is not tolerable. Clearly, God is the only absolute owner. Hence, we have in Thomas some key notions that are antecedents of radical solidarity, reciprocity and identification with the least ones. Yet, Aquinas's ideas remain rooted in the hierarchical understanding of governance that flows from his stress on the transcendence of God. Law made by a single prince is preferable to democracy.¹⁴¹ Thomas does not address the participation of the poor in determining their own destiny. To this extent, again one finds only an analogous connection between Aquinas's notion of the common good and the understanding of social mutuality advocated by contemporary Christian feminists.

JOHN DUNS SCOTUS

Mutuality in Scotus: Mary Elizabeth Ingham's Thesis

The notion of mutuality permeates the entire philosophical and theological system framed by John Duns Scotus.¹⁴² Scotus sees all as relational in light of his

---

¹³⁹*ST*, I-II.90.2.

¹⁴⁰*ST*, II-II.66.2 and 7.

¹⁴¹"De regimine principum, Chapter 3, in *St. Thomas Aquinas On Politics and Ethics: A New Translation, Backgrounds and Interpretations*, ed. and trans. Paul E. Sigmund (New York: W. W. Norton and Company, 1988), 18.

¹⁴²I am grateful to Mary Elizabeth Ingham of Loyola Marymount University, Los Angeles, CA for her scholarly development of this insight; an insight I had known only at an intuitive level from reading portions of Scotus's work in the context of a variety of scholarly and spiritual Franciscan sources. I first became aware of Ingham's work through her paper, "The Harmony of Goodness: Mutuality as a Concept For Scotus' Moral Discussion," presented at a symposium held at the Franciscan Institute, St. Bonaventure, NY, June 24-28, 1992. The paper has been published in *Spirit and Life* 3 (1993): 55-82. Ingham makes no direct connection between Scotus's work and the four feminists' notion of mutuality

"essential order."[143] According to Mary Elizabeth Ingham, Scotus never used the term "mutuality." However, in his discussion of the "essential order," in his *Tractatus de primo principio*, Ingham claims Scotus offers a type of mutuality:

> I do not take essential order, however, in the strict sense as do some who say that what is posterior is ordered whereas what is first or prior transcends order. I understand it rather in its common meaning as a relation which can be affirmed equally (relatio aequiparantiae dicta) of the prior and posterior in regard to each other. In other words, I consider prior and posterior to be adequate division of whatever is ordered, so that we may use terms order and priority or posteriority interchangeably.[144]

Ingham aligns Scotus's statement with her own working definition of "mutuality" which is: "a dynamic state of relatedness existing between two or among three or

---

examined in this dissertation, nor does she suggest that mutuality is a formal moral norm.

[143]*John Duns Scotus: God and Creatures - Quodlibetal Questions*, trans. Felix Alluntis and Allan B. Wolter (Princeton: Princeton University Press, 1975), 503: "Order exists between two or more things if one can be said to be either prior or posterior to the other. If this is based on something accidental such as time, motion, place, size, etc., the order is accidental. If the priority or posteriority relationship stems from the nature or the essence, it is essential. Though Scotus treats of the essential order in all of his works, only in the *De Primo Principio* is there an attempt to treat the various types of essential order exhaustively under two headings of eminence and dependence. The first obtains if one essence is more perfect than another; the second holds if one essence can exist without the other, but not vice versa. This may be because the first is the efficient, final, formal or material cause of the second; or because of two effects of a common cause, the existence of the first is the predication of the second. Where several causes are required to produce a particular effect, they may not be essentially ordered to one another in producing that effect."

[144]John Duns Scotus, *Tractatus de primo principio, 1:15*, in *John Duns Scotus: A Treatise on God as First Principle*, trans. Allan B. Wolter (Chicago: Franciscan Herald Press, 1966), 2, cited by Ingham in her "John Duns Scotus: An Integrated Vision," in Kenan B. Osborne, ed. *The History of Franciscan Theology* (St. Bonaventure, NY: The Franciscan Institute, 1994), 211.
   In this chapter, I rely on translations of the original Scotus sources by internationally recognized Scotus scholars Allan B. Wolter and Mary Elizabeth Ingham.
   No complete critical edition of Scotus's works exists.
See Mary Elizabeth Ingham, *Ethics and Freedom: An Historical - Critical Investigation of Scotist Ethical Thought* (Lanham, MD: University Press of America, 1989), 4-5. Since there are several versions of the original Scotus material, some citations provide notation for the text in more than one manuscript. With these limitations in mind, in the citations below, I first give the original source and then indicate the source of the English translation. The notation: *Ordinatio* I.17.n.20 (Vatican 201.5-6) trans. Wolter, *Will and Morality*, 234 indicates *Ordinatio*, Book I, distinction 17, paragraph 20, found in the Vatican edition, page 201, lines 5 and 6. The English translation can be found in *Duns Scotus on the Will and Morality* by Allan B. Wolter, page 234. Some translations occasionally use other manuscripts, and these are indicated in the source I have cited.

more individuals. While the individuals are not necessarily equal, the relationship can be predicated equally of each. Mutuality also includes something in common among the related members."[145] In Scotus's works, God and humans are "related as essences within the order of being."[146] Since neither can exist outside of that order, God never exists outside of a relationship to humanity. This ontological relationship found within nature, within the will, and between the intellect and the will, Ingham has named a "weak mutuality."[147] Where beings are able to freely choose to enter into relationship with one another, create relationships or establish order, a "stronger mutuality" exists. This "stronger mutuality" is a profound sort of relationship which Ingham describes as a communion which is exemplified by the Trinitarian life, the Covenant, the Incarnation, the divine graciousness and liberality of *acceptatio* and the order of merit.[148]

Ingham notes the uniqueness of Scotus:

> as typified by necessity of nature and universal eternal and a
> Against a philosophical perspective which emerged from the 13th
> century abstract truths, Scotus elaborates an understanding of
> reality imbued with freedom, contingency, and attention to the
> particular. The basis of his emphasis on the superiority of theology
> over philosophy is precisely his preference for freedom over natural
> necessity as foundation for the cosmic order. Yet, superiority does
> not mean independence of theology from philosophy, for the fruits
> of natural reflection are necessary in speculation on the data in
> revelation.[149]

---

[145] Ingham, "Integrated Vision," 211.

[146] Ibid.

[147] Ibid.

[148] Ibid., 211-12.

[149] Ibid., 198. See also Ordinatio II.d.3.n.251. (Vivès 7:514) in Duns Scotus' Early Oxford Lectures, trans. Allan B. Wolter (Santa Barbara: Old Mission, 1992), xxvii. While philosophy was marked by necessary relationships and abstract considerations theology's marks are free acts of self-revelation and the value of the concrete.

The Basis for Mutuality: Scotus's Philosophy

Haecceitas

In order for one subject to be related to another, it must first be known for what it is in itself. Scotus's principle of *haeccitas*[150] (individuation or "thisness") provides the philosophical foundation for all created reality being specified. *Haecceitas* makes a singular thing what it is and differentiates it from all other things (of common nature) to which it may be compared (because of its commonality).[151]

As Ingham concludes, Scotus's concept of *haecceitas* sheds light on his thinking in several ways.[152] For our purposes, *haecceitas* is important because it makes possible individuation, and mutuality is a relationship between or among distinct beings. *Haecceitas* affects human relating in general because it affects how one understands contingent reality, one's capacity for the beatific vision, God, freedom, and the value of all elements of the cosmos.

Cognitive Theory

Scotus's cognitive theory emerges from the theological context. Significant for our purposes is how Scotus applied this theory to the human capacity to know and be known by God. He studied the question concerning the kind of knowledge Christ experienced while on this earth, and by extension, he drew conclusions concerning the cognitive capacity of human nature. In Scotus, metaphysical reflection (which focuses on abstraction and the formal order) is attention given to the conceptual framework

---

[150] Alluntis/Wolter, "Glossary," *God and Creatures*, 511: "*haecceitas*, (from the Latin *haec*, this): The term means literally, 'thisness.' It designates the unique formal principle of individuation that makes the nature, which all individuals of the same species have in common, to be just this or that individual and no other. Scotus regards it as a distinct positive formality over and above the common nature of the individual (*natura communis*)."

[151] Eric Doyle, "Duns Scotus and Ecumenism," *De Doctrina I. Duns Scoti*, vol. III, Acta Congressus Scotistici Internationalis Oxonii et Edimburgi, 11-17 September 1966 celebrati, Camille Bérubé, ed., (Roma: Cura Commissionis Scotisticae, 1968), 460: "The uniqueness, the unrepeatable something of all things, is what gives them their intrinsic and eternal value. There is about everything, every person, an originality that gives new insight into reality, another aspect that has never been seen before. Each person enters into a new enriching relationship of knowledge and love with every new person met, with every new thing encountered."

[152] Ingham, "Integrated Vision," 210.

which grounds concrete experience. Theology, in Scotus (which focuses on intuition and the contingent order) deals with the contingent experiences of God revealed in scripture.[153]

Intuition is possible due to the presence of the object "in all its proper intelligibility" and not via a mental representation.[154] Intuitive cognition is judged superior to abstractive cognition because it is immediate knowledge and it does not depend upon a mental species or phantasm.[155] Intuitive cognition grasps the object solely in itself and in the act of experience.[156] On the one hand, intuitive cognition can only occur with an existing object.[157] On the other hand, abstractive cognition can occur with an existing as well as a non-existing object. Abstractive knowledge is proper to scientific reflection as understood by Aristotle. Intuitive intellection is imperfect, however in the beatific vision, both abstractive and intuitive knowledge will be perfected (more below).[158]

Significant for our purposes is the manner in which Scotus applied the above distinction to the human capacity to know and be known by God. Intuitive knowledge is caused by an object that one observes face to face, and which communicates itself to the person through its actual existence and presence.[159]

---

[153] Ingham, *Ethics and Freedom*, 13-17.

[154] *Quodlibet* 14.n.10, trans. Alluntis/Wolter, 325.

[155] John Duns Scotus, *Tractatus de primo principio* IV.4.89 trans. Wolter, *First Principle*, 149.

[156] Sebastian Day, *Intuitive Cognition: A Key to the Significance of the Later Scholastics* (St. Bonaventure, NY: Franciscan Institute, 1947), 82. See T.F. Torrance, "Intuitive and Abstractive Knowledge: From Duns Scotus to John Calvin," in *De Doctrina Ioannis Duns Scoti*, ed. C. Bérubé, Acta Congressus Scotistici Internationalis Oxionii et Edimburgi, Sept. 11-17, 1966 celebrati, (Roma: Caria Commissionis Scotisticae, 1968), 291-305. Also, Richard Dumont, "Intuition: Prescript of Postscript in Scotus' Demonstration of God's Existence," in *Deus et Homo ad mentem I. Duns Scoti* Acta Tertii Congressus Scotistici Internationalis, Vindebonae, 28 Sept.-2 Oct. 1970, (Romae: Societas Internationalis Scotistica, 1972), 86.

[157] *Quodlibet* 7.n.8 (Alluntis 7:22) trans. Alluntis/ Wolter, 167.

[158] *Quodlibet* 14.n.12 (Alluntis 14:43) trans. Alluntis/ Wolter, 327.

[159] *Ordinatio* II.d.3.q.9.n.6.7; III.d.14.q.3.n.7. The key phrase is "causari in intellectu."

Therefore, the actual understanding gained through this kind of intellectual knowledge is necessarily a real and actual relation connecting it to the object itself.[160] Here two additional distinctions Scotus makes are also important to clarifying how humans know God.

Scotus distinguishes (1) perfect and imperfect intuition and (2) a voluntary from an involuntary object. In perfect intuitive knowledge, the object is always present and it is its own evidence. In imperfect intuitive knowledge, the object may be remembered or anticipated, known or mediated through evidence outside of the object itself.[161] There are also two kinds of objects giving rise to human knowledge.[162] A voluntary or supernatural object is known by the human mind when through its (the object's) willed activity the object makes itself known to the human mind (not through any natural relation of the mind to it, the object). A natural object, by contrast, is known to the human mind by the mode of necessary causality.

Referring to Augustine's De Trinitate IX, Scotus indicates that human knowledge of God is contingent upon Divine will. When a person knows God, a movement of the will of both God and the person is involved. A mutual relation is thus established between the knower (human) and the known object (God).[163] Human knowledge of God is not necessary knowing as is the case with our knowledge of natural objects. However, Scotus holds that when the human mind encounters God's self-communication and apprehends it, it cannot withhold its assent to the truth of God's reality.[164]

---

[160] Quodlibet q.13.n.34, trans. Alluntis/Wolter, 291-92: "Of the thing as existing, must include in itself a real and actual relation to the object itself."

[161] Quodlibet q.7.n.8; q.13.n.8.9; q.14.n.10, trans. Alluntis/Wolter, 166-67; 290-92; 324-25.

[162] Quodlibet q.13.14, trans. Alluntis/Wolter, 295.

[163] Ordinatio prol. n.72; I.d.3.n.486-493; II.d.3.q.8.n.17.

[164] Metaphysics IX.q.15.n.6, trans. Wolter, Will and Morality, 145. See also Quodlibet q.16.n.6, trans. Alluntis/Wolter, 375-76.

Now, God does not communicate with humans in just any way or at any time at random. Rather, because God's nature and mode of being is personal, says Scotus, God communicates in a personal manner. Here Scotus (in contrast to Aquinas, who follows Boethius' idea of person) aligns himself with Richard of St. Victor and derives his understanding of person from reflection on the economic Trinity.[165] For Scotus, "person" is properly understood as both relational and an ontological concept. The relationship is not simply a product of our understanding, but it is an inherent and ontological determination, as well.[166] Since human logic and abstractive knowledge cannot achieve that understanding, thus prohibiting us from knowing God in her/his own personal mode of being, God must be spoken of in terms of imperfect intuitive knowledge.

On the one hand, because the nature and mode of God's being is personal, true knowledge of God must include real and actual relation to the Divine as its proper object. But on the other hand, humans cannot have perfect intuitive knowledge of God in this life.[167] To resolve this dilemma, Scotus distinguishes five different grades of knowledge, stressing that God is the proper object of knowledge at all levels.[168] Because God is at the first level, complete and intuitive knowledge of Self and is Her own completely adequate and proportionate object, all other levels of knowledge are both dependent upon and contained in the first level. Thus, Scotus speaks of theology in two ways: *theologia in se*--the pure science of theology as it is in God, and *theologia in nobis*-- the knowledge humans can have of God as object.[169] Human

---

[165]*Ordinatio* 1.d.23.n.15; *Reportatio* 1.d.23.q.un.n.7; *Quodlibet* q.3.n.17, trans. Alluntis/Wolter, 74-75. See also *Reportatio* 1.d.25.q.2.n.5.6.7.14; *Quodlibet* q.3.n.3, trans. Alluntis/Wolter, 69-79.

[166]*Ordinatio* I.d.4.n.11-13; *Reportatio* I.d.25.q.2.n.5.14; d.26.q.5.n.5; *Quodlibet* q.3.n.4.6.9; q.13.n.11; q.19.n.20, trans. Alluntis/Wolter, 64-5, 68; 292-93; 435-36.

[167]*Quodlibet* q.7.n.8; q.13.n.11, trans. Alluntis/Wolter, *166-67; 292-93*.

[168]*Reportatio* prol. q.2.n.17.

[169]*Tractatus de primo* 4.n.36, trans. Wolter, *First Principle*, 98. See also Ordinatio prol.n.141.168.

knowledge of God, Scotus calls a *scientia practica* because it functions through his several gradations of the knowledge of God, each level tending toward the ultimate end, God.

The process of knowing God remains real, actual and personal, however because God freely chooses to manifest Self to us, and we, upon apprehending God as proper object, will to yield our minds to Truth and God-likeness.[170]

In addition, God reveals Self to us in Holy Scripture as the one who knows the Divine's own name and who can reveal it to us.[171] Humans are also infused with the inclination toward the Divine.[172] In the beatific vision, the most complete exercise of human cognition takes place. The beatific vision is not an added level of knowledge, but rather it is a gift of the free choice of the divine will. God can reveal Self to the created intellect as an immediate object of vision. In the beatific vision the human intellect will enjoy both abstractive knowledge and knowledge of the essence of God, as well as the intuitive certainty of being in the presence of God. The fullness of human cognitive powers will not be realized until then.[173]

Human knowledge of God is then worked out in mutual relationship between God and humans. The process of humans coming to know God is mutual because it is a real, actual and personal exchange between divine and human beings; it is freely chosen by each; and it is rooted in the univocity of being to be perfected in eternity.

Moral Theory

In Scotus's ethical thought, the discussion of free choice is supported by the primacy of contingent reality. The focus is on the person; the object of moral science

---

[170]*Ordinatio* prol.n.314-15; n.210-12; III.d.1.q.1.n.8.9; *Quodlibet* q.19.n.19, trans. Alluntis/Wolter, 423.

[171]*Tractatus de primo* 1.n.1, trans. Wolter, *First Principle*, 2.

[172]*Ordinatio* IV.d.23.q.1.n.10.11; d.25.q.1.n.9.

[173]*Quodlibet* 14.10, 14.36, trans. Alluntis/Wolter, 324-5.

is the perfection of the moral person.[174] For Scotus, the will is the sole rational faculty capable of self-determination and self-movement. It can will, nil or refrain from passing judgment on any object.[175] Because the affection for justice (*affectatio justitiae*) within, the will seeks to love according to the absolute value of the object of loving, and the superiority of the will is a rational superiority. *Affectatio commodi* seeks to love for the relative value of possession or use, and is "tempered" by *affectatio justitiae*.[176] According to Scotus's argument in *Quodlibet* 18, right reason determines the demands of justice.

The morally good act and its circumstances are determined by right reason or prudence and must be suitable to the agent, have a suitable object, and be performed under suitable circumstances (end, manner, time and place).[177] Love for God is, for Scotus, the self-evident first principle of praxis. He demonstrates in *De Primo Principio* that God is infinite being and therefore also infinite goodness.[178] Then he restates the Aristotelian/Stoic maxim, "Good is to be pursued, evil avoided," as the theological principle, *Deus diligendus est*. That God is to be loved is necessarily true because God is infinite goodness and as such, is worthy of all love. Therefore, love

---

[174]*Ordinatio* prol.5.q.1-2.n.262 (Vatican I 177.11-12).

[175]*Quaestiones Metaphysicam IX*, q.15, trans. Wolter, *Will and Morality*, 145-47. See also *Ordinatio* IV.49.1.10.n.10. (Vivès 21:333b). Wolter views this position in light of self-determination or rational self-direction which ideates the will from potency to act. See his essay "Native Freedom of the Will Key to the Ethics of Scotus," in Marilyn McCord Adams, ed., *The Philosophical Theology of John Duns Scotus* (Ithaca: Cornell University Press, 1990), 152.

[176]*Ordinatio* II.d.6.q.2.n.8. (Vivès 12:353) trans. Wolter, *Will and Morality*, 463.

[177]*Quodlibet* 18.1.n.3.18.8 trans. Alluntis/Wolter, 400.

[178]*Tractatus de primo principio*, 4:87-4:94, trans. Wolter, *First Principle*, 146-151. See also *Ordinatio* III.suppl.d.27, trans. Wolter, *Will and Morality*, 425: "As for the first, I say that to love God above all is an act conformed to natural right reason, which dictates that what is best must be loved most; and hence such an act is right in itself; indeed, as a first practical principle of action, this is something known *per se*, and hence its rectitude is self evident. For something must be loved most of all, and it is none other than the highest good, even as this good is recognized by the intellect as that to which we must adhere the most."

of God is the first commandment of the Decalogue and belongs to natural law *stricte loquendo*.[179]

The love of neighbor is commanded in the second table of the law, and it belongs to natural law *large loquendo*. The commandments of the second table are in harmony (*consona*) with the first principle, though not merely derived from it. Rather, the laws of the second table follow the intent of the divine Legislator and as such, they can indeed admit of exceptions in certain specific cases (God's command to Abram to kill Isaac; God's command to the Hebrews to plunder Egypt). If God, the first cause, were not free, there would be no way to account for human free choice or explain why contingent reality exists at all.[180]

God's power is manifested in two manners: *potentia absoluta* which allows God to act with indifference toward creation and *potentia ordinata* which requires conformity to rules predetermined by divine wisdom or motivated by the divine will.[181] Scotus understands human power on analogy to God's power. It is this difference which allows Scotus to determine different modes of divine activity. Scotus extends a similar kind of power to humans. However, while God cannot act in a contradictory fashion, humans can.[182]

While God can choose to act in one of several modes, in the divine revelation of the Decalogue, there is a clear indication of the ordinary mode (natural law) which

---

[179]*Ordinatio* IV.46.q.1.n.3 (Vivès 20:400) trans. Wolter, *Will and Morality*, 239-53. See also *Ordinatio* III.37.un.n.5 (Vivès 15:826a) trans. Wolter, *Will and Morality*, 269.

[180]For insight concerning Scotus's position on this issue see Mary Elizabeth Ingham, "The Condemnation of 1277: Another Light on Scotist Ethics," *Zeitschrift für Philosophie und Theologie* 37 (1990): 91-103; Edward Grant, "The Condemnation of 1277, God's Power, and the Physical Thought in the Late Middle Ages," *Viator* 10 (1979): 211-244; and John F. Whippel, "The Condemnations of 1270 and 1277 at Paris," *Journal of Medieval and Renaissance Studies* 7 (1977): 169-201. Also see Robert Prentice, "The Contingent Element Governing the Natural Law on the Seven Last Precepts of the Decalogue According to John Duns Scotus," *Antonianum* 42 (1967): 258-92.

[181]*Ordinatio* III.37 trans. Wolter, *Will and Morality*, 269. See also *Tractatus de primo principio*, 4:15 trans. Wolter, *First Principle*, 82. Also see *Ordinatio* I.44 trans. Wolter, *Will and Morality*, 255.

[182]Ingham, *Ethics and Freedom*, 79-80, cites *Ordinatio* II. n.18 (Vivès XII.394a).

the divine will prefers. Any exception to this ordinary mode involves first, God's choice of a new order making what is normally illicit, licit. Certainly, natural law remains the overall norm.[183] However, this ultimate freedom of God prevents any deontological perspective of morality, according to which a particular principle is the ultimate decisive factor for all time and all cases.[184] Rather, we see here an opening for communication between God and the human moral agent (discernment), a participative process through which the moral act is defined either in affirmation of the natural law, or as an exception--based on some solid indications, which are ultimately ordered to the first principle, *Deus diligendus est*. It is here that Scotus's unique blend of theology and philosophy emerges to frame a theological synthesis in which mutuality is normative.

Paradigms of Mutuality in Scotus's Theology

A deep concern found throughout Scotus's thought is to unify all of reality, both human and divine. He demonstrates a dynamic state of reciprocity that can be chosen by both human and divine partners which leads to the optimal thriving of humanity, while protecting the ultimate freedom of God. The suggestion of a relationship named by modern feminists as "mutuality" can be found in Scotus's metaphysical commitment to the univocity of being[185] in the essential order and his definition of moral goodness as the harmony of circumstances under the direction of right reason. These metaphysical constructs work in tandem with the paradigms of divine mutuality which he draws from divine revelation.

---

[183]Ingham considers it inappropriate to apply what Scotus says of God to the human political head. In fact, Scotus developed no political theory, as such. See Ingham, *Ethics and Freedom*, 113-45, esp. 119-21.

[184]See Thomas A Shannon, "Method in Ethics: A Scotistic Contribution,"*Theological Studies*, 54(1993):272-93.

[185]*Tractatus de primo principio*, 1.8, Pars I, q.3.n.89 (IV, 195.16-18), trans. Ingham, *Ethics and Freedom*, 20: ". . . a concept is univocal if it is sufficiently one so that it would be contradictory to affirm it or to deny it of the same object, or if taken as a middle term of a syllogism, two terms may be linked through it without fallacy of equivocation."

Scotus's metaphysical constructs are grounded in his apprehension of the nature of God, the divine essence which is expressed both as person and in the communion of the Trinity. Each trinitarian person images God's essence, but the three persons together reflect the divine in a way not possible for the single person. Divine revelation discloses several paradigmatic relationships between God and humankind of interest for our exploration of mutuality. These are the life of the Trinity, *imago Dei*, the Incarnation, Covenant with Moses, and acceptance in the order of merit.

Trinity

Scotus's entire understanding of reality is informed by his relational apprehension of the doctrine of the Trinity. Particularly rich is the distinction he makes between the activity of the Trinity *ad intra* and *ad extra*. The life of the Trinity *ad intra* is the incommunicable aspect of trinitarian life in which God functions necessarily only in relation to the other persons of the Trinity. The life of the Trinity *ad extra* is that aspect whereby the Trinity expresses its divine will, freely choosing creation, Incarnation and *acceptatio*.[186] Scotus asserts that the essence of God involves both aspects, however. Of the two dimensions, the incommunicable dimension is seen as the logical *suppositum* which is necessary for the *ad extra* relationship.

In Scotus's view, the basis for the relationship among the three persons reveals an important aspect of God's essence. In the *Lectura* discussion of *Ordinatio* I, 26 on the constitution of the divine persons, Scotus argues for some kind of constitutive cause for each person of the Trinity.

> Holding this position, it must be said that persons are not constituted by relationships, but by something absolute, and so three persons in God are first absolute, then referred to by relationship.[187]

We see that Scotus finds both person and communion essential to the divine life. By insisting on the integrity of each person of the Trinity in the absolute sense, he

---

[186]*Acceptatio* is the acceptance of a human act by God as a meritorious act. This will be detailed below.

[187]Ingham, "Integrated Vision," 213. Ingham cites *Lectura* n.54.

designates the basis upon which he can later assert that God's essence is also communion. There can be no relationship without at least two terms joined in interaction.[188]

Scotus is most clear about how God's essence is also communion in his discussion of the topic in the fourth of the *Quodlibetal Questions*. First, the Franciscan explains that:

> One can conceive of the *suppositum* within a relationship of origin prior to that relationship without any contradiction. One cannot, however, abstract from all relationships whatsoever and still retain a conception which possesses cognitive content. This is the case with persons of the Trinity. To say anything at all, there must be a *suppositum* or metaphysical entity of which relationship can be predicated.[189]

He then makes application of the metaphysical concept to the triune God, who "involves three persons whose personhood exists as substantial *suppositum* for any predication."[190]

Scotus's discussion of the Trinity is significant for understanding mutuality as a formal norm for several reasons: First, Scotus's affirmation of both the individual personhood of each member of the Trinity as a *suppositum* of divine relations makes it possible for the Trinity to also stand as a paradigms for human relations. Second, the individuality Scotus claims for each person of the Trinity provides the metaphysical basis for mutuality; the persons of the Trinity are constituted *as persons* through the relationship (*ad intra*) of mutuality. Insofar as the Trinity as a

---

[188]Ingham, "Integrated Vision," 214. Ingham cites *Quodlibet 1*.n.3. (Alluntis 1:5-6) trans. Alluntis/Wolter, 6-7.

[189]Ingham, "Integrated Vision," 217. Ingham cites *Quodlibet* 4.n.28 (Alluntis 4:61) trans. Alluntis/Wolter, 103-104.

[190]Ingham, "Integrated Vision," 217. Ingham cites *Quodlibet* 4.n.29 (Alluntis 4:63) trans. Alluntis/Wolter, 104.

communion of persons models the goal for human community, the Trinity models the relationship of mutuality as the goal of all human activity.[191]

Creation and *imago Dei*

Even though humans may come to realize that their source is God, they cannot naturally and fully grasp the image of God within the human soul. The limitations of human cognition allow humans to know only one aspect of the God/human relationship, from the human side. In addition to what philosophy can tell us, revelation (such as Genesis 2) is needed in order for us to grasp some notion of how we are related to God.[192] Scotus relies on revelation to further explicate that relationship between God and humans in his discussion of the divine action *ad extra*, specifically the Incarnation and *acceptatio*.

Incarnation

The Subtle Doctor joins a long line of Franciscan scholars in maintaining that the Word would have become incarnate even if *adam* had not sinned.[193] *Adam*'s sin was not the *sine qua non* for the Incarnation. Scotus stresses the importance of the humanity of Jesus as preordained for the glory of union with the second person of the Trinity.[194] This foreordaining of Christ was part of the manifestation of divine glory.

---

[191] Ingham, "Integrated Vision," 218.

[192] *Quodlibet* 14.nn.23-24 (Alluntis 1:83) trans. Alluntis/ Wolter, 338-9.

[193] See Robert North, "The Scotist Cosmic Christ," in *De Doctrina Ioannis Duns Scoti*, vol. III, 194-198. Positions of key Franciscans concerning the reason for the Incarnation are: Alexander of Hales (1200)--it would have been suitable had there been no sin; Matthew of Aquasparta (1282)--it was supposed for the perfection of the natural order; Raymond of Lull (1289)--its primary aim was to show forth the love of God; Roger Marston and William of Ware both believed it would have taken place "apart from sin"; Bonaventure affirmed that either position was orthodox, but he opted for the traditional Anselmian solution which held sin as the cause.

[194] Scotus's position on the Incarnation is articulated in his *Reportatio* and *Ordinatio* III.7.3. See Allan B. Wolter, "John Duns Scotus on the Primacy and Personality of Christ," in *Franciscan Christology: Selected Texts, Translations and Essays*, Franciscan Sources No. 1, ed. Damian McElrath (St. Bonaventure, NY: Franciscan Institute Publications, 1980), 147-55. See also Antonio Aranda, "La Cuestión Teológica de la Encarnatión del Verbo: Relectura de Tres Posiciones Caracteristicas," *Scripta Theologica* 25 (1993): 49-94.

In Scotus's view, the Incarnation was not necessitated by human choice to sin, for that would effectively subject God to the permission of sin. Rather, the Incarnation represents the manifestation of God's eternal glory and God's intent to raise human nature to the highest point of glory by uniting it with divine nature. Understood in this way, the Incarnation is a paradigm for generative mutuality.

> Mutuality between God and humanity was foreseen from eternity, begun in the Incarnation and is to be fully realized in the future when Christ will be "all in all." The summit of creation is the communion of all persons with one another and with God. . . . Christ is the very person in whom the human and divine achieve mutuality.[195]

Christ embodies the divine message that human actions are pleasing to God, human persons are pleasing to God and humans are loved by God. The fact that, according to Scotus, God's freedom and liberality inspired the Incarnation provides a positive enhancement of human nature that is not possible in a sin-centric understanding of the doctrine. God, in Scotus's view, is a creative artist who selected the human nature as the "material" most fitting to receive the highest glory of subsisting in the person of the Word.[196] This divine message provides the basis for Scotus's understanding of divine *acceptatio* and the order of merit.

Divine *acceptatio* and the Order of Merit

God is the source of all creation. God's essence is freedom to create, to reveal Godself, and to accept. *Acceptatio* is the fulfillment of divine freedom for creation. At the summit of creation is the human person, created by and for love. The *acceptatio* of the divine will is the acceptance of human actions inspired by charity and the establishment of a reward for those actions. In the order of merit, the human

---

[195]Ingham, "Integrated Vision," 222.

[196]*Ordinatio* III.7.q.3, trans. Wolter "On the Primacy," 151: "Now the sequence in which the creative artist evolves his plan is the very opposite of the way he puts it into execution. One can say, however, that in the order of execution, God's union with a human nature is really prior to his granting it the greatest grace and glory. We could presume, then, that it was in the reverse order that he intended them, so that God would first intend that some nature, not the highest, should receive the highest glory, as he bestowed natural perfection. Then secondly, as it were, he willed that this nature should subsist in the Person of the Word, so that the angel might not be subject to a [mere] man."

moral act is informed by charity and the reward intended by God is established by the divine will. In the process of the acceptance of human acts by the divine will, the human moral act is judged worthy for divine acceptance, enhanced by divine liberality, then rewarded beyond the action's natural value.[197]

In contrast to the naturally good act, the moral act must be chosen freely in accord with right reason, deal with an appropriate object, and be embellished with the theological virtues.[198] Scotus attempts to determine the precise capacity of humans for good.[199] He concludes that the human capacity for goodness, based on love, extends automatically to acts of charity or generosity out of love for God.

Scotus sets up the dialogical model for human/divine relationship in the prayer at the beginning of *Tractatus de primo principio*, referring to the establishment of the Covenant with Moses in Ex. 3:15:

> O Lord our God, true teacher that you are, when Moses your servant asked you for your name that he might proclaim it to the children of Israel, you, knowing what the mind of mortals could grasp of you, replied:'I am who am,' thus disclosing your blessed name. You are truly what it means to be, you are the whole of what it means to exist. This, if it be possible for me, I should like to know by way of demonstration. Help me then, O Lord, as I investigate how much natural reason can learn about that true being which you are if we begin with the being which you have predicated of yourself.[200]

---

[197]*Ordinatio* I.17.n.142 (Vatican 5:208) trans. Ingham, *Ethics and Freedom*, 217: "Here it can be said that in the meritorious act (about which we are now talking) I consider two, namely, that which precedes the notion of meritorious and in this level is included the substance of the act and its intensity and its moral rectitude; beyond that, I consider the very notion itself of the meritorious which is to be accepted by the divine will relative to a reward or to be acceptable or worthy to be accepted."
See also *Ordinatio* I. 17.n.144 (Vatican 5:208-9) trans. Ingham, *Ethics and Freedom*, 218: "... the aspect of merit is not completely had unless the aspect of worth is had or by being worthily able to be ordered to the reward (which is beatitude) and is worthily according to commutative or retributive justice ... therefore, such order according to justice is only from the divine will gratuitously ordering, and so the aspect of merit will be completely from the divine will ordering this act toward the reward."

[198]*Quodlibet 17* trans. Alluntis/Wolter, 388-98.

[199]Fernand Guimet, "Conformité a la droît raison et possibilité surnaturèlle de la charité," in *De Doctrina I. Duns Scoti*, vol. III, Acts Congressus Scotistici internationalis Oxonii et Edimburgi 11-17 Sept. 1966 celebration, Camille Bérubé, ed., (Roma: Cura Commissionis Scotisticae, 1968), 539-97.

[200]*Tractatus de primo principio*, trans. Wolter, *First Principle*, 2.

Here is found the metaphysical framework for his entire theory. Scotus defines merit as a relationship to divine acceptance which confers reward upon the human act. The order of merit is the fullness of mutuality between the divine and human wills.[201] As Ingham explains:

> God in no way merits for the person, nor does divine acceptance provide the entire basis; the act must be inspired by charity and performed by right reasoning. The meritorious act is truly mine. . . . 'the act of merit is in my power, supposing general influence, if I have use of free will and grace.' The divine act completes the human by ordaining it to the end to which natural reason aspires but is incapable of attaining: full union with God. . . . 'but completion of the essence of merit is only in my dispositive power, finally to be so disposed that from divine disposition there follows the completion of my action.'[202]

The unknown element in the order of merit is how much beyond its value God will reward a meritorious act (divine liberality). As Scotus concludes:

> [I]t must be known that [it is] by eternal divine acceptance, by which God from eternity, seeing this act elicited from such principles, has willed to ordain it toward the reward, has willed its merit; which when considered accordingly by such divine acceptance, would not, according to strict justice, be worthy of such reward from its intrinsic goodness from its own principles; proof, because the reward is always greater than the good in merit and strict justice does not render a greater for a lesser good. And so it is well said that God always rewards beyond worth, universally beyond certain worth which an act merits,--since that such be worthy of merit, this is beyond nature and its intrinsic goodness, from gratuitous divine acceptance; and even more, beyond that other which normally would be accepting the act, whenever God rewards by pure liberality.[203]

Divine liberality is a cause for optimism and hope for the future of humanity. It is free relationship, which exists within reality for both the human and the divine, that constitutes the dignity of the person and the value of each human act. In charity

---

[201]*Ordinatio* I.17.n.146 (Vatican 5:209) trans. Ingham, *Ethics and Freedom*, 223-24.

[202]Ingham, "Integrated Vision," 224. Ingham quotes her translation of *Ordinatio* I.d.17.n.146 (Vatican 5:209).

[203]*Ordinatio* I.17.n.149 (Vatican 5, 210-211) trans. Ingham, *Ethics and Freedom*, 225.

and freedom humans choose the "good" and God rewards their efforts out of divine liberality and *acceptatio*.

Divine revelation characterizes Jesus Christ as "the image of the invisible God" (Col. 1:15-18) who unites all of creation with God and one another. In Eph. 1:3-10, St. Paul speaks of "God's hidden plan" the intent of which was from the beginning, to bring everything together under Christ. Here then, we see the divine intention is to bring all of creation to grace and glory along two distinct but unifying paths (1) the Incarnation and (2) Divine *acceptatio* in which, through grace, humans are rewarded beyond the demands of justice.[204] Both paths also serve as ground for mutuality between God and humankind.

Feminists' Notion of Mutuality and Scotus's Thought

Cosmic Mutuality

Scotus's positive view of creation and the Incarnation includes not only humans, but the entire cosmos. The notion of *haecceitas* not only defines individuality, but it also points to an aspect of each element of the universe that is known only to God. We find here grounds for cosmic mutuality. "Thisness" denotes the profound uniqueness of each element that shapes the relationship between God and the whole of creation, because of its origin in the one Creator. "Thisness" is enhanced by the Incarnation insofar as all are joined to the one who fulfills "God's hidden plan" (Eph. 1:3-10). We discover here in Scotus then, the basis for a fluid dynamism between God, all of creation and humans with the entire cosmos that respects the boundaries of the individual elements, yet which also empowers each element toward the maximal thriving of all in proper relation to God.

Gender Mutuality

Scotus gives a very mixed message concerning what we have defined as gender mutuality. On two separate occasions he addressed the issue of the ordination of women; on yet another occasion, he challenged Aristotle's theory of the totally passive role of women in human procreation.

---

[204]Ingham, "Integrated Vision," 226.

151

In his *Opus oxoniense* of 1304 and his *Reportatio parisiensis* of 1303, Scotus contends that it is the will of Christ that women not be admitted to Holy Orders.[205] Now, Scotus reasoned that the Church and the apostles could never deprive anyone of anything ordinarily considered necessary or beneficial for salvation, unless it was *also* the will of Christ. Thus, since Christ is the Lord of all and the only authority worthy of making such a prohibition, barring women from ordination must be the will of Christ.[206]

In addition, Scotus argues that women are not capable of teaching and preaching as is required of those in Holy Orders, and therefore are excluded from consideration for ordination.[207] To illustrate his point further, Scotus holds up the Virgin Mother of Christ. Certainly, he argues, if anyone deserved Holy Orders, she did. Since she was not given the grace of Holy Orders, certainly other women (of lesser stature) should not expect to be called to Orders, either.[208]

On the other hand, in the context of his discussion of the real motherhood of Mary and the Incarnation, Scotus makes a surprisingly modern sounding argument for the active role of women in the process of human procreation. Unlike Aquinas, Scotus rejects the Aristotelian biological theory that claims only a passive role for women in the human act of procreation. In his critique of Aristotle's theory of human procreation, Scotus presents four strong arguments in defense of women's active role in the procreative process.[209] In the course of his argument, Scotus stresses that the positive active influence of a woman can be so great that her son can become more like his mother than his father.

---

[205] *Opera omnia*, vol.19, *Opus oxoniense* and vol.24, *Reportatio parisiensis*, (Paris: L. Vivès, 1895-).

[206] *Opus oxoniense*, 19.140.

[207] *Reportatio* 24.370 (Vivès).

[208] *Reportatio 24.370-371 (Vivès).*

[209] *Ordinatio* III.d.4.n.2.1-4 in *John Duns Scotus: Four Questions on Mary*, Latin and English texts trans. Allan B. Wolter (Santa Barbara, CA: Old Mission Santa Barbara, 1988), 77-79.

Given his otherwise balanced and open system, one can only speculate concerning the inconsistent approach to the status of women in Scotus's thought. Certainly one must look to the Condemnations of 1277 and to Scotus's efforts to remain orthodox (that is, not to be perceived as associating himself with some heretical groups who ordained women) for partial answers.[210] Yet, given the wide influence in his day of Aristotle's biological misunderstanding of women and their role in human procreation, Scotus's strong challenge to that theory can reasonably be viewed as an antecedent of gender mutuality as defined by modern feminists.

Generative Mutuality

The optimistic view of humankind found in Scotus ultimately flows from his refusal to identify human sin as sole the reason for the Incarnation. As we have seen, Scotus's cognitive theory outlines how humans become privy to insights concerning God's nature and actions in history. In the relationship which is willed by both God and humans, there is a fluidity and continuity of Divine initiative and human response in love, which advances in a redemptive fashion in history toward the glory of the Beatific Vision. Scotus's moral theory demonstrates how the human will is constituted to respond to not only God's initiative, but to all good it encounters (*affectiones commodi* and *affectiones justitiae*). All human efforts toward doing good are perfected in the order of merit through God's *acceptatio*, the acceptance and reward of human actions inspired by charity. Thus we have in Scotus an antecedent of generative mutuality, the human/divine partnership in ongoing creation and redemption.

---

[210] See the discussion of the divine *potentia absoluta*, above. It seems that Scotus would interpret this prohibition by Christ, in an otherwise open sacramental system, as an exception similar to the command of Abraham to kill Isaac or the plunder of the Egyptians. Moreover, evidence that Scotus crafted his system well within the boundary of the 1277 Condemnations would indicate that he would not venture to move beyond the status quo on this issue. See John Hilary Martin, "The Injustice of Not Ordaining Women: A Problem For Medieval Theologians," *Theological Studies* 48 (1987): 303-316. Martin notes 304, n.2 that: "Wyclif, or Wyclifites, seemed to have countenanced, even encouraged, sending out women priests and preachers" according to Thomas Netter of Walden (1370-1430).

Social Mutuality

Three aspects of Scotus's thought combine to form the basis for social mutuality: (1) his views on the economic Trinity (2) the moral principle, *Deus diligendus est*, and (3) his political and economic theory.

Scotus's understanding of trinitarian relations forms the grounding of his understanding of the love of neighbor, which in turn, strongly implies the concept of social mutuality articulated by modern feminists. While each person of the Trinity is distinct, each is constituted in relation to one another. This is also the case with humans in relationship to God and one another.

At the heart of the relationship of humans to God and one another is love; not a possessive, domineering or jealous love, but rather a dynamic, reciprocal love that empowers and enhances life *ad intra* and *ad extra*. This love is expansive and inclusive.[211] Since the nature of the love of the God, the Font of All Goodness, requires that the lover seek only what enhances the well-being of the beloved, we find here in Scotus not a minimalistic concern for the other, but a radical, generous, overflowing sort of identification with the needs of the other (including the lesser ones) by the lover. In such an identification we find an analogy of social mutuality.

Scotus did not write a systematic treatise on society or politics. In the context of his treatise on the sacrament of penance, however, we find the discussion of whether or not restitution for sin is necessary prior to licitly receiving the sacrament. Within this discussion we find also a treatment of the origin of civil authority and the use and ownership of property.[212] Scotus insists that the best form of government is a form in which the people who are the subjects of governance participate in determining its structure and give it authority over them.[213]

---

[211]Ordinatio III.suppl.d.37.10, trans. Wolter, *Will and Morality*, 283: "Hence it follows that if God is to be loved perfectly and orderly, then the one loving God must will that his neighbor love God; but in so willing, he is loving his neighbor."

[212]Ordinatio IV in *Duns Scotus' Political and Economic Philosophy*, Latin Edition and English Translation, trans. Alan B. Wolter (Santa Barbara, CA: Old Mission Santa Barbara, 1989).

[213]Ordinatio IV.1, trans. Wolter, *Political*, 39.

In the realm of economic life, Scotus's fundamental assumptions are that "the earth is the Lord's and the fullness thereof" and that it is only human law that allows the concept of "mine" into the human vocabulary.[214] True to Francis of Assisi, who admonished that we are to live in the world as "strangers and guests" (Lv. 25:23), Scotus, did not identify use and ownership, even in the case of fungibles.[215] According to Scotus, money is to be viewed as a fungible because by its nature it is essentially a medium of exchange, which is "consumed" in the process of exchange for other goods. Scotus also joined in the condemnation of usury.

While Scotus's simple approach to economics seems almost naive and unbefitting such a great mind, in reality, if his very basic principles were ever followed they could radically and positively impact the quality of economic and political life. The participation of the governed in a context where there is no absolute ownership and where material wealth and goods are considered the generous bequest of a Gracious Host, suggests a radical contrast to the modern political and economic reality. Here there is rather, an open acknowledgement of the contingent nature of wealth, and a radical recognition of the sole purpose of material goods, namely, the divinely ordained well-being of the entire cosmos. Both political and economic decisions must be made through the participation of the entire community, with the common good as the first and foremost criterion.

At the heart of the economic and political philosophy of this Franciscan lies consideration for the poor. Because all humans are but caretakers and borrowers of a common creation, to use material goods unjustly is effectively to steal, especially from the poor. The poor most often suffer the repercussions of injustice disproportionately. Thus, it is the poor who require repayment when circumstances

---

[214] Ordinatio 1, trans. Wolter, *Political*, 35.

[215] Ordinatio IV.1, trans. Wolter, *Political*, 51. See Ibid., 105, n.'s 5 and 6. See also St. Francis of Assisi, *Regula bullata (1223)*, Chapter 4-6, trans. Regis J. Armstrong and Ignatius C. Brady, in *Francis and Clare: Complete Works*, The Classics in Western Spirituality (New York: Paulist Press, 1982), 140-41.

prevent the person who has been wronged from being repaid directly.[216] In these instances, Scotus's political and economic philosophy provides analogs to the modern feminist notion of social mutuality.

CONCLUSIONS

Our purpose in this chapter has been to illustrate selected moments in the history of Christian thought that serve as antecedents and analogs to modern feminists' notion of mutuality. The two major figures treated here, Aquinas and Scotus, need to be understood against the whole backdrop of the twelfth and thirteenth centuries.[217] It is beyond the scope of this project, to elaborate that background or to compare and contrast the two figures in detail;[218] however, some brief comparative comments are in order.

Modern feminists have leveled a great deal of criticism at Aquinas. Scotus, as we have shown, created a system laced with the notion of mutuality. In comparison to Aquinas, however, Scotus has had far less influence upon Christian thought.[219] This lack of influence can partly be accounted for, by the fact Scotus died before he could edit his meticulously and subtly reasoned thought into a stylized systematic work comparable to Thomas's *Summa theologiae*.[220] Scotus's work simply has not been as prominent as Aquinas's and the work of the Subtle Doctor has not attracted extensive attention or criticism from feminists. In recent years, with the

---

[216] Ordinatio IV.4, trans. Wolter, *Political*, 79-87.

[217] For a concise review of these periods see *Dictionary of the Middle Ages*, s.v. "Philosophy and Theology, Western: 12th Century. See also Ibid., s.v. "Philosophy and Theology, Western: 13th Century Crisis." In addition see, Ibid., s.v. "Philosophy and Theology, Western: Late Medieval."

[218] Indeed, such a comparison is largely inappropriate. Most Scotus scholars including Paul Vignaux, Camille Bérubé, and Dom Ordon Lottin prefer to examine Scotist thought in light of Henry of Ghent rather than of Aquinas. Any comparison of Aquinas and Scotus must take into account the fact that Aquinas wrote with the express purpose of developing a moral theory and Scotus did not. See also Ingham, *Ethics and Freedom*, 239-58 for a discussion on comparing the thought of Scotus and Aquinas.

[219] Ingham, *Ethics and Freedom*, 1-5.

[220] Ibid., 3-5.

partial completion of a critical edition of Scotist sources, Scotus is receiving more scholarly attention. A feminist criticism of Scotus will, no doubt, be forthcoming.

We have shown several differences between Scotus and Aquinas, differences suggesting that Scotus's thought is somewhat more compatible with Christian feminist mutuality than is Aquinas's. To recall but one example, Aquinas's starting point for discussing the Trinity is *theologia* rather than *oikonomia*. That combined with his Boethian notion of person makes for a transcendent God and a theoretical relationship between humans and the divine. Scotus on the other hand, begins his treatment of the Trinity by examining both the economic and theological Trinity, and concludes that the essence of the Trinity is both "person" and "communion." Scotus's notion of person is modeled on the economic Trinity. This being the case, it seems easier to find in Scotus the support feminists seek for the positive value of immanence and embodiment than it is in Aquinas.

Clearly, this and other points of comparison between Aquinas and Scotus requires further and extensive analysis. Nonetheless, what we have shown here gives convincing evidence that modern Christian feminists are solidly within the Christian tradition when they build upon the antecedents and analogs in the theological systems of Aquinas and Scotus that we have illuminated in this chapter.

CHAPTER 3

TWENTIETH CENTURY ANTECEDENTS TO CHRISTIAN FEMINISTS' NOTION OF MUTUALITY MARTIN BUBER AND H. RICHARD NIEBUHR

INTRODUCTION

The purpose of this chapter is to examine two instances in twentieth century Christian thought in the wherein antecedents of Christian feminists' notion of mutuality may be found. I first evaluate major aspects of Martin Buber's dialogical philosophy. Next, I review central aspects of H. Richard Niebuhr's ethic of responsibility. Finally, I draw conclusions concerning how specific aspects of the modern Christian feminists' notion of mutuality are found in the works of Buber and Niebuhr.

MARTIN BUBER: MUTUALITY IN HIS DIALOGICAL PHILOSOPHY

This frequently quoted passage from Buber's *I and Thou* readily sums up his dialogical thought.

> Relation is mutual. My Thou affects me, as I affect it. We are moulded together by our pupils and built up by our works. The "bad" man, lightly touched by the holy primary word, becomes one who reveals. How we are educated by children and animals! We live our lives inscrutably included within the streaming life of the universe. . . . In the beginning is relation.[1]

---

[1]Martin Buber, *I and Thou*, trans. Ronald Gregor Smith (New York: Charles Scribner's Sons, 1958), 15-16. Smith's choice of "mutuality" for the German, Gegenseitigkeit is not uncontested. See Martin Buber, *I and Thou*, trans. Walter Kaufmann (New York: Charles Scribner's Sons, 1970), 67-69: "Relation is reciprocity." A typical comparison of the Kaufmann and Smith translations of *Ich und Du* is James A. Moran, "Book Review: *I and Thou* by Martin Buber. A New Translation, With Prologue and Notes by Walter Kaufmann," *New Scholasticism* 46 (1972): 268-70.

The preferred German translation of "mutuality" is Gegenseitigkeit. See *The New Cassel's German Dictionary: German/English-English German*, 1962 ed., s.v. "mutuality." See also *Langenscheidt's New College German Dictionary: German/English-English German*, 1990 ed., s.v. "mutuality." Cf. *Cassel's* s.v. "reciprocity," is "gegenseitige Beziehung; die Gegenseitigkeit; Wechselwirkung, Reziprozität." Cf. *Lagenscheidt's*, s.v. "reciprocity," is "Reziprozität; die Gegenseitigkeit." Smith consistently translates all of these terms as "mutuality."

At the heart of a cluster of books Martin Buber published (1923-54) delineating and elaborating his dialogical philosophy is *Ich und Du*, which explicates the core of the philosophy.[2]

Buber's Basic I - Thou Philosophy
Word Pairs (Wörtpaare): I-It (Ich-Es) and I-Thou (Ich-Du)

Buber's opening assertion in Ich und Du (*I and Thou*) is:
To man the world is twofold, in accordance with his twofold attitude. The attitude of man is twofold, in accordance with the twofold nature of the primary words which he speaks. The primary words are not isolated words, but combined words. The one primary word is the combination I-Thou. The other primary word is the combination I-It; wherein, without a change in the primary word, one of the words He and She can replace It. Hence the I of man is also twofold. For the I of the primary word I-Thou is a different I from that of the primary word I-It.[3]

Buber does not claim a dualism in reality, but rather dual relations within reality; an I-It and an I-Thou relation. Buber maintains that the "I" of the I-It relation relates to the other as an objective, detached observer, while the "I" of the I-Thou relationship

---

I follow Smith, using "mutuality" as the preferred translation for several reasons. First, in the Kaufmann *and* Smith translations of *I and Thou*, in the "Postscript" passages (where Buber clarifies his understanding of the "in between" of the two fold relation) "mutuality" is used rather than "reciprocity." Secondly, "mutuality" does not bear the connotations of bargaining or contractual arrangements as strongly as does "reciprocity." In addition, when one of Buber's most faithful interpreters, Emil L. Fackenheim addressed the nature of the I-Thou relationship (in May 1974, after Kaufmann's translation was readily available) he cited Buber's *Werke*, and consistently used "mutuality" as the preferred term. See Emil L. Fackenheim, "Martin Buber: Universal Aspects of the I-Thou Philosophy," *Midstream* 20 (1974): 46-56. Finally, Maurice S. Friedman, perhaps the worlds foremost Buber scholar has stated concerning the I-Thou relation: "It is characterized by mutuality, directness, presentness, intensity, and ineffability." See Maurice S. Friedman, "Martin Buber's Theory of Knowledge," *The Review of Metaphysics* 8 (1954): 268. See also Friedman's "Walter Kaufmann's Mis-meeting With Martin Buber," *Judaism* 31 (1982): 232-39.

²Buber, *I and Thou* (K), 183. Kaufmann names these works: *Ich und Du* (1923), *Zweisprache* (1930), *Die Frage an den Einzelnen* (1936), *Über das Erzieherische* (1926), *Das Problem des Menschen* (1943), *Urdistanz und Beziehung* (1950), and *Elemente des Zwischenmenschlichen* (1954).

³Buber, *I and Thou* (S), 3. Cf. Buber, *I and Thou* (K), 53. Cf. "Ich un Du," *Martin Buber: Werke*, vol. 1, *Schriften zur Philosophie* (München: Kösel-Verlag KG und Heidelberg: Verlag Lambert Schneider GmbH, 1962), 79. Feuerbach's "I-Thou" influenced Buber's thought. See Martin Buber, *Between Man and Man*, trans. Ronald Gregor Smith (New York: Macmillan Publishing Company, 1965), 148.

relates to the other with commitment and involvement.[4] The I-Thou relation is the relationship between subject and subject which involves the whole being of each[5]. The I-It relation is a polarity of subject and object and the experience of the object is within the subject.

The World of Relation

The Three Primary Spheres

The world of relation exists in three primary spheres.[6] The first sphere is the relation between humans and nature, a relationship is expressed in silence. The second sphere is the relation between human persons. The third sphere of relation is between humans and spiritual forms. One can encounter these three spheres of relation from either the I-It or the I-Thou attitude.[7]

The Dynamics of Relating: Meeting and Dialogue

Buber uses the metaphors "dialogue," "speaking," "hearing," "responding," and "being addressed" to describe the dynamics of the exchange between the two subjects in the I-Thou relationship.

---

[4] Buber, "Ich und Du," *Werke I*, 79-80; cf. Buber, *I and Thou* (K), 53-55; cf. Buber, *I and Thou* (S), 3-4.

[5] Buber's notion of wholeness is ties directly to the idea of the original relation. See *I and Thou*(S), 4,18. There is no "I" that stands by itself. In any relationship, each party brings every aspect of itself (including its history) to the relationship. See Maurice Freedman, *Martin Buberlife of dialogue*, Phoenix edition (Chicago: University of Chicago Press, 1976), 30-33,90-97,esp.92.
For a discussion of the major influences on Buber's development of the concepts of "I" and "Thou," see Friedman,*Life of Dialogue*, 34-53; Will Herberg, ed., *The Writings of Martin Buber* (New York: The World Publishing Company, 1968),11-39; Paul Pfuetze, *The Social Self* (New York: Bookman Associates, 1954),117-227. See Buber *Between Man and Man*. 148. Buber credits Feuerbach with influencing his thought the most. Feuerbach holds that it is the whole person, not cognition that is the beginning of philosophizing. Understood the person as an individual who is always in relation. In addition, see Buber's criticism of Kirkegaard's notion of the "single one," n.21 below. Also see Fackenheim, "Martin Buber: Universal Jewish Aspects of the I-Thou philosophy," 46-56.

[6] Buber, "Ich und Du," *Werke I*, 81; cf. Buber, *I and Thou* (S), 6; cf. Buber, *I and Thou* (K), 56-57.

[7] The notion of mutuality is an issue only in I-Thou relationships. Robert E. Wood, *Martin Buber's Ontology*, Northwestern University Studies in Phenomenology and Existential Philosophy, ed. John Wild (Evanston: Northwestern University Press, 1969), 42 discusses the I-It relation.

Buber elaborated his basic concept of "meeting" (*Vereinigung*) in several works which followed *Ich und Du*.[8] Buber classifies three types of dialogue.[9] First, there is genuine dialogue in which both participants are fully mindful of the other and each turns to the other intending to establish a lively, mutual relationship between her/himself and the other. Second, there is technical dialogue which is utilitarian in that the purpose of the relation is objective understanding. Finally, there is the monologue, disguised as a dialogue. Here, an individual is at the same location as are others (in terms of time and space) but s/he, under the impression that s/he has escaped isolation, speaks to the other but fails to truly encounter the other and is ultimately left to her/his own resources.

In genuine dialogue in order for two persons to move from mere communication to communion or "meeting" (*Vereinigung*), an evocative continuity needs to be established between "I" and "Thou." Without either person relinquishing his/her substance or being absorbed into the other, each comes to live within the other. The fundamental movement in genuine dialogue is a "turning towards the other."[10] This meeting is characterized by a sacredness, a sacramentality that fills both persons with wonder and grace.[11] This "turning" effects an "inclusion" (*Umfassung*) that enables the I-Thou relationship to happen. "Inclusiveness is the complete

---

[8] See n. 2 above. "Meeting" is a kind of social communion considered as a primary act of being. See Martin Buber, "Replies to My Critics," in *The Philosophy of Martin Buber*, Library of Living Philosophers ed. Paul Arthur Schilpp and Maurice Friedman (La Salle, IL: Open Court Publishing, Co., 1967), 705. Also, Emmanuel Levinas, "Martin Buber and the Theory of Knowledge," in Ibid., 136-39. Cf. Buber, "Ich und Du," *Werke I*, 85. Cf. Buber, *I and Thou* (S), 11.

[9] Buber, "Zwiesprache," *Werke I*, 192. See Ibid., 180: "Dialogue" is a conversation between two subjects. Each turns to the other, listening to the other as if nothing else mattered. Cf. Buber, "Dialogue," in *Between Man and Man*, 8.

[10] Buber, "Dialogue," in *Between Man and Man*, 22. Cf. Buber, "Zwiesprache," *Werke I*, 195: "Die Dialogische Grundbewegung is Hinwendung."

[11] Buber, "Zwiesprache," *Werke I*, 177-78. Cf. Buber, "Dialogue," in *Between Man and Man*, 4-6. Here Buber describes such an encounter.

realization of the submissive person, the desired person, the partner, not by the fancy but by the actuality of being."[12]

This realization of the other by both partners in genuine dialogue can take place within any of the three primary spheres. Buber states: "The first rests on an abstract but mutual experience of inclusion."[13] In this form of the relationship, inclusion is so basic that it can flow in unexpected moments of understanding even between those who disagree; it is acknowledgement of the other connected to the spiritual aspect of the person.[14]

Two other forms of the genuine dialogue relationship deal with the full reality of human life and being. One is typical of helping relationships which are necessarily one-sided, and is grounded in "a concrete, but one sided experience of inclusion."[15] The other is typical friendship and is "based on a concrete and mutual experience of inclusion."[16]

The false dialogue or monologue moves toward the "I" viewing the other as an "It," but that extreme is not quite reached. The other is reoriented within the province of the "I"'s self. Here the "I" is reflexive in that it turns what is outward back into the self (in contrast to the situation of meditation where the "I" brings itself to dwell in the other.) The other is not viewed in her/his uniqueness, but rather is seen as serving the purposes of the "I." Buber gives several illustrations of this

---

[12]Buber, "Education," in *Between Man and Man*, 97. Cf. Buber, "Über das Erzieherische," *Werke I*, 801.

[13]Buber, "Education," in *Between Man and Man*, 99. Cf. Buber, "Über das Erzieherische," *Werke I*, 804: "Die eine beruht auf einer abstrakten, aber gegenseitigen Umfassungfahrung."

[14]Buber, "What is Common to All," trans. Maurice Friedman in *Knowledge of Man: Selected Essays*, ed. Maurice Friedman (Atlantic Highlands, NJ: Humanities Press International, 1988) 79. Cf. Buber, "Dem Gemeinschaflichen Folgen," *Werke I*, 454.

[15]Buber, "Education," *Between Man and Man*, 99. Cf. Buber, "Über das Erzieherische," *Werke I*, 804. Educational relationship is discussed below.

[16]Buber, "Education," in *Between Man and Man*, 101. Cf. Buber, "Über das Erzieherische," *Werke*, 806:" . . . auf die konkrete und gegenseitige Umfassungserfahrung gegründet."

relationship--the self-aggrandizing conversationalist, the aggressive orator, or the self-bedazzled lover.[17]

Martin Buber's Notion of Mutuality
Definition and Translation Issues

Walter Kaufmann (who translated *I and Thou* at the request of Rafael, Buber's son) most consistently translated *Gegenseitigkeit, Wechselwirung, gegenseitigte Beziehung* as "reciprocity," while Ronald Gregor Smith translated the terms as "mutuality." Just as in English "reciprocity" and "mutuality" bear a similar meaning and are frequently used synonymously, such is the case with these several terms in German. Indeed, Buber used several words (*die Gegenseitigkeit, die Wechselwirkung, gegenseitige Beziehung*) synonymously to express the relational aspect of the "between."

Buber's "*Nachwort*" (postscript), to *Ich und Du* is useful in clarifying the more precise meaning of these terms in relation to his broader enterprise.[18] In the *Nachwort* one finds nearly total agreement between Smith's and Kaufmann's translation of various terms. Here too, Buber is more direct in his meaning, utilizing anglicized "*Mutualität*" and "*Reziprozität*" to clarify the text.

Mutuality: Its Modes In Buber's Three Spheres of Relation
Sphere of Human Relations

According to Buber, a person, in the interhuman sphere, is being vis-a-vis one to the other, and the explication of this sphere is the dialogical form. Buber's notion of the "between" is the nature of "the meaningful dialogue itself that proceeds between [the] two men and into which the acoustic and optical events fit, the dialogue that arises out of the souls and is reflected in them . . ."[19] To be engaged in the vis-a-

---

[17]Buber, "Dialogue," in *Between Man and Man*, 19-21. Cf. Buber, "Zweisprache," *Werke I*, 192-93.

[18]München: Kösel-Verlag KG, 1962, 161-70.

[19]Buber, "Replies to My Critics," in Schilpp, *Philosophy of Buber*, 707.

vis situation is to be embedded in mutuality or "entering mutuality."[20] The partners in a situation of mutuality are the "I" and the "Thou" and they are established through mutuality: "I become through my relation with Thou; as I become I, I say Thou."[21] The status and character of personality itself is established in the sphere of human mutuality.[22] Buber claims that mutual relations between humans are an irreducible fact.

In the interhuman sphere of relation each subject brings his/her whole person to the encounter; s/he is addressed as "Thou" and addresses the other as "Thou." It is this sort of "meeting" that Buber considers the apex of human relating. "No deception penetrates here; here is the cradle of real life. . . . All real living is meeting."[23] Not only do two individuals relate to one another, but they are formed and shaped by one another as they are present to one another. The moment the other becomes an object in any way--one sees the other in terms of her/his goodness, physical characteristics, or profession, for example--the relationship reverts to an I-It relation.

Helping Relations

Buber discusses three interhuman relationships in which full mutuality can never be fully achieved; the helping relationships between teacher and student, therapist and patient, and priest and penitent.

In the situation between the teacher and the student,". . . the pupil cannot experience the educating of the educator. The educator stands at both ends of the

---

[20]Buber, "Education," in *Between Man and Man*, 87. Cf. Buber, "Über das Erzieherische," *Werke I*, 791.

[21]Buber, *I and Thou* (S), 11. Cf. Buber, "Ich und Du," *Werke I*, 85. Buber reacts to Kierkegaard in "The Question of the Single One," in *Between Man and Man*, 65: "The single one is the man for whom the reality of relation with God as an exclusive relation includes and encompasses the possibility of relation with all others . . ."

[22]Buber, *I and Thou* (S), 27, 62. Cf. Buber, "Ich und Du," *Werke I*, 96.

[23]Buber, *I and Thou* (S), 9, 11. Cf. Buber, "Ich und Du," *Werke I*, 83 and 85: "Hierher langt kein Trug: hier ist die Wiege des Wirklichen Lebens . . . Alles wirkliche Leben ist Begegnung".

common situation, the pupil at only one end. In the moment when the pupil is able to throw himself over and experience from over there, the educative relation would burst asunder, or change to friendship."[24] In Buber's view, education is based on "a concrete but considered experience of inclusion."[25] He believes that the educational relationship simply cannot endure if the pupil lives through the shared experience from the teacher's perspective: "Whether the I-Thou relation comes to an end or assumes the altogether different character of friendship, it becomes clear that the specifically educational relationship is incompatible with complete mutuality."[26] The limits to the student/teacher relationship are necessary if the teacher is to teach and the student is to learn. Buber reasons that the teacher is the medium for transmitting knowledge and experience to the student. Though full mutuality is absent, teacher and student can still relate as I-Thou. However, the education process precludes any full partnership that disrupts the pedagogical relationship.[27] It appears that Buber finds "degrees" in the extent to which mutuality is necessarily absent in the student/teacher relationship, depending on the age and maturity of the student. He even makes reciprocity a priority for adult education.[28]

---

[24]Buber, "Education," in *Between Man and Man*, 100-101. Cf. Buber, "Über das Erzieherische," *Werke I*, 806.

[25]Buber, "Education," in *Between Man and Man*, 97-98. Buber's notion of "inclusion" acknowledges three degrees: (1) focusing of attention on the other (2) acting to make the other present (3) entering into full dialogue with the other, experiencing the situation from the position of the other as well as from one's own. The fullness of dialogue is the ideal state of being mutual. Cf. Buber, "Über das Erzieherische," *Werke I*, 802-803.

[26]Buber, *I and Thou* (S), 131-32. Cf. Buber, "Ich und Du," *Werke I*, 166-67.

[27]Numerous educators challenge Buber's rigid approach here, both in terms of professional teaching styles and kinds of friendship. Brian Hendley's "Martin Buber on the Teacher/Student Relationship: A Critical Appraisal," *Journal of Philosophy of Education* 12 (1978): 141-48 cites Elizabeth Telfer who argues that friendship defined under certain specific conditions can contribute to the education process.

[28]Ibid., 146. Hendley cites Buber, "A Venture in Adult Education," in *The Hebrew University of Jerusalem* Silver Jubilee Volume (Jerusalem: The Hebrew University Press, 1952), 117: "Contact is the root and basis of education . . . a connection between personalities, so that one human entity confronts another. . . . What is wanted is true reciprocity
. . . a truly reciprocal conversion in which both sides are full partners. The teacher leads and directs it,

In the relation between therapist and patient, the patient calls out to the self of the doctor "that selfhood that is hidden under the structures erected through training and practice."[29] The therapist's role is definitively that of the helper who enters "into the elementary situation between the one who calls and the one who is called."[30] Buber rejected the "objective" Freudian styles of therapy. He held that psychological illness resulted from impaired or broken relationships between persons. The therapist, by entering into a genuine, though nonmutual dialogue with the patient, meets the patient in the abyss of human existence between the helper and the one in need. Buber concluded that through the process of relating, healing can take place: "The utmost that can be expected of him, as I have said, is only this: that the reaching out beyond his familiar methods, he conduct the patient, whose existential guilt he has recognized, to where an existential help of the self can begin."[31]

The third relation to which Buber denies the possibility of full mutuality is that between one holding a sacerdotal position and the penitent.[32] Placing this denial in context with Buber's notions of personal guilt, confession, and repentance it seems that the sacerdotal reference is to the Christian priesthood in which lies the particular power to absolve the confessed sins of the penitent.[33] By virtue of ordination, the priest is given the power to dispense absolution, imparting Christ's healing grace to the penitent, enabling her/him to forgive her/himself of wrong doing. The process

---

and he enters it without any restraint. I call this the "dialogue principle" in education."

[29] Martin Buber, *Believing Humanism: My Testament 1902-1965*, Credo Perspectives, trans. Maurice Friedman (New York: Simon and Schuster, 1967) 140.

[30] Ibid.

[31] Buber, "What is Man?," in *Between Man and Man*, 148.

[32] Buber, *I and Thou* (S), 133. Cf. Buber, *I and Thou* (K), 179. Cf. Buber, "Ich und Du," *Werke I*, 168: "Am nachdrucklichsten ware die normative Beschränkung, der Mutualität wohl am Beispiel des Seelsrogers darzulegen, weil hier eine Umfassung von der Gegenseite her die sakrale Authentiztät des Auftrags antsasten würde. Jedes Ich-Du-Verhältnis innerhalb einer Beziehung, die sich als ein zielhaftes Wirken des einen Teils auf den andern spezifiziert, besteht kraft einer Mutualität, der es auferlegt ist, keine volle zu werden."

[33] Zvi E. Kurzweil, "Buber on Education," *Judaism* 11 (1962): 48.

includes the penitent seeking out the priest in order to benefit from his/her power to absolve. The Priest/penitent turns to the other in an I-Thou relationship that is conditioned by the need for mediation and the power to mediate between the penitent and God. Certainly, both partners in the relationship practice inclusion, but unequally.

In distinguishing the three "nonmutual" relationships, Buber does not insist on the complete absence of (any degree of) mutuality, for some degree of mutuality is essential to relation as such. Rather, he sets the conditions of each relationship such that in each of the situations maximal opportunities for the student, the patient and the penitent are opened up and each is enabled to move toward a more full form of reciprocity and to mutuality with others (beyond the helping relationship). In short, mutuality is the ultimate goal of each helping relationship and thus, temporary limitation of each relationship is required and placed in the service of this goal. This fits Buber's broader enterprise which is to promote the optimal humanizing of all human meeting.

Friendship

Friendship is definitive of "the true inclusion of one another by human souls."[34] Friendship is the particular and unique relation in which both partners are constantly addressed by the other. It is in true friendship that trust is engendered and nourished, making possible other kinds of loyalties; even faith in God.

Of the three forms of dialogue (genuine, technical and false), inclusion is most complete in the genuine dialogue that takes place between friends. In friendship there is direct participation in the partners lives, not physically, but ontically.[35] The immediate connectedness of the partners goes beyond empathy (in which one 'transposes' one's feelings into the other from one's interior) and is the opposite of empathy in that it: "is extension of one's own concreteness, the fulfillment of the actual situation in life, the complete presence of the reality in which one

---

[34]Buber, "Education," in *Between Man and Man*, 101.

[35]Buber, "What is Man?," in *Between Man and Man*, 170.

participates."³⁶ In friendship a partner will be able to extend him/herself to live through an event in the lived activity of the other, without forfeiting anything of the felt reality of her/his own activity. Though the inclusion of each partner by the other is deep and whole, each remains distinct and independent within the meeting. In friendship, mutuality is most complete. The "Thou" of each partner relates the "I" of each back to the other. That means each partner apprehends the experience of the other from the other side (exterior) and reflects information about that experience back to the other.

Mutuality In The Nonhuman Spheres of Relations

Buber deals with mutuality in two other spheres of I-Thou relations. In nonhuman relations, the fundamental mark of the I-Thou relation is not full-blown mutuality of address and response, but the intuition on the human side of the full ontological dimension of the other.³⁷ In order to distinguish the modes of mutuality in the nonhuman spheres, we need to examine more closely Buber's 1957 "*Nachwort*" (postscript) to *Ich und Du* (*I and Thou*) where he defines several "degrees" or modes of mutuality. There Buber first, distinguishes mutuality from reciprocity. "*Reziprozität*" is used to express the operative dynamic of the ideal of mutuality and refers to any situation where two (or more) beings act upon one another.³⁸ "*Mutualität*" is the ideal of the "between" or the positive value of the nearness of relations possible when both partners are human beings.³⁹ Here each partner

---

³⁶Buber, "Education," in *Between Man and Man*, 97.

³⁷Wilhelm Dilthey's distinction between methodologies of natural and human sciences influenced Buber on this point. Objectivity and detachment characterize the former and personal participation the later. In Dilthey's *Lebensphilosophie* human experience (and thus necessarily, human sciences) is embedded in (and can only be understood by) participation in the stream of life. See Buber, "The Question of the Single One," in *Between Man and Man*, 40-82. Also Buber, "Replies to My Critics," in Schilpp, *Philosophy of Buber*, 693. Cf. Diogenes Allen, *Philosophy for Understanding Theology* (Atlanta: John Knox Press, 1985), 270-71.

³⁸Buber, "Ich und Du," Werke I, 163. Cf. Buber, *I and Thou* (S), 126.

³⁹Buber, "Ich und Du," Werke I, 162, 163-64, 165, 166. Cf. Buber, *I and Thou* (S), 124-25, 126, 127.

experiences an event both from his/her own side and from the side of the other. As such, "*Mutualität*" is considered a form of grace for which one must always be prepared and which one never gains as an assured possession.[40] Buber names three levels of mutuality which result from the inborn, *a priori* quest for all beings toward mutuality in relation: full mutuality, threshold, and prethreshold.

In his study on mutuality within the sphere of non-human relations, Donald L. Berry, working from the schema presented in Buber's *Nachwort* to *Ich und Du*, divides the sphere of Nature into three categories: (a) Threshold [zoological] (b) Pre-threshold [botanical] and (c) Subthreshold [Empedoclaen elements--earth, air, water, fire].[41] Berry studies references to nature in the primary Buber sources and analyzed each, considering their appearance in "early" or "late" Buber--whether prior or following *Ich und Du*, 1923; and four functions they serve in Buber's broader enterprise. Berry notes that as Buber's thought on relationality developed, increasingly he used animals as examples to illustrate the meaning of mutuality. There are more references to the Empedoclaen elements in Buber's early mystical works than in his later, more mature writings. The line of demarcation between "early" and "late" is his discovery of the "in between." "Early and late Buber will insist that no thing or being, in and of itself, is necessarily excluded from being that with which I find myself in relation."[42]

Threshold of Mutuality

Buber distinguished relationships with animals as being at "*die Schwelle der Mutualität*" (the threshold of mutuality) because animals are not twofold like humans.[43] The evidence that twofoldness is latent in them is seen in that they do "turn" toward another being and contemplate objects, as did the horse, cat and dog

---

[40] Buber, "Ich und Du," Werke I, 166. Cf. Buber, *I and Thou* (S), 127.

[41] Donald L. Berry, *Mutuality: The Vision of Martin Buber* (Albany: State University of New York, 1985).

[42] Ibid., 23.

[43] Buber, "Ich und Du," *Werke I*, 162. Cf. Buber, *I and Thou* (S), 126.

Buber observed.[44] With himself vis-a-vis the animals, Buber discovered the foundational elements of relation: (a) the "primal setting at a distance" which presumes each one in the relation has become an "independent opposite" and (b) an "entering into relation" in which one becomes detached from one's own being *(Sein)* "what is" *(das Seiende)* and enters into relation with it.[45] While animals are capable of the former, they are only latently capable of the latter. While humans can be aware of their own present and future, as well as the future of the *world* beyond them, the animal's concern in Buber's estimation is confined to its present, future, the future of its young, and its immediate environment. Thus, the extent of mutuality possible in a relation with animals is limited.[46]

On the positive side, Buber discovered significant tendencies toward mutuality in the interchange from the side of the horse, the cat and the dog. The otherness of the horse is preserved, the horse can invite communication (as well as respond) and it can affirm the other. The cat's communication with its eyes is significant for Buber; the glance is a powerful medium of relation.[47] In the instance with the dog, there was a definite exchange "between" the child and the dog, that didn't have a conceptual nature. The child *knew* in the depths of her/his being an exchange had taken place, but only upon reflection and an attempt to articulate the occurrence was the experience conceptually framed. It is doubtful that a dog would attempt the later step, and therein lies a difference in the capacity for mutuality at the threshold level.

---

[44]Buber, "Dialogue," in *Between Man and Man*, 22-23 (horse); *I and Thou* (S), 96 (cat); Martin Buber, "Interrogation of Martin Buber," conducted by Maurice Friedman, in *Philosophical Interrogations*, ed. Sydney Rome and Beatrice Rome (New York: Harper Torchbooks, 1970), 47 (dog).

[45]Martin Buber, "Distance and Relation," trans. Ronald Gregor Smith. *The Hibbert Journal* 49 (1951): 105-107.

[46]Ibid., 106-107.

[47]Buber, *I and Thou* (S), 96-97.

Prethreshold Mode of Mutuality

Buber's "prethreshold" mode of mutuality is characteristic of the sphere that reaches from the "stones to [the] stars."[48] While animals are able to participate in mutuality to the extent that they can "turn toward the other being and contemplate objects," botanical entities participate in a mode of mutuality by simply being. It is, for example, the beholder of the tree who grants the tree "the opportunity to manifest" its living wholeness and unity.[49] Buber provides several illustrations of this relationship. There is a tree which "has to deal with me as I must deal with it, only differently."[50] In this example it is made clear that the two basic features of this "prethreshold" relation are particularity and wholeness. "I encounter no soul or dryad of the tree, but the tree itself."[51] The nature of the encounter is also purposeless, nonutilitarian and gratuitous; the "I" moves toward the "other" and allows the "other" to be itself, not assimilating the other into her/his world. A second example is that of a meeting with a fragment of mica.[52] It is through this experience of making contact with the mica that Buber realized the potential mutuality with prethreshold beings: "But when one that is alive arises out of things, and becomes a being in relation to me, joined to me by its nearness and its speech, for how inevitably short a time it is nothing to me but Thou!"[53] Buber clearly realized a particularity or distinctness of each "other," a "between" amid himself and the mica; in other words, a relationship. In both of these examples, mutuality is present, though not full blown. The "I" does not take the "other" into him/her/itself and the "Thou" manifests itself by simply being.

---

[48] Buber, *I and Thou* (S), 126. Cf. Buber, "Ich und Du," *Werke I*, 163.

[49] Ibid.

[50] Buber, *I and Thou* (S), 8. Cf. Buber, "Ich und Du," *Werke I*, 82.

[51] Ibid.

[52] Buber, *I and Thou* (S), 98-99. Cf. Buber, "Ich und Du," *Werke I*, 144-45.

[53] Buber, *I and Thou* (S), 98. Cf. Buber, "Ich und Du," *Werke I*, 145.

The Subthreshold of Mutuality

Donald L. Berry, in his analysis of subhuman things and beings referenced in Buber's works, asserts that the subhuman entities can be grouped according to their ability to respond to human presence.[54] Humans, as expected, are deemed most responsive, followed by animals, plants and finally by the Empedoclaen elements. Berry further claims a category within the sphere of nature for the Empedoclean elements (in addition to those distinguished in Buber's *Nachwort*) which he names "subthreshold." This category emerged from Berry's analysis which included Buber's criteria for distinguishing one being from the other in their discreetness. Berry notes that Buber was concerned to develop an epistemological approach which was more hospitable to the linkage he saw between humans and the world than was the traditional subject-object approach. This problem is resolved in Buber's early works, by the notion of "oneness" (*"Über Jakob Boehme"*) and the notion of "unity" (*Daniel*).[55] In early Buber, the elements--sea, mica, lake-- were viewed from a perspective of traditional German nature mysticism.[56] From that perspective the "other" (elements) cannot say "Thou" in response to the gaze of the "I," nor "step", in their overagainstness, in relation to me.[57]

Mutuality in the Sphere of *geistige Wesenheiten*

The third sphere of relation in which mutuality is present is that of "spirit in phenomenal forms" (*geistige Wesenheiten*).[58] There are three areas in which the

---

[54] See Wood, *Buber's Ontology*, 70-71.

[55] Berry, *Mutuality*, 16.

[56] Maurice S. Friedman, *Martin Buber: The Life of Dialogue*, 3rd revised ed. (Chicago: University of Chicago Press, 1976), 27-30. Early influences on Buber were Meister Eckhart and Jakob Boehme.

[57] Berry, *Mutuality*, 23.

[58] There is no really good way to translate this term from the German, and Buber's elaborations on the idea are scattered through his works. Robert E. Wood, *Buber's Ontology*, 42-45 and 50-52, is credited with clarifying Buber's meaning. Wood supports "forms of the spirit" as the better translation. He states: "'Form' suggests something broader than essence, for form includes all aspects of human

forms "of the spirit" are realized: knowledge, art and action.[59] Humans respond to the forms of the spirit by "forming, thinking, and acting."[60] When a human stands overagainst an other in the sphere of the forms of the spirit, s/he relates either in terms of I-It or I-Thou. In so doing the person enters the world of the spirit in which s/he will encounter the "demanding silence of forms."[61] Buber understands our response to this encounter as the source of speech, even though the encounter is "supralinguistic." Buber also speaks of the forms of the spirit as the "transcending mystery of Being," and as the eternal Thou that shines through all other relations.[62] Human relation to "spirit in phenomenal forms" (*geistige Wesenheiten*) is something which addresses us through all things, something that transcends the world, an incipient relation to God. From such encounters come expressions of knowledge, art, and ultimately, faith in the transcendent Thou.[63] We now examine more closely two manifestations of *geistige Wesenheiten*, art and the Eternal Thou.

Mutuality and Art

Buber seems to assume that the area of art includes thought and action--the creative activity of humans.[64] Both thinking and living are in Buber's view a kind of

---

creativity.... `Spirit' and `spiritual' (Geist and geistig) in German thought furnish an exact correlate to `form.' Hence the solidity of the suggested translation `forms of the spirit'." Wood also cites Ronald Gregor Smith, *Martin Buber* Makers of Contemporary Theology Series (Richmond: John Knox Press, 1967), 6, n.19, where Smith states that in a letter of December 6, 1957, Buber told him that geistige Wesenheiten means "spirit in phenomenal forms."

[59]Buber, *I and Thou* (S), 40-42. Cf. Buber, "Ich und Du," *Werke I*, 104-06.

[60]Buber, *I and Thou* (S), 6. Cf. Buber, "Ich und Du," *Werke I*, 81.

[61]Buber, *I and Thou* (S), 102. Cf. Buber, "Ich und Du," *Werke I*, 147.

[62]Buber, "Who is Man?," in *Between Man and Man*, 177. Cf. Buber, "Des Problem des Menschen," *Werke I*, 375. See also Buber, "Man and His Image-work," in *Knowledge of Man*, 153-55. Cf. Buber, "Der Mensch und Sein Gebuild," *Werke I*, 437-38.

[63]Buber, "Man and His Image-work," *Knowledge of Man*, 153-55.

[64]Ibid., 152. Poetry is different from other art forms. It engages one beyond any single sense. Buber acknowledged poetry as a unique sphere in the tradition of romanticism rooted in the "primal structure of man as man" and expressed through language that transcends space and time.

art. Both are a Gestalt which encounters the human person and draws her/him to embody it in a work.[65] The world meets the "other" and a work of art arises as witness to the realm of the spirit that encompasses nature and points to the transcendent mystery of being.[66] There is a danger that in the objectification necessary in embodiment, the work will become a mere It. But, embodiment is necessary to secure the vision in the work; "it [c]ould be said that every thing in the world, either before or after becoming a thing, is able to appear to an I as its Thou."[67] It is the inspired words and works that constitute human creativity and human contribution to the community of the world.

Mutuality in this sphere is found in the disposition of the artist to be taken hold of by the form and the response that is evident in the subsequent work of art. The form that is met is drawn out of the spaceless, timeless, present into the spaciotemporal world through the creative activity of the artist. It enters the common world of humanity as an It which can then become a Thou in relation to others who observe or interact with the creation.

Mutuality and the Eternal Thou

The relationship between the human and the divine marks the apex of the I-Thou relationship in the sphere of geistige Wesenheiten.[68] Where only movement and silence (due to the inability to "speak") distinguishes the human/nature relationship,

---

[65]Buber claims in his "Distance and Relation," in *Knowledge of Man*, 110: "Art is neither the impression of natural objectivity nor the expression of spiritual subjectivity, but it is the work and witness of the relation between substantia humana and substantia rerum, it is the realm of 'between' which has become form." Cf. Buber, "Urdistanz und Beziehung," *Werke I*, 418.

[66]Buber, "Who is Man?," *Between Man and Man*, 177.

[67]Buber, *I and Thou* (S), 17-18. Ibid.: "The It is the chrysalis, the Thou the eternal butterfly--except that situations do not always follow one another in clear succession, but often there is a happening profoundly twofold, confusedly entangled." Cf. Buber, *I and Thou* (K), 69. Cf. Buber, "Ich und Du," *Werke I*, 89.

[68]Insofar as God is also a Person, "Mutualität" is also possible between humans and God; the relationship between God and humans includes humans being addressed by God in every biographical and historical event, empowered, and enabled to respond to God. This relationship cannot be proven any more than can the existence of God. Buber, *I and Thou* (S), 136-37. Cf. Buber, "Ich und Du," *Werke I*, 169-70.

and dialogue denotes the intrahuman relationship, the human/divine relationship is characterized by silent awe that is beyond speech. Here, the human stands at the brink of a relationship with God, the Eternal Thou (that which addresses her/him and to which s/he replies). Here it is only fitting that it is the whole being that speaks this basic utterance.[69] It is in this sphere that humans meet directly what is present indirectly in all other I-Thou relations, the "Eternal Thou." The Eternal Thou is present in all relations as a horizon against which each partner gazes; it is present in every Thou addressed; all spheres are included in it, yet, it is contained in none of them. The Eternal Thou can never dissolve into an "It" because there is no way that the human can actually objectify or alienate it.

> The Eternal Thou can by its nature not become It; for by its nature it cannot be established in measure and bounds, not even in the measure of the immeasurable, or the bounds of boundless being; for by its nature it cannot be understood as a sum of qualities, not even as an infinite sum of qualities raised to a transcendental level; for it can be found neither in nor out of the world; for it cannot be experienced, or thought; for we miss Him, Him who is, if we say "I believe that He is"--"He" is also a metaphor, but "Thou" is not.[70]

Buber understands the human/divine dialogue as something that is readily accessible to all people; indeed, dialogue is the way of humanity.[71] In revealing Godself to

---

[69]Buber, *I and Thou* (S), 6. Cf. Buber, "Ich und Du," *Werke I*, 81.

[70]Buber, *I and Thou* (S), 112. Cf. Buber, "Ich und Du," *Werke I*, 154: "Das ewige Du kann seinem Wesen nach nicht zum Es werden; weil es seinem Wesen nach nicht in Maß und Grenze, auch nicht in das Maß des Unermeßlichen und die Grenze des Unbegrenztseins gesetzt werden kann; weil es seinem Wesen nach nicht als eine Summe von Eigenschaften, auch nicht als eine unendliche Summe zur Transzendenz erhobener Eigenschaften gefaßt werden kann; weil es weder in noch außer der Welt vorgefunden werden kann; weil es nicht erfahren werden kann; weil es nicht gedacht werden kann; weil wir uns an ihm, dem Seienden verfehlen, wenn wir sagen: "Ich glaube, daß er ist"--auch "er" ist nicht eine Metapher, "du" aber nicht."

[71]See Paul E. Pfuetze, *The Social Self* (New York: Bookman Associates, 1954), 118. Influenced by Kant, Buber asserted that "the ultimate transcendental reality, the Ding an sich, can only be `realized' in the lived life." See Will Herberg, *The Writings of Martin Buber* (New York: The World Publishing Company, 1956), 12. "Realization" and "orientation" are related. "Orientation" is the objective attitude that orders the environment for knowledge and use. "Realization" is the approach that brings out the inner meaning of life in intensified perception and existence. Buber criticizes Kant's purely ethical position. He maintains the paradoxes found in the ultimate unknowability of the ultimate notions of God and life on the one hand, and the immediate personal relationship the believer may have with God,

humanity, God chose to do so in a personal and dialogic manner. This is not to reduce God to the personal, but rather to believe what God revealed to Moses in the theophany recounted in Exodus.

On the one hand, God is infinite and humans are finite, standing over and against God. On the other hand, God is absolute, yet *also* a whole and holy *person*. This paradox that God is an "Absolute Person" is both antinomy and a marvelous truth held by the Hasidim.[72] Buber translated Exodus 3:14, *Ehyeh asher ehyeh*, as "I shall be there as I shall be there."[73] In Buber's view, God doesn't make a metaphysical statement here, but rather a statement concerning care, presence, response and mutuality. Buber asserts that God is at the same time both "inclusive" (a person) and "exclusive" (transcendent).

---

as well as her/his intuitive *knowing*, on the other. Cf. Martin Buber, *Pointing the Way*, trans. Maurice S. Friedman (New York: Harper and Brothers, 1956), 27-29. Buber explains the Hebrew sense of "to know" is to "embrace lovingly." "Realization" is related to mystical, unifying kind of knowing of the hero, poet, sage or prophet for whom, a reality arises from their experiences, which allows them to embrace all things.

[72]Martin Buber, "The Love of God and the Idea of Deity," in *The Eclipse of God: Studies in the Relation Between Religion and Philosophy*, trans. Robert M. Seltzer (1988; reprint, Atlantic Highlands, NJ: Humanities Press International, Inc., 1989), 60. Cf. "Gottesfinsternis," *Werke I*, 548: ". . . [daß] er als Person liebt und als Person geliebt werden will. Und ware es nicht anders, so ist er als er den Menschen schuf, Person geworden, um ihn zu lieben und von ihm geliebt zu werden, um mich zu lieben und von mir geliebt zu werden. Denn mag es zu sein, daß auch Ideen geliebt werden: nur Personen lieben. Und auch der vom Glauben überwaltigte Philosoph, der--das System auch jetzt noch, ja heftiger als je mit beiden Händen umklammernd--die Liebe zwischen Gott und Mensch als Liebe zwischen Idee und Person deutet, bezeugt doch jene in ihrer Wirklichkeit, die aus Gegenseitigkeit besteht. Auch die Philosophie, die, um das Sein Gottes rein zu halten, ihm das Dasein abspricht, weist gegen ihren Willen auf den Brückenbogen des Dasein hin, der sich über den beiden Pfeilern, dem allmächtigen und dem hinfälligen, unerschütterlich spannt."
See also Buber, *I and Thou* (S), 135. Cf. Buber, "Ich und Du," *Werke I*, 169: "Dieser Grund und Sinn unseres Daseins konstituiert je und je eine Mutualität, wie sie nur zwischen Personen bestehen kann. Der Begriff der Personhaftigkeit ist freilich völlig außerstande das Wesen Gottes zu deklarieren, aber es ist erlaubt und nötig zu sagen, Gott sei *auch* eine Person . . . in die Sprache eines Philosophen, die Spinozas, übersetzen wollte, müßte ich sagen, von Gottes unendlich vielen Attributen seinen uns Menchen is nicht zwei, wie
Spinoza meint, sondern drei bekannt: zu Geisthaftigkeit . . . und Naturhaftigkeit . . . als drittes das Attribut der Personhaftigkeit . . . Und nur dieses Dritte, das Attribut der Personhaftigkeit, gebe sich uns in seiner Eigenschaft als Attribut unmittelbar zu erkennen."

[73]Martin Buber, "Der Brennende Dornbusch," in *Martin Buber: Werke*, vol. 2, *Schriften zur Bibel* (München: Kösel-Verlag KG und Heidelberg: Verlag Lambert Schneider, 1964), 61-62.

Summary of Buber's Notion of Mutuality

To summarize Buber's understanding of mutuality, we must return to each of three the spheres of relations: human/human, nature/human and human/*geistige Wesenheiten*. We have seen how Buber understands the capacity for entering into meeting with the other (things or beings) as an *a priori* for humanity and humanity alone[74] and that there are different grades of the capacity for mutuality.[75] Repeatedly, Buber names mutuality as the essential ingredient of the I-Thou relation in all the spheres of relating. He is most clear that mutuality is real, if not full in both human and nonhuman I-Thou relations.

Buber is forthright in admitting the difficulties this presents and the vagueness that still remains in his notion of mutuality. However, he repeatedly asserts: "Relation is mutual." (*Beziehung ist Gegenseitigkeit.*)[76] He pleads his case for not abandoning the quest for full mutuality in spite of limitations, both human and natural: "I am concerned that the I-Thou relation be realized where it can be realized, and I cannot declare where it cannot be realized. I am concerned that the life of man be determined and formed by it. For I believe that it can transform the human world, not into something perfect, but perhaps into something very much more human, according to the created meaning of man, than exists today."[77]

It is clear that in Buber's view mutuality involves a stance that opens both parties of a relation to an exchange which allows each to become more whole (or distinct) as a result of the exchange. In the case of humans, the effect is an enrichment of the person. In the case of the nonhuman it is a bodying forth that addresses the human, enabling him/her to address the entity in return, calling it "Thou." In the most full and most clear mode of mutuality, there is a "turning" of one

---

[74]Buber, "On the Landscapes of Leopold Krauer," in *Believing Humanism*, 120.

[75]Rome and Rome, "Interrogation," 37.

[76]Buber, *I and Thou*, 15-16. Cf. Buber, "Ich und Du," *Werke I*, 88.

[77]Rome and Rome, "Interrogation," 38-39.

person to the other, the naming each "Thou" by each. In the least full and least clear mode of mutuality, such as with nonhuman entities, there is an attitude required which disallows a utilitarian objectification of the other. Mutuality requires humans to appreciate the wholeness of the other, in and of itself.[78] It is this profound appreciation that obligates humans: to practice sound ecology which respects threshold mutuality in animals and prethreshold mutuality in plants and elements; to see the "Divine Spark" in human persons regardless of physical or mental capacity; and to place the human in perspective with the wider cosmos, and value all accordingly.

Mutuality as a Norm in Buber's Work

Buber definitely understands mutuality as real and normative for ethical life. For Buber, norms are implicit in the I-Thou relationship. Norms take on absoluteness because the Eternal Thou is part of every I-Thou relationship. Buber is critical of dogmas and universal norms, as such.[79] His notion of responsibility is key to understanding his criticism. In Buber's view, the responsibility of an "I" to a Thou" is similar to Kant's second formulation of the categorical imperative: `Never treat one's fellow as a means only but always also as an end of value in himself.'[80] Also, according to the Hasidim, each person is responsible for coming to know her/himself in relation to the Torah *and* community.[81] Buber's notion of what motivates ethical

---

[78]See Hiam Gordon, "A Method of Clarifying Buber's I-Thou Relationship," *Journal of Jewish Studies* 27 (1976): 71-83. Gordon relates stories in which a personal experience clarifies the meaning of mutuality in the I-Thou relationship.

[79]Buber, "Dialogue,"in *Between Man and Man*, 16: "Even the most universal norm will at times be recognized only in a very special situation. There is a direction, a `yes,' a command hidden even in a prohibition, which is revealed to us in moments like these. In moments like these the command addresses us really in the second person, and the Thou in it is no one else but one's own self. Maxims command only the third person, the each and the none."

[80]Friedman, *Life of Dialogue*, 200.

[81]From an early age, themes of the Hasidim are constant in Buber's thought: Community--life together in spiritual harmony; Personal responsibility for one's actions in community; Individual value-- all bears the *nitzotz* (Divine Spark); God's accessibility to all, especially the *am ha-aretz* (simple poor); Reinterpretation of messianism--Judaism is religion and ethical practice; and A metaphysically positive attitude toward language--*"Shema, Yisroel!"* starts a dialogue between God and creatures. See Maurice

behavior is rooted in his understanding of the ontological reality of "life between man and man." He thus stresses the concern for the other as an end in him/herself, which is rooted in one's direct relation to the other and to a higher end which s/he serves.[82] In Buber's "dialogical ethics," "is" and "ought" are joined "without losing their tension in the precondition of authentic human existence--making real the life between man and man."[83]

While the two person model (I-Thou relation) for the fullness of mutuality shows some of the same limitations which exist in other spheres of relations, it also brings into relief those situations where mutuality is possible at all. Humans are capable of relating at all of the levels of mutuality, but more fully, because humans are rational, self-aware beings. Buber considers mutuality as a normative requisite for human life itself: "And in all the seriousness of truth, listen: without It a human being cannot live. But whoever lives only with that is not human."[84] Since it is in the "It World" that humans experience the breakdown of mutuality, and in I-Thou relations that mutuality is at its fullest, mutuality is necessary for maximum human flourishing. Buber also points to mutuality as characteristic of a life of fuller and deeper thriving, using the term to affirm what is optimally possible in an encounter. I suggest that in an ecologically and spiritually threatened age like our own, Buber would readily call mutuality normative for any ethical system: "The experience from which I have proceeded and ever again proceed is simply this, that one meets another."[85] Buber's

---

Friedman, *Martin Buber's Life and Work*, 3 vols. (New York: Dutton, 1981-83).

[82]Friedman, *Life of Dialogue*, 201.

[83]Ibid.

[84]Buber, *I and Thou* (K), 85. Cf. Buber, *I and Thou* (S), 34. Cf. Buber, "I und Du," *Werke I*, 101.

[85]Rome and Rome, "Interrogation," 47. See also Maurice Friedman, "The Bases of Buber's Ethics," in *The Philosophy of Martin Buber*, 171-200. Ibid., 177, Friedman cites Buber's *Eclipse of God*, 93: "One can believe in and accept a meaning or value . . . only if it has been revealed to me in my meeting with being, not if I have freely chosen it for myself from among the existing possibilities and perhaps have in addition decided with a few fellow creatures: `This shall be valid for me from now on'." Regarding moral norms, Friedman cites Buber's *Between Man and Man*, 114: "No responsible person

broader enterprise was to do away with human alienation. An ethical stance that regards mutuality as a formal norm is strongly implicit in his entire system of thought. "If I face a human being as my Thou, and say the primary word I-Thou to him . . . he is Thou and fills the heavens. . . . All else lives in his light."[86]

H. RICHARD NIEBUHR'S RESPONSIBILITY: ANTECEDENT TO MUTUALITY

Helmut Richard Niebuhr is indebted to Martin Buber for his emphasis on the encounter with the Thou in the I-Thou relationship as the key to understanding reality.[87] The importance of the "thous" for the self in Niebuhr's view is the fact that the self is conditioned by the presence of other selves. Niebuhr, like Buber, understands the believer as a self-in-community. The responsible self must therefore decide on the fitting response in light of the data received from the "thous" s/he encounters and in relation to the Eternal Thou.[88] With a unique blend of Christian monotheism and the I-Thou philosophy of Buber, Niebuhr focused on the self as the central locus for his ethics of responsibility. Responsibility is Niebuhr's interactional framework for an ethics that keeps intact the relationships of religion with morality and the individual with society. Niebuhr assumed, however, that morality is primarily located in the experiences and relationships of the feeling, thinking, deciding self. He

---

remains a stranger to norms. But the command inherent in a genuine norm never becomes a maxim and the fulfillment of it never a habit. Any command that a great character takes to himself in the course of his development does not act in him as apart of his consciousness or as material for building up his exercises, but remains latent in a basic layer of his substance until it reveals itself to him in a concrete way."

[86]Buber, *I and Thou* (S), 8.

[87]See Claude Welch, "Review Essay: H. Richard Niebuhr-- *Faith on Earth: An Inquiry into the Structure of Human Faith*," *Religious Studies Review* 17 (1991): 292. See also Libertus A. Hoedemaker, *The Theology of H. Richard Niebuhr* (Philadelphia: Pilgrim Press, 1970), esp. Chapters 1 and 2.

[88]H. Richard Niebuhr, *Responsible Self: An Essay in Christian Moral Philosophy*, Paperback ed., ed. Richard H. Niebuhr (New York: Harper and Row, Publishers, 1978), 72, 100-107. Buber concentrates on the grace of the I-Thou relationship itself, but Niebuhr focuses on the influence of the "Thou" in forming the other. Niebuhr also follows George Herbert Mead's approach to human behavior.

therefore, concentrated the greater portion of his attention on the study and understanding of the responsible self.

Niebuhr stressed God as the center of value and the importance of relation--"what is fitting." He demonstrated the usefulness of an ethical methodology based on the relational and relatedness, while avoiding the pitfalls of pure situationalism.[89] Niebuhr's notion of responsibility opens the way for modern Christian feminists' placing of mutuality as a central normative concept in Christian social ethics.

Niebuhr's Key Theological Assumptions/ Theory of Responsibility

We begin our study of possible antecedents to mutuality in Niebuhr's works by examining some key theological assumptions that undergird his theory of responsibility. Niebuhr's central theological concern is the meaning of existence for an individual in the concrete situation in which the self emerges as a free, rational-moral being and for whom the quest for meaning is a forced option.

From Natural Faith to Monotheism

Niebuhr began by observing that all people are believers; all people have faith in something. He distinguished the natural faith of daily life from religious faith in that the latter makes life worth living.[90] Niebuhr's idea of religious faith included *fiducia* and *fidelitas*--personal trust and reliance on some thing or someone (Luther,

---

[89]James Gustafson, "Christian Ethics and Social Policy," in *Faith and Ethics: The Theology of H. Richard Niebuhr* Paul Ramsey, ed. (New York: Harper and Row, 1957), 120-22. See Paul Ramsey, "The Transformation of Ethics," in Ibid., 142. Ramsey states: "The words 'relational' and 'related' better represent Niebuhr's position than the words 'relative' and 'relativism' which he uses more frequently. Indeed, the technical philosophical designation of objective relativism' is not really adequate to describe the point of view of relational value theory; and ought perhaps to be replaced by some such expression as 'subjective relatedness' or preferably 'relational objectivism'." Also Ibid., 151-172.

[90]H. Richard Niebuhr, *Radical Monotheism and Western Culture*, (New York: Harper and Row, 1960), 16 [hereafter cited as *Radical Monotheism*]: "[Faith is] a fundamental personal attitude . . . apparently universal or general enough to be recognized . . . the attitude and action of confidence in, fidelity to, certain realities as the sources of value and objects of loyalty." Also Ibid., 118: ". . . no man lives without living for some purpose, for the glorification of some god, for the advancement of some cause." See also Niebuhr's *Meaning of Revelation* (New York: Macmillian Publishing Company, 1941; reprint, New York: Macmillian Paperbacks Edition, 1960), 17. Niebuhr quotes Luther: "Trust and faith of the heart alone make both God and idol. . . . For the two, faith and God, hold close together. Whatever than thy heart clings to . . . and relies upon, that is properly thy god."

Schleiermacher, Ritschl) and loyalty (Royce) with a lesser emphasis on *fides*--intellectual assent to propositions, teachings or doctrines.[91] Faith takes many forms. Faith on Earth is always attached to some object, a god, in which one of three basic configurations of trust and loyalty takes shape. In henotheism faith is placed in one god among many, and while the center of value is a finite society. Niebuhr illustrated the object of henotheistic faith as the nationalism of any social unit that: is a community and commands human trust and loyalty both as a center of value and as the focal point of all service.[92] The horizon of these closed societies is always less than universal. When henotheism breaks down due to various types of treason and disaster, polytheism usually emerges. Polytheism is the simultaneous or successive faith in many gods in which there are multiple sources of meaning and a proliferation of commitments. Polytheism is manifest in egoism and other efforts to know, create, or love in order to prove one's self-worth (since there is no attachment to a single community that provides the individual with support and affirmation). Polytheism is also manifest in various kinds of piety, where faith is placed in a single aspect of the Christian doctrine to the neglect of the whole belief system. For example, one seeking affirmation of his/her own self-worth places faith in *only* Jesus, *only* the Holy Spirit, *only* guardian spirits, or *only* a compassionate virgin.[93] Multiple causes such as Truth, Beauty, Justice, Peace, Love, Goodness or Pleasure are the focus of the activities of the polytheist.

The third and preferred form of faith is radical monotheism. Radical monotheism is faith in the One beyond the many and it is characterized by universal trust and universal loyalty. Here the center of value is being itself and the cause is the principle of value. The principle of value and the principle of being are identical. Since all being participates in the same One that is the center of value, whatever is,

---

[91]H. Richard Niebuhr, *Faith on Earth: An Inquiry into the Structure of Human Faith*, ed. Richard R. Niebuhr (New Haven: Yale University Press, 1989), 47-48.

[92]H.R. Niebuhr, *Radical Monotheism*, 24.

[93]H.R. Niebuhr, *Radical Monotheism*, 29-30.

is good. According to Niebuhr, the ultimate identification of being and value in radical monotheism is a point of departure, not a deduction.[94]

Value always has a relational property, in Niebuhr's view --things have value in relation to God and God is always related to all things. Worth and meaning inhere in reciprocal relationships of being good for another and of receiving good from another.[95] Radical monotheism is exemplified by Moses, the prophets of Israel and Jesus as "a concrete expression in a total human life of radical trust in the One and of universal loyalty to the realm of being."[96] God's universal impartation of value creates a universal community of valued things and valuing beings.[97]

Humanity the Sinner/God the Giver of Grace

The fundamental human problem is that people routinely place faith in the limited and non-universal gods of heontheism and polytheism. The honotheistic and polytheistic gods are neither absolute nor eternal, thus, when trusting these gods, humans pervert their own being and enter into a rebellious relationship with their creator.[98] Sin, in Niebuhr's view, is not to be equated with immorality, but it is rather, disloyalty to God in the form of a false loyalty which ultimately diminishes any chance for mutuality. According to Niebuhr, the central issue of sin concerns human dependence on God, not human freedom.[99] What is significant is accounting for how humans come to know first, the fact and then the consequences of their disloyalty to God, and finally, that there is hope through utter dependence upon God.

---

[94]Ibid., 112.

[95]Ibid., 105-06.

[96]Ibid., 40.

[97]H.R. Niebuhr, *Responsible Self*, 86-89, 171-172.

[98]See H.R. Niebuhr, "Man the Sinner," *Journal of Religion*, 15 (1935): 272-280. See also H.R. Niebuhr, "An Attempt at a Theological Analysis of Missionary Motivation," *N.Y.C. Missionary Research Library Occasional Bulletin*, 14 (1963): 3.

[99]H.R. Niebuhr, "Responsibility and Christ," in *Responsible Self*, 172-73 and 100-06.

Even as sinners, people can ultimately realize the limited nature of the gods of henotheism and polytheism; when they do so they are cast into a void of meaninglessness where God is seen as the "Enemy." The key question then becomes, "How does one move from `God the Enemy' to `God the Companion and Friend?'." Niebuhr claims that the solution to this dilemma of meaning lies in the discovery of that which is the enemy of all of our causes, namely idolatry--placing our ultimate trust in someone or something other than God.[100]

The movement from experiencing the "void" of "God the Enemy" to knowing "God the Companion and Friend" is the result of grace. Niebuhr asserts that the crucial element is an encounter with Jesus Christ. Because humans are historical creatures, the existence of God cannot be proven through metaphysics or an abstract system of morality.[101] He explains, "what we mean by the revelation of God can be indicated only as we point through the medium in which we live."[102]

Niebuhr's approach to revelation employed Kant's distinction between two kinds of history: internal and external.[103] The distinction enabled Niebuhr to conclude

---

[100] H.R. Niebuhr, *Radical Monotheism*, 122: "We may not be able to give a name to it, calling it only the `void' out of which everything comes and to which everything returns, though that is also a name. But it is there--the lasting shadowy and vague reality, the secret of existence by which things come into being, are what they are, and pass away. Against it there is no defense."

[101] Ibid., 124.

[102] H.R. Niebuhr, *Meaning of Revelation*, 48.

[103] H. Richard Niebuhr, *Meaning of Revelation*, 44-54. See also Hans W. Frei, "The Theology of H. Richard Niebuhr," in *Faith and Ethics*, 89-94. See Immanuel Kant, *Critique of Pure Reason*, 2nd ed., trans. N.K. Smith (New York: St. Martin's Press, 1933) and *Critique of Practical Reason and Other Writings In Moral Philosophy* trans. and ed. L.W. Beck (Chicago: University of Chicago Press, 1949).

External history is encompassed by the realm of theoretical reason and events of history are observed from the outside by an objective disinterested observer. This approach to history is impersonal, concerned with objects, and produces results in the form of descriptive knowledge. The value of an event is measured in terms of its strength and valency and time is measured serially. Society is understood as an association of individuals related only by an external bond. Buber's I-It relation describes the subject and object relations here.

Internal history is encompassed by the realm of practical reason and concern is oriented to the meaning of events for human life. The approach to history is subjective and participative, concerned with the subject and results in normative knowledge. Value is measured in terms of worth for selves and time

that revelation can take place in history, yet go undetected as anything miraculous or revelatory by an outside observer. Niebuhr located revelation in internal history but asserted that the Christian community needs to be open to knowledge and critique from external sources because God is sovereign over all history. The church must attempt to view itself as God does, careful to recognize that not all internal history is revelation. Revelation is only given by grace.[104] Though humans are historically conditioned, they can perceive things outside of history which are historically mediated.

Christology

First, God compels faith by Self-revelation particularly in Jesus' life, death and resurrection.[105] Then follows the decision of the self, the revolution of the mind and the leap of faith. The encounter with the Christ event transforms and revolutionizes henotheistic and polytheistic human faith into radical monotheism. In spite of the apparent absurdity involved in believing that God would first allow Jesus to be crucified, and then demonstrate divine power and loyalty in raising him from the dead, the resurrection of Jesus Christ has a persuasive impact on the person of faith.[106]

Niebuhr carefully distinguished the role of Jesus from the ultimate objective of revelation. While the believer needs to seek the triumph of Christ's cause, s/he must not "substitute the Lordship of Christ for the Lordship of God."[107] In Niebuhr's view, Christ's sonship and his fidelity to the Father indicate there is One beyond him

---

is the duration in which both past and future are present as memory and possibility. Society is understood as a community of selves who are personally and internally related. Buber's I-Thou relation describes the subjective relationship here.

[104] H.R. Niebuhr, *Meaning of Revelation*, 68.

[105] Lonnie D. Kliever, "The Christology of H. Richard Niebuhr," *The Journal of Religion* 50 (1970): 33-57.

[106] H. Richard Niebuhr, *Christ and Culture* (New York: Harper and Row, Publishers, 1951; reprint, New York: Torchbooks, 1975), 254. "What is irrational here is the creation of faith in the faithfulness of God by the crucifixion, the betrayal of Jesus Christ, who was utterly loyal to Him."

[107] H.R. Niebuhr, *Radical Monotheism*, 59-60. See also H.R. Niebuhr, *Christ and Culture*, 11. Niebuhr distinguishes *following* from *believing in* Christ.

to whom he summons humanity. Christ elicits three "notes" of faith from the believer: (1) that the valuing, saving power in the world is being itself (2) that the ultimate principle of being gives, maintains, and re-establishes worth (3) that believers have been called upon to make the cause of God their cause.[108] God is universal--"God-in-Christ" and redemptive--"Christ-in-God."

Niebuhr describes Jesus primarily in three ways: the moral Son of God, the incarnation of radical faith, and the paradigm of responsibility. Jesus the moral Son of God possesses five virtues, love, obedience, hope, faith, and humility. These virtues receive their significance from Christ's unique devotion to God. Niebuhr asserts they must be taken together in order to adequately portray Jesus' character and teachings.[109]

Niebuhr underscored the significance of the Incarnation with his definition of the event as "the coming of monotheistic faith into our history, meaning by it the concrete expression in a total human life of radical trust in the One and of universal loyalty to the realm of being."[110] The Incarnation reaffirmed God as the absolute center of value. Therefore, the worth of every plant, animal, animate or inanimate object is to be reverenced because of and in relation to God.[111]

For our purposes, most significant is Jesus the "paradigm of responsibility" who always did what fit the divine action. He interpreted all of his interactions as a sign of God's activity and he recognized the universal omnificent One as his Father.[112] By the singular focus of his life, death and resurrection on the complementary communication between God and humanity, Jesus released humanity from false gods and introduced them to a right relationship with the One Creator. Jesus' action

---

[108] H.R. Niebuhr, *Radical Monotheism*, 43-44.

[109] H.R. Niebuhr, *Christ and Culture*, 14-27, 28.

[110] H.R. Niebuhr, *Radical Monotheism*, 40-42.

[111] Ibid., 32-33. See also H.R. Niebuhr, *Christ and Culture*, 239-41.

[112] H.R. Niebuhr, *Responsible Self*, 162.

effectively stressed a common humanity in relation to one God, opening the way for mutuality.

H. Richard Niebuhr's Theory of Responsibility

H. Richard Niebuhr's first use of the term, "responsible self" came early in his discussion concerning how the church can meet the expectations of society and serve civilization. Niebuhr contended that the real question was that of how the church "can be true to itself: that is to its Head. What must it do to be saved?" [113] Niebuhr argued: "This question is not a selfish one; it is only the question of a responsible self."[114] Here Niebuhr's use of the term is indicative of a member of the Christian community who takes her/his commitment to the discipline of the church seriously and who feels obligated to assert to his/her beliefs when the mission of the church is in question. Implicit in the discussion is that this "responsible self" is not closed to the critique of outside sources, but rather, welcomes it. On the other hand, there is an identity to be maintained, namely, that of one who is a believer whose primary identity is with God. To be responsible here, means to be open to criticism and judgment from the outside, but only to the extent that it does not impose upon one's core ideal.

Niebuhr's early use of the term "responsibility" occurred within the discussion of church unity. In his view denominationalism is a scandal of Christianity. He asserted: "It [the church] becomes an organization intent upon promotion of its own interests, without a sense of its responsibility to the world as a social whole."[115] Here Niebuhr's use of the term suggests that simple adjustment to social conditions by the church of the early twentieth century is not fruitful. He claims that by failing to allow itself to be in true dialogue with the world outside of Christianity, it has cut itself off from the very goal it seeks namely, universality. Two aspects of mutuality are implicit

---

[113] H. Richard Niebuhr, "The Question of Church," in *The Church Against the World* by Francis P. Miller, H. Richard Niebuhr, Wilhelm Pauck. (Chicago: Welleth, Clark and Company, 1935), 4.

[114] Ibid.

[115] H. Richard Niebuhr, *The Social Sources of Denominationalism* (New York: The World Publishing Company, 1929), 274-75.

here. First, it is necessary for each partner in the dialogue to maintain his/her/its identity. Secondly, only distinct and whole partners can "respond" to each other, rather than become identified with one another.

In 1946 and again, in the context of a discussion on the role of the church in society, Niebuhr began to formulate his interpretation of Christian ethics in terms of responsibility and response.[116] He based his position on two central convictions: first, that the church must be understood as a movement, rather than only as an institution and second, a dialectical movement must take place between worship of the Sovereign God and work to transform the world. The significant point Niebuhr argues here is that responsibility is a universal feature of human social life and it consists in a double movement: (a) what people are responsible for in a community is determined by (b) what they respond to as a community.

> The idea of responsibility, with the freedom and obligation it implies, has its place in the context of social relations. To be responsible is to be a self in the presence of other selves, to whom one is bound and to whom one is able to answer freely; responsibility includes stewardship or trusteeship over things that belong to the common life of the selves. The question about the one to whom account must be rendered is of equal importance with the question about the what for which one must answer.[117]

In Niebuhr's view, "responsibility" in the Christian community must consist in a response to the Sovereign God, revealed in Jesus Christ. It naturally follows that Christians are also responsible for God's inclusive and regenerative Kingdom. Such a universal response precludes limited spiritualism, elitist moralism, and automatonistic individualism and worship of anything other than the Sovereign God.[118]

---

[116]H. Richard Niebuhr, "The Responsibility of the Church for Society," in Kenneth Scott Latourette, ed. *The Gospel, the Church and the World* (New York: Harper and Brothers, 1946) 111-133.

[117]Ibid., 114-15. "To be responsible is to be able and required to give account to someone for something."

[118]Ibid., 119-20.

In his Robertson Lectures on the Responsible Self, H. Richard Niebuhr states that his primary concern in setting forth his phenomenology of responsibility is to understand human moral life. He clearly owns his perspective as "Christian," however, he is quick to add that Christianity is not his sole focus.[119] Set in the context of his theology, Niebuhr believed that morality is necessarily understood in relation to God and as an active dimension of faith.

H. Richard Niebuhr defines "responsibility" as:

[t]he idea of an agent's action as response to an action upon him in accordance with his interpretation of the latter action and with his expectation of response to his response; and all of this in a continuing community of agents.[120]

This notion of responsibility is central to Niebuhr's moral philosophy and it is deeply rooted in his concept of radical monotheism. In light of his monotheism, the symbol most appropriate for the human person is "man-the-answerer," one who "responds" to the dynamic gift of grace of the One revealed in Jesus Christ.[121] The human person is thus, ideally, one who has a style of life that engages her/him in Niebuhr's

---

[119]H.R. Niebuhr, *Responsible Self*, 42, 45-46. Niebuhr believed his notion of responsibility was equally insightful for analyzing styles of morality and systems of ethics. Like the four feminists whose notions of mutuality are our focus, he recognized that all analysis is done from a particular perspective; no analysis is totally objective. He is informed by sources both within and outside of classical Christianity--psychology, sociology and history, as well as dogma and scripture--thus, widening the universe of discourse and broadening the possibility to influence and be influenced by others. Such inclusivity is foundational for mutuality as understood by the four Christian feminists whose works are addressed in this thesis.

[120]Ibid., 65.

[121]Ibid., 48-56. Niebuhr contrasts the Aristotelian and Thomistic symbol for humanity, "man-the-maker" and the accompanying teleological ethics, as well as the Barthian symbol for humanity, "man-the-citizen" living under the law and the accompanying deontological ethics with Niebuhr's own "man-the-answerer" and his own "cathēkontic ethics." See Ibid., 55-60.

The teleological ethics of "man-the-maker" is primarily concerned with the goal to be achieved. This symbol is inadequate because it underestimates human penchant for making life as easy as possible, doesn't acknowledge the resistant unpredictability of life, and fails to comprehend how the past impacts the present and the future.

The deontological ethics of "Man-the-citizen" queries, "What is the law to be obeyed?" "Man-the-citizen" is inadequate in that it: is not fully aware of the temporality and solidarity of moral existence, fails to appreciate ambiguous life, and fails to apprehend the novelty of history. Deontological theories fail to inform the anxiety, freedom and change that occurs within the moral life.

See also Richard E. Crouter, "H. Richard Niebuhr and Stoicism," *Journal of Religious Ethics* 2 (1974):129-46; see esp. 130.

cathēkontic ethics (the ethics of the fitting) and who addresses the primary question: "What is going on?." This question is necessary because all of life's activity takes place within a context or universe and because all behavior is observed by and affects others in the universal community (outside of the individual or group involved in the particular activity in question).

Niebuhr's question points to the biblical pattern of "responsible action," as exemplified by Isaiah (Is. 10).[122] Niebuhr's intent is not to replace teleology or deontology entirely, but to place them in perspective with what is currently more apt to serve as a model and guide for moral conduct, namely, the symbol of responsibility.[123] In support of this position Niebuhr argues that the notion of responsibility is grounded in the latest psychological, sociological, biological and historical premises; it is most adequate for dealing with issues concerning tragedy, pain and suffering; and it is consistent with the biblical ethos.[124]

Niebuhr outlined four components to his notion of responsibility, naming the first component, "response." All human action is response to action upon others in both personal and social situations.[125] While moral and ethical decisions are made partly on logical bases, moral responsiveness is emotionally evoked, as well. The imagination plays a major role ordering human feelings and passionate responses toward moral decisions.[126] In all instances the self becomes aware of the certain limitations to her/his ability to respond and the self is defined. Niebuhr illustrates how

---

[122]H.R. Niebuhr, *Responsible Self*, 67. The prophet "calls to their attention the intentions of God present in hiddenness in the actions of Israel's enemies."

[123]Ibid., 54-56, 60-61, 131.

[124]Ibid., 56-60, 65-67.

[125]Ibid., 62-63. Niebuhr believes the very ability for moral discernment and judgment is actualized in response to others. See Ibid., 69-89 where Niebuhr cites George H. Mead, Josiah Royce and Martin Buber.

[126]Ibid., 58. See also 168-70 where Niebuhr discusses the process of decision making in the Hebrew and Stoic systems and illustrates the affinities of the two with Christian ethics.

personal suffering is one of the most common occasions for the growth of self-awareness.[127]

Drawing meaning from occasions of suffering points to the second element of Niebuhr's notion of responsibility, "interpretation." Interpretation, which normally requires some sort of dialogue, distinguishes moral action from other human actions.[128] The process of analyzing a response includes consideration of "what is going on" and "the fitting," as well as "the right" and "the good." The dialogic and inclusive character of Niebuhr's ethic requires a sensitivity to the value scales and notions of duty held by other parties with whom one relates. The context in which the response takes place is also, always significant.

"Accountability" marks the third aspect of Niebuhr's notion of responsibility. Niebuhr perceives the human as one who can anticipate the answers others give to his/her answers. People can anticipate the consequences of their own actions, and thus, some actions can be judged more fitting than others. The responsible person, therefore, is held accountable for interpreted actions insofar as they are taken in anticipation of responses to his/her ethical dilemma. To be accountable is to be constant, consistent and dependable, always accepting the consequences of one's actions.

The fourth element of responsibility is "social solidarity." A substantial continuity in the agency of selves and communities is necessary to form the basis of responsible action. Responsive interpretation attempts to establish the real connections among things in a given context. The attempt to discover "what is going on" in a setting discloses the connections of the self to society, to time and to its absolute dependence on something beyond itself. Social solidarity gives expression to the pressures of the actual situation on the self's interpretation and its sense of accountability. "Our action is responsible it appears, when it is response to action

---

[127]Ibid., 60.

[128]Ibid., 64. See also H. R. Niebuhr, *Meaning of Revelation*, 79-80.

upon us in a continuing discourse or interaction among beings forming a continuing society.[129] Niebuhr's four components address the God/human relationship from the human side.

Patterns of God's Actions and Human Response

There are discernable patterns in human response based on a view from God's side. All action upon humankind whether personal, natural or historical is, in Niebuhr's view, God's action.[130] Niebuhr understands the trinitarian God as One who simultaneously acts as Creator, Governor and Redeemer. All human activity is to be judged and measured in light God's action in the three roles.

As Creator, God is in the ordered goodness in the world and in the activity of humans when they act in the world as the nurturers of the emergence of human culture. "Whatever is, is good," was Niebuhr's way of expressing the foundational appreciative and affirmative disposition of God (and thus, humanity) toward the world.[131] From God's viewpoint, each thing is affirmed in its particularity and all things are good in relationship to one another. Several attitudes significant for ethics follow from this positive disposition: (1) People can "merely accept what is," realizing that God's judgment is final and significant. (2) It is possible to affirm and understand oneself, one's neighbor, nature, and even one's enemy. (3) Human beings can be the cultivators of an emerging unfashioned world.[132] Humans thus respond to the Creator by participating in a limited manner in God's creative action.[133]

---

[129]H.R. Niebuhr, *Responsible Self*, 65.

[130]James M. Gustafson, "Introduction," in Ibid., 25-41.

[131]Ibid., 29-32.

[132]Ibid., 30-31.

[133]Ibid., 31-32. The human temptation is to idolatry: to forget that humanity is merely a responder to God and is able to create only because God empowers them to do so.

As limited and finite creatures, humans are sustained and governed by God.[134] Humans are limited by other beings, individual capacities of intelligence and strength, as well as economic, political and social circumstances. Within this world of limitations God's governing and sustaining activity takes place. The choice is for humanity to respond to God, nature and others with self-restraint and to live and serve others, or to resist the Sovereign with a sense of disdainful futility. In all cases human failure to acknowledge God as Governor and Sustainer leads to defensive or aggressive action that destroys human potential to experience the joy, goodness and affirmation of God and others.

Human limitation is universal, but so is the human inclination to have faith in something or someone. In Niebuhr's view, this is positively significant for ethics because ultimately humans can attain a monotheistic faith. In faith, humans can interpret powers that limit them as present only by the power of God, and therefore, as sustaining powers which fundamentally serve God. Niebuhr suggested two means of response to conflict, limitation, and suffering: self denial and the restraint of the evil of others.[135]

It is by the redeeming love of God that humans become free, responsible and loving persons.[136] God as Redeemer opens the way for an ethics of redemption, not redemptive ethics which seeks to redeem, confusing God's action with human acts. The initiative of redemption remains with God and it is constantly dynamic in the world. Any person or group who lays claim to the ethics of redemption is in error.[137] The effect of God's redemption is that humans are empowered and transformed such that all valuation in life falls in order with God's will. In transformed human

---

[134]Ibid., 32-36.

[135]Ibid., 34-36.

[136]Ibid., 36-40.

[137]Ibid., 39.

relationships ". . . it impregnates our actions with freedom and love so that we are driven toward the creative responses to others that realize the good."[138]

Ethics, therefore, in Niebuhr's view is based on God's activity as Creator, Governor and Redeemer, as well as the human response to it, whether that action be direct, through nature, or through other human persons. The notion of responsibility provides for an adequate report of human experience and is thus an instructive instrument of analysis. Responsibility can only direct self-determination, however. Responsibility needs to work hand in hand with radical monotheistic faith as the organizing principle that places God as the center of value and frames the responsible life.

The Normative Nature of "Responsibility"

One criticism leveled against H. Richard Niebuhr's theory of responsibility is that it fails to provide any substance or content toward the formulation of norms or prescriptive ethics.[139] The criticism is based on a literal interpretation of Niebuhr's use of terms such as "relative" and "relativism" and on an unnuanced understanding of the theocentrism and conversionism that ground his relational value theory.

There is another way to interpret Niebuhr's theory of responsibility that does clearly support the formulation of norms and prescriptive ethics.[140] Niebuhr treated the normative lawful element of ethical reflection as a means to an end.[141] Because God is both the center of value and the center of being, "the good" is presupposed in

---

[138]Ibid., 40.

[139]See E. Clinton Gardner, "Responsibility and Moral Direction in the Ethics of H. Richard Niebuhr," *Encounter* 40 (1979): 143-68. Also, Timothy F. Sedgwick, "Faith and Discernment: Directions in Theological Ethics in the Thought of H. Richard Niebuhr," *Andover Newton Quarterly* 18 (1977): 111-21.

[140]Beverly Wildung Harrison, "H. Richard Niebuhr: Towards a Christian Moral Philosophy," (Ph.D. diss., Union Theological Seminary, 1974), 310-47.

[141]See n. 118 above. The content of Christian ethics can be found in other systems, in Niebuhr's view. I use the case of the monotheistic Christian as an illustration.

"what is right." The fittingness of how we interpret what is going on is a reflection of how we understand the good.

In faith, the Christian monotheist voluntarily and thoroughly identifies with Jesus Christ; her/his cause is identical to Christ's cause (God's cause).[142] The value content of the life and ministry of Jesus is also the value content utilized by the responsible self. Therefore, the Christian knows God's constraint on human behavior (and perceives how human finitude disrupts God's intentions, as well). Niebuhr believed that valuation establishes our orientation to the good. For the Christian monotheist, totally oriented to Jesus Christ, value is never individualized, but rather measured for the social self in the context of community.[143] So valuation includes both determining and interpreting what is going on (context), and making choices about how to respond (personal).

Niebuhr is clear about the content for the ethics of responsibility in his discussion of biblical ethics.[144] Laws and imperatives such as the ten commandments, Covenant Law, injunctions of the Hebrew prophets, the Sermon on the Mount, and the Pauline admonitions (Rom. 12-15) all provide content for what is responsible.[145] Niebuhr is clear that seeking what is good and living belong together.[146] God's constant activity in the world (as with ancient Israel) indicates a continual transvaluing, broadening, deepening and universalizing of God's law of love in the world.[147] Jesus exemplified the interpretation of indicatives and imperatives of the covenant law, redefining "the neighbor," and challenging *both* oppressed and

---

[142] H.R. Niebuhr, *Responsible Self*, 43-44.

[143] H.R. Niebuhr, *Radical Monotheism*, 104.

[144] H. Richard Niebuhr, "Introduction to Biblical Ethics," in Waldo Beach and H. Richard Niebuhr, eds., *Christian Ethics: Sources of the Living Tradition*, 2nd ed. (New York: The Ronald Press Company, 1973), 10-45.

[145] Ibid.

[146] Ibid., 24.

[147] Ibid., 23-26.

oppressor, where earlier prophets had focused on the oppressors.[148] The monotheistic Christian can follow Jesus by interpreting imperatives and indicatives in the modern world because God is ever present (Ps.139) to assist with love, mercy, forgiveness, and kindness.[149] The dialectic between love of God and love of neighbor allows for the ongoing refinement of the content of responsibility within relationships to God, the self and others.[150] It is in these relations that values come to be and moral actions take place.

The substantive normativity of responsibility for Niebuhr can be claimed on the basis of other areas of argument.[151] First, Niebuhr, by the very fact of asserting his concept of radical monotheism, indicates an idea of how things ought to be. The assumptions Niebuhr brings to this vision are value laden indicatives of a formal norm. To say that all is "relative" to the Sovereign God is not to necessarily exclude an ordering or a standard of measure from being used to judge what is "other than God." In fact, the very process by which all else becomes "relative" to God is to become the creature *related* to God the Creator, Governor, and Redeemer by being gifted with grace and then responding to God from within that relationship. All that is "other than God" is viewed by God as elemental in the universal Reign of God, and subject to the norm of the Kingdom, responsibility.

A second case can be made for the normative nature of responsibility, when one attends to the significance Niebuhr gives the imagination and symbol. Even if one

---

[148]Ibid., 34-35.

[149]Ibid., 33.

[150]Ibid., 42-44. See H. Richard Niebuhr, "Reflections on Faith, Hope, and Love," *Journal of Religious Ethics* 2 (1974): 152-53. Also H. Richard Niebuhr, *Kingdom of God in America* (New York: Harper and Row, Publishers, Inc., 1937; reprinted, Middletown, CT: Wesleyan University Press, 1988), 112-115.

[151]Some who hold that Niebuhr's notion of responsibility is normative are: Paul Ramsey, "The Transformation of Ethics," in *Faith and Ethics*, 140-172; James Gustafson, "Christian Ethics and Social Policy," Ibid., 129-139; D. Don Welch, Jr., "A Niebuhrian Contribution to Normative Ethics," *Encounter* 44 (1983): 341-51; and Thomas R. McFaul, "Dilemmas in H. Richard Niebuhr's Ethics," *Journal of Religion* 50 (1974): 35-50.

were to agree that Niebuhr's tendency is toward relativism, it must be recognized that Niebuhr's intent was to establish a standard framework within which moral decisions are made. Images, symbols and paradigms hold a power in human thought and decision processes that is equal to (and likely, beyond) the power of laws and principles.[152] Christ as the "paradigm of responsibility" is recognized by Christians, but he also has a universal appeal.[153] Jesus as a model and his parabolic teachings are powerful frames within which the Christian (and others) consciously measure their valuations, actions and choices in suffering and death. In this sense, responsibility is normative in Niebuhr's thought.

Niebuhr claimed, "God is acting in all actions upon you. So respond to all actions upon you as to respond to his action."[154] In relational value theory "value is present wherever one existent being with capabilities and potentialities confronts another existence that limits or completes or complements it."[155] If value is relational and if God is acting in every relation, then the possibility for judging the order and quality of any given value is present in all relationships. The fittingness of a response lies not only in the character of the agent, but in the relation of the act to the context in which the response occurs, as well. The obligation of the agent is to decide on a response and define her/his accountability in line with the interpretation of which demand is most in accord with social solidarity. Here is Niebuhr's framework for approaching an ethical dilemma.

Niebuhr's reluctance to set down specific maxims need not be interpreted as his intending nothing normative. His concern was to maintain an attitude of humility and openness, avoiding egoistical judgment which often entraps ethical systems that

---

[152] H.R. Niebuhr, "Metaphors and Morals," in *Responsible Self*, 149-178.

[153] Ibid., 155-56. "Again Jesus Christ is the symbolic form with which the self understands itself, with the aid of which it guides and forms itself in its actions and its sufferings."

[154] Ibid., 126.

[155] H.R. Niebuhr, *Radical Monotheism*, 103.

are delineated more concretely. Humility demands that divine and human law remain in perspective, not that there be no law articulated.

Responsibility: Antecedent to the Feminist Notion of Mutuality

Feminists agree that false consciousness attendant to polytheism and henotheism needs to be challenged in assertive dialogue. Responsibility as a norm opens such a dialogic dynamic in relationships. However, responsibility is only an antecedent of mutuality. The dimension of accountability in responsibility requires a one for one measure on the behavioral level, only. While Niebuhr acknowledges the value of emotions and imagination, he provides no ordered process for their inclusion in the accounting process.[156] Interpretation is also portrayed as a singularly cognitive process, although Niebuhr does acknowledge an affective aspect may be involved there. The power dynamic entailed in responsibility defined as "stewardship or trusteeship over things" is one of "power-over."[157] Rather than serving to maximize human thriving, the dynamics of "power-over" readily become oppressive. Finally, the "expectation of a response" is viewed by Niebuhr as a cognitive process to the exclusion of the intuitive. Mutuality requires an intuitive, flexible ebb and flow of affect between partners, in addition to cognitive relating.

MUTUALITY IN BUBER, NIEBUHR, AND MODERN CHRISTIAN FEMINISTS

Some General Considerations: Buber

Buber's dialogical philosophy and his interpretation of divine/human relations is foundational to the thought of Reuther, Heyward, Harrison and Johnson concerning mutuality. These scholars find Buber's twofold conception of relationality the most viable expression of all forms of human relationship because, as we have shown, mutuality is central to I-Thou relations.

---

[156] Ruether, *Sexism and God-Talk*, 89-91. Cf. Ruether's evaluation of mathematical forms of measure.

[157] H.R. Niebuhr, "Responsibility and Christ," in *Responsible Self*, 174-75. Emphasis is mine.

Ruether claims I-It relations form the structure of alienation in society, particularly in its form of sexism and abusive sexual relations.[158] Buber's conception of the Eternal Thou as a metaphor for God is also significant for Ruether because it is gender-inclusive and relational, in contrast to classical Christian images of God. God, exclusively imagined as male and/or as a transcendent ideal (not as a person), establishes a paradigm for power in relations in which subordinates (women) are treated as objects--an I-It relation.[159] I-Thou relationships, which affirm the right of each life form to exist in interdependent relationship with God and other elements of creation, are necessary for the healing of our spiritually and ecologically ravaged world.[160]

Buber's dialogical philosophy and his Hasidic interpretation of God, covenant, and messianism heavily influence Heyward's theology of mutual relation. In contrast to the transcendent, male God named in complex philosophical terms in classical theology, a God of I-It relation, Buber's God is also a person of immanent covenant relations, involved in history and in every I-Thou relation.[161]

For Heyward, the I-Thou relation is the relationship found in the Jewish covenant and the Christian extensions of the covenant--love, justice and mutuality. In the I-Thou relation between God (also a person) and humans, God needs humans to fulfill the personality of the Eternal Thou, and humans need one another and all of creation in order to know the most complete expression of the Eternal Thou.[162] According to Heyward the incarnation is a paradigm of the I-Thou relation. The Christic power of Jesus of Nazareth was a power for mutuality, rooted in I-Thou

---

[158]Ruether, *Liberation Theology*, 29. See Ruether, *Sexism and God-Talk*, 174.

[159]Ruether, *Sexism and God-Talk*, 61, 128, 174. See Rosemary Radford Ruether, "Sexism and the Theology of Liberation: Nature, Fall and Salvation as Seen From the Experience of Women, *The Christian Century*, 90 (1973): 1225.

[160]Ruether, *Gaia and God*, 228. See also Ibid., 302, note 36.

[161]Heyward, *Redemption of God*, 1-7.

[162]Ibid., 7.

relationships with God, humans, and all of creation--the kind of relationship available to all healthy persons.[163] As exemplified by Jesus, Christian love and justice is active and needs to be delimited by mutuality which is central to all I-Thou relations.

Harrison values particularly Buber's understanding of the dynamics of hate and love in human relationships. It is tremendously empowering for women to comprehend anger and hatred in a positive sense. This means that, as Buber suggests, hate and anger can be recognized as embodied signals of unhealthy relationships. Upon heeding those signals, choices can be made concerning how to channel one's anger or hate toward relations of mutuality. As Buber says: ". . . whoever hates directly is closer to a relation than those who are without love and hate."[164]

Johnson finds Buber's conception of God rich, and useful toward her broader goal of speaking of God as both immanent and transcendent and in gender inclusive terms. She finds Buber's stories exhibiting the breadth and depth of God's character and personality stimulating for the imagination.[165] Buber's interpretation of *'ehyeh 'asher 'ehyeh* (Ex.3:14) as a pledge of God's presence, "I shall be there, as who I am, shall be there with you," is significant for Johnson because it creates an image of God that is at the same time relational and historical.[166] Extending Buber's interpretation, this image of God presents the possibility of mutual relations with God, and among all elements of creation.

---

[163]Heyward, *Touching Our Strength*, 15. Buber's work exploring the need for strong relational bonding between people in community provides impetus for modern psychological and theological research toward improving healing of broken persons and relationships. Such is the work of the Stone Center. See Heyward, *Staying Power*, 88, 161 n. 13. See also Carter Heyward, *When Boundaries Betray Us: Beyond Illusions of What is Ethical in Therapy and Life*, (New York: Harper Collins Publishers, 1993), 146, 250 n. 12.

[164]Harrison, "Power of Anger," 50. Harrison cites Buber, *I and Thou* (K), 67-68.

[165]See Johnson, *She Who Is*, 43-44 and Johnson, *Consider Jesus*, 61-62.

[166]Johnson, *She Who Is*, 241. Johnson cites Buber's *Eclipse of God*.

Some General Considerations: Niebuhr

H. Richard Niebuhr's theory of responsibility holds several positive implications for the feminist notion of mutuality. First, in light of the confessional motif in his ethics he viewed defensiveness concerning one's own version of the truth to be sinful.[167] Niebuhr's understanding of history allows for a true dialogue in which each partner is open to be influenced and changed by the truth of the other.[168] Such dialogue is a condition necessary for mutuality.

Secondly, Niebuhr placed Christian thought within the realm of practical reason, and thus, he stressed the significance of the "reasons of the heart" in making value judgments and deciding religious issues.[169] This alignment opens the way for inclusion of the non-mathematical and the non-linear (images, symbols, embodiment) in Christian theology and ethics along with the classical, abstract, theoretical notions.[170]

Third, Niebuhr's thesis is that the chief rival to monotheism is henotheism. He thus challenges some deeply established patriarchal oppressive (especially for women) interpretations of Christian piety, Christian institutional practices, and the weight given to Christian dogma in relation to contextual factors, while more egalitarian interpretations of those same tenets are possible.[171] This blatant fact of patriarchal

---

[167] Daniel Day Williams, "A Personal and Theological Memoir," *Christianity and Crisis* 23 (1963): 211-12.

[168] Ibid., 212: "He did believe, I know, that when Christ is accepted in cultures other than those of the West, we should expect some radically new forms of Christianity to emerge." It is difficult to believe that Williams insight concerning "cultures other than those of the West" would not also apply to the feminist "culture."

[169] H.R. Niebuhr, *Meaning of Revelation*, 69: "It does mean that the reason which is correlate with revelation is practical reason, or the reason of a self rather than of impersonal mind; it implies that the conflict of practical reason is with practical irrationality as pure reason is at war with irrationality in the head and not with reason of the heart."

[170] Carl Michalson, "The Real Presence of the Hidden God," in *Faith and Ethics*, 254.

[171] The substance of this critique is corroborated by Winifred Legerton, "H. Richard Niebuhr's Radical Monotheism and Christian Feminism," *Religion in Life* 45 (1976): 427-435. Recent illustrations of this point: Karen Jo Torjesen, *When Women Were Priests* (San Francisco: Harper, 1993; Virginia

dominance is challenged headlong by Niebuhr's radical faith: "No special places, times, persons or communities are more representative of the One than any others are."[172] Niebuhr specifically addresses two types of henotheism.[173] In church-centered henotheism the center of value is shifted from God to institutional laws and the pronouncements of institutional leaders. In Christ-centered henotheism the center of value deviates from God to particularities of Christ's person, teaching, life and ministry--such as his maleness--resulting in a cultic Jesuology. Such loss of God as the center of value precludes the true universal nature of Christianity (Gal 3:28) as well as the possibility of mutuality. In Niebuhr's terms, only when monotheism is made concrete in daily life will the flux and flow of mutuality (as understood by modern feminists) be possible.

Most distinctive in Niebuhr's approach to ethics is his assertion that the context of human relations is a central consideration for ethics. Humans are social beings, members of multiple communities in which claims are exchanged. Women's experiences have affirmed Niebuhr's insight and relationality is central to feminist thought.[174]

Four Forms of Mutuality: Modern Feminists, Buber, and Niebuhr

Buber does not directly address the equality of genders that is central to the feminists' notion of gender mutuality. The hasidimic principle of the *nitzotz* (the glory of God) borne by all creatures (unless they directly turn from God's law) only implies

---

Ramey Mollenkott, *The Divine Feminine: The Biblical Imagery of God as Female* (New York: Crossroad, 1991); Mary Ann Rossi, "Priesthood, Precedent, and Prejudice," *Journal of Feminist Studies in Religion* 7 (1991): 73-94; Rosemary Radford Ruether, *Sexism and God-Talk: Toward a Feminist Theology* (Boston: Beacon Press, 1983); Elizabeth Schüssler Fiorenza, *In Memory of Her: A Feminist Reconstruction of Christian Origins* (New York: Crossroad, 1983); Carroll Stuhmueller, ed., *Women and Priesthood: Future Directions* (Collegeville, MN: The Liturgical Press, 1978).

[172]H.R. Niebuhr, *Radical Monotheism*, 52.

[173]Ibid., 58 and 59-60.

[174]Of the four feminists studied here, all acknowledge Niebuhr's influence upon them except Elizabeth A. Johnson. It is clear, however, that she is in broad agreement with much of what Niebuhr holds regarding human sociality and the importance of context in ethical reflection.

a fundamental equality in dignity. Nothing in Buber's thought would deter his full support of the patriarchal structures that overshadow this equality of dignity in life.

Ruether finds Niebuhr's confessional approach to Christology significant for mutual gender relations.[175] The historical kenosis of patriarchy is visible in Jesus' life and ministry when he is viewed as the paradigm of responsibility. The notion of gender mutuality is also supported by extension in Niebuhr's discussion the democratic belief in human equality as an issue for church and state.[176] A henotheistic interpretation of Christianity supports the ideology of sexism. In principle, sexism is comparable to the white supremacy condemned by Niebuhr because like white supremacy, sexism is grounded in false logic and emotional appeals to the limited loyalty and dependent confidence of people.[177]

Niebuhr's approach to divine/human relations acknowledges some limited participation of humans with God in creation and redemption, because God affirms all of life. Heyward joins Niebuhr in holding a generally optimistic view of humanity.[178] She, however, parts with him in how social sin is overcome. Both agree that social sin is misplaced loyalty and trust in another god. Niebuhr holds self-denial and combat with sin is a solution. Heyward looks to mutual relationship with God who initiates and sustains relationships (the power in mutual relation) as the solution to sin (which is separation from relatedness). In mutual relation with God, humans are co-creators and co-redeemers--generative mutuality.

---

[175]Ruether, *Sexism and God-Talk*, 127-38.

[176]Ibid., 72.

[177]Ibid., 75-76. "The doctrine of supremacy of a special group is a faith, too, in the sense that it expresses loyalty to a cause and a community. The accompaniment of the denigration of other groups is always a call for solidarity in the supposedly superior group." See Legerton, "Monotheism and Feminism." 434-35.

[178]Common intellectual ancestors of Niebuhr and Heyward are Frederick Schleiermacher and F.D. Maurice. See Robert H. King, "Review Essay: H. Richard Niebuhr - *Faith on Earth: An Inquirery into the Structure of Human Faith*," *Religious Studies Review* 17 (1991): 295. Also, Heyward, *Redemption of God*, 37, 63 n. 26, 115. See H.R. Niebuhr, *Responsible Self*, 34-36. See Heyward, *Speaking of Christ*, 15-25.

In Buber's thought cocreative activity is found in all I-Thou relations. The partners participate with the Eternal Thou turning toward and forming one another, redeeming one another from the alienation of the I-It world.

Mutuality is central to Buber's notion of "the in between" of the I-Thou relation. Full mutuality is possible in interhuman relations; threshold mutuality is possible between animals and with humans; prethreshold mutuality is possible in relations with plants and non-living beings. Buber's notion that the Eternal Thou undergirds all forms of mutual relation finds near identity with the modern feminists' concept of cosmic mutuality. Niebuhr included nature as part of the triadic dialogue of the self, social companions, and natural events.[179] While his focus is on the self, there is clear recognition of the relatedness of humans with the entire cosmos that anticipates the modern feminists' cosmic mutuality.

A critical assumption that is present in Buber's twofold world is the necessity of community; there is no healthy isolated individual. God's covenant relationship is paradigmatic for the community. Since God is accessible to all, especially the *am ha-aretz* (simple poor) so too, the responsible person in community must engage in ethical practices to include the poor in the thriving of the community.[180] This practice includes relinquishing power and claiming power as is necessary for relating as I-Thou; it thus involves social mutuality.

In Harrison's view, Niebuhr's central bequest to ethics is his reconstruction of the "dialectical interaction between self-emergence and social process" and his clarification of how "the intentions, purposes, and values of persons interact with the `givenness' of social systems in the direction of change."[181] This contribution opened the way for further development of social mutuality as a social ethical norm. His process of ethical interpretation allowed analysis of the dynamics of social institutions

---

[179]H.R. Niebuhr, *Responsible Self*, 80-83.

[180]See n. 81 above.

[181]Harrison, "H. Richard Niebuhr," diss., 345.

and economic forces to determine the effect of the powerful upon the less powerful. "What is fitting" for the love of neighbor may then be measured and acted upon.[182] Jesus, the paradigm of responsibility, challenging oppressors and the oppressed to relinquish or take up power, is key to Niebuhr's understanding of biblical ethics, which provides the standard for what is fitting.[183] A recognition of the use of power for good or ill is necessary for engaging in social mutuality toward the thriving of all.

In this chapter I have explained how antecedents of the modern feminist notion of mutuality are found in the thought of Buber and Niebuhr. Next, I will show that mutuality is a formal norm in light of definitions given by Lisa Sowle Cahill, Josef Fuchs, and Timothy E. O'Connell.

---

[182]Ibid., 346. Harrison is critical of Niebuhr's heavy dependence upon God the "Determiner" which resulted in the loss of emphasis in his later work upon solidarity, mutuality and common service as guiding principles for the moral life.

[183]See n. 147, above.

CHAPTER 4

THE MORAL STATUS OF MUTUALITY: A FORMAL NORM

INTRODUCTION

The purpose of this chapter is to demonstrate that mutuality is a formal norm for Christian social ethics. I will make the case for understanding mutuality as a formal norm based upon the evidence illuminated and analyzed thus far, and in light of the definition of "formal norm" given by Lisa Sowle Cahill, Josef Fuchs, and Timothy E. O'Connell.[1]

I demonstrate my claim by first, presenting a brief exposition of the definition of "formal norm" found in the work of Cahill, Fuchs and O'Connell. Next, I compare and contrast the normative treatment of mutuality by the four modern feminists with definitions of "formal norm" offered by Cahill, Fuchs, and O'Connell. Having determined that mutuality is a formal norm, I show its distinctiveness and its relationship to love and justice. Finally, in anticipation of the case study to be presented in Chapter 5, I suggest how mutuality, love and justice function together as foundational formal norms for Christian social ethics.

---

[1] I situate my treatment and use of formal norms within the context of post-Vatican II revisionist Roman Catholic moral theology. There has been a rigorous debate over the absolute nature of moral norms. A wide range of positions have been taken concerning the specificity and material content of moral norms, as well. See a sample of this discussion in *Readings in Moral Theology* No. 1, *Moral Norms and Catholic Tradition* ed. Charles E. Curran and Richard A. McCormick (New York: Paulist Press, 1979). See also Vincent MacNamara, *Faith and Ethics: Recent Roman Catholicism* (Washington, DC: Georgetown University Press, 1985). In addition, see *Readings in Moral Theology* No.2, *The Distinctiveness of Christian Ethics* ed. Charles E. Curran and Richard A. McCormick (New York: Paulist Press, 1980). Despite these lively debates concerning the potential absoluteness of various sorts of norms, one finds a great deal of consensus on the possibility of absolute status at the level which I have here called "formal."

FORMAL NORM: DEFINITIONS AND DESCRIPTIONS
Formal Norm: A Basic Definition

Thus far, I have utilized as working definitions Richard M. Gula's basic definition of "norm" and Timothy E. O'Connell's definition of "formal norm."[2] While these have served our general discussion and enabled us to see the general normative status of mutuality in the thought of four modern feminists, in order to claim mutuality as a formal norm distinct from love and justice, a closer examination of the notion of "formal norm" is now required.[3]

As Daniel C. Maguire has suggested, moral norms hold the moral memory of the community's collective and experiential wisdom.[4] Beyond the individual's wisdom, the community's wisdom adds breadth and depth illuminating personal and communal insight in moral decision-making, providing stability and consistency in judging wrong/right, bad/good. Moral norms carry no sanctions as such, but they do challenge individuals and communities to be accountable to others for the common good.

While there are several sources of moral norms, the most common source for Christians is the teaching, life, and ministry of Jesus.[5] The focal point of Jesus' teaching is a call to conversion, to live within and toward the fullness of the Reign of God. Compliance with the command to love God and neighbor is the behavioral expression of that *metanoia*. Jesus' life and death demonstrate for all time the

---

[2]See Introduction, n.'s 12 and 14.

[3]Several discussions of the basic definition of formal norm exist in introductory texts of Christian ethics. I review the key points here for the sake of clarity. See Gula, *Reason Informed by Faith*, 283-89. Also see Gula, *What About Moral Norms*, 55-58. In addition see O'Connell, *Principles For a Catholic Morality*, 180-84.

[4]Daniel C. Maguire, *The Moral Choice* (Minneapolis: Winston Press, 1979), 220-21.

[5]See Introduction, n.13.

meaning of love and he stands as a exemplar of Christian discipleship.[6] Moral norms assist in carrying a standard through the ages which enables Christians to live out the double love command in their time and place. These moral norms are generally categorized in two groups: "formal norms," that relate to character (virtues/vices) and "material norms" (behavioral principles). Our concern here is with formal norms, more specifically, formal norms characterized as moral absolutes.[7]

Formal norms have an absolute character because they express values that are common, beyond the distinctiveness of gender, culture, or history and are indicative of enduring notions of divine revelation, as well as that which is universal to human person.[8] Formal norms express the character of what ought to be, but they do not express the exact content of the behavior required to achieve that standard.[9]

Some formal norms are expressed in synthetic terms; terms which "refer to the material content of an action, but at the same time formulate a moral judgment."[10] When norms are formulated in synthetic terms they are absolute because they are tautological, that is, they name immoral behavior as immoral.[11] Some ethicists, for example John Finnis, vigorously dispute any attempt to dissolve or limit absolute moral norms to tautological, synthetic statements.

There are other kinds of formal norms such as the Golden Rule (Matt 7:12; Lk. 6:31) or the Double Love Command (Matt. 22:37-40; Mk. 12:29-34). Formal

---

[6]See e.g. Karl Rahner, *Love of Jesus and the Love of Neighbor* trans. Robert Barr (New York: Crossroad, 1983). See also Karl Rahner, "Reflections on the Unity of the Love of Neighbor and the Love of God," in *Theological Investigations* vol.6, *Concerning Vatican Council II* (New York: Crossroad, 1982), 231-49.

[7]Gula, *Reason Informed by Faith*, 286-87. Cahill, Fuchs, O'Connell understand the absoluteness of material norms to be conditioned by the intention of the moral agent and the circumstances of the moral dilemma. Formal norms are characteristically absolute.

[8]Ibid., 287-88.

[9]Cf. the discussion of material norms Ibid., 289-97.

[10]Ibid., 288. Gula cites Louis Janssens, "Norms and Priorities in a Love Ethics," *Louvain Studies* 4 (1977): 216. Examples of synthetic terms: murder, lie, adultery, etc.

[11]Gula, *Reason Informed by Faith*, 288.

norms can be stated positively (be loving, be just, be merciful, be honest) or negatively (do not be egotistical, proud, selfish). These norms exhibit "fixed points in divine revelation" or indicate what is universal to humankind and that which reaches beyond culture and history.[12] For our four feminists, mutuality is a formal norm, though not explicitly called such. This is so because, as was demonstrated in Chapter One, it is a characteristic of the Reign of God and because it is foundational to all healthy human relationships.

According to Gula, Fuchs, Cahill, and O'Connell, formal norms, though absolute, need to be combined with material norms and considerations of the intention of the moral agent as well as the circumstances of the moral dilemma in order to make an adequately reasoned ethical decision or any determinations concerning the morality of an action.

Yet, formal norms have significant value in themselves, because "they provide motivation, exhortation, and challenge to do what we already know to be right."[13]

Formal Norm: Timothy E. O'Connell

Timothy E. O'Connell describes the value of "formal norms" as meaningful for ethical practice in this way:

> They take the meaning of humanity, with its challenge of intellect and freedom. They further specify that meaning to a particular area of human life (for example, property rights). And they declare, in pithy form, what I already know but tend to forget or neglect: Do not steal. By presenting me with that challenge, almost in aphoristic style, formal norms serve me in those moments of human weakness and temptation that are so much a part our sin-affected situation.[14]

In O'Connell's view, formal norms play a definitive role in the application of evaluative knowledge to the facts of a situation.[15] Moral decision-making requires the

---

[12] Ibid., 287.

[13] Ibid., 289.

[14] O'Connell, *Principles For a Catholic Morality*, 182.

[15] See O'Connell's discussion of evaluative and speculative knowledge in Ibid., 58-64.

science of the established facts of a situation, but also the art/science of understanding the value of a person, thing and circumstances of a situation. O'Connell holds that formal norms are "self-evidently exceptionless," "they speak without fear of contradiction."[16]

In O'Connell's view, formal norms are virtues that define the moral person. They are general abstract terms that give no new information about a situation. Though they give no new information, they focus the goals of the human enterprise, challenge, motivate, and prompt people to move forward with moral choice-making in daily life.

O'Connell goes so far as to claim that formal norms are "more important than material norms."[17] He argues first, that "the primary force of Catholic natural law is precisely that moral obligation is objective . . . that its ultimate metaphysical basis is . . . existential reality."[18] He points to modern thinkers such as Levi-Strauss, Chomsky, and Piaget, who have submitted models for universal understandings of values.[19] Further, O'Connell shows that there is cross-cultural consensus concerning some important values and that these find expression as formal norms in all cultures-- e.g., "the truth must be told." O'Connell's third argument is based on "the phemonological fact that moral dilemmas are more commonly the result of the "weakness of the will" than of "darkness of intellect."[20] Moral motivation, provided by formal norms, is more frequently required and therefore more significant than the moral information typical of material norms.[21]

---

[16]Ibid., 183.

[17]O'Connell, "The Question of Moral Norms," *The American Ecclesiastical Review* 169 (1975): 383.

[18]Ibid.

[19]Ibid., 386. O'Connell also names Erickson, Kohlberg, Berne, and Maslow as providers of such models.

[20]Ibid.

[21]Ibid., 388.

As he later clarified, O'Connell's real concern is that the comparative complexity and more frequent discussion of material norms should not serve to de-emphasize the significance of the parenetic discourse articulated in formal norms.[22] The two types of norms have different purposes. Formal norms involve parenetic discourse, reminding us of the right and exhorting us to do it. Material norms entail explanatory discourse, attempting to state specifically what is said aphoristically.

Formal norms found in scripture are not unique to Christianity, nor is the content of Christian morality uniquely Christian in O'Connell's view.[23] He has, however, maintained that Christianity does hold a particular vision and motivation for life.[24]

Formal Norm: Josef Fuchs

German Jesuit revisionist ethicist Josef Fuchs has been one of the most significant figures in the post-Vatican Council II renewal of Catholic moral theology. To follow his thought is to also follow the progression of the key moments and controversies raised by the Council.[25]

Published at the start of Vatican II, Fuchs's most extensive work, *Theologia Moralis Generalis*, was one of the last manual-style works in moral theology.[26] In this work (*Theologia*) Fuchs attempted to develop a style of moral theology that differed from neo-Scholasticism. The early Fuchs can be distinguished from the later Fuchs in that his understanding of grace changed, particularly under the influence of

---

[22] O'Connell, *Principles For a Catholic Morality*, 275, n. 7. O'Connell credits Richard A. McCormick with helping him to clarify his position here. See Richard A. McCormick, "Notes on Moral Theology," *Theological Studies* 37 (1976): 72-74.

[23] O'Connell, *Principles For a Catholic Morality*, 244-48.

[24] Ibid., 248-53.

[25] See John A. Gallagher, *Time Past, Time Future: An Historical Study of Catholic Moral Theology* (New York: Paulist Press, 1990), 176-81, 212-14.

[26] Josef Fuchs, *Theologia Moralis Generalis* editio altra (Roma: Editrice Universita Gregoriana, 1963).

Karl Rahner.[27] Fuchs understood the Christian to be subject to the law of Christ (moral law). The imperative for obedience to that law was the external explication of the internal grace-filled movement of the Holy Spirit within each believer.[28] Also significant in early Fuchs is his consideration of human personal existence, rather than the traditional human nature of neo-Scholasticism. The human person thus became the norm of morality and the moral law became a dictate of practical reason.[29] Fuchs understood the natural law as an element in the law of Christ, not as separate from it. The moral law is thus accessible to all.[30] Whereas neo-Scholastics considered natural law a philosophical entity, Fuchs considered it a theological tenet.[31]

Heavily influenced by Rahner, the later Fuchs changed his thinking concerning the metaphysical basis for natural law, now grounding his natural law theory in transcendental Thomism. The person in the world can discover what is needed to protect and enhance human dignity and that is the discovery of the natural law.[32] Fuchs explains:

> [*a priori* moral norms] relate primarily to man's personal, responsible, social and historical nature which, as in all human behavior, demands consideration in the realization of his mandate and desire for progress. These general moral principles are of considerable importance and have their consequences in all human conduct, but alone they scarcely produce concrete guide-lines for human behavior and human progress. More concrete guide-lines presuppose experience and knowledge of

---

[27]See Josef Fuchs, "Moral Truths--Truths of Salvation," in *Christian Ethics in a Secular Arena* trans. Bernard Hoose and Brian McNeil (Washington, DC: Georgetown University Press, 1984), 48-65. See esp. 65, n. 6.

[28]Fuchs, *Theologia Moralis*, Prima Pars, 62 cited in Gallagher, *Time Past, Time Future*, 178.

[29]Ibid., 3-38, 59 cited in Gallagher, *Time Past, Time Future*, 178.

[30]Ibid., 62-68 cited in Gallagher, *Time Past, Time Future*, 178.

[31]Josef Fuchs, *Natural Law: A Theological Investigation* trans. Helmut Reckter and John A. Dowling (Dublin: Gill and Son, 1965) 6-7, 60.

[32]Josef Fuchs, *Human Values and Christian Morality* trans. M.H. Heelman, M. McRedmond, E. Young and G. Watson (Dublin: Gill and Macmillan, 1970), 181-83.

concrete reality and its possible method of realization--together with the consequences.³³

Fuchs's ethics after Vatican Council II became more, not less, Christocentric; only now the law of Christ does not impose any new moral requirements apart from the natural law. He sees the distinctiveness of Christian morality as a qualitative not quantitative difference. The Holy Spirit, alive in the Christian, permeates her/his entire life and is given expression in the law of Christ. Through the Holy Spirit the Christian receives grace, the power of the Spirit, the same Spirit that is in Christ, and becomes a sharer in the Spirit of Christ.

> If one is carried by the grace of the Spirit of Christ, the imperative of being man-in-Christ will be one's own willing and loving. The more one allows oneself to be caught up by the grace of Christ, the more will this imperative, which is based on both natural law and the supernatural order, become one's own concern, one's inner law. What constitutes the law of Christian life and conduct, is not so much the being and obligation that are derived from Christ, but rather the striving and loving that flow from the grace of the Spirit of Christ.³⁴

Christ is the animating principle.³⁵ The animating function of Christ, according to Fuchs is the grace of his Spirit working within the Christian, motivating her/him to lead a moral life of love toward redemption. This basic stance concerning norms is significant for our purposes, as we shall see.

Fuchs examined scripture, magisterial teaching, and natural law and concluded that they contain no moral absolutes.³⁶ He claims that what is found in scripture is a series of transcendental norms and objective values. He claims the scriptures have a *parenetic* scope (useful in exhortation) and a *maieutic* scope (explicitly affirm

---

³³Ibid., 187.

³⁴Fuchs, *Human Values*, 83.

³⁵Ibid., 65.

³⁶Josef Fuchs, "The Absoluteness of Moral Terms," *Gregorianum* 52 (1971): 415-33. See also *Christian Morality: The Word Becomes Flesh* trans. Brian McNeil (Washington, DC: Georgetown University Press, 1987) 3-18. Also "Historicity and Moral Norms," in *Moral Demands and Personal Obligations* trans. Brian McNeil (Washington, DC: Georgetown University Press, 1993), 102-104.

eternally high values).³⁷ The *parenetic* and *maieutic* presentations in the scriptures are sporadic and not systematic, which makes it difficult to glean material norms from the texts. The magisterium and natural law do generate material norms, but they are culturally and historically bound. In the interpersonal context within which Fuchs understands morality, moral decisions are part of the on-going creation of human persons and human cultures. God is the primary absolute and the secondary absolutes are formal norms.³⁸

Fuchs believes that formal norms are "nothing more than the formal formulation of man's ethical self-understanding."³⁹ Formal norms can be applied to a variety of spheres of life. Formal norms are universal. They have pedagogical value as a tool for moral reflection. They are useful toward achieving a greater truth and therefore a grater objectivity in making moral decisions or as a guide for one who has lost her/his way and is returning to social responsibility and community.⁴⁰

Fuchs holds that Christian formal norms have motivational value but no unique moral content.⁴¹ St. Paul demonstrated that potential when he invoked the special dignity of the body and the mutual relationships of Christians in Christian community as motivation for morality (1 Cor. 6:12-20; Eph. 4:25). Formal norms expressed in cult, ritual, faith, hope, contemplation, prayer and love are religious in Fuch's opinion, but they can inspire moral actions. For Fuchs, the theological and the moral life exist

---

³⁷Josef Fuchs, "Christianity, Christian Ethics, and the Crisis of Values," in *Christian Ethics*, 21-22.

³⁸Fuchs, "Absoluteness of Moral Terms," 437, 418.

³⁹Ibid., 452.

⁴⁰Ibid., 456.

⁴¹Josef Fuchs, "Is There a Christian Morality?," in *The Distinctiveness of Christian Ethics*, Readings in Moral Theology No. 2, ed. Charles E. Curran and Richard A. McCormick (New York: Paulist Press, 1980), 15. Cf. Fuchs, *Human Values*, 120-31.

in one another; this holds true for all people. Therefore, when one pursues what is good, s/he pursues the absolute, or God.[42]

Formal Norms: Lisa Sowle Cahill

Known for her work in sexual ethics; her insistence on an integrated methodology that balances major sources of Christian ethics (revelation and human experience); and her work pertaining to biblical ethics and state-supported violence (war)--Lisa Sowle Cahill has defined several types of moral norms as they have appeared in the post-Vatican Council II ethics literature. Cahill has isolated four types of norms involved in the discussions of "exceptionless norms."[43] The impetus for the debate about "exceptionless norms" has been the challenge of *Gaudium et spes*, 4 and 5 which stressed the need for a personal approach to natural law and to consider the "signs of the times" in moral reflection.[44]

Among the four types of norms Cahill delineates, are:

> Formal moral norms, such as "Be honest," "Be just," and "Respect persons." These principles are absolute: dishonesty, injustice, and disrespect for persons are wrong without exception. However, these norms are formal in that they do not tell us exactly what is concretely to count for these wrongs. . . . Even after general moral absolutes have been defined, their substantive meaning remains to be filled out.[45]

Unfortunately for our purposes, Cahill does not elaborate further on this category, but rather devotes the remainder of her discussion to three other types of norms.

Cahill does however, address the fact that formal norms are found in the

---

[42]Fuchs, *Human Values*, 148-77.

[43]Lisa Sowle Cahill, "Contemporary Challenges to Exceptionless Norms," in *Moral Theology Today: Certitudes and Doubts*, (St. Louis: The Pope John XXIII Medical-Moral Research and Education Center, 1984), 123. These discussions followed the debates of the 1950's and 1960's concerning situation ethics.

[44]Ibid., 122.

[45]Ibid., 123. Cahill appeals to Richard A. McCormick, Charles E. Curran, Josef Fuchs, Bruno Schüller, and Louis Janssens as those who share this view.

scriptures.[46] She admits that "the contribution of the Bible to ethics is at the level of community formation, not primarily as that of rules or principles . . . ."[47] In her view, the New Testament focus on the Kingdom of God and the struggle of the primitive Christian communities to meet the challenges implied therein is morally significant and instructive. The very tension created in the New Testament by the transcendent nature of the Reign of God and Jesus' challenge to perfection is what gives value to the formal norms of love, justice, equality, mercy, forgiveness or solidarity in the historical situation. As Cahill points out, the failure of the early communities to live out the perfection to which Jesus called them did not stop them from creating communities that attempted to be loving, just, mutual, etc. Indeed, Christians were successful to the extent that on many occasions they were able to project their quality of life into the wider society and effectively achieve social justice by drawing these notions (formal norms) into higher relief.[48]

The relationship of the formal norms presented in the past in the New Testament, the desire of persons in the present to follow Jesus, and the transcendental nature of the standards that mark the Reign of God is a relationship that is at once controversial and provocative, and therefore valuable in Cahill's view.[49] The Christian cannot but be disquieted by the formal norms presented in the context of the scriptures. Cahill observes:

> [W]e may conclude that at a minimum, kingdom futurity as divine transcendence and sustenance is required by New Testament eschatology as a prototype for the faith texture of discipleship. The Kingdom is both present and immanent in our experience, and

---

[46] Lisa Sowle Cahill, *Love Your Enemies: Discipleship, Pacifism, and Just War Theory* (Minneapolis: Fortress Press, 1994), 8-9, 15-38. Cahill does not explicitly state she is discussing formal norms here. By her own definition that is the case, however. She supports her claim drawing on a wide range of contemporary historical critical biblical scholarship. See her "Moral Methodology: A Case Study," *Chicago Studies* 19 (1980): 173-79, esp. 174.

[47] Cahill, *Love Your Enemies*, 244. Material norms are not given in scripture.

[48] Ibid., 245.

[49] Ibid., 246.

> transcendent in that it is graciously enabled by the saving inauguration of a new divine-human interaction, a mutually responsive relationship profoundly beyond human creation and control.[50]

Cahill notes that because of the divine-human relationship which is the context for living out the formal norms of the Reign of God, grace is available to all to enter into that Reign. Those who turn from grace by despairing of the transformation now or simply pretending to move toward the Reign of God, utilizing purely humanitarian means, will indeed be judged.

From all of this we can conclude that in Cahill's view, formal norms are significant for the shaping of the broad moral milieu. The encounter with formal norms, which function to challenge, motivate, and inspire, provides the occasion for divine-human relationship or judgment.

Formal Norm: Consensus Among Cahill, Fuchs, and O'Connell

A broad consensus on the definition of "formal norm" can be found among Cahill, Fuchs, and O'Connell. Formal norms are exceptionless norms that describe the shape of the style of how a person ought to be or act in a particular sphere of life. Human reason can adduce formal norms from ordinary life experiences. Christian sources of formal norms such as the magisterium or scripture, while providing no new content for moral norms, present them in a manner that gives them a qualitative uniqueness for the believing person. Formal norms function to provide motivation, inspiration, vision and instruction for all people. In the Christian community, however, there is a qualitative difference in that the intentionality of the community is focused on the Reign of God and working toward its fullness.

ARGUMENT FOR MUTUALITY AS A FORMAL NORM

In general, feminist theology arose as a corrective to classical theologies which stressed transcendent, patriarchal, or male images of God to the near exclusion of the immanent, egalitarian, female images. As feminists have developed theologies, they have shown that classical notions of love and justice are not adequate to

---

[50]Ibid.

accommodate the kinds, degrees, and qualities of relationship that emerge as imperative, if Christians are to be faithful to the images of God presented in the whole of their tradition.

As has been illustrated thus far in this dissertation, there is evidence of the emergence of a norm that is a corrective and complement to the traditional notions of love and justice, namely the notion of mutuality. All four forms of mutuality (as I have defined them) address areas of relationship that were degraded, discounted, or entirely ignored in classical theology because they required serious consideration of "things female" or "feminine" in a theological system biased against women.

Four Feminists' Evidence for the Normative Status of Mutuality

As we saw in Chapter One, Rosemary Radford Ruether, (Isabel) Carter Heyward, Beverly Wildung Harrison, and Elizabeth A. Johnson all utilize mutuality in a normative fashion in their works. The question remains whether the four feminists' normative understanding of mutuality is identical to the consensus definition of formal norm we discovered in Cahill, Fuchs, and O'Connell.

For Ruether, mutuality describes the form and style of human relationships to other humans, earthcreatures, the earth itself and the entire cosmos.[51] She views mutuality as a moral absolute in that without mutuality, the dynamics of power-over readily become abusive and oppressive. Ruether has illustrated how the formal norm of mutuality is accessible to all by reason through the principles of the natural sciences of ecology, astrophysics and quantum physics. From a specifically Christian perspective, mutuality is a formal norm because it is characteristic and formative of the Reign of God. For Christians (as well as non-Christians) "mutuality" expresses what it means to be in a healthy thriving relationship with all things and all beings.

Heyward's assertions about mutuality meet the criteria defining it as a formal norm.[52] Employing psychological data, Heyward has explained how no healthy

---

[51] See Chapter One, after n. 36.

[52] See Chapter One, after n. 99.

relationship lacks mutuality. She has also pointed to ecology, astrophysics and quantum physics as sources through which reason has access to the notion of mutuality as a necessity for life. Heyward's primary sources for mutuality are scripture and Christian tradition which reveal a God of mutual relation and Jesus as its exemplar. In addition, she has shown how the lack of mutuality, particularly in sexual relationships, allows for power-over that leads to abuse and oppression. Mutuality as Heyward describes it is an exceptionless formal norm.

Harrison is clear that mutuality sets the conditions for genuine love and justice by limiting the dynamics of power in those relationships to power-with rather than power-over.[53] What Harrison claims concerning mutuality is defined by Cahill, Fuchs, and O'Connell as the terms of a "formal norm."[54] Harrison, whose eye is always toward the dynamics of power in the economic, political, and social arenas, views the capacity for mutuality as a common power residing in each person as a function of the *imago Dei*, grounded in the sociality that is innate in humanity. She concurs with Heyward in affirming mutuality as a moral norm for sexual relations, asserting that non-mutual relations are harmful and oppressive. Implied in the human/divine relationship is our relationship to others. Since God's relations to us are mutual, we too, must engage in mutual relations with others.

Johnson's notion of mutuality is a formal norm according to the consensus definition of our three moralists.[55] Based on human experience, particularly the affiliation patterns of women, Johnson has observed that mutuality is normative. Primarily, she understands God's relations *ad intra* and *ad extra* as mutual. Johnson forcefully argues that because God's relationships *ad intra* and *ad extra* are mutual, human relationships need also be normatively mutual. This means that for Johnson, mutuality is a formal norm.

---

[53]See Chapter One, after n. 174.

[54]See Harrison's understanding of norms, Chapter One, n. 197.

[55]See Chapter One, after n. 217.

Distinctiveness/Relationship: Love, Justice and Mutuality

Love

For our purposes in distinguishing love, justice and mutuality, the distinctions made by Ruether and Heyward concerning love are most revealing. Ruether stresses the necessity of a healthy self-love and the perception of equality among the lovers/beloved as conditions for love, which she describes as "[seeking] the total welfare and personal growth of the other."[56] Heyward agrees with Ruether and emphasizes (as does Ruether invoking the prophetic tradition) the unity of the three classical aspects of love (*eros, agape, philia*) in practical *action* rather than focusing on *concepts* of love. Feminists turn to these distinctions, qualifications, and emphases to counter many longstanding interpretations of sacrificial love, which in the world of women frequently translated into unhealthy self-denial and passive subordination.[57]

Beginning with Valerie Saiving Goldstein's watershed article on the relationship of sacrifice and sin in the moral lives of women and men, modern feminists have roundly rejected notions of love that see *only* sacrifice in the Christian notion of *agape*.[58] As was shown in Chapter One, feminists prefer a definition of love that is *conditioned by* the formal norm, mutuality. Traditional and *unqualified* definitions of love referring to the classical Greek notions of *agape, eros,* and *philia* rooted in the philosophy of Aristotle and Plato are repudiated by our feminists.[59]

Rooted in the Hebrew and Christian scriptures the feminist notion of love involves first, a healthy self-esteem that is grounded in knowledge of God's

---

[56] See Chapter One, n.'s 61-62.

[57] See Gudorf, "Parenting," *Women's Consciousness*.

[58] Valerie Saiving Goldstein, "The Human Situation: A Feminine View," *The Journal of Religion* 40 (1960): 108-11.

[59] See the discussion of Aristotle's and Thomas's understandings of these classical notions, Chapter Two, after n. 62 and after n. 116. Lawrence C. Becker and Charlotte B. Becker (New York: Garland Publishing, Inc., 1992). See also *Webster's*, s.v. "love." "strong affection for another arising out of kinship or personal ties; attraction based on sexual desires; affection based on admiration, benevolence, or common interests."

unconditional love for each person (1 Jn. 4:19) and a relational anthropology.[60] This self-esteem includes a balanced self-confidence that acknowledges one's gifts and talents, but also one's limitations and failures to be assertive. Self-love requires that one meet one's basic needs (not wants) such as food, clothing, shelter, health care, basic education, rest to the highest degree possible (within the bounds of justice).[61] No healthy love of self can be sustained outside of some sort of communal affiliation, because humans are naturally social beings. Here is where love of neighbor finds its source and its end. Created in the image and likeness of a God who is in mutual relation *ad intra* (Johnson), but who "is also a person" (Buber), humans are related to one another in the kinship of humanity and the common Parenthood of God. Love of neighbor is to be as an intense desire for the good of the other as one's love for oneself (Matt. 2:39-40).

Jesus extended the boundaries of what love requires to include love of enemies and anyone in need (Matt. 5:46; Lk. 6:32-34; Matt. 5:43; Lk. 10:29-37). In making that extension, Jesus moved to the deepest challenge of love, namely to the place where the common ground of foes is their humanity itself. It is in the attempt to love the enemy that the Christian finds her greatest strength, in the "power to be powerless" (Cf. Mk. 10:35-45). From a feminist perspective this means that if the Christian is not to be ruled by the power-over that is of the enemy, s/he must move to a stance of power-with; relinquishing power-over, but also asserting the common humanity s/he and the enemy share. Once the enemy is viewed as an equal, true affection can be given to her/him. The move that has been made constitutes a change of stance to mutuality.

It is in the "love of enemy" where the relation between love and mutuality perhaps becomes most clear. As Ruether has pointed out, there can be no real love between those who do not understand themselves as equals in some form. This does

---

[60]For a fine explication of biblical love see Daniel C. Maguire, *The Moral Core of Judaism and Christianity* (Minneapolis: Fortress Press, 1993), 208-30.

[61]June Jordan, "Where is the Love?," in *Civil Wars* (Boston: Beacon Press, 1981), 142-44.

not mean, as in the case of Aristotle, that only social/political/ economic peers can love. It does mean that the basic dynamic and attitude toward power in the relationship of love needs to be one of "power-with." The dynamic that names the exchange constitutes mutuality; what is exchanged is love (affection). This exchange is more accurately called mutual love. Only when one chooses self-denial toward a goal of greater mutuality (out of mutual love) is sacrifice healthy. All other motives for self-denial can be traced back to selfishness or sloth, or worse, self-hatred. Love then, is the exchange of affection between acknowledged equals, toward the maximum well-being of the other(s), in the context of mutuality.

Justice

In the Introduction I reviewed and gave a general critique of three major categories of theories of justice: positivist, utilitarian, and natural law.[62] The general criticisms of those justice theories given there represent the key criticisms feminists raise against them. The four Christian feminists in this study fundamentally agree that the most adequate theory of justice is found instead, in the biblical justice outlined within the Hebrew and Christian scriptures.[63]

These feminists stress the relational nature of justice and contrast their understanding of justice, which focuses on ethics of care, with concepts of justice focusing on ethics of rights.[64] Heyward's definition of justice, for instance, centers on the Hebrew notion of *hesed*. While Heyward translates the word as "righteousness," it can also be translated as compassion, caring, or fidelity.[65] The interhuman

---

[62]See Introduction, at n. 42.

[63]A fine summary of biblical justice is Daniel C. Maguire, *The Moral Core of Judaism and Christianity* (Minneapolis: Fortress, 1993), 126-65.

[64]See particularly Heyward's and Johnson's ideas concerning justice, Chapter One, after n. 145 and after n. 253.

[65]José Miranda, *Marx and the Bible: A Critique of the Philosophy of Oppression* (Maryknoll: Orbis Books, 1974), 46-47. Miranda states: "In the Hebrew Bible, *hesed* appears together with justice (*ṣedaḳah*) and/or right (*mišpat*) in synonymic parallelism or in hendiadys in the following instances: Jer. 9:23; Isa. 16:5; Mic. 6:8; Hos. 2:21-22; 6:6; 10:12; Zech. 7:9; Pss. 25:9-10; 33:5; 36:6-7; 36:11; 40:11; 85:11; 88:12-13; 89:15; 98:2-3; 103:17; 119:62-64." See *The Oxford Companion to the English*

compassion that is *hesed* is possible only through knowledge of God, who is a God of covenant and mutual relations.

Johnson refers to Gilligan's ethic of care, which suggests that justice is done when relationships are converted from either total dependence or independence to interdependence.[66] Utilizing the image of a web, Gilligan suggests that all humans are related to one another and the entire universe. Perfect justice happens when everyone and everything is responded to and included in a manner that serves the maximum thriving of all; no one is hurt or left out. Justice, then, is not only a matter of equality, but also a matter of interconnection. Justice then becomes a matter of power-with grounded in the common power of mutual relation, rather than power-over rooted in coercion. It is mutuality that forms the strands of the web that hold everyone and everything in relation.

Mutuality requires justice to address both rights and needs. Traditionally, self-interest was viewed as the root motivator of society's ills and in many cases as the fundamental justification for hierarchical, coercive social structures.[67] In the face of the persistence of self interest, rights language, which tends to focus on individuals, delineates minimum standards and boundaries that must not be violated. The traditional role of justice is to supervise and protect those boundaries. When the good is understood in terms of relationality, however, justice needs to address persons in the context of the groups to which they belong. Mutuality, which views the person as part of social-historical relations, requires justice to consider those social-historical

---

Language, s.v. "hendiadys." "A term in rhetoric for equal words joined by *and* instead of a one word modifier (nice and warm rather than nicely warm), and similar words joined by *and* where one might have been enough, usually for emphasis . . . ."

[66]See Chapter One, n. 257 for references to Carol Gilligan, et. al.

[67]See Reinhold Niebuhr, *Man's Nature and His Communities* (New York: Charles Scribner's Sons, 1965), 39, *The Self and the Dramas of History* (New York: Charles Scribner's Sons, 1955), 165, *The Children of the Light and Children of Darkness* (New York: Charles Scribner's Sons, 1944), 62.

relations to correct historical wrongs as well as immediate infractions, and to restore and reconcile relationships.[68]

What Mutuality as a Formal Norm Illuminates/Delimits

We have said that formal norms function to motivate, exhort, provide vision, and give instruction for the moral life. Just how mutuality functions to illuminate certain aspects of the moral life will demonstrate further its status as a formal norm.

Mutuality, as these feminists define it, is a dynamic process and not a static situation. Set within a dynamic world view, an emerging feminist ethic of mutuality has implications for ethicists' appreciation of truth and truth claims. In a recent essay Leonard Swidler helpfully analyzes the relation between truth and mutuality, highlighting truth's praxis, interpretive, and perspectival dimensions.

Parties in mutual relation are oriented to the needs of the other and maintain an intentionality directed to the well-being of the other(s).[69] Mutuality then requires a "praxis view of truth" in which the truth is conditioned by the intentions of the relationship.[70] What is true is related to the action-oriented intention of the speaker.[71]

Mutuality is a relationship between two or more parties, each of whom has a distinctive particularity and history. Sustaining the relationship requires a perspectival view of truth in which the various standpoints determined by culture, gender, history, economics or politics are taken into account. For mutual relations it is necessary to recognize that language is limited in the meaning it can bear. As Wittgenstein has

---

[68]Cf. Abraham Edel and Elizabeth Flower, "Economic Justice: Notes and Queries," *The Journal of Value Inquiry* 19 (1985): 257-58.

[69]See Leonard Swidler, "Mutuality: The Matrix For Mature Living," *Religion and Intellectual Life* 3 (1985): 105-19.

[70]Ibid., 108.

[71]Ibid. Swidler cites the epistemological theories of Max Scheler and Karl Mannheim as the basis for this statement.

argued, human language can bear only one or two perspectives at once.[72] What is true needs to be understood in a context.

From Gadamer and Ricoeur, Swidler adduces evidence that knowledge of any text is also an interpretation of the text. In sustaining a mutual relation, this interpretive view of the truth needs to be acknowledged lest there be false absolutizing of unintended information or action.[73]

Having identified several views of truth that can affect the understanding of mutuality as well as the sustaining of a mutual relationship--praxis, perspectival, interpretive--the need for a fourth kind of truth becomes clear, namely a dialogic truth. As one acts, speaks, and interprets with another there are moments when the "I" and the "Thou" combine to form the "We." It is in those moments that mutuality reaches its apex. If we are not open and ready for these kinds of truth and the moment of true mutuality that happens in the "between" of dialogue, we live in a false reality. We assume what are indeed only elements of truth to be the full truth.

How does one counter the obvious risk of lapsing into relativism when considering conditioned aspects of truth? As Swidler suggests, clear acknowledgement of one's own presuppositions is significant in identifying the biases or lenses through which one interprets information and actions.[74] Further, he suggests that one should purposefully seek out viewpoints other than one's own and probe them for what challenges and enlightens one. He also suggests a full measure of modesty concerning one's own viewpoint--it is the rare human being who has a corner on the full truth.[75] In the Christian milieu, the concurrence of scripture/tradition, Church teachings and the *sensus fidelium* provide additional safeguards.

---

[72]Ibid., 109.

[73]Ibid., 110.

[74]Ibid., 111.

[75]Ibid., 111-12.

Besides transforming our understanding of truth, mutuality shifts ethics' understanding of the moral subject by focusing on the sociality of the human person. No longer is the person's action evaluated as if s/he is constituted as an isolated unit. Rather moral actions are considered in light of culture, history, and the social context of the situation. As H. Richard Niebuhr so forcefully argued, we are always in a situation of response to others.[76] Our actions make sense in relationship to others. The structure of a relationship is key to its moral value.

Mutuality also expands the idea of the moral subject from one bearing a status (human nature) to one who develops, experiences, and transforms value and who is, in turn, developed and transformed by valuing. The moral capacity of the self, the motivation for sacrifice, and the motivation for justice is understood in terms of mutuality in relationships. Mutuality, further, focuses on reciprocity in moral agency. In the situations of mutuality, the moral subject constantly exchanges valuing and being valued. We are enabled "to grasp our dependence on each other and our social institutions and relations for our moral self-regard and moral power."[77]

Along with renovating ethicist's view of truth and moral agency, the notion of mutuality modifies what is understood as "good." As we have seen in the discussion of the four feminists, mutuality moves the starting point for ethical reflection to a radically inclusive place, where literally everyone and everything is included. The Christian vision of the "new heavens/new earth" stands behind the notion of mutuality as it is drawn from Christian sources. There is a two-fold context for the vision, the present history and the future. "Goods" based on atomistic individualism and patterns of competition, adversarial relations, exploitation, authoritarianism, or paternalism are ruled out because they diminish or deny the fundamental mutual relation that exists between God and humans and that needs to exist between humans, and with all of creation.

---

[76]H.R. Niebuhr, *Responsible Self*, 70-71.

[77]Ruth L. Smith, "Morality and Perceptions of Society: The Limits of Self-Interest," *Journal for the Scientific Study of Religion* 26 (1987): 289.

Human good needs to fit in with all other "goods" in the cosmos with an eye toward the maximum flourishing of all--not just human thriving. This means mutuality requires an integration of independent and responsible acts as well as interdependent and relational activities. It means that in achieving the "good" what must be overcome is whatever isolates, completely separates, arouses disinterest and atomistic individualism. There is one good that permeates both private and public spheres; mutuality empowers by including everything and everyone in the social/political/economic equation.[78]

"Good" measured in terms of mutuality can be promoted by society and institutions in a manner analogous to the way rugged individualism has historically been promoted in the United States. Every human is born in need of relationships. When relations are such that needs and rights are not met and honored, injustice occurs and it is accompanied by self-doubt, mistrust or resentment on the part of the victim. The practice of justice in society also, therefore, needs to include mutual practices of reconciliation among the parties involved, as Margaret Cotroneo states:

> The dialogue context requires that each partner be able to state his or her needs and expectations to the other in terms of the present. It is a process of mutual accountability. Reestablishing a dialogue on this basis in an injured relationship is a form of giving. By asking for something, a person says he or she continues to care enough about the relationship to risk rejection. It is the extending of trust in order to open up the possibility of rebalancing the "ledger" of exploitative or unjust relation through the reciprocal giving of the other. Giving through asking is a claim on the other for reciprocal consideration of one's own needs and expectations. Because the claim is in the form

---

[78]Ibid., 288-91. It could be argued that the formal norm, mutuality actually disempowers one because human finitude does not allow any person to *always* deal with *everything* and *everyone*. While humans are indeed, limited, the purposeful creation and maintenance of community, solidarity, friendship, ecological and spiritual relationships can assist one in staying focused on the goal of an evermore perfect praxis of mutuality. In the Jewish and Christian contexts, it is understood that God's grace undergirds all efforts toward perfect mutuality. (Recall for example Buber's notion of the Eternal Thou and Duns Scotus's notion of *acceptatio*.) In the case of non-believers, human reason concerning a course toward basic survival and a high quality of life can provide the impetus for striving toward a more perfect praxis of mutuality. Like the formal norms of love and justice, mutuality provides a standard and source of motivation, inspiration, vision and instruction. To not consider mutuality, however, is to neglect a whole realm of moral responsibility and possibility.

of asking, it is an acknowledgement of the other's capacity for trustworthy giving. Asking . . . in dialogue . . . invites the partner to respond.[79]

When mutuality is not recognized by both parties, and an impasse results, an ethics of care does not abandon the effort. Rather it moves to confront the deeper social-psychological blockages and tries again and again. An ethic of mutuality may then knowingly choose to love sacrificially in order to act-the-other-into-life, moving toward greater mutuality.

Mutuality, Love, and Justice: Foundational Formal Norms

As has been implied, feminists elevate mutuality from being considered as any other value to being understood as a formal norm. The special attention to mutuality does not replace love and justice as norms, but complements and corrects them. In relation to love and justice, mutuality is the prior recognition of the common power, in all of creation and in relation to the divine, to make reciprocal claims on one another.

Mutuality brings justice to love. It does so in two ways. First it liberates and affirms the self in meeting her/his own needs. Indeed, as we have seen, mutuality requires the partners in a relationship be whole, distinct individuals. Mutuality challenges moral agents to integrity of character.[80] For the Christian, the *imago Dei* and the unconditional mutual relation with God lies at the heart of such integrity. From a stance of inner justice, a healthy self-esteem, the person is able to move outward to others within affection rooted in their common power. In maintaining personal integrity, justice plays the role of calling the person to honesty; to deal with her/himself as a whole embodied being--physical, emotional, spiritual, mental--in all its strengths and weaknesses. On this personal level, the challenge mutuality brings to love is similar to the dynamics that are at work in the love of one's enemies, only here, the "enemy" may be within. Those aspects of every person that bring alienation

---

[79]Margaret Cotroneo, "A Contextual Catholic Ethics," Ph.D. diss. (Temple University, Philadelphia, PA, 1983), 248.

[80]See the contrast of character Jesus presents Lk. 18:10-17.

in any form and which militate against personal wholeness are challenged forth for confrontation and healing. Positively, the call of justice mutuality brings to love is for the perfection of the self; for the self to inclusively embrace what one/it is.[81]

A second way mutuality brings justice to love is in the way it requires one to love one's neighbor. In light of what was just stated, the motivation for love of neighbor can be made more clear if one addresses this question to herself: "Am I a neighbor?". The test of that question is honesty within one's self and the challenge to cease projecting outward what is not whole within. If one views oneself as like another, one must first see the common power and common limitations one shares with the other. Mutuality dictates that all humans share a common power in relationship by virtue of the *imago Dei*. By not being a "neighbor," in a real way I deny my own humanness. If this is so, I am not capable of a human love or an inner justice, and I am plagued with disease that requires healing. Only after healing takes place can I be free enough to be influenced and motivated to be a neighbor. As a neighbor, I can give and receive mutual love and choose to serve others in dignity with integrity.

Justice tempered by mutuality saves love from condescension in that mutuality requires a reverence for the common dignity that is shared and/or an appreciation of the relatedness of all creation to the divine and to one another. Mutuality requires that the boundaries of any relationship be set together by all involved in the relationship. A noteworthy example of this dynamic can be seen in Jesus' approach to others in many of the healing stories.[82]

We have seen how mutuality serves justice and love. Mutuality and love also serve justice. Justice restrains mutuality from "value free" agreement (Rawls) that could point a relationship in a direction that detracts and harms the common good by failing to direct individual needs toward the well-being of all. Justice keeps mutuality

---

[81] See Matt. 5:44-48.

[82] See Mk. 10:46-52; Lk. 8:22-26; Mk. 9:14-29.

real by holding forth concrete needs which must be filled in order to satisfy human dignity and the common good. Love prevents mutuality from regressing to a utilitarian exchange, a mere reciprocity by holding up *communio* as the standard (telos) of relationship.

In the functioning of love, justice and mutuality then, we have the formal norms that create the value framework for Christian feminist social ethics. In the final chapter I will demonstrate how this framework, which includes mutuality as a formal norm, leads to greater flourishing of all involved in an ethical dilemma than is possible when the formal norm of mutuality is neglected.

CHAPTER 5

MUTUALITY A FORMAL NORM FOR CHRISTIAN SOCIAL ETHICS: A CASE STUDY

INTRODUCTION

Thus far in this study we have uncovered a Christian feminist definition of mutuality, examined its antecedents in medieval and contemporary Christian thought, and made a case for its status as a formal moral norm. In this chapter, I hope to illustrate the probative value of including mutuality in an interpretive framework for moral decision-making.[1] I will show how considering mutuality (along with love and justice) when resolving an ethical dilemma is more likely to lead to practical actions that promote, provide, and/or sustain optimum human flourishing, a flourishing set within the interdependent context of the whole of creation.

To illustrate the effects of mutuality in moral reflection and judgment, I wish to evaluate three ethical analyses of U.S. involvement in the Persian Gulf War in 1991 which employ the Just War Tradition. Utilizing the definition formulated in this study, I will show instances where consideration of mutuality and its four forms, (or failure to consider mutuality) in ethical reflection concerning the justification of the use of force influences moral judgment. Specifically, I will examine essays[2] on the subject by

---

[1] Some would argue that this practical application is contradictory to the definition of formal norm given in Chapter Four. I maintain that in this case mutuality is utilized as a formal norm. My stance is that a Christian *ought* to act mutually in every situation (also lovingly and justly). Given this, s/he must, as a moral agent, raise specific questions concerning whether or not those who called the Gulf War a "just war" considered the norm of mutuality when evaluating the war. Justice and love can be both formal and material norms; such is the case with mutuality. The formal norm of mutuality calls for its consideration in the material case.

[2] The three essays are from *But Was It Just?: Reflections on the Morality of the Persian Gulf War*, ed. David E. Decrosse (New York: Doubleday, 1992).

the ethicists George Weigel,[3] Jean Bethke Elshtain,[4] and Stanley Hauerwas.[5] I will close by offering conclusions concerning ways in which mutuality as a formal norm qualitatively affects moral decision-making.

Given the confines of this format, I will not attempt to analyze the implications mutuality holds for the validity of the just war theory, as such.[6] The three ethicists whose works we will examine here all accept to some degree the usefulness of the just war theory. Our purpose is to see where and how mutuality enters into their analyses, and what effect it has upon their final judgments.

The limitations of this study also preclude a comparison of every point of the three scholars' analyses. I have therefore elected to focus my analysis on each scholar's evaluation of three just war criteria: *jus ad bellum*--just cause; *jus in bello*--proportionality of means and discrimination.[7]

Although neither George Weigel, Jean Bethke Elshtain, nor Stanley Hauerwas explicitly discuss mutuality in their essays, I analyze the content of their arguments

---

[3]George Weigel is president of the Ethics and Public Policy Center in Washington, DC. He is a Catholic theologian specializing in social ethics. His past publications include: *Tranquillitas Ordinis: The Present Failure and Future Promise of American Thought on War and Peace*.

[4]Jean Bethke Elshtain is formerly Centennial Professor of Political Science at Vanderbilt University in Nashville, TN. She is currently professor of social ethics at the University of Chicago Divinity School. Her expertise include moral philosophy, the history of political thought, contemporary political and social theory, and women's studies. Publications by Elshtain include: *Public Man, Private Woman: Women in Social and Political Thought, Power Trips and Other Journeys: Essays in Feminism as Civic Discourse, Antigone's Daughters*, and *Women and War*.

[5]Stanley Hauerwas is Professor of Religious Ethics at Duke University, Durham, NC. His work focuses on an ethic of virtue or character. In 1984 he delivered the Père Marquette Theology Lecture, "Should War Be Eliminated?: Philosophical and Theological Investigations." Publications by Hauerwas include *A Community of Character: Toward a Constructive Christian Social Ethic* and *The Peaceable Kingdom*.

[6]See J. Bryan Hehir, "Just War Theory in a Post-Cold War World," *Journal of Religious Ethics* 20 (1992): 237-57. See also Lisa Sowle Cahill, "Theological Contents of Just War Theory: A Response to J. Bryan Hehir," *Journal of Religious Ethics* 20 (1992): 259-65.

[7]The most common set of just war criteria includes eight principles. *Jus ad bellum* includes: just cause, right intention, competent authority, proportionality of ends, and last resort. *Jus in bello*: proportionality of means and discrimination.

utilizing the definitions of mutuality I have gleaned from Ruether, Heyward, Harrison, and Johnson. The **basic definition** I have adduced from these writers is:

Mutuality is the sharing of "power-with" by and among all parties in a relationship in a way that recognizes the wholeness and particular experience of each participant toward the end of optimum flourishing of all.

I have also noted four forms of mutuality:

Cosmic Mutuality: *the sharing of "power-with" by and among the Creator, human beings, all earth elements, and the entire cosmos in a way that recognizes their interdependence and reverences all.*

Gender Mutuality: *the sharing of "power-with" by and among women and men in a way that recognizes the full participation of each in the imago Dei, embodied in daily life and through egalitarian relationships.*

Generative Mutuality: *the sharing of "power-with" by and among the Divine, human persons, and all creation in the on-going co-creation and redemption of the world.*

Social Mutuality: *the sharing of "power-with" by and among members of society in a way that recognizes the foundational dignity of each and the obligation to attain and maintain for each what is necessary to sustain that dignity.*

"FROM LAST RESORT TO ENDGAME: MORALITY, THE GULF WAR, AND THE PEACE PROCESS" BY GEORGE WEIGEL

Review of the Content

George Weigel's essay expresses his enthusiastic support of U.S. policy in the Gulf, and his unambiguous endorsement of the just war theory and its capacity to determine that the Gulf War was, indeed just.[8] Weigel believes the purpose of the just war theory is to forge moral, political, and strategic links between the limited use of armed force and the pursuit of peace with freedom, security, and order.[9] The just war theory, in Weigel's view, does not offer clear-cut answers to administrators or military leaders. He draws an analogy between an ethicist's interpretation of the norms of the just war theory and a conductor's rendition of the notes in a musical score.

---

[8] "From Last Resort to Endgame: Morality, the Gulf War, and the Peace Process," 19-41, at 19.

[9] Ibid., 20.

Weigel systematically moves through the eight classical criteria of the just war tradition, stating in an unequivocal fashion his claim that actions before, during, and after the Gulf War sufficiently met each criterion of *jus ad bellum* and *jus in bello*.

Analysis of the Essay

The method of analysis used in Weigel's essay is deontological, measuring all activity of the U.S./Coalition side against the criteria of the just war theory, seeking a one to one correspondence between just war norms and U.S./Coalition activities. In Weigel's analysis, the arguments for/against an action meeting a criterion are mounted in natural, rational, philosophical or secular terms. Following Aquinas (whom he terms "the first Whig"), Weigel does not argue his case on the basis of Christian love. He rather asserts his claims of right and wrong in relation to right order, natural duties, and minimum requirements. Weigel's language is, at times, laced with self-assuredness and is "rights language:"

> Claims from certain 'conflict resolution specialists,' who asserted that Saddam's attempted incorporation of Kuwait into Iraq could have been reversed by more active 'win-win' diplomacy, simply puts one in mind of Orwell's famous observation, that some propositions are so preposterous that only intellectuals could possibly believe them.[10]

And, another example:

> Listening to some of the critics of the Gulf War, one would have thought that the United States should have done penance for the past sins of the Near Eastern Bureau by leaving Saddam Hussein in possession of Kuwait. But that is, *prima facie*, a morally absurd position.[11]

Weigel uses language that presses human concern, but it appears to be accidental in relation to more weighty, hard core, strategic considerations.

The criterion of **just cause** for U.S. and Coalition intervention was met, Weigel contends, for four reasons.[12] Iraq did invade Kuwait--a violation of

---

[10] Ibid., 24-25.

[11] Ibid., 25.

[12] Ibid., 21.

international law. However, Weigel never indicates what or if historical, economic, cultural, religious or any other factors might mitigate what appears to be a blatant violation, and he thus forestalls any use of the norm of mutuality. Weigel relates that Amnesty International and other reliable sources reported widespread terror and torture perpetrated by Iraqis upon Kuwaitis. While such behavior is intolerable, he does not consider past documented violations of Kuwaitis toward Iraqis, which were equally dreadful.[13] He states that Iraq was clearly engaged in a quest for weapons of mass destruction that threatened peace beyond its borders. Again, Weigel fails to consider the context for Iraq's activity, or to ask about the perceived threats that might have motivated such actions. Weigel's fourth reason does exhibit some attention to human solidarity. He asserts that Iraq's economic threat to control forty per cent of the world's oil supply was potentially most devastating for the world's poorest nations. (While that is certainly true, it could be argued that the Coalition nations would have had far more to lose/gain.) In the face of Weigel's total argument, this consideration proves to be a minor point and falls short of our definition of mutuality.

Weigel also systematically works through an analysis of *jus ad bello*. The criterion of **proportionality of means** was hotly debated during numerous deliberations before, during and after the war, according to Weigel. The force used by the U.S. side was clearly targeted at the Hussein regime, Weigel contends. It is a tragic fact of life that power grids and water supplies destroyed by U.S. forces happened to supply both the Iraqi people and Saddam Hussein. Weigel's judgment stated in terms of the principle of double effect, is that the U.S. action to halt Hussein's aggression had a moral goal; destruction of power grids and water supplies was not the direct intent of the war; there was greater good in removing Saddam Hussein than evil incurred by bombing power grids and water supplies.

---

[13] See G. Simon Harak, "Hypertexting the Gulf War," *Cross Currents* 41 (1991): 506-20. Harak cites numerous sources that substantiate that there have been atrocities on all sides of this conflict.

Given these facts, the norm of mutuality would require an evaluation of how the destruction of power grids and clean water supplies would serve the dignity and optimum thriving of all. It would also require consideration of the environment itself, as well as how environmental destruction would ultimately impact human thriving for generations to come. Mutuality would also seek power-with the Iraqi people. Given the sophistication of the Coalition's military capabilities, mutuality would combine with the proportionate means criterion and weigh in favor of a strategy that would indeed make a "surgical strike" at the Hussein regime. Perhaps a covert operation, combined with overt support of the Kurds and the Shiites would have provided a greater proportionality.

Certainly, mutuality would raise questions concerning how coalition forces were "kept from harm's way" by primary reliance on air forces, flying beyond the range of most Iraqi air capabilities. Mutuality would require even greater proportionality, and a more equal risk of the loss of life on both sides. The effect of mutuality is to delimit power-over. In a consideration of violence, which is definitively a situation of struggle for power-over, mutuality strains against dominance. While these considerations certainly raise no easy answers to very complex questions, introducing the criterion of mutuality has a sobering effect on the discussion by bringing a more profound realism to the fore. Mutuality requires that the "enemy" be contemplated in the personal terms of shared human dignity and participation in a common power toward the optimal flourishing of all.

The Iraqi soldiers killed in the last stages of the war could have surrendered instead of being attacked, in Weigel's view.[14] The moral responsibility for the Iraqi

---

[14]See Wm. M. Arken, Damian Durrant, and Marianne Cherni, *On Impact: Modern Warfare and the Environment - A Case Study of the Gulf War*, A Greenpeace Study prepared for a "Fifth Geneva" Convention on the Protection of the Environment in Time of Armed Conflict, London, U.K., June 3, 1991 (Washington, DC: Greenpeace, 1991), 107-13. This resource has numerous footnotes citing the same horrific facts from sources representing all sides of the war. The massacre at al-Mutlaa Ridge and "The Highway to Hell" took place Feb. 25-27 near the junction of two roads exiting Kuwait City. U.S. forces were ordered to block the withdrawal of enemy forces. Strategic bombing left the Iraqis one way out of the city, resulting in a two-mile traffic jam of over 2,000 military vehicles and personnel. That the Iraqis were virtually the target of a U.S. "turkey shoot" was widely reported. A similar event took place on March 1, the third day of the ceasefire, on Highway 8, west of Basra. It was widely reported that the

soldiers killed at the front is Saddam Hussein's. Had mutuality appeared as a substantive consideration here, it would have required far greater or perhaps total restraint on the side of the Coalition forces, especially in the latter stages of the conflict. Even by the most conservative reports, the Coalition forces overwhelmingly out-gunned the Iraqis.[15] The rush to end the war and the need to "really kick butt" prevailed. Measuring the activity of Coalition forces on February 25-27 and March 1 against the norm of mutuality could have disclosed the potential of an outright massacre of Iraqi forces should the Coalition proceed as they intended.

The criterion of **discrimination** was met as well, in Weigel's estimation. U.S. strikes were precise and bombs were not dropped indiscriminantly. Iraqi civilian casualties are a cause for sorrow, not guilt; the guilt is Saddam Hussein's. Hussein's tactics of housing military command posts and civilian shelters in the same locations; parking military equipment near religious and archeological sites; and using civilians to camouflage missile launchers made it extraordinarily difficult for the U.S. side to avoid harming non-combatants. The risk, however needed to be taken, in Weigel's view, in order to avoid a greater evil.[16]

Mutuality demands a wholistic view of the parties involved in any relationship. It requires an examination of how all parties participate in the thriving or the lack of thriving of the others. The clear-cut transfer of responsibility and guilt away from a perpetrator of violence is not possible, because everything and everyone are interconnected in the web of life.

The multifaceted and complex implications the norm of mutuality illuminates serve to place an even greater burden of proof on the perpetrator of violence. S/he must show that in exercising violent power-over a more healthy relatedness will

---

Iraqis fired "a couple of rockets" to clear a path for their exit via the causeway across the Euphrates. The U.S. forces responded, and in less than two hours, destroyed 187 Iraqi armored vehicles, 25-50 tanks, and more than 350 military trucks, killing some 2,000 Iraqi soldiers.

[15]See Richard P. Stevens, ed., *The Iraqi Invasion of Kuwait: American Reflections* (Washington, DC: International Education and Communications Group, 1993).

[16]"From Last Resort to Endgame: Morality, the Gulf War, and the Peace Process," 28-29.

result, rather than a wider relational gap between parties. It raises for serious reflection the difficulty of restoring a relationship, once violence is used; and the need for the intentional and careful work in months and years ahead to repair and restore affiliations. Mutuality requires a response to the query: "How can a first world power claim to have a focused adversarial relationship with one small group of people (Saddam Hussein and his regime), but then willfully destroy hundreds of thousands of relationships (lives) immediately, and potentially even more lives, well into the future?"[17] When, as in the Gulf War, discrimination between combatants and non-combatants was nearly impossible, mutuality presses against the use of force.

---

[17]See *On Impact*, 15, 40-61, at 15: "The human toll can be summarized as follows: 151,000-183,000 people--Iraqis, Kuwaitis and allied soldiers lost their lives as a result of the Gulf War as of the beginning of May. 100,000-120,000 Iraqi military deaths occurred, 5,000-15,000 Iraqi civilians died during the war, and 4,000-6,000 civilians died since the end of the war due to wounds, lack of medical care, or malnutrition. 49,000-76,000 Iraqi civilians have died as of the beginning of May. During the month long civil war, 20,000 Iraqis are estimated to have died, and another 15,000-30,000 Kurds and other refugees have died on the roads or in camps. Of Iraq's 100,000-120,000 military deaths, some 50 percent were killed during the 100-hour ground battle between February 24-28, and during a military engagement on March 1 after the ceasefire. Only 10-20 percent of the civilian casualties occurred during the 43-day air and ground war. Eighty to ninety percent occurred after the war ended, in the aftermath, in the civil war, and during the refugee exodus. This percentage will increase, as the number of post-war deaths escalates. Assuming military and civilian deaths just during the 43-day war, about 110,000-135,000 Iraqis died, or an average of 2,500-3,000 people a day. This is almost three times the daily average of deaths during the Vietnam War, based on the estimate of 3,000 North Vietnamese, Cambodian and Laotian deaths in a seven year, four month period (1965-74).
Ibid., at 44-5: In contrast to the above mentioned figures, "A total of 343 allied soldiers died, and some 563 were wounded in the six months of the war. The best estimate of allied casualties is as follows: The U.S. death toll for the six-month operation was 266, with 122 accidental (non-combat) deaths occurring since the deployment of forces for Desert Shield. Another 357 U.S. soldiers were wounded in action, six remain missing. British casualties total 44 dead, 25 in action, 19 killed in non-combat accidents; 43 British soldiers were wounded in action. Two French soldiers died, and 28 were wounded. One Italian soldier was killed in a non-combat accident. Twenty-nine Saudi soldiers were killed, 53 were wounded, and nine were missing in action. Nine Egyptian soldiers were killed, and 74 were wounded. Six soldiers from the United Emirates were killed in action. Eight Senegalese soldiers were wounded in action. Iraq released allied POWs starting 4 March, and by 13 March, all 47 allied military prisoners that were held by Iraq were repatriated.

"JUST WAR AS POLITICS: WHAT THE GULF WAR TOLD US ABOUT CONTEMPORARY AMERICAN LIFE" BY JEAN BETHKE ELSHTAIN

Review of the Content

Elshtain believes that the resort to force by the U.S./Coalition in the Gulf War was justifiable under the just war criteria, narrowly applied.[18] She is, however, highly critical of the conduct of the war. She contends that just war reasoning seeks to affirm a shared humanity across enemy lines and it knows mercy, as well as justice. Elshtain argues forcefully against the contention that U.S./Coalition strikes on water and power supplies were just. She argues that a gross lack of responsibility was displayed in the Coalition's failure to provide immediate humanitarian assistance, and to support the Shiites and Kurds.[19] She also raises particular concerns about the use of women in the military by the Bush administration to popularize and promote the war in the media.

Analysis of the Essay

Elshtain's method of ethical reflection could be classified as mixed-consequentialist. She engages in a dialogical process, identifying values and seeking guidance from norms to direct action protecting those values. She weighs carefully the consequences of possible choices and judges whether a proportion exists between the premoral evil that exists along side the good sought from the action in question. In this case, she weighs the command to love neighbors against the necessity to use force and kill to prevent a greater evil.

In her discussion Elshtain appeals several times to Augustine's intention, which undergirds the just war theory, that all acts in a just war remain within the purview of

---

[18]"Just War as Politics: What the Gulf War Told Us About Contemporary American Life," 43-60.

[19]See *On Impact*, 49. The history of the Kurds and the Shiites in relation to Iraq and Kuwait is long and complex. What is significant here is that the U.S. had encouraged Shiite and Kurd leaders to rebel against Hussein. After the Coalition withdrawal, Hussein turned his elite Republican Guard on the rebellious Kurds (north) and Shiites (south), driving hundreds of thousands of civilians from their homes. The U.S. and other forces eventually joined in the relief efforts, but the estimated three million refugees immediately overwhelmed their attempts. This occurrence was judged by many as "too little, too late."

love. Elshtain is strong in her critique of the simplistic use of the just war criteria in public discourse about **just cause** for the war:

> What is remarkable about the subsequent response to Iraqi aggression is the way the just war considerations framed so much of the debate. Here, the argument went, was a clear-cut case of unjust aggression: the paradigmatic instance of a *causus belli*. Responding to such aggression, in turn, fit the criteria of just cause. Sanctions were tried, so the war could be declared a last resort. Just war insists that war be declared by legitimate authority--and what could be more proper and more legitimate than a twenty-seven-nation coalition, acting under the imprimatur of the United Nations and in the name of collective security? Ticking off criteria for *jus ad bellum* added up to a knockdown case for a defensive war to deny the fruits of aggression to a dictator who tortured his own people and was certain to be even less cautious in his treatment of peoples in an occupied territory.

She continues:

> This, at least, is one plausible version of the story. But just war principles are ambiguous and complex. Evaluations have to be made at each step along the way. New facts may alter previous assessments. Greater and lesser evils must be taken into account.[20]

Elshtain concurs with Bryan Hehir, who argues that though most would certainly agree that there was a *just cause* for U.S. engagement in the Gulf War, the questions of *proportionate means*, environmental damage, assault on the human spirit or other *jus in bello* criteria may indicate otherwise.[21] She deplores the fact that, "[m]uch of this complexity fell out of the argument in the weeks preceding the beginning of the aerial bombardment and in the crucial early days of the war."[22]

Invoking St. Augustine, Elshtain recalls that there is no earthly order that is free from sin and therefore, what is judged as "just" or "good" in this world can never be claimed with absolute certainty. She finds the fact that President Bush publicly demonized Saddam Hussein and proclaimed that the U.S./Coalition forces were on

---

[20] Ibid., 47-8.

[21] Ibid., 48. Elshtain quotes from Hehir's article, "Baghdad as Target: An Order to Be Refused," *Commonweal* (October 26, 1990): 603.

[22] "Just War as Politics: What the Gulf War Told Us About Contemporary American Life," 48.

"the side of God," particularly egregious. Elshtain also recalls St. Augustine's words declaring that war and strife, regardless of how just the cause, arouses temptations to ravish and devour in order to ensure peace.

This acknowledgment of and caution concerning common human limitations, implicitly draws upon the norm of mutuality. If there is common ground in human powerlessness (sinfulness), can there not also be common power in humanness (*imago Dei*)? Elshtain's criticism attempts to recognize ordinary humanity, dignity across battle lines, thereby precluding a moral triumphalism that breaks human relationships. Such concern for human relationships reveals a concern for mutuality, as well.

Elshtain admits that many efforts were made to observe the just war criterion of **discrimination**, such as the barring of indiscriminate bombing. She is dismayed, however, by the disturbing gloating about just how "smart" U.S. bombs were:

> Framed by the celebrations of our know-how, the loss of life in the Baghdad bomb shelter became a temporary blip on the screen. This tragedy *should* have been addressed by the President and our military spokesmen in language of deep regret and acknowledgement of responsibility--a responsibility ironically magnified precisely *because* our bombs were so "smart."[23]

This acknowledgement of responsibility is certainly a recognition of human relatedness. The evidence supporting a presumption against gloating over the suffering of the "enemy" would increase diametrically if the question were framed in terms of mutuality instead of simply responsibility. Such gloating certainly fractures relationships. Therefore, mutuality would insist that power-over should not be used this way, if at all.[24]

Elshtain's use of the discrimination criterion takes an interesting twist. She contends that given Hussein's tactics of placing noncombatants at or dangerously near

---

[23]Ibid., 51. Emphasis is Elshtain's.

[24]Like perfect love and perfect justice, perfect mutuality is directed toward the maximum well-being of all involved in a relationship. Since mutuality acts as a corrective to power-over, it bears a presumption against violence, because violence by definition breaks apart healthy relationships. Mutuality does not preclude all power-over in relating; it does delimit and direct power-over to power-with and toward greater mutuality (e.g. teacher/student, parent/child, mentor/protégé relationships).

logical military targets, it was nearly an impossible task to insure this criterion was being met in this war. Publicly, much rhetoric swirled around the fact that noncombatants were *not actual targets* of the Coalition forces. The effect of the rhetoric was to divert attention from the ironic failure of sophisticated weapons, and from the disorder, horror, and brutality that actually occurred. Here, the norm of mutuality brings an honesty to justice. Mutuality calls forth a confrontation with the concrete reality, not just intellectualized rhetoric or a rationalization of theoretical intent.[25]

Mutuality requires an evaluation of specific actions and their effects not only the present moment, but also on the prospects of future relating, survival and flourishing. Elshtain criticizes the haste and rush to a judgment that bombing the unspecified, but life-sustaining infrastructure of Iraqi society--water and power supplies, communications and other services--was justified. In Elshtain's view, the just war criteria require a far greater specificity and assurance of equitable consequences than was allowed for in the Gulf War.

Elshtain shows concern for the possibilities of a future peace--the restoration of relationships. She asserts that the just war theory precludes a punitive peace: ". . . it is blatantly inconsistent with just war as politics to torment this people further in order to bring the dictator to heel. The war did not dislodge him. A just peace must not try to do so over the malnourished bodies of Iraqi children."[26]

In applying the criterion of **proportionality** to the war, Elshtain makes a imaginative and revealing application to the domestic scene as well as to the battle sites abroad. She states:

> [If] . . . just war incorporates a wider theory of just politics, and that politics rests on a recognition of our sociality and on the essential

---

[25]Mutuality requires constant consideration of the common humanness of the "enemy" by any potential perpetrator of violence. In this sense, mutuality is almost always incompatible with the just war criteria, which assumes violence as an option.

[26]Ibid., 52. Elshtain cites the Geneva Protocol (1977) which bars war activities that cause malnutrition, starvation, or epidemics resulting from tainted water, inadequate food or medicine supplies. She also cites a Harvard study estimating 170,000 children would die from delayed effects of the war.

> integrity of human relationships at the most fundamental levels of families, friendships and communities, it follows that political actions and public policies can and must be assessed by looking at their impact upon families and communities, and by examining what effect these policies have on our most vital and fragile human relationships.[27]

Here is a reflection on relationship that begins to concretize the impact of war. It is rather one-sided (perhaps even self-serving), yet it redirects the discussion from strategies about power-over the "enemy" to the balancing of the loss of valued power-with in relation, with the gains made by the exertion of force. This kind of deliberation is necessary in order to reach a point of pondering the wholeness and the particular experience of the others and the flourishing of all involved, and it reveals Elshtain's consideration of mutuality.

Elshtain alters what is normally considered under the just war proportionality criterion (weighing the losses in human relationship against the gains of the use of force upon the "enemy") by including an analysis of the use of women by the government and the military media under that category. Elshtain posits that the U.S. government not only was not just in its treatment of the "enemy," but it also violated its own people in several ways. Had mutuality been a consideration in its deliberations, government officials could have confronted the unhealthy nature of such behavior. She contends that both U.S. servicewomen and the children of military personnel were the victims of war on the U.S. side.

While maintaining rules within the U.S. armed forces that skew the chance for advancement in favor of those who have participated in combat--only males, the military media produced glamorous images of women toting M-16's and used them to "sell" the war to the public. The war was an occasion to brandish all of the supposed new opportunities the military had opened for women. What was not flaunted were the effects of military rules that effectively left "children from 17,500 families without the custodial single parent who usually cares for them or without

---

[27]Ibid., 55.

both parents . . . '."²⁸ This consideration is certainly an invocation of the norm of gender mutuality. What is at issue here is a recognition of the full dignity of women and men that is embodied in daily life. Creating conditions in which women in the military must choose between the care of children, equal opportunity for advancement, rights, and power is a violation of gender mutuality, and it is particularly repugnant when it is done in the guise of promoting a just war.

"WHOSE JUST WAR? WHICH PEACE?" BY STANLEY HAUERWAS
Review of the Content

Hauerwas contends the just war theory was invoked by U.S. government and military officials in support of the Gulf War, but only to serve as a cloak for an immoral military campaign motivated by power politics and crusading patriotism.[29] He believes that the just war "theory" is not a tool that can be applied ahistorically by anyone anywhere. Hauerwas has maintained that the just war theory can serve a great good if properly used by Americans for moral reflection.[30] He contends that the Christians who drew up the just war criteria over the centuries did so out of their nonviolent convictions and with the presumption that the burden of proof that violence was justified was upon those who wished to act with force. In Hauerwas's view, there are great differences in the historical application of just war criteria (e.g. in the Middle ages by confessors disciplining Christians who participated in war; by princes of the Holy Roman Empire to their wars of expansion; by Grotius in developing the nation-state system; and by the U.S. in the Gulf War). In the modern period, out of the hands of Christians and others committed to nonviolence, the just war criteria have become "illusory moral objectivity" that serve to "hide from us the reality of what was done in the Gulf War."[31] In this essay, Hauerwas deals mainly

---

[28]Ibid., 58. Elshtain cites the *Washington Post*, February 15, 1991.

[29]"Whose Just War? Which Just Cause?," 83-105.

[30]Ibid., 89.

[31]Ibid., 85.

with a distinctively Christian stand toward the use of force, in general. He illustrates his points using examples from the Gulf War and the just war criteria.

Analysis of the Essay

Hauerwas's method is that of the deontologist. He does his analysis from the perspective of a Christian pacifist. For Hauerwas pacifism means obeying the teaching and example of Jesus, who was merciful, forgiving, and radically inclusive. The Christian is called to witness to the God's love in practical ways, loving both neighbors and enemies, as well as challenging unjust social structures, even beyond the dictates of common reason. Hauerwas joins his voice on the one hand, with Lutheran just war theorist Paul Ramsey who reserves the just war criteria for application by Christians committed to nonviolence, and on the other, with Mennonite theologian John Howard Yoder who criticizes the ahistorical and often hypocritical application of the criteria by modern democratic societies.

Hauerwas opens his essay with the declaration that "there is a lot more to this 'war thing' than just 'just war'."[32] He places the judgment that there was **just cause** for the Gulf War in perspective with a brief review of U.S. foreign policy. Particularly, he focuses on Reinhold Niebuhr's theological justification for political realism and Paul Ramsey's ability to defend the just war theory as a coherent practice (but based on the presumption that, in a Christian civilization, the goal would always be to protect the innocent--even if that meant greater losses for the U.S. side).

Hauerwas holds that Niebuhr's and Ramsey's intent was to help Americans to think about war in a morally disciplined fashion. There has been, however, no consistent adherence to either political realism or just war theory in determining U.S. involvement in war. For Hauerwas this all leads to a conclusion that:

> The war in the Gulf was prosecuted by a military that was shaped by realist presumptions, justified by the crusade rhetoric of the Cold War, and determined not to repeat Vietnam. Americans were able to fight the war in the Gulf as an allegedly just war, not because America is a nation whose foreign and military policies are formed by just war

---

[32]Ibid., 83.

doctrine, but because America is a nation whose military has been shaped by realists to serve the crusade against communism. American Christians, undisciplined as they are by serious reflection on the morality of war, enthusiastically backed this war as a provisional instance of good versus evil.[33]

Hauerwas likens the sudden and abstract use of the just war criteria by the U.S. to "justify" the Gulf War to like children on a playground who assume questions of right/wrong turn on whether or not a rule has been broken.

Hauerwas elaborates:

> When just war is construed in such an abstract way, we forget the social, political, and economic considerations that are necessary for the serious use of the theory. It is no wonder that the Administration found it useful to make just war criteria appear as if they are generally agreed-upon presumptions that can be used by any right-thinking people. Those who possess hegemonic power always claim to represent universal morality. Such universal claims are meant to create a social and historical amnesia that is intended to make us forget how the dominant achieved power in the first place.[34]

Considering all of this, Hauerwas argues that the decision to go to war was not based on just war criteria, but rather on the self-interest of the U.S. and the Coalition nations. He points to the fact that U.S. troops were committed to the Gulf on a massive scale long before Americans knew about it. The American people were given information (in many cases disinformation, information subjected to "spin control" to use Yoder's terms) about the intended war *after* U.S. forces were already in the Gulf.[35] Citizens, therefore, were unable to determine the justice of that war or influence its execution in any way before the deed was done. That left the power for deciding the war had a just cause as well as the determination of the justice of its course, squarely in the hands of a few military leaders and politicians who pursued "U.S. interests," in Hauerwas's view.

---

[33]Ibid., 94.

[34]Ibid., 95.

[35]Hauerwas cites John Howard Yoder, "Just War Tradition: Is It Credible?," *Christian Century* [March 13, 1992], 295-98, in "Whose Justice? Whose Peace?," 96.

Precisely how does the norm of mutuality affect Hauerwas's judgment concerning just cause? Mutuality requires that the distinctive parties in a relationship have and maintain a real and honest self-understanding. It requires that self-interest be contextualized with the needs of the others involved. The dynamics of power in that contextualization process include a relinquishing of sole concern with power-over, and a taking up of power-with. In this case it would require the U.S./Coalition governments to place their self-interest within the broader purview of the common humanity shared with the "enemy," particularly the Iraqi citizens, and the rest of the world. Mutuality also calls for a self-critical, honest assessment of motivation which measures self-interest against the need for the survival and flourishing of all.

Hauerwas contends that the American administration and military incorrectly judged their Gulf War activities to be in compliance with the just war criterion of **proportionate means.** That misjudgment was the direct result of the drastic deterioration of traditional Christian just war theory's high standard of what is tolerable or fair, and therefore what is considered proportionate. He supports his contention by first placing the Gulf War in historical perspective with the Vietnam War and the Cold War. Hauerwas claims that the Vietnam War illustrated how it has gradually become impossible for Americans to think about war in a disciplined manner. The experience of Hiroshima and Nagasaki set the precedent for the U.S. demanding the unconditional surrender of the enemy. That concept, during the Cold War, was mixed with a total villainizing of the "enemy" and the adoption of a "crusade mentality" that called on the defenders of freedom and democracy to ward off the demonic "enemy." The experience of Vietnam added to the equation. Horrific television images transmitted live from the battlefield gave large numbers of average Americans an immediate experience of the pain and suffering of war. It contributed to destablizing the U.S.'s self-image as the good, honorable, and able defender of freedom and democracy; still, the villainized Communists "won" the ambiguous Vietnam War.

In Hauerwas's view, then, most Gulf War activity was not, in fact, decided and prosecuted on the basis of the just war criterion of proportionate means. The decisions were rather political ones, based upon the need for the U.S. to fight a "good war"--one that achieved a total victory over a totally evil enemy in the self-interest of the U.S. and without significant numbers of U.S. casualties. The need to meet these all encompassing requirements skewed the presumptions undergirding just war criterion of proportionate means to the extent that it was ineffective in influencing judgments made in the Gulf War.

In this part of Hauerwas's analysis, the norm of mutuality underpins his judgment that the social-psychological and political motivations of the U.S. were suspect. As we saw in Heyward's work particularly, healthy relationships require mutuality. When fear, insecurity, self-interest, greed, or any other phenomenon presses humans to isolate themselves from others in a self-righteous manner that discounts a need for self-criticism or evaluation by peers, a sense of reality is lost and the possibility of their considering the common good is grossly diminished. Delusions of grandeur preclude any real relating and serve to impair moral judgments.

Hauerwas claims the inability for the U.S. to properly grasp the proportionate means criterion had a direct influence on the discernment of **discrimination** criterion. He recalls Paul Ramsey's judgment regarding the bombing of Hiroshima and Nagasaki: "It would have been better for more Japanese and American soldiers to die on the beaches of Japan than for noncombatants to be killed at Hiroshima and Nagasaki."[36] Hauerwas agrees that one must be willing to make such judgments if one is to credibly maintain that the purpose of just war criteria is the protection of the innocent. How else is one to distinguish killing in war from murder, he asks? He also suggests that how one understands morality and prudence has a great deal to do with how one distinguishes just and unjust discrimination.

Hauerwas argues that the distinction between what is moral and what is prudent in war, such as some made to justify the bombings of Hiroshima and

---

[36]Ibid., 92.

Nagasaki, is illusional and based upon the abstraction of moral principles from their roots in concrete communities and practices.³⁷ He recommends a test for determining if discrimination was properly carried out in the Gulf War suggested by Michael Baxter:

> They [who assume the distinction between prudence and morality is intelligible for judging the Gulf War on just war grounds] should ask themselves what they might possibly learn about how the war was conducted that might make them change their minds and deem the war unjust. If, for example, the United States' primary goal was to make Iraq withdraw from Kuwait, then was the bombing policy pursued in Iraq itself just? Why was it necessary at the same time the United States pursued the war in Kuwait to also try to eliminate Saddam Hussein's nuclear capacity? Surely the potential to make nuclear weapons is not itself unjust, as otherwise the American policy in that regard would be problematic. The implications of American bombing policy in Iraq, moreover, must surely raise questions about the principle of discrimination, since such policy was clearly meant to disrupt the social infrastructure of Iraq. And if any of these considerations lead just war theorists to conclude that the Gulf War was (at least in part) unjust, then there is a further question to face; what will the United States do to make reparation for those parts of the war, which in hindsight, were morally unjust?³⁸

These sorts of questions are the kinds of questions that can be raised only by someone who has a view toward mutuality. Such a person considers the "more" about war that Hauerwas suggested is necessary. Mutuality's probative value is that it moves moral reflection into a wider frame of reference, considering the concrete reality that understands each person, each people, the land each calls home as part of the whole interconnected cosmos.

CONCLUSIONS: THE PROBATIVE VALUE OF MUTUALITY

The probative value of the formal norm, mutuality, is multifaceted. First and foremost, it requires the moral agent to deal concretely in moral reflection and moral decision-making. Specific and careful attention needs to be given to the reality

---

³⁷Ibid., 101.

³⁸Ibid., 102-3.

revealing questions--what?, why?, how?, who?, where?, when?, What are the foreseeable effects?, What are the viable alternatives?--in the concrete, as well as in the abstract. Second, mutuality requires the moral agent to probe the dynamics of power in an ethical dilemma and to seek out ways to shape those dynamics to serve power-with. It is a complement to and corrective of love and justice. Third, engaging the norm of mutuality presses the moral agent toward inclusivity drawing into the process of moral reflection concern for the thriving and flourishing of all involved.

Engaging the concerns of mutuality personalizes and concretizes the situation, blatantly reminding the moral agent that s/he is dealing with the relationships of real lives and real people. Such probing also raises the necessity of an historical perspective since relationships between humans, non-humans, the earth and the cosmos have a history with a beginning, middle and an end. Since the probing of relationships reveals a cosmic interconnectedness, the norm of mutuality brings a wider world view into play that calls for radical inclusiveness. Mutuality calls to account those exercises of power-over that fail to unite and nurture, but isolate and destroy the flourishing of living beings. Because mutuality assumes the wholeness of the individual parties in a relationship, it demands honesty and integrity from those involved. Without such integrity relationships are destructive for all involved, including the perpetrators of force.

More than the norms of love and justice, mutuality places humanity in a perspective within the whole of creation. As we have seen, cosmic mutuality defines the relationship of humans with their Creator, other earth elements, and the entire cosmos. Gender mutuality ensures the equal and full participation of women and men in the *imago Dei* and directs that to be realized in daily life. Generative mutuality recognizes the value of each aspect of creation in the wider view of the Creator sharing the Holy power to create and to redeem what is yet incomplete or broken. Social mutuality governs the social exchange of power that "raises up the lowly, and casts the mighty from their thrones," and frees the human family to relate with one another in justice and love. Attention to these forms of mutuality promises to have a qualitative impact on moral reasoning about the use of force and on any moral question.

MORE QUESTIONS

This study has only begun to explore the wealth of ethical understanding that lies in the formal norm of mutuality. No doubt the time will come when there will be the same plethora of works addressing mutuality as exists today discussing love and justice. I have only suggested how mutuality relates to sin and finitude in the case of the moral analysis of Persian Gulf War. Other questions arise. Might mutuality have any real effect on limiting violence? How do the value systems of other cultures and other religions effect mutuality as a formal norm? How may mutuality be dealt with, if at all, as a material norm? Precisely how could mutuality function to counter the utilitarian and other negative influences modernity has wrought upon Christian moral decision-making? What effect can our understanding of mutuality have upon current notions of ecclesiology? What would a more focused study of the biblical roots of mutuality reveal? What can be learned by studying other levels of mutuality such as Buber's threshold and prethreshold dimensions? Clearly to understand mutuality and its implications presents a potential lifetime scholarly agenda.

Within the ambit of this project, we have seen how Rosemary Radford Ruether, (Isabel) Carter Heyward, Beverly Wildung Harrison, and Elizabeth A. Johnson define and use "mutuality." I have shown that the notion of mutuality is deeply rooted in Jewish and Christian thought, as illustrated in the work of Thomas Aquinas, John Duns Scotus, Martin Buber and H. Richard Niebuhr. My claim that mutuality is a formal norm was tested against definitions of "formal norm" given by Josef Fuchs, Lisa Sowle Cahill, and Timothy E. O'Connell. The formal norm, mutuality has been employed in a case study and found to have probative value in uncovering the necessity for concrete, personalized attention to human and ecological relationships in which the dynamics of power are defined as power-with, rather than power-over. I conclude, therefore, that mutuality is a formal norm for Christian social ethics, that functions along with love and justice to promote a balance of power that is required for optimum human flourishing, a flourishing set within the interdependent context of the whole of creation.

BIBLIOGRAPHY

Aelred of Rievaulx. *Spiritual Friendship*. Cistercian Fathers Series 5. Trans. Mary Eugenia Laker. Washington,DC: Cistercian Publications Consortium Press, 1974.

Aranda, Antonio. "La Cuestión Teológica de la Encarnatión del Verbo: Relectura de Tres Positiones Caracteristicas." *Scriptura Theologica* 25 (1993): 49-94.

Aristotle. *Nicomachean Ethics*. In *Commentary on Aristotle's Nicomachean Ethics: St. Thomas Aquinas*. Trans. C. I. Litzinger. Notre Dame: Dumb Ox Books, 1993.

Arken, Wm. M., Damian Durrant, and Marianne Cherni. *On Impact: Modern Warfare and the Environment - A Case Study of the Gulf War*. A Greenpeace Study prepared for a "Fifth Geneva" Convention on the Protection of the Environment in Time of Armed Conflict, London, U.K., June 3, 1991. Washington, DC: Greenpeace, 1991.

Augustine. *City of God*. Trans. Marcus Dods. New York: Modern Library, 1950.

Baier, Annette C. "The Need For More Than Justice." *Canadian Journal of Philosophy* Supplementary 13 (1987): 41-56.

Berry, Donald L. *Mutuality: The Vision of Martin Buber*. Albany: The State University of New York, 1985.

Betz, H.D. *Galatians*. Philadelphia: Fortress Press, 1979.

Bianchi, Eugene C. and Rosemary Radford Ruether. *From Machismo to Mutuality: Essays on Sexism and Man-Woman Liberation*. New York: Paulist Press, 1976.

Bolton, Benda M., et.al. *Women in Medieval Society*. Ed. Susan Mosher Stuard. Philadelphia: University of Pennsylvania Press, 1976.

Boston Women's Health Collective. *Our Bodies, Ourselves*. New York: Simon and Schuster, 1973.

Brock, Rita Nakashima. Review of *Speaking of Christ: A Lesbian Feminist Voice*; *Touching Our Strength: The Erotic as Power and the Love of God*, by Carter Heyward. *Journal of Religion* 72 (1992); 130-31.

Brown, Lester, et. al. *State of the World 1992: A Worldwatch Institute Report on Progress Toward a Sustainable Society* New York: W.W. Norton and Co., 1993.

Buber, Martin. *Believing Humanism: My Testament 1902-1965*. Credo Perspectives. Trans. Maurice Friedman. New York: Simon and Schuster, 1967.

-----. *Between Man and Man*. Trans. Ronald Gregor Smith. New York: Macmillan Publishing Company, 1965.

------. *Die Frage an den Einzelnen*. Berlin: Schocken Verlag, 1936.
------. "Distance and Relation." Trans. Ronald Gregor Smith. *The Hibbert Journal* 49 (1951): 105-13.
------. *The Eclipse of God: Studies in the Relation Between Religion and Philosophy*. Trans. Robert M. Seltzer. Atlantic Highlands, NJ: Humanities Press International, Inc., 1988. Reprint, Atlantic Highlands, NJ: Humanities Press International, Inc., 1989.
------. "Elemente des Zwischenmenschlichen." *Merkur* Neue Folge 21 (1954): 593-608.
------. *I and Thou*. Trans. Walter Kaufmann. New York: Charles Scribner's Sons, 1970.
------. *I and Thou*. Trans. Ronald Gregor Smith. New York: Charles Scribner's Sons, 1958.
------. "Interrogation of Martin Buber." Conducted by Maurice Friedman. In *Philosophical Interrogations*. Ed. Sydney Rome and Beatrice Rome. New York: Holt Reinhart and Winston, 1964.
------. *Martin Buber: Werke*. Erster Band. *Schriften zur Philosophie*. München: Kösel-Verlag KG und Heidelberg: Verlag Lambert Schneider GmbH, 1962.
------. *Martin Buber: Werke*. Zweiter Band. *Schriften zur Bibel*. München: Kösel-Verlag KG und Heidelberg: Verlag Lambert Schneider GmbH, 1964.
------. *Pointing the Way*. Trans. Maurice S. Friedman. New York: Harper and Brothers, 1956.
------. *Rede über das Erzieherische*. Berlin: Lambert Schneider Verlag, 1926.
------. "Replies to My Critics." In *The Philosophy of Martin Buber*. Library of Living Philosophers. Ed. Paul Arthur Schilpp and Maurice Friedman, 689-744. LaSalle,IL: Open Court Publishing, Co., 1967.
------. "Urdistanz und Beziehung." *Studia Philosophica* 10 (1950): 7-19.
------. "A Venture in Adult Education." In *The Hebrew University of Jerusalem*. Silver Jubilee Volume. Jerusalem: The Hebrew University Press, 1952.
------. "What is Common to All." Trans. Maurice Friedman. In *Knowledge of Man: Selected Essays*. Ed. Maurice Friedman. Atlantic Highlands,NJ: Humanities Press International, 1988.
------. *The Writings of Martin Buber*. Ed. and Trans. Will Herberg. New York: The World Publishing Company, 1956.
------. *Zweisprache*. Berlin: Schochen Verlag, 1932.
Cahill, Lisa Sowle. "Contemporary Challenges to Exceptionless Norms." In *Moral Theology Today*. St. Louis: Pope John XXIII Medical-Moral Research Center, 1984.
------. *Love Your Enemies: Discipleship, Pacifism, and Just War Theory*. Minneapolis: Fortress Press, 1994.
------. "Moral Methodology: A Case Study." *Chicago Studies* 19 (1980): 173-79.
------. "Notes On Moral Theology: 1989--Feminist Ethics." *Theological Studies* 51 (1990): 49-64.

------. "Theological Contents of Just War Theory: A Response to J. Bryan Hehir." *Journal of Religious Ethics* 20 (1992): 259-65.
Carmody, John. Review of *Christ in a Changing World: Toward an Ethical Christology*, by Tom Driver; *To Change the World: Christology and Cultural Change*, by Rosemary Radford Ruether. *Horizons* 9 (1992): 372-73.
Chenu, M.D. *Nature, Man, and Society in the Twelfth Century: Essays on New Theological Perspectives in the Latin West*. Trans. and Ed. Jerome Taylor and Lester K. Little. Chicago: University of Chicago Press, 1968.
Chodorow, Nancy. *The Reproduction of Mothering*. Berkeley: University of California Press, 1978.
Chopp, Rebecca S. "Seeing and Naming the World Anew: The Works of Rosemary Radford Ruether." *Religious Studies* 15 (1989): 8-11.
Christ, Carol P. and Judith Plaskow, eds. *Weaving the Visions: New Feminist Spirituality*. San Francisco: Harper and Row, Publishers, 1989.
Cizewski, Wanda. "Reading the World as Scripture: Hugh of St. Victor's *De tribus diebus.*" *Florilegium* 9 (1987): 65-88.
------. "Friendship With God? Variations on a Theme in Aristotle, Aquinas, and Macmurray." *Philosophy and Theology* 6 (1992): 369-81.
Coleman, John A. Review of *New Woman, New Earth: Sexist Ideologies and Human Liberation*, by Rosemary Radford Ruether. *Union Seminary Quarterly Review* 32 (1977): 192-94.
Cone, James H. *God of the Oppressed*. New York: Seabury Press, 1975.
Cotroneo, Margaret. "A Contextual Catholic Ethics." Ph.D. diss. Temple University. Philadelphia, 1983.
Crouter, Richard E. "H. Richard Niebuhr and Stoicism." *Journal of Religious Ethics* 2 (1974): 129-46.
Crysdale, Cynthia S. W. "Gilligan and the Ethics of Care: An Update." *Religious Studies Review* 20 (1994): 21-28.
Curran, Charles E. and Richard A. McCormick, eds. *Readings in Moral Theology*. No. 1. *Moral Norms and Catholic Tradition*. New York: Paulist Press, 1979.
------. *Readings in Moral Theology*. No. 2. *The Distinctiveness of Christian Ethics*. New York: Paulist Press, 1985.
Davies, Paul. *The Cosmic Blueprint: New Discoveries in Nature's Creative Ability to Order the Universe*. New York: Simon and Schuster, 1988.
Day, Sebastian. *Intuitive Cognition: A Key to the Significance of the Later Scholastics*. St. Bonaventure, NY: Franciscan Institute, 1947.
Dennis, Marie, et.al. *St. Francis and the Foolishness of God*. Maryknoll: Orbis Books, 1993.
Dermott, Rose. "The Legal Condition of Women in the Church: Shifting Politics and Norms." JCD diss. The Catholic University of America, 1979.
Deutsch, George and Sally P. Springer. *Left Brain, Right Brain*. San Francisco: Freeman, 1981.
Devall, Bill and George Sessions. *Deep Ecology: Living as if Nature Mattered*. Salt Lake City: Peregrine Smith Books, 1985.

Diamond, Irene and Gloria F. Orenstein. *Renewing the World: The Emergence of Ecofeminism.* San Francisco: Sierra Club Books, 1990.
Dowd, Michael. *Earthspirit: A Handbook for Nurturing an Ecological Christianity.* Mystic,CT: Twenty-Third Publications, 1991.
Doyle, Eric. "Duns Scotus and Ecumenism." In *De doctrina Ioannis Duns Scoti.* Vol. 3. Acta Congressus Scotistici Internationalis Oxonii et Edimburgi, 11-17 September 1966, celebrati. Studia scholastico-Scotistica. Ed. Camille Bérubé. Romae: Cura Commissionis Scotoisticae, 1968.
Driver, Tom F. *Christ in a Changing World: Toward an Ethical Christology.* New York: Crossroad, 1982.
Dumont, Richard. "Intuition: Prescript of Postscript in Scotus' Demonstration of God's Existence." In *Deus et homo ad mentum I. Duns Scoti* Acta tertii Congressus Scotistici Internationalis, Vindebonae, 28 Sept.-2 Oct. 1970. Romae: Societas Internationalis Scotistica, 1972.
Edel, Abraham and Elizabeth Flower. "Economic Justice: Notes and Queries." *The Journal of Value Inquiry* 19 (1985): 251-61.
Eisenstein, Zella R., ed. *Capitalist Patriarchy and the Case For Socialist Feminism.* New York: Monthly Review Press, 1979.
Elshtain, Jean Bethke. "Just War as Politics: What the Gulf War Told Us About Contemporary American Life." In *But Was It Just?: Reflections on the Morality of the Persian Gulf War.* Ed. David E. Decrosse. New York: Doubleday, 1992.
Englebert. Omer. "A Time For War, A Time For Servitude." In *The Francis Book: Eight Hundred Years With the Saint From Assisi.* New York: Collier Books, 1980.
Fackenheim, Emil L. "Martin Buber: Universal and Jewish Aspects of the I-Thou Philosophy." *Midstream* 20 (1974): 46-56.
Farley, Margaret. "Feminist Ethics in the Christian Ethics Curriculum." *Horizons* 11 (1984): 361-72.
Farley, Wendy. Review of *Gaia and God: An Ecofeminist Theology of Earth Healing,* by Rosemary Radford Ruether. *Theology Today* 50 (1993): 461-464.
Finkel, Asher. *The Pharisees and the Teacher of Nazareth.* Leiden: E.J. Brill, 1964.
Follett, Mary Parker. *Creative Experience.* New York: Longman, Green and Company, 1924.
------. *Dynamic Administration.* New York: Harper and Brothers, 1942.
Francis of Assisi. *Regula bullata (1223).* Chapter 4-6. In *Francis and Clare: Complete Works.* The Classics in Western Spirituality. Trans. Regis J. Armstrong and Ignatius C. Brady. New York: Paulist Press, 1982.
Frei, Hans W. "The Theology of H. Richard Niebuhr." In *Faith and Ethics: The Theology of H. Richard Niebuhr* Ed. Paul Ramsey, 65-115. New York: Harper and Brothers, 1957.
Freire, Paulo. *Pedagogy of the Oppressed.* Trans. Myra Bergman Ramos. New York: Herder and Herder, 1970.

Friedman, Maurice S. *Martin Buber: Life of Dialogue*. Chicago: University of Chicago Press, 1976.
------. *Martin Buber's Life and Work*. 3 Vols. New York: Dutton, 1981-83.
------. "Martin Buber's Theory of Knowledge." *The Review of Metaphysics* 8 (1954): 264-80.
------. "Walter Kaufmann's Mismeeting With Martin Buber." *Judaism* 31 (1982): 229-39.
Fuchs, Josef. "The Absoluteness of Moral Terms." *Gregorianum* 52 (1972): 415-33.
------. *Christian Morality: The Word Becomes Flesh*. Trans. Brian McNeil. Washington, DC: Georgetown University Press, 1987.
------. "Historicity and Moral Norms." In *Moral Norms and Personal Obligations*. Trans. Brian McNeil. Washington, DC: Georgetown University Press, 1993.
------. *Human Values and Christian Morality*. Trans. M.H. Heelman, M. McRedmond, E. Young and G. Watson. Dublin: Gill and McMillian, 1970.
------. "Is There a Christian Morality?." In *The Distinctiveness of Christian Ethics*. Readings in Moral Theology No. 2. Ed. Charles E. Curran and Richard A. McCormick. New York: Paulist Press, 1980.
------. "Moral Truths--Truths of Salvation." In *Christian Ethics in the Secular Arena*. Trans. Bernard Hoose and Brian McNeil. Washington, DC: Georgetown University Press, 1984.
------. *Natural Law: A Theological Investigation*. Trans. Helmut Reckter and John A. Dowling. Dublin: Gill and Son, 1965.
------. *Personal Responsibility and Christian Morality*. Washington, DC: Georgetown University Press, 1983.
------. *Theologia Moralis Generalis*. Editio altra. Roma: Editrice Universita Gregoriana, 1963.
Fulkerson, Mary McClintok. Review of *She Who Is: The Mystery of God in Feminine Discourse*, by Elizabeth A. Johnson. *Religious Studies Review*. 21.3 (1995): 21-25.
Gallagher, John A. *Time Past, Time Present: An Historical Study of Catholic Moral Theology*. New York: Paulist Press, 1990.
Gardner, E. Clinton. "Responsibility and Moral Direction in the Ethics of H. Richard Niebuhr." *Encounter* 40 (1979): 143-68.
Gilligan, Carol. *In A Different Voice: Psychological Theory and Women's Development*. Cambridge: Harvard University Press, 1982.
------. "Moral Orientation and Moral Development." In E.F. Kittay and D.T. Meyers, eds. *Women in Moral Theory*. Totowa, NJ: Rowman and Littlefield, 1987.
Gilligan, Carol, N.P. Lyons, and T.J. Hammer. *Making the Connections: Relational Worlds of Adolescent Girls at Emma Willard School*. Cambridge: Harvard University Press, 1989.
Gilligan, Carol, J.V. Ward and J.M. Taylor, eds. *Mapping the Moral Domain*. Center for the Study of Gender, Education, and Human Development. Cambridge: Harvard University Press, 1988.

Gillman, Gerald. *The Primacy of Love in the Moral Life*. New York: Newman Press, 1959.

Glennon, Lynda M. *Women and Dualism: A Sociology of Knowledge Analysis*. New York: Longman and Green, 1979.

Godsey, John D. *The Promise of H. Richard Niebuhr*. Philadelphia: J.B. Lippincott Company, 1970.

Goodenough, E. "The Political Philosophy of Hellenistic Kingship." In *Yale Classical Studies*. Vol. 1. New Haven: Yale University Press, 1928.

Gordon, Hiam. "A Method of Clarifying Buber's I-Thou Relationship." *Journal of Jewish Studies* 27 (1976): 71-83.

Gore, Al. *Earth in Balance: Ecology and the Human Spirit*. New York: Houghton Mifflin Co., 1992.

Grant, Edward. "The Condemnation of 1277, God's Power, and the Physical Thought on the Late Middle Ages." *Viator* 10 (1979): 211-44.

Green, Robert. *Sexual Identity Conflict in Children and Adults*. New York: Basic Books, 1974.

Grey, Mary. "Claiming Power-in-Relation: Exploring the Ethics of Connection." *Journal of Feminist Studies in Religion* 7 (1991): 7-18.

Gudorf, Christine E. *Body, Sex, and Pleasure: Reconstructing Christian Sexual Ethics*. Cleveland: The Pilgrim Press, 1994.

------. "Parenting, Mutual Love and Sacrifice." In *Women's Consciousness, Women's Conscience: A Reader in Feminist Ethics* Ed. Barbara Hilkert Andolson, Christine E. Gudorf, Mary D. Pellauer, 175-91. Minneapolis: Winston, 1985.

Guimet, Fernand. "Conformité a la droit raison et possibilité de la charité." In *De doctrina Ioannis Duns Scoti*. Vol. 3. Acta Congressus Scotistici Internationalis Oxonii et Edimburgi, 11-17 September 1966, celebrati. Studia scholastico-Scotistica. Ed. Camille Bérubé, 539-97. Romae: Cura Commissionis Scotoisticae, 1968.

Gula, Richard M. *Reason Informed By Faith: Foundations of Catholic Morality*. New York: Paulist Press, 1989.

------. *What Are They Saying About Moral Norms?*. New York: Paulist Press, 1982.

Gustafson, James M. "Christian Ethics and Social Policy." In *Faith and Ethics: The Theology of H. Richard Niebuhr*. Ed. Paul Ramsey, 119-39. New York: Harper and Brothers, 1957.

------. "Introduction." In *The Responsible Self: An Essay in Christian Moral Philosophy*. Paperback Edition. Ed. Richard R. Niebuhr, 6-41. New York: Harper and Row Publishers, 1978.

Gutierrez, Gustavo. *A Theology of Liberation: History, Politics and Salvation*. Trans. Caridad Inda and John Eagleson. Revised Edition with New Introduction. Maryknoll: Orbis Books, 1988.

Haney, Eleanore Haney. "What is Feminist Ethics: A Proposal For Continuing Discussion." *Journal of Religious Ethics* 8 (1980): 115-24.

Harak, G. Simon. "Hypertexting the Gulf War." *Cross Currents* 41 (1991): 506-20.

Harrison, Beverly Wildung. "Agendas for a New Theological Ethics." In *Churches in Struggle: Liberation Theologies and Social Change in North America.* Ed. Wm. K. Tabb. New York: Monthly Review Press, 1986.

------. "Dream of a Common Language: Toward a Normative Theory of Justice in Ethics." *The Annual of the Society of Christian Ethics.* (1983): 1-25.

------. "H. Richard Niebuhr: Towards a Christian Moral Philosophy." Ph.D.. diss., Union Theological Seminary, 1974.

------. "Human Sexuality and Mutuality: A Fresh Paradigm." *Journal of Presbyterian History* 6 (1983): 142-61.

------. "Human Sexuality and Mutuality." In *Christian Feminism: A Vision of a New Humanity.* Ed. Judith L. Weidman. San Francisco: Harper and Row, 1984.

------. "Keeping the Faith in a Sexist Church: Not For Women Only." In *Making the Connections: Essays in Feminist Social Ethics.* Ed. Carol S. Robb. Boston: Beacon Press, 1985.

------. "Misogyny and Homophobia: Unexplored Connection." *Church and Society* 73 (1982): 20-33.

------. *Our Right to Choose: Toward a New Ethic of Abortion.* Boston: Beacon Press, 1983.

------. "The Politics of Energy Policy." In *Energy Ethics.* Ed. Dieter T. Hessel. New York: Friendship Press, 1979.

------. "The Politics of Energy Policy." In *Making the Connections: Essays in Feminist Social Ethics.* Ed. Carol S. Robb. Boston: Beacon Press, 1985.

------. "The Power of Anger in the Works of Love: Christian Ethics for Women and Other Strangers." *Union Seminary Quarterly Review* 36 (1981 Supplement): 41-57.

Hauerwas, Stanley. "Whose Just War? Which Just Cause?." In *But Was It Just?: Reflections on the Morality of the Persian Gulf War.* Ed. David E. Decrosse. New York: Doubleday, 1992.

Hehir, Bryan J. "Just War Theory in a Post-Cold War World." *Journal of Religious Ethics* 20 (1992): 237-57.

------. "Baghdad as Target: An Order to be Refused." *Commonweal* 117 (1990): 602-04.

Hendley, Brian. "Martin Buber on the Teacher/Student Relationship: A Critical Appraisal." *Journal of Philosophy of Education* 12 (1978): 141-48.

Hennecke, Edger and Wilhelm Schmeemelcher, eds. "The Gospel of Hebrews." *New Testament Apocrypha.* Vol. 1. Philadelphia: Westminster Press, 1963.

Herlihy, David. "Land, Family and Women in Continental Europe, 700-1200." In *Women in Medieval Society.* Philadelphia: University of Pennsylvania Press, 1976.

Heyward, Carter. "Can Anglicans Be Feminist Liberation Theologians?." In *The Trial of Faith: Theology and the Church Today.* Ed. Peter Eaton. West Sussex: Churchman Publishers, Ltd., 1988.

------. "Heterosexism: Enforcing Male Supremacy." *The Witness* 69 (1986): 18-20.

------. "Heterosexist Theology: Being Above It All." *Journal of Feminist Studies in Religion.* 3 (1987): 29-38.
------. "How My Mind Has Changed: The Power of God-With-Us." *Christian Century* 107 (1990): 275-78.
------."Lent and Easter Upside Down." *Christianity and Crisis* 51 (1991): 75-76.
------. *Our Passion For Justice: Images of Power, Sexuality and Liberation.* Cleveland: The Pilgrim Press, 1984.
------. *A Priest Forever.* New York: Harper and Row, 1976.
------. *The Redemption of God: A Theology of Mutual Relation.* New York: University Press of America, 1982.
------. *Speaking of Christ: A Lesbian Feminist Voice.* Ed. Ellen C. Davis. New York: The Pilgrim Press, 1989.
------. *Staying Power: Reflections on Gender, Justice and Compassion.* [Uncorrected 12/1/94 page proofs.] Cleveland: The Pilgrim Press, 1995.
------. *Touching Our Strength: The Erotic and the Love of God.* San Francisco: Harper and Row, 1989.
------. "An Unfinished Symphony of Liberation: The Radicalization of Christian Feminism Among US Women--A Review Essay." *Journal of Feminist Studies in Religion* 1 (1985): 99-118.
------. *When Boundaries Betray Us: Beyond Illusions of What is Ethical in Therapy and Life.* New York: HarperSanFrancisco, 1993.
Hill, Brennan, Paul Knitter and William Madges. *Faith, Religion and Theology: A Contemporary Introduction.* Mystic, CT: Twenty-third Publications, 1993.
Hislop, Ian. "The Anthropology of St. Thomas." In *St. Thomas and Nietzsche.* Ed. F.C. Copleston, 3-10. Ditchling, Sussex: Blackfriars, 1955.
Hoedemaker, Libertus A. *The Theology of H. Richard Niebuhr.* Philadelphia: Pilgrim Press, 1970.
Hollenbach, David. *Justice, Peace, and Human Rights: American Catholic Ethics in a Pluralistic World.* New York: Crossroad, 1990.
Huff, Margaret Craddock. "The Interdependent Self: An Integrated Concept From Feminist Theology and Philosophy." *Philosophy and Theology* 2 (1987): 160-72.
Hugh of St. Victor. *On the Sacraments of the Christian Faith.* Trans. Roy J. Deferrari. Cambridge: Medieval Academy of America, 1951.
Hughs, Lewis M. "Charity as Friendship in the Theology of St. Thomas." *Angelicum* 52 (1975): 164-78.
Ingham, Mary Elizabeth. "The Condemnation of 1277: Another Light on Scotist Ethics." *Zeitschrift für Theologie und Philosophie* 37 (1990): 91-103.
------. *Ethics and Freedom: An Historical-Critical Investigation of Scotist Ethical Thought.* Landham, MD: University Press of America, 1989.
------. "The Harmony of Goodness: Mutuality as a Concept For Scotus' Moral Discussion." In *Spirit and Life* 3 (1993): 55-82.

------. "John Duns Scotus: An Integrated Vision." In *The History of Franciscan Theology*. Ed. Kenan B. Osborne, 185-230. St. Bonaventure, NY: The Franciscan Institute, 1994.
Irish, Gerry A. *The Religious Thought of H. Richard Niebuhr*. Atlanta: John Knox Press, 1983.
Jaggar, Alison M. "Feminist Ethics: Some Issues For the Nineties." *Journal of Social Philosophy* 20 (1990): 91-107.
James, E.O. *The Cult of the Mother Goddess: An Anthropological Documentary Study*. New York: Barnes and Noble, 1959.
Janssens, Louis. "Norms and Priorities in a Love Ethics." *Louvain Studies* 4 (1977): 207-38.
Jeramias, Joachim. *The Parables of Jesus*. New York: Scribner's, 1955.
John Duns Scotus. *Duns Scotus: Philosophical Writings*. 2nd Ed. Indianapolis: Hackett Co., 1987.
------. *Duns Scotus' Political and Economic Philosophy*. Trans. Allan B. Wolter. Santa Barbara, CA: Old Mission, 1989.
------. *Duns Scotus on the Will and Morality*. Trans. Allan B. Wolter. Washington, DC: Catholic University of America Press, 1986.
------. *John Duns Scotus' Early Oxford Lectures on Individuation*. Trans. Allan B. Wolter. Santa Barbara, CA: Old Mission, 1982.
------. *John Duns Scotus: Four Questions on Mary*. Trans. Allan B. Wolter. Santa Barbara, CA: Old Mission, 1988.
------. *John Duns Scotus: A Treatise on God as First Principle*. 2nd Ed. Trans. Allan B. Wolter. Chicago: Franciscan Herald Press, 1981.
------. *John Duns Scotus: God and Creatures, The Quodlibetal Questions*. Paperback Edition. Trans. Felix Alluntis and Allan B. Wolter. Washington, DC: Catholic University of America Press, 1981.
------. *Opera omnia*. Editio nova. 26 Vols. Parisiis: L. Vivès, 1895-. Farnborough, England: Gregg International Publishers, 1969.
------. *Opus oxoniense*. Vol. 24. Paris: L. Vivès, 1895-.
Johnson, Elizabeth A. *Consider Jesus: Waves of Renewal in Christology*. New York: Crossroad, 1992.
------. "The Incomprehensibility of God and the Image of God Male and Female." *Theological Studies* 45 (1984): 441-65.
------. "Marian Tradition and the Reality of Women." *Horizons* 12 (1985): 116-35.
------. *She Who Is: The Mystery of God in Feminist Discourse*. New York: Crossroad, 1992.
------. *Woman, Earth, Creator Spirit*. 1993 Madeleva Lecture. New York: Paulist Press, 1993.
Johnson, Luke Timothy. "Something Fundamental is Afoot." Review of *She Who Is: The Mystery of God in Feminist Theological Discourse*, by Elizabeth A. Johnson; *Speaking the Christian God: the Holy Trinity and the Challenge of Feminism*, ed. by A.F. Kinel. *Commonweal* 120 (29 Jan 1993): 17-22.

Jonsen, Albert R. *Responsibility in Modern Religious Ethics.* Washington, DC: Corpus Books, 1968.

Jordon, June. "Where is the Love?." In *Civil Wars.* Boston: Beacon Press, 1981.

Kant, Immanuel. *Critique of Practical Reason and Other Writings in Moral Philosophy.* Trans. L.W. Beck. Chicago: University of Chicago Press, 1949.

------. *Critique of Pure Reason.* 2nd ed. Trans, N. K. Smith. New York: St. Martin's Press, 1933.

Kater, John L. Jr. Review of *Our Passion for Justice: Images of Power, Sexuality, and Liberation,* by Carter Heyward. *Anglican Theological Review* 67 (1985): 207-210.

Kierkegaard, Soren. *Works of Love.* Trans. Howard and Edna Hong. New York: Harper and Row, 1965.

King, Richard H. "Review Essay: H. Richard Niebuhr--*Faith on Earth: An Inquiry into the Structure of Human Faith.*" *Religious Studies Review* 17 (1991): 293-95.

King, Ursala. Reviews of *Sexism and God-Talk: Toward a Feminist Theology,* by Rosemary Radford Ruether; *In Memory of Her: A Feminist Theological Reconstruction of Christian Origins,* by Elisabeth Schüssler-Fiorenza. *Religious Studies* 20 (1984): 699-702.

Klapish-Zuber, C. "Zacharias; or the Ousting of the Father: The Rites of Marriage in Tuscany from Giotto to the Council of Trent." In *Ritual, Religion and the Sacred.* Vol.7. Ed. R. Forester and O. Ranum. Baltimore: John Hopkins University Press, 1978.

Kliever, Lonnie D. "The Christology of H. Richard Niebuhr." *The Journal of Religion* 50 (1970): 33-57.

------. *H. Richard Niebuhr.* Makers of the Modern Theological Mind. Waco, TX: Word Books Publisher, 1977.

Koehane, Michelle Z. et. al. *Feminist Theory: A Critique of Ideology.* Chicago: University of Chicago Press, 1982.

Kurzweil, Zwi E. "Buber on Education." *Judaism* 11 (1962): 44-55.

LaCugna, Catherine Mowry. *God For Us: The Trinity and Christian Life.* 1993 Paperback Edition. San Francisco: Harper Collins, 1991.

Laeuchli, Samuel. *Power and Sexuality: The Emergence of Canon Law at the Synod of Elvira.* Philadelphia: Temple University Press, 1972.

Lassen-Williams, James. Review of *Touching our Strength: The Erotic as Power and Love of God,* by Carter Heyward. *Anglican Theological Review* 72 (Summer 1990): 347-351.

Legerton, Winifred. "H. Richard Niebuhr's Radical Monotheism and Christian Feminism." *Religion in Life* 45 (1976): 427-35.

Lerner, Ralph and Muhsin Mahdi, eds. Trans. Ernest L. Fortin and Peter D. O'Neal. *Medieval Political Philosophy: A Sourcebook.* New York: Free Press of Glencoe, 1963.

Levinas, Emmanuel. In *The Philosophy of Martin Buber*. Library of Living Philosophers. Ed. Paul Arthur Schilpp and Maurice Friedman, 133-50. LaSalle, IL: Open Court Publishing, Co., 1967.
Loomer, Bernard. "Two Kinds of Power." *Criterion* 15 (1976): 12-28.
Lovelock, James. *The Ages of Gaia: A Biography of Our Living Earth*. New York: W.W. Norton and Co., 1988.
McCormick, Richard A. "Notes on Moral Theology." *Theological Studies* 37 (1976): 72-74.
McDonald, D. R. *There is No Male or Female*. Philadelphia: Fortress Press, 1987.
McDonough, Elizabeth. "Women and the New Church Law." *Concilium* 85 (1986): 73-81.
McFaul, Thomas R. "Dilemmas in H. Richard Niebuhr's Ethics." *Journal of Religion* 50 (1974): 35-50.
McGlone, Jeanette. *The Behavior and the Brain Sciences*. 3 (1980): 215-63.
McGuire, Brian Patrick. *Friendship and Community: The Monastic Experience 350-1250*. Cistercian Studies Series 95. Kalamazoo: Cistercian Publications, Inc., 1988.
MacNamara, Vincent. *Faith and Ethics: Recent Roman Catholicism*. Washington, DC: Georgetown University Press, 1985.
Maguire, Daniel C. "A Feminist Turn in Ethics." *Horizons* 10 (1983): 341-47.
------. "The Feminization of God and Ethics." *Christianity and Crisis* 42 (1982): 59-67.
------. *The Moral Choice*. Minneapolis: Winston Press, 1979.
------. *The Moral Core of Judaism and Christianity: Reclaiming the Revolution*. Minneapolis: Fortress Press, 1993.
------. *A New American Justice*. Minneapolis: Winston Press, 1980.
------. "The Primacy of Justice in Moral Theology." *Horizons* 10 (1983): 72-85.
Maguire, Daniel C. and Fargnoli, A. Nicholas. *On Moral Grounds: The Art/Science of Ethics*. New York: Crossroad, 1991.
Martin, John Hilary. "The Injustice of Not Ordaining Women: A Problem For Medieval Theologians." *Theological Studies* 48 (1987): 303-16.
Mauer, Armand A. *Medieval Philosophy*. The Etienne Gilson Series 4. Second Edition. Toronto: Pontifical Institute of Mediaeval Studies, 1982.
Maurice, F.D. *Theological Essays*. London: James Clarke, 1957.
Mendes-Flohr, Paul, ed. *Land of Two Peoples: Martin Buber on Jews and Arabs*. New York: Oxford University Press, 1983.
Merriell, Juvenal D. *To The Image of the Trinity: A Study in the Development of Aquinas' Teaching*. Studies and Texts. Toronto: Pontifical Institute of Mediaeval Studies, 1990.
Michalson, Carl. "The Real Presence of the Hidden God." In *Faith and Ethics: The Theology of H. Richard Niebuhr* Ed. Paul Ramsey, 245-67. New York: Harper and Brothers, 1957.

Micks, Marianne H. Review of *To Change the World: Christology and Cultural Criticism*, by Rosemary Radford Ruether. *Theology Today* 39 (1982); 214-15.

Milhaven, John Giles. *Hadewijch and Her Sisters: Other Ways of Loving and Knowing*. Albany: State University of New York Press, 1993.

Miller, Jean Baker. "What Do We Mean by Relationships?." *Work in Progress* no. 22. Wellesley: The Stone Center Working Paper Series, 1986.

Miranda, José. *Marx and the Bible: A Critique of the Philosophy of Oppression*. Maryknoll: Orbis Books, 1974.

Mollenkott, Virginia Ramey. *The Divine Feminine: The Biblical Image of God as Female*. New York: Crossroad, 1991.

------. "Who's Redeeming Whom?" Review of *The Redemption of God: A Theology of Mutual Relation* by Isabel Carter Heyward. *Christianity and Crisis* 43 (1983): 123-24.

Money, John and Patricia Tucker. *Sexual Signatures*. Boston: Little Brown, 1975.

Moran, James A. Review of *I and Thou* by Martin Buber. A New Translation, With Prologue and Notes by Walter Kaufmann." *New Scholasticism* 46 (1972): 268-70.

Morley, John F. *Vatican Diplomacy and the Jews During the Holocaust 1939-43*. New York, KTAV, 1980.

Morrison, D. *The Juridic Status of Women in Canonical Law and in United States Law*. Rome: Gregorianum, 1965.

Mott, Stephen Charles. *Biblical Ethics and Social Change*. New York: Oxford University Press, 1982.

Mowinchel, Sigmund. *He That Cometh*. New York: Blackwell and Abingdon, 1955.

Mullins, Mary. Review of *New Woman, New Earth: Sexist Ideologies and Human Liberation*, by Rosemary Radford Ruether. *Horizons* 6 (979): 129-30.

Nash, James. *Loving Nature: Ecology, Integrity, and Christian Responsibility*. Nashville: Abingdon Press, 1991.

Nelson, James B. *Embodiment: An Approach to Sexuality and Christian Theology*. Minneapolis: Augsburg Publishing House, 1979.

Niebuhr, H. Richard. "An Attempt at a Theological Analysis of Missionary Motivation." *N.Y.C. Missionary Research Library Occasional Bulletin* 14 (1963): 3.

------. *Christ and Culture*. New York: Harper and Row, Publishers, 1951. Reprint, New York: Harper Torchbooks, 1975.

------. *The Kingdom of God In America*. New York: Harper and Row, Publishers, Inc., 1937. Reprint, Middletown, CT: Wesleyan University Press, 1988.

------. "Man the Sinner." *Journal of Religion* 15 (1935): 272-80.

------. *The Meaning of Revelation*. 1941. Reprint, New York: Collier Books, 1960.

------. "The Question of the Church." In *The Church Against the World* by Francis P. Miller, H. Richard Niebuhr, Wilhelm Pauck, 1-16. Chicago: Welleth, Clark and Company, 1935.

------. *Radical Monotheism and Western Culture*. 1943. Reprint, New York: Harper Torchbooks, 1970.

------."Reflections on Faith, Hope, and Love." *Journal of Religious Ethics* 2 (1974): 151-56.

------. *The Responsible Self: An Essay in Christian Moral Philosophy*. Paperback Edition. New York: Harper and Row Publishers, 1978.

------. "Responsibility in Christ." In *The Responsible Self: An Essay in Christian Moral Philosophy*. Paperback Edition. Ed. Richard R. Niebuhr, 161-78. New York: Harper and Row Publishers, 1978.

------. "The Responsibility of the Church for Society." In *The Gospel, the Church and the World*. The Interseminary Series Vol. 3. Edited by Kenneth Scott Latourette, 111-33. New York: Harper Brothers, 1946.

------. *The Social Sources of Denominationalism*. 1929. Cleveland: Meridian Books, 1962.

Niebuhr, H. Richard and Beach, Waldo. *Christian Ethics: Sources of Living Tradition*. 2nd Ed. New York: The Ronald Press Company, 1973.

Niebuhr, Reinhold. *Children of the Light and Children of Darkness*. New York: Charles Scribner's Sons, 1944.

------. *Man's Nature and His Communities*. New York: Charles Scribner's Sons, 1965.

------. *Nature and Destiny of Man: A Christian Interpretation*. Vol.II. New York: Charles Scribner's Sons, 1943.

Niebuhr, Richard R., ed. *Faith on Earth: An Inquiry into the Structure of Human Faith By H. Richard Niebuhr*. New Haven: Yale University Press, 1989.

Nolan, Albert. *Jesus Before Christianity: The Gospel of Liberation*. Capetown: Philip David, 1976.

North, Robert. "The Scotist Cosmic Christ." In *De doctrina Ioannis Duns Scoti*. Vol. 3. Acta Congressus Scotistici Internationalis Oxonii et Edimburgi, 11-17 September 1966, celebrati. Studia scholastico-Scotistica. Ed. Camille Bérubé. Romae: Cura Commissionis Scotoisticae, 1968.

Nygren, Anders. *Agape and Eros*. 2 Vol. Trans. Philip S. Watson. London: S.P.C.K House, 1932, Part I; 1938, Part II, Vol.1; 1939, Part II, Vol.2. Reprint, New York: Harper and Row Publishers, 1969.

O'Connell, Timothy E. *Principles For A Catholic Morality*. Rev. ed. San Francisco: Harper, 1990.

------. "The Question of Moral Norms." *The American Ecclesiastical Review* 169 (1975): 377-88.

O'Connor, June. Reviews of *Sexism and God-Talk: Toward a Feminist Theology* by Rosemary Ruether; *Metaphorical Theology: Models of God in Religious Language*, by Sally McFague; *The Sacred and the Feminine: Toward a Theology of Housework*, by Kathyrn Allen Rabuzzi. *Religious Studies Review* (1986): 202-05.

O'Neill, Mary Aquin. Review of *She Who Is: The Mystery of God in Feminist Theological Discourse*, by Elizabeth Johnson. *Religious Studies Review* 21.1 (1995): 19-21.

Osborne, Kenan B. *Sacramental Theology: A General Introduction.* New York: Paulist Press, 1988.
Outka, Gene. *Agape: An Ethical Analysis.* New Haven: Yale University Press, 1972.
Parvey, Constance. "Women in the New Testament."In *Religion and Sexism: Images of Women in Jewish and Christian Traditions.* Ed. Rosemary Radford Ruether. New York: Simon and Schuster, 1974.
Patai, Raphael. *The Hebrew Goddess.* Philadelphia: KTAV, 1967.
Pauw, Amy Planinga. "Braiding a New Footbridge: Christian Wisdom, Classic and Feminist." Review of *She Who Is: The Mystery of God in Feminist Theological Discourse,* by Elizabeth A. Johnson. *Christian Century* 110 (1993); 1159-62.
Petchesky, Rosalind Pollack. *Abortion and Women's Choice: The State, Sexuality, and Reproductive Freedom.* New York: Longman, 1984.
Peterson, Ingrid J. *Clare of Assisi: A Biographical Study.* Quincy, IL: Franciscan Press, 1993.
Pfuetze, Paul E. *The Social Self.* New York: Bookman Associates, 1954.
Pieper, Joseph. *Justice.* Trans. Lawrence E. Lynch. New York: Pantheon Books, 1955.
Plant, Judith. *Healing the Wounds: The Promise of Ecofeminism.* Philadelphia: New Society Publications, 1989.
Porter, Jean. *The Recovery of Virtue: Relevance of Aquinas For Christian Ethics.* Louisville: Westminster/John Knox, 1990.
Prentice, Robert. "The Contingent Element Governing the Natural Law on the Seven Last Precepts of the Decalogue According to John Duns Scotus." *Antonianium* 42 (1967): 258-92.
Principe, Walter. "Affectivity of the Heart." In *Spirituality of the Heart.* Ed. Annice Callahan. New York: Paulist Press, 1990.
Quitslund, Sonya A. Review of *Mythological Woman: Contemporary Reflections on Ancient Religious Stories,* by Denise Lardner Carmody; *She Who Is: The Mystery of God in Feminist Theological Discourse,* by Elizabeth A. Johnson; *Gaia and God: An Ecofeminist Theology of Earth Healing,* by Rosemary Radford Ruether; *Church in the Round: Feminist Interpretation of the Church,* by Letty M. Russell; *The Annual Review of Women in World Religions, Vol. 1, Heroic Women, Vol 2,* ed. by Arvind Sharma and Katherine K. Young; *She Flies Beyond: Memories and Hopes of Women in the Ecumenical Movement,* by Pauline Webb; *Sisters in the Wilderness: The Challenge of Womanist God-Talk,* by Delores S. Williams; *An Anthology of Sacred Texts by and about Women,* ed. by Serenity Young. *Journal of Ecumenical Studies.* 31 (1994): 190-92.
Rabuzzi, Kathryn Allen. "The Socialist Feminist Vision of Rosemary Radford Ruether: A Challenge to Liberal Feminism." *Religious Studies* 15 (1989): 4-8.
Rahner, Karl. "Current Problems in Christology." *Theological Investigations.* Vol. 1. New York: Crossroad, 1961.
------. *The Dynamic Element in the Church.* New York: Herder and Herder, 1964.

------. *Love of Jesus and the Love of Neighbor.* Trans. Robert Barr. New York: Crossroad, 1983.

------. "Reflections on the Unity of the Love of Neighbor and the Love of God." In *Theological Investigations.* Vol. 6. Concerning Vatican Council II. New York: Crossroad, 1982.

Ramsey, Paul. "The Transformation of Ethics," In *Faith and Ethics: The Theology of H. Richard Niebuhr.* Ed. Paul Ramsey, 140-72. New York: Harper and Brothers, 1957.

Rich, Adrienne. "Compulsory Heterosexuality and Lesbian Experience." *Blood, Bread, and Poetry: Selected Prose 1979-85.* New York: W.W. Norton, 1986.

Ricoeur, Paul. *The Symbolism of Evil.* Boston: Beacon Press, 1967.

Robb, Carol S. "A Framework For Feminist Ethics." *Journal of Religious Ethics* 8 (1981): 48-68.

------. Review of *Sexism and God-Talk*, by Rosemary Radford Ruether. *Union Seminary Quarterly Review* 40 (1985): 62-72.

Robinson, James M., ed. "The Gospel of Philip." In *Nag Hammadi Library in English.* New York: Harper and Row, 1977.

Roll, Susan K. Review of *She Who Is: The Mystery of God in Feminist Theological Discourse*, by Elizabeth A. Johnson. *Louvain Studies* 18 (1993): 374-75.

Rossi, Mary Ann. "Priesthood, Precedent and Prejudice." *Journal of Feminist Studies in Religion* 7 (1991): 73-94.

Rowling, Marjorie. *Everyday Life in Medieval Times.* New York: Dorset Press, 1987.

Ruether, Rosemary Radford. "Beginnings: An Intellectual Biography." In *Journeys: The Impact of Personal Experience on Religious Thought.* ed. Gregory Baum. New York: Paulist Press, 1975, 34-56.

------. *Disputed Questions: On Being a Christian.* Journeys in Faith. Ed. Robert A. Raines. Nashville: Abingdon, 1982.

------. *Gaia and God: An Ecofeminist Theology of Earth and Healing.* San Francisco: Harper, 1992.

------. *Liberation Theology: Human Hope Confronts Christian History and American Power.* New York: Paulist Press, 1972.

------. *New Woman/New Earth: Sexist Ideologies and Liberation.* New York: Seabury, 1983.

------. "Rich Nations/Poor Nations: Towards a Just World Order in the Era of Neo-Colonialism." In *Christian Spirituality in the United States: Independence and Interdependence.* Ed. Francis A. Eigo. Villanova, PA: Villanova University Press, 1978.

------. *Sexism and God-talk: Toward a Feminist Theology.* Boston: Beacon Press, 1983.

------. "Sexism and the Theology of Liberation: Nature, Fall and Salvation as Seen From the Experience of Women." *The Christian Century* 90 (1973): 1224-29.

------. *To Change the World: Christology and Cultural Criticism.* New York: Crossroad, 1989.

------. "Witness to Hope in a Demonic World." *Sojourners* 20 (1991): 22-23.

Saiving Goldstein, Valerie. "The Human Situation: A Feminine View." *The Journal of Religion* 40 (1960): 100-12.
Schüssler-Fiorenza, Elisabeth. *Bread Not Stone: The Challenge of Feminist Biblical Interpretation*. Boston: Beacon Press, 1984.
------. "Justified by All Her Children: Struggle, Memory and Vision." *Concilium* (1990/1): 27-34.
------. *In Memory of Her: A Feminist Theological Reconstruction of Christian Origins*. New York: Crossroad, 1983.
Sedgwick. Timothy F. "Faith and Discernment: Directions in Theological Ethics in the Thought of H. Richard Niebuhr." *Andover Newton Quarterly* 18 (1977): 111-21.
Shannon, Thomas A. "Method in Ethics: A Scotistic Contribution." *Theological Studies* 54 (1993): 272-93.
Smith, Ronald Gregor. *Martin Buber*. Makers of Contemporary Theology Series. Richmond: John Knox Press, 1967.
Smith, Ruth L. "Morality and Perspectives of Society: The Limits of Self-Interest." *Journal for the Scientific Study of Religion* 26 (1987): 279-93.
Stevens, Richard P., ed. *The Iraqi Invasion of Kuwait: American Reflections*. Washington, DC: International Education and Communications Group, 1993.
Straus-Feuerlicht, Roberta. *The Fate of the Jews: A People Torn by Israeli Power and Jewish Ethics*. New York: Time Books, 1983.
Stuhmueller, Carroll, ed. *Women and Priesthood: Future Directions*. Collegeville, MN: The Liturgical Press, 1978.
Swahnberg, Ann. Review of *Gaia and God: An Ecofeminist Theology of Earth Healing*, by Rosemary Radford Ruether. *Journal of Religion* 74 (1994): 580-81.
Swidler, Leonard. "Mutuality the Matrix for Mature Living: Some Philosophical and Christian Theological Reflections." *Religion and Intellectual Life* 3 (1985):105-119.
Thomas Aquinas. *Commentary on Aristotle's Nicomachean Ethics: St. Thomas Aquinas*. Trans. C.I. Litzinger. Notre Dame: Dumb Ox Press, 1993.
------. *De regimine principum*. In *St. Thomas Aquinas On Politics and Ethics: A New Translation, Backgrounds and Interpretations*. Trans. and Ed. Paul E. Sigmund. New York: W.W. Norton and Company, 1988.
------. *Summa theologiae*. Black Friars Edition. New York: McGraw-Hill Book Company, 1968.
Thudy, Zacharias P. "Clandestine Marriages in the Late Middle Ages." In *New Images of Medieval Women: Essays Toward a Cultural Anthropology*. Medieval Studies Vol. 1. Ed. Edelgard E. DuBruck. Lewiston, NY: The Edwin Mellin Press, 1989.
Torjesen, Karen Jo. *When Women Were Priests*. San Francisco: Harper, 1993.

Torrence, T.F. "Intuitive and Abstractive Knowledge: From Duns Scotus to John Calvin." In *De doctrina Ioannis Duns Scoti*. Vol. 3. Acta Congressus Scotistici Internationalis Oxonii et Edimburgi, 11-17 September 1966, celebrati. Studia scholastico-Scotistica. Ed. Camille Bérubé. Romae: Cura Commissionis Scotoisticae, 1968.

Trash, Haunani-Kay. *Eros and Power: The Promise of Feminist Theory*. Philadelphia: University of Pennsylvania Press, 1986.

Trible, Phyllis. *God and the Rhetoric of Sexuality*. Philadelphia: Fortress Press, 1978.

Varga, Andrew C. *On Being Human: Principles of Ethics*. New York: Paulist Press, 1978.

Vermes, Geza. *The Dead Sea Scrolls in English*. New York: Penguin Books, 1962.

------. *Jesus the Jew*. New York: Collins, 1973.

Weber, Theodore R. Review of *New Woman New Earth; Sexist Ideologies and Human Liberation*, by Rosemary Ruether. *Theological Studies*. 37 (1976): 358-61.

Weeks, Jeffery. *Sexuality and Its Discontents: Meanings, Myths and Modern Sexualities*. London: Routledge and Kegan Paul, 1985.

Weigel, George. "From Last Resort to Endgame: Morality, the Gulf War, and the Peace Process." In *But Was It Just?: Reflections on the Morality of the Persian Gulf War*. Ed. David E. Decrosse. New York: Doubleday, 1992.

Weinbaum, Batya. *The Curious Courtship of Women's Liberation and Socialism*. Boston: South End Press, 1978.

Welch, Claude. "Review Essay: H. Richard Niebuhr--*Faith on Earth: An Inquiry into the Structure of Human Faith*." *Religious Studies Review* 17 (1991): 289-92.

Welch, D. Don. "A Niebuhrian Contribution to Normative Ethics."*Encounter* 44 (1983): 341-51.

Whipple, John F. "The Condemnations of 1270 and 1277 at Paris." *Journal of Medieval and Renaissance Studies* 7 (1977): 169-201.

Williams, Daniel Day. "A Personal and Theological Memoir." *Christianity and Crisis* 23 (1963): 209-13.

Wolter, Allan B. "John Duns Scotus on the Primacy and Personality of Christ." In *Franciscan Christology: Selected Texts, Translations and Essays*. Franciscan Sources No.1. Ed. Damian McElrath, 147-55. St. Bonaventure, NY: Franciscan Institute Publications, 1980.

Wood, Robert E. *Martin Buber's Ontology*. Northwestern University Studies in Phenomenology and Existential Philosophy. Ed. John Wild. Evanston, IL: Northwestern University Press, 1969.

Wright, John H. Review of *She Who Is: The Mystery of God in Feminist Theological Discourse*, by Elizabeth A. Johnson. *Theological Studies* 54 (1993): 371-73.

Young, Robin Darling. "She Who Is: Who is She?" Review of *She Who Is: The Mystery of God in Feminist Theological Discourse*, by Elizabeth A. Johnson. *The Thomist* 58 (1994): 323-33.

INDEX

adam, creation of woman, 107, dominion, 8; sin in Aquinas, 125-26; sin in Scotus, 146-47
ad extra. See Trinity
ad intra. See Trinity
Aelred of Rievaulx, 99, 102, 108-111
affectatio commodi in Scotus, 141, 152
affectatio justitiae in Scotus, 141, 152
agape, Ruether's critique, 40-41
Alan of Lille, 103
am haretz, 177n.81, 203
amicitia, Aquinas and, 117
Amnesty International, 235
amor procedens, 89
analytical theories of justice, 17-18
Anath. *See* Canaanite deities
anthropology. *See* Ruether, Rosemary Radford
Aristotle: biology in Scotus, 150-51; body/spirit dualism, influences of, 30n.25; friendship, 86, 112-13, 115-20; hierarchy, Heyward's critique of, 43; in Thomas Aquinas, 112, 129-30: justice, 16-17; man the maker, 188n.121
Nicomachean Ethics, 113n.49, 116-18 *passim*
art, in Buber, 172-73
Augustine of Hippo: *De Trinitate*, anthropology, 113; knowledge of God, 138 essence and existence, 24n.4; platononic influence, 53; redemption, 52-53; war, 241; women, 25
Baal. *See* Canaanite deities.
balance of power, 6-8

Barth, Karl, 24n.4
Baxter, Michael, 248-49
Berry, Donald L., 168-69
Beziehung, 162, 176
biophilic mutuality, 23,34
Boethius' notion of person, 139, 156
boundaries: setting of, 4-5, 55; solidarity and, 58
Buber, Martin: analogical notions, 9-10; *geistige Wesenheiten*, 171-75;
art, 172-73; Eternal Thou, 173-75;
Harrison, and, 197-98;
Heyward, and, 22, 46, 198-99; Human relations, 162-67; helping relations, 163-66; friendship, 166-67
I and Thou, 22; philosophy and, 158-62
Johnson and, 199
mutuality, 162-79: cosmic, 202; definition and translation, 162; gender, 202; generative, 198-99, 202; social, 203
non-human relations 167-71; threshold of mutuality, 168-69; pre-threshold of mutuality, 170; sub-threshold of mutuality, 171
Ruether and, 198
Word Pairs, 158
World of Relation, 159-61; primary spheres, 159; meeting and dialogue, 159-61
Bush, George, 239, 240
Cahill, Lisa Sowle, 205, 208; formal

Bush, George, 239, 240
Cahill, Lisa Sowle, 205, 208; formal norms, 214-16; scripture, 214-16
Calvin, John, and the Fall, 25
Canaanite tradition, 31; deities, 40
capax Dei, woman as: Johnson, 77; Ruether, 33
caritas, Aquinas and, 118-19
cathēkontic ethics, 189, 188n.121
causus belli. *See* Just War Tradition
Chalcedon (451 C.E.), 42
Chartres, 103
Christian feminists, 2-3 *See also* Harrison, Heyward, Johnson, Ruether
Christic power: defined, 45-46; and generative mutuality, 52, in mutual relations, 52
Christology: Ruether, 28-30, 32-33; Heyward, 43-46; Johnson, *See* Jesus Sophia; low Christologies of Segundo, Solle, and Miranda, 66; in Heyward, 43, 45n.89
H.Richard Niebuhr, 184-86
Cicero, 102, 108
classical theology, 77n.216
coaptationem, 127
co-creating, creation and, 50; and generative mutuality, 94; in Heyward, 53-54; in Ruether, 36-37; with Mother-Sophia, 81-82
Code of Canon Law, 13-14
Cold War, 247
common good, 54
compositum, 103
Condemnations of 1277, 100, 142n.180, 152
conscientization, 40
consona in Scotus, 142
Constantine, 30n.25

covenant, 68: and society, 41; creation, 41; God of fidelity, 42; New Covenant, 42-43
cosmic interdependence, 100
cosmic mutuality, analysis question, 21; brief description, 10; consensus of feminists, 92-93; defined, 93; in Aquinas, 131; in Buber, 203; in Harrison, 67-79; in Heyward, 49-50; in Hugh of St. Victor, 110; in Johnson, 78; in H.R. Niebuhr, 203; in Ruether, 35; in Scotus, 150
Cotroneo, Margaret, 226
Creator: in H.R. Niebuhr, 191, 95
criteria, just war. *See* Just War Tradition
delectio, 128
De sacramentas christiainae fidi, 104-108
desiderium, 128
De spirituali amicitia, 109-111
De trinitate, *See* Augustine of Hippo
deificet, 119
Deus diligendus est, in Scotus, 141, 142-43, 153
dialogue, and meeting. See Buber
discrimination. *See* Just War Tradition
double love command, 14, 207
dualism: platonic, 32, 36, 36n.47, 69; aristotelian, 30n.25; Harrison's critique of, 63-64
dunamis, 44
ecojustice, in Ruether, 41
ecological ethic, 30-33
Ehyeh asher ehyeh, 175, 199
Elshtain, Jean Bethke, 232, 239-44
embodiment, and Be-ing, 62n.160, 62-64; defined, 63n.163; Doing, 62n.160, 62-64; and embodied reason, 61-64; in Harrison's socialist

feminist ethics, 61-64; and
lovemaking, 59-60, 66n.150
emeth, 42
empedoclaen elements, 168, 171
en christō, 93
Enuma Elish, 34
equality: consensus of feminists, 92;
    defined, 4; Harrison and, 72-
    3; Heyward and, 57; Johnson
    and, 85; Ruether and, 38;
    synonymous use and, 4
essence and existence, 24, 24n.4
essentia, 120, 121
Eternal Thou, 173-75
ethics of care. *See* Carol Gilligan
Eusebius of Ceasarea, Christology
    and, 30n.25
Eusebius of Pamphilis, Christology
    and, 30n.25
exousia, 44
experience of women, 24, 24n.3
Fall: interpretations harmful to
    women, 25; sexuality and, 50-
    51, 50n.106
Finnis, John, 207
formal norms, 229, consensus
    definition, 216; *See also*
    Cahill, Fuchs, O'Connell
Francis of Assisi, 35
friendship, 101. *See also* Buber,
    Harrison, Heyward, Johnson,
    Ruether, spiritual friendship,
    friendship with God
friendship with God, 101; in Aquinas,
    112-113; in Buber, 166-67; in
    Johnson, 85-87
Fuchs, Josef, 205, 208; and formal
    norms, 210-13
gegenseitige, 162
Gegenseitigkeit, 162, 176
geistige Wesenheiten, 171-75
gender mutuality: in Aelred of
    Rievaulx, 111; analysis
    question, 21; in Aquinas, 131-
32; in Buber, 201; consensus
of feminists, 93; defined, 93,
98; in Harrison, 69-70; in
Heyward, 50-52; in Hugh of
St. Victor, 112; in Johnson,
79-81; in H.R. Niebuhr, 202;
in Ruether, 35-36; in Scotus,
150-52
generative mutuality: analysis
    question, 21; in Aelred of
    Rievaulx, 111; in Aquinas,
    132; in Buber, 203; consensus
    of feminists, 93-94; defined,
    94, 99; in Heyward, 52-54; in
    Hugh of St. Victor, 109;
    in Johnson, 81-82; in H.R.
    Niebuhr, 202; in Ruether, 36;
    in Scotus, 152
Gilbert of La Porree, 104
Gilligan, Carol: ethics of care, 89;
    defined, 89n.257, 222
Gloria Dei vivens homo, mulier, 88
God: Being Itself, 86; Christ,
    Wisdom of, 80-81;
    community of love, 83;
    Creator, 191-92, 195;
    Companion and friend, 183;
    Divine Wisdom, 30-32; the
    enemy, 183; friends of, 82;
    Governor, 191-93, 195;
    Harrison's critique of
    metaphors for, 65, 65n.170;
    Holy Spirit, 82, 90, 94; Holy
    Wisdom, 85; Jesus-Sophia,
    81; Messianic King, 30-32;
    Mother, 81; Mother Sophia,
    81; as person in Buber, 175,
    198, 220; procession of,
    82n.232; Redeemer, 192-93,
    195; in Scotus:
        acceptatio,
        100, 144, 146, 147-
        50; *potentia absoluta*,

and *potentia ordinata*, 142;
Sophia-God, 78;
Spirit-Sophia, 82, 84;
subsistant relations, 82;
triune, 83; *See also* Christology, panentheism, trinity
Godfrey of St. Victor, 103
Gods/Goddeses, God, God/ess, in Ruether, 26-27
Golden Rule, 207
Goldstein, Valerie Saiving, 219
Governor, 192-93, 195
Grotius, 244
Gudorf, Christine, 16
Gula, Richard M., 206
Gutierrez, Gustavo: in Ruether, 40-41; in Heyward, 55n.129
haeccitas. *See* John Duns Scotus
Harrison, Beverly Wildung: and Aquinas, 132; biographical data, 61; and Buber, 199; Christology, 66; equality and, 72-73; and forms of mutuality, 9-11; Heyward and, 65, 66, 68, 68n.185, 68, 73, 76; mutuality: basic definition, 66-67; cosmic, 66-69; gender, 69-70; normative status, 71-72, 217, 218; social, 70-71

H.R. Niebuhr and, 22, 203; reciprocity and, 73; social feminist theory and, 61-64; solidarity in, 73; theology in, 64-65 works analyzed, 3n.4
Hauerwas, Stanley, 232, 244-49
Hehir, J. Bryan, 240
heretical groups, 25
hesed, 42, 60, 221-22

heterosexism, 51, 51n.111
Heyward, Isabel Carter:
anthropology, 46-47; Aquinas and, 132; biographical data, 41-42; Buber and, 46, 198-99; Christology and, 43-46; equality in, 57; friendship in, 58-59; justice in, 221; love in, 219; mutuality: basic definition, 47-48; cosmic, 49; four forms of, 9-10; gender, 50-52; generative, 52-54; normative status, 56-57, 217, 218 social, 54-55;

Niebuhr, H.R. and, 202; reciprocity and, 57-58; solidarity and, 58; theology in, 42-43; works analyzed, 3n.4
hierarchy: Heyward's critique of, 50; Jesus' critique of, 28; oppressive, 36; sexism and, 27; women's relations and, 32
Hiroshima, 247-48
Holocaust, 14
Holy Spirit, source of justice, 88-89. *See* Spirit-Sophia
Hugh of St. Victor: aristotelian biology and, 106; God in creation, 100-07; Incarnation and, 104-05; marriage, 107-08, 109; mutuality in, 109-111; "not the deflowering...", 107;Virgin Birth, 105-06, 109
human relations, 162-67
Hussein, Saddham, 234-49, *passim*
Ich und Du. See Buber, I-Thou
Ich-es. See Buber, I-It
I-It. *See* Buber
imago Dei: Aelred of Rievaulx and,

111; Aquinas and, 113-14; common power and, 228; embodiment and, 10; feminist anthropology and, 25, 30, 32, 33; gender mutuality and, 21, 50; humanness, 241; integrity and, 227; marriage and, 108; one in Christ and, 80; patriarchical Christianity and, 24-25; Scotus and, 144; Virgin Birth and, 106

Incarnation: in Aquinas, 124-28; economy of salvation and, 124-26; love incarnate, 126-28; in H.R. Niebuhr, 185; in Scotus, 146-47

in divinis. See Trinity

intimus, 128

Iraq, 234-49, *passim*

Irenaeus of Lyons, 52-53

isos, 117

I-Thou. *See* Buber

Jesus: friends of, 87; Jesus-Sophia, 81; Liberator, 28; maleness of, 28, 28n.20; ministry and women, 30; norm for Christian ethics, 56; power in mutual relation, 52; radical mutuality, model of, 68-70; redemption and, 52-53; solidarity with poor and, 88

John Duns Scotus: *acceptatio*, 147-50; analogical notion of mutuality, 9; cognitive theory, 136-39; *hacceitas*, 136, 150; Incarnation in, 146-47; moral theory and, 141-42; mutuality: cosmic, 150; gender, 150-52; genera-time, 152; Ingham's theory, 133-35, 136-38, *passim*; social, 153-55
order of merit, 147-50;
philosophy, 136-42; theology, 143-49; trinity in, 144-45

Johnson, Elizabeth, A.: Aquinas and, 132; biographical data, 76-77; Buber and, 199; equality, 87; four forms of mutuality and, 9-10; friendship in, 85-87; justice and, 222; love and, 219-20; mutuality: basic
definition, 78; cosmic, 78-79; gender, 79-81; generative, 81-82; normative status, 83-85, 217, 219; social, 82-83
reciprocity, 87-88; solidarity, 88

jus ad bello. See Just War Tradition

jus ad bellum. See Just War Tradition

just cause. See Just War Tradition

justice: relationship to love, 12; relationship to mutuality and love: consensus of four
feminists, 90-91; Harrison, 75; Heyward, 60; Johnson, 88; Ruether, 39-40;
theories of, 17-18; tripartite nature of, 11

Just War Tradition: *causus belli*, 240; criteria of, 232, 232n.7; discrimination, 237, 241, 248; *jus ad bellum*, 232, 234, 240; *jus in bello*, 232, 234, 240; just cause, 234, 240, 245; proportionality of means, 235, 240, 242, 247

Kant, Immanuel, 183-84

kenosis, of patriarchy: gender mutuality and, 93; Jesus' maleness and, 820 in Ruether, 37; social mutuality and, 94

King, Martin Luther, Jr., 70
koinonia, 81, 93
Kurds, 236, 239
Kuwait, 233-49
large loquendo, 142
love: relationship to justice, 12; relationship to mutuality and justice: feminists' consensus, 91-92; in Harrison, 73-75; in Heyward, 59-60; in Johnson, 88-90; in Ruether, 39-40
Luther, Martin: esssence and existence, 24n.4; the Fall, 25; monotheism, 180
machismo, 10, 22
Macmurray, John, 46, 46n.93
Madeleva Lecture 1993, Elizabeth A. Johnson, 78
Maguire, Daniel C.: function of moral norms, 206; relation of love and justice, 12
Marx, Karl: Harrison's appropriation of, 62; socialist feminism and, 62n.158
Mather, Cotton, 13
Meeting and dialogue. *See* Buber
Messiah: Davidic, 29; Jesus' role, 30
metanoia, 206
metaphysics of being, in Aquinas, 120
Metz, J.B., solidarity in Johnson, 88
Microcosmos, 103
mišpat, 221n.65
moral norms: sources for, 5; Harrison's definition, 72n.197
mutua inhaeso, 127
mutual love: defined, 75n.207; in Harrison, 75-76; in Heyward, 60-61, 60 n.151; in Johnson, Spirit-Sophia, 84; in Ruether, 39-40
Mutualität, 162, 167-68
mutuality: argument for status as formal norm, 216-29; forms of, 9-12; as complement and corrective, 12-18, 227-29; complexity of, 11-12; definition: as formal norm, 95-97; in Harrison, 66-67; in Heyward, 47-48; in Johnson, 78
Nothwehr's definition, 233; ontological status of, 1; probative value and, 249-51; sociality and, 225; truth and, 223-24; See also cosmic mutuality, gender mutuality, generative mutuality, social mutuality
mutuus amor, 89-90 *See also* mutual love
nachtwort, 162, 167
Nagasaki, 247-49
natural law theories of justice, 17-18
Nature, 101
new heaven/new earth, 79
Nicea (325AD), 30n.25
Nicomachean Ethics. See Aristotle
Niebuhr, Helmut Richard, 179-197; Buber and, 179-80; center of value, 180-81; Christology, 184-86; fitting, 180; God, 191-92; grace, 182-84; Harrison and, 9, 11, 203; Heyward and, 202; henotheism, 181; Incarnation, 185; monotheism, 181-82; mutuality, 201-04; patterns of God' action, 191-93; polytheism, 181; *Responsible Self*, 179-204, *passim*; responsibility: antecedent of mutuality, 197; normative nature of, 193-97; sin, 182-84; sociality, 225; theory of, 186-91; Ruether

and, 202
Niebuhr, Reinhold, 6n.15, 245
nitzotz, 177n.81, 201
non-human relations, 167-71
normative status of mutuality: in Aquinas and Scotus, 155-56; in Buber, 177-79; consensus of four feminists, 94-95; in Harrison, 71-72; in Heyward, 56-57; in Johnson, 83-85; in Niebuhr, 193-97; in Ruether, 37-38
norms. *See* Jesus; *See also* moral norms
Nygren, Anders, 75
O'Connell, Timothy E., 5, 205; and formal norms, 208-210
oikonomia, 120, 156
Outka, Gene, 60
panentheism, 92
parousia, 43
patriarchy: in advanced capitalism, 46-47; in classical theology, 95; as evil, 57; Johnson's critique of, 79-81, 82-84; See *kenosis* of patriarchy
Persian Gulf War, 231-51, *passim*
personalist ethics, 29, 29n.26, 38n.54
philein, Aristotle and, 116-17
philia, Aristotle and, 116-17
philioi, 117
platonic dualism: Harrison's critique, 69-70; Heyward's critique, 43, 43n.80, 50; influence on Augustine, 52-53
pope, interpretations of Fall, 25.
potentia absoluta, 142
potentia ordinata, 143
power: act-each-other-into-well-being, 75; Loomer's two kinds, 7; Harrison's definition, 67n.177, 68-69; See also *exousia* and *dunamis*
power-over: Heyward's definition, 48n.100; erotic desire and, 51, 51n.109; love-making and, 60; obedience to God and, 65-66; parent/child relationship and, 58n.139; relinquishment of, 37; responsibility and, 57-58, 197; social mutuality and, 54-55
power-to. *See* power-with
power-with: cosmic mutuality and, 92-93; dynamics of, 12-13; gender mutuality and, 93; generative mutuality and, 93-94; Heyward's definition, 48n.100; limits by mutuality, 91-92; love and, 70-71; morality and, 65-66; normative nature and, 94-95; social mutuality and, 94; solidarity and, 58;
prethreshold of mutuality, 170
primary spheres. *See* Buber
probative value. *See* mutuality
process theology, 53-54
proportionality of means. *See* Just War Tradition
Ramsey, Paul, 245
Rahner, Karl, 210-11
rationalist theories of justice, 17-18
reciprocity: consensus of four feminists, 91; defined, 4; in Harrison, 73; in Heyward, 57; in Johnson, 87-88; in Ruether, synonymous use, 4
Redeemer, 192-93, 195
redemption, 28, 52-53
reditus, 130
Reign of God: biblical vision, 41; community and, 79-80; Ruether's Christology and, 29
responsibility: antecedent to mutuality, 197; normative nature of, 193-97

Reziprozität, 162, 167
Richard of St. Victor, 139
Ritschl, 181
Robertston Lectures. See
    Responsible Self
Royce, Josiah, 181
Romero, Oscar, 70
Ruether, Rosemary Radford:
    anthropology, 24-27;
    Aquinas and, 132;
    biographical date, 23;
    biophilic mutuality, 23,
    34; Buber and, 198;
    Christology, 28-30;
    ecological ethics, 30, 33;
    equality and, 38; basic
    definition of mutuality, 33-34
    friendship, 38-39; forms of
    mutuality, 9-10; love, 219,
    220-21; mutuality: cosmic,
        34-35; gender, 35-36;
        generative, 36-37;
        normative, 37-38,
        223-24; social, 37;
    naming God, 26-27;
    Niebuhr, H.R. and, 202;
    personal sin, 27; reciprocity
    and, 39; redemption, 28;
    sin for women, 27; social sin,
    27; solidarity and, 39; works
    analyzed, 3n.6
sacrificial love, 89-92
Schleiermacher, F., 181
scientia practica, 140
Scriptum super Sententiis, Aquinas
    and, 113
ṣedaḳah, 221n.65
sexism: heterosexism, 51, 51n.111;
    oppression of women, 30;
    personal and social, 36; as
    sin, 27, 27n.15
shalom, 29, 41
Shiits, 236, 239
sin: for men, 27; in H.R. Neibuhr,
    182-84; for women, 27 *See
    also* sexism
Smith, Ronald Gregor, 162
socialist feminism, 62n.158
social mutuality: in Aelred of
    Rievaulx, 109-11; analysis
    question, 21; in Aquinas, 132-
    33; in Buber, 203; consensus
    of four feminists, 94; defined,
    94; in Harrison, 70-71; in
    Heyward, 54-55; in Hugh of
    St. Victor, 110-11; in
    Johnson, 82-83; in H.R.
    Niebuhr, 203-04; in Scotus,
    153-55
Society of Christian Ethics, 73
solidarity; consensus of four
    feminists, 91; defined, 4; in
    Harrison, 73; in Heyward, 58;
    in Johnson, 88; in Ruether,
    39; synonymous use, 4
Song of Songs, 40
Sophia-God, 78-79
spheres of relation, 162-75
spiritual friendship, 101-02, 108-09
Stone Center, studies by, 46
stricte loquendo, 142
subthreshold of mutuality, 171-75
suppositum, 144-45
Swidler, Leonard: the good and
    mutuality, 226-27; sociality
    and mutuality, 225; status of
    moral subject, 225; truth
    and mutuality, 223-24
symbolism, of St. Victor, 103
Tertullian, on women, 25
theologia, 119, 156
theologia in nobis, 139
theologia in se, 139
theories of justice, 17-18
Thomas Aquinas: anacedent of
    mutuality and, 9;
    anthropology, 113-14;
    biology, Harrison's critique

of, 64n.164; essence and
existence, 24n.4;
friendship with God, 112-19;
friendship with God,
Johnson's critique of, 85-87;
God: exemplar cause, 114-15;
feminist notion of mutuality
and, 129-33; friend, 117-19;
Incarnation, 124-28; micro-
ordering of universe, 8;
theory of justice, 16-17;
Trinitarian relations, 119-24;
women, 25
threshold of mutuality, 168-69
Tillich, Paul, 26
Timaeus, 34, 103
Trinity: in Aquinas, 119-24; *ad
intra/ad extra*, 120-
21; divine missions,
122-24; metaphysics
of being, 120; names
of God, 121;
in Heyward, *ad intra*, 60
n.152; *in divinis*, 121
in Johnson, *ad extra*, 84; *ad
intra*, 82-83;
hypostases, and
gender, 85;
hypostasis, as male or
female, 85; as highest
ideal, 84n.237;
in Ruether, *ad intra*, 33;
in Scotus, 143-46, 153
Umfassung, 160
universitas, 102, 104
US/Coalition forces, 234-49, *passim*
utilitarian theories of justice, 17-18
Vatican State, 14
vereinigung. See meeting and
dialogue
vestigium, 113
Vietnam War, 245, 247
Virgin Birth, 105
Wechselwirkung, die, 162

Weigel, George, 232, 233-38
William of Conches, 103
women, as "devil's gateway," 25n.7
world of relation. *See* Buber
Wortpaare. See Buber
Yoder, John Howard, 245-46